COMMUNICATION AND MASS MEDIA

Culture, Domination, and Opposition

MICHÈLE MARTIN
Carleton University

with contributions by
GRAHAM KNIGHT
McMaster University

translated by
BENOÎT OUELLETTE

Prentice Hall Allyn and Bacon Canada
Scarborough, Ontario

Canadian Cataloguing in Publication Data

Martin, Michele, 1944-
    Communication and mass media : culture, domination, and opposition

Translation of: Communication et medias de masse.

ISBN 0-13-376807-4

1. Mass media. 2. Mass media - Social aspects.
3. Mass media - Influence. 4. Sex role in mass media.
5. Popular culture. I. Knight, Graham. II. Title.

P90.M3713   1997   302.23 C96-932518-5

 © 1997 Prentice-Hall Canada Inc., Scarborough, Ontario
A Division of Simon & Schuster/A Viacom Company

Translated and adapted with the authorization of the Télé-université. Original French
edition entitled *Communication et média de masse: Culture, domination et opposition*,
© 1991, Collection Communication et Société, published by the Télé-université/Presses
de l'Université du Québec. Translated to English by Benoît Ouellette.

Prentice-Hall, Inc., Upper Saddle River, New Jersey
Prentice-Hall International (UK) Limited, London
Prentice-Hall of Australia, Pty. Limited, Sydney
Prentice-Hall Hispanoamericana, S.A., Mexico City
Prentice-Hall of India Private Limited, New Delhi
Prentice-Hall of Japan, Inc., Tokyo
Simon & Schuster Southeast Asia Private Limited, Singapore
Editora Prentice-Hall do Brasil, Ltda., Rio de Janeiro

ISBN 0-13-376807-4

Vice President, Editorial Director: Laura Pearson
Acquisitions Editor: Cliff Newman
Developmental Editor: Imogen Brian
Production Editor: Amber Wallace
Copy Editor: Carol Glegg
Production Coordinator: Julie Preston
Permissions: Marijke Leupen
Art Director: Mary Opper
Cover Design: Kyle Gell/Julia Hall
Page Layout: April Haisell

1 2 3 4 5   RRD   01 00 99 98 97

Printed and bound in the United States.

Visit the Prentice Hall Canada web site! Send us your comments, browse our
catalogues, and more. **www.phcanada.com** Or reach us through e-mail at
phabinfo_pubcanada@prenhall.com

Contents

Acknowledgments ix

GENERAL INTRODUCTION 1

Communication, Mass Media and Society 1

Mass Media Concepts 2

PART 1 MASS MEDIA AND SOCIETY: THEORETICAL APPROACHES

INTRODUCTION TO PART 1 10

CHAPTER 1 The Coming of Mass Media: Print and Radio Broadcast 11

Introduction 11

The Coming of Print 12

The Manuscript 12

The Printed Book 15

The Coming of Oral Mass Media 21

The Telephone 21

Radio Broadcast Throughout the World 22

The Production of Radio Programme Content 26

Conclusion 27

CHAPTER 2 Mainstream Models in Mass Communication Research 28

Introduction 28

The American Models 29

A Psychological Theory: The hypodermic model 29

Functionalist Models 31

Critique of Functionalist Models 37

The Canadian School of Communication Model   39
> Communication Bias   39
> Hot and Cool Media   42

Conclusion   45

CHAPTER 3 Power, Control and Resistance in Mass Media   46

Introduction   46
Capitalist Society: Social Classes, Ideology and Resistance   47
Mass Production and Liberation: The Frankfurt School Viewpoint   51
The Power Relations in the Organization of Mass Media   53
> Forms of Control and of Accessibility
>   to Mass Media   54
> Economics and Politics as Factors in Media Production:
>   Resistance to Forms of Control   59

Conclusion   64

CHAPTER 4 Ideology, Culture and Opposition in Mass Media   66

Introduction   66
Ideology and Culture: Interrelated Concepts   67
> Ideology   67
> Culture   70

Forms of Culture   71
> Dominant Culture   72
> Popular Culture   72
> Mass Culture   74

International Culture: Exportation of Media Content   77
Are Mass Media Democratic?   79
Conclusion   81

CHAPTER 5 Power Relations and Sexual Discrimination in Media Production   83

Introduction   83
Media Industries: Capitalist Production   84
Socialization of Individuals   86
Social Construction of Masculinity and Femininity   89
Women in Patriarchal Capitalist Production Processes   95
Power Relations in the Production Process of Mass Media   97
Conclusion   103

CHAPTER 6 Capitalism and Patriarchy as Concepts in Media Consumption Analysis 104

Introduction 104

Modernity: A Myth in the Service of Capital 105

    Creation and History of the Modern Housewife 106

    Obsolescence and Eternity in Modernity 108

    Elements of the Myth of Modernity 109

Capitalism and Patriarchy as Concepts in Audience Analysis 112

    Female Television Audiences 112

    The French Feminist Model: Soap Operas,
      "Temporal" Pleasure and Resistance 114

    The North American and English Model:
      Soap Operas, "Illicit" Pleasure and Resistance 116

    Female Fandom: From Spectators to Participants 120

    Female Audiences and Participants in Television Game Shows: "Subversive"
      Pleasure and Resistance 122

Conclusion 126

Conclusion to Part 1 127

PART 2 COMMUNICATION AND SOCIETY: EMPIRICAL CASES

INTRODUCTION TO PART 2 130

CHAPTER 7 What does Cultural Television Reflect? 131

Introduction 131

Images Conveyed in Television Content 132

    Television Violence 133

    The Image of Women on Television 134

Gender Representation in Soap Operas 137

    Once Upon a Time . . . Radio: The Birth of Soap Operas 137

    The Classic Soap Opera Formula 138

    The Construction of Québec Soap Operas 139

The Soap Opera: An International Cultural Product 140

    Dallas: A Cross-cultural Analysis 141

    Dynasty: An Interclass Analysis 145

The Promotion of the Dominant Ideology By Way of the Family 147

    Soap Operas as a Source of Confusion 148

Conclusion 149

CHAPTER 8 Popular Literature: From Harlequins to Detective Novels   151

Prologue   151

Introduction   152

Harlequin Romance: A Recipe For Success   153

The Enterprise   153

The Characters   156

Space and Time   158

The Scenario   158

Confrontation and Marriage   160

The Harlequin "Romance": A Modern Story?   160

Harlequin Romance: Escape for as Little as $2.99   162

Escape or Pornography?   162

The Disappearing Act   164

Illicit Pleasure: The Escape From Everyday Life   167

Detective Novels: Women Dying to Be Killed!   170

Heroes: Faster than a Speeding Bullet   171

Heroines: In the Hero's Shadow, If Not at His Feet   172

Harlequin Romances and Detective Novels: A Comparative Analysis   173

Conclusion   175

Epilogue   176

CHAPTER 9 Comics: Children's Literature?   177

Introduction   177

Comics: A Worldwide Phenomenon   177

Comics in English Canada   178

Comics in Québec   179

Comics in French-Speaking Europe   180

Comics in the United States   182

The Wonderful World of Disney: Dreams Presented as Reality   183

The Worldwide Presence of Disney   183

The Production of the World of Disney   185

Are Donald and Mickey Impostors?   187

The Invisible Adults: Father and Mother   187

The Noble Savage   188

The Missing Production Process   189

Donald the Worker   191

The World of Disney: "New" Simply Means More of the Same   192

Donald the Impostor   193

The Deconstruction of Donald the Impostor 194

Are Comics Infantile Literature? 196

Conclusion 198

CHAPTER 10 Advertising as Mass Culture 199

Introduction 199

The Transformation of Advertising into Mass Culture 199

  Advertising in the Mass Media 201

  What is Hidden Behind Advertising? 202

The Image of Women in Advertising 203

  The Social Construction of Women in Advertising 204

  Representations of the "New" Woman 205

  Is Advertising Sexist? 206

The Image of Men in Advertising 209

  Male Advertising: Neo-sexism? 211

The Image of Cultural Minorities in Advertising 212

  Multiracial Representation in Advertising in Montéal 214

The Power of Advertising 215

Is Advertising Related to Softcore Porn? 216

  The Pornographic Look 218

  Advertising is not Pornography 219

Conclusion 220

CHAPTER 11 The News: Show, Propaganda or Consent? 238

Introduction 238

The News World: A Male World 239

  The Image of Women in the News 241

The News in Canada: Some Basic Facts 242

  Who Wields the Power? 245

  Objectivity in the News: A Myth? 247

  The News as Show 249

  The International News: An American Production 251

The American International News: Propaganda and Disinformation 251

  The Profit Orientation of the Mass Media 252

  Advertising: The Primary Source of Income of the Media 253

  Political Leaders, Private Enterprise and Experts as Sources of Information for
    the Media 253

  Criticism and Discipline of the Media 254

  Anticommunicsm as a Control Mechanism 255

Information as Propaganda: A Manipulation of "Worthy" and "Unworthy"
Victims in the News   255

   Coverage of the Murders of Popieluszko in Poland and
      Romero in El Salvador   256
   News Coverage of Elections in El Salvador, Guatemala
      and Nicaragua   258

Conclusion   260

CHAPTER 12 New Mass Communication Technologies   262

Introduction   262

Videotex   263

   Difficulties in Videotex Implementation   264
   A New Form of Social Control   266

E-mail   267

   Definitions   267
   More than One Information Highway?   268
   The "Internet"   269
   Economic and Political Implications   270
   Technological Illiteracy   272
   The Issue of Data Base Construction   273

Video: An Emerging Medium   276

   The Piracy Problem   278

New Forms of Television   281

   Pay Television   281
   Interactive Television   282

Conclusion   283

General Conclusion   285

Bibliography   288

Index   294

Acknowledgments

I would like to thank all the people who have helped me with this textbook. First, the research assistants: Isabelle Gusse, Jean Leblond, Richard Pitre, and Ariane Brunet for the French version, and Shawn Yerxa for the English version. In addition, I would particularly like to thank the translator, Benoît Ouellette, whose patience and professionalism are reflected in this book, and Carol Glegg whose editing has been very helpful. I would also like to acknowledge the contributions of the following reviewers: Kelly Cusinato, University of Windsor; Graham Knight, McMaster University; Ted Madger, York University; Joan McKibbin, St. Lawrence College; Robert M. Pike, Queen's University; and Gregory S. Yelland, St. Thomas More College. Finally, Shoshana Goldberg and Amber Wallace at Prentice Hall helped me with the burden of producing such a translation. All remaining errors or mistakes are my responsibility.

GENERAL INTRODUCTION

COMMUNICATION, MASS MEDIA AND SOCIETY

The relationship between the mass media and the different forms of communication they produce—as expressed in various cultural practices—is a very complex one. It is important, however, to understand the factors at play in this relationship in order to make better use of media. The mass media have an influence on many aspects of our lives at home, school, work, etc. While almost everyone uses the media to some degree, this experience varies from one person to the next. Moreover, very few people know the source of the media's content, under what conditions it is produced, or what impact it has on audiences.

Most of our knowledge of the world comes to us either directly through the media, or through someone who uses them. This would not be a matter of concern if the mass media provided an accurate portrait of reality. But each mass medium presents, or codifies, reality in its own particular way. For example, someone watching a news bulletin on one television network may receive information that differs—perhaps only slightly, but maybe greatly—from what is broadcast on another network. The same holds true for entertainment shows. Each network has its own internal policies, based on a set of social and ideological values, that determine the types of entertainment they showcase. Some networks, such as Radio-Québec and TVOntario, focus more on educational programming than others that lean towards popular programming. Media content, therefore, cannot be considered as neutral, that is, not conveying any social values. Every medium communicates certain values, beliefs, myths or prejudices that are founded either in the economic conditions, or political and ideological tendencies they support.

The importance of the mass media becomes apparent when we consider the average number of hours young people spend using different media during their elementary and high school years. Such an analysis reveals that children and adolescents are exposed to many forms of communication from different media. Moreover, young people spend an average of 15,000 hours watching television and another 10,500 hours listening to popular music, as compared with 11,000 hours in school (Ontario Ministry of Education, 1989: 5). And although few children are interested in the news, they see an incalculable number of films and, especially, commercials (they are exposed to an average of seven hours of advertisements a week). Adults, by comparison, spend 23.4 hours a week watching television (*La Presse*, April 12, 1991).

Since the media are used by children at a very young age, they play a pivotal role in the social processes that shape our values and perceptions. The media not only provide local and international news, but also suggest ways of looking at the world and of understanding it which may indirectly, or even insidiously, foster, for example, sexist or racist world views. This aspect of the media challenges the belief that their only role is to provide audiences with news, information and entertainment. Given that the media play a formative as well as informative role, it is important for audiences to be aware of the

1

inequalities in terms of knowledge and power that exist between those who produce and control information in their own interests, and those who candidly consume this information as news or entertainment.

The goals of this book are to inform readers about the workings of various mass media so that they will use them in a more critical way, and to instill in readers a healthy dose of scepticism regarding mass media content. To these ends, the book examines how the mass media are organized, how their content is produced, and how the mass media create meaning and construct their own version of reality.

Knowing how mass media content is produced is indispensable for those who wish to keep a critical distance from mass culture and resist media manipulation. An audience that is aware of the social, cultural, political and economic implications of media content and messages can better decode these, and consequently take better advantage of the cultural practices and social values they convey. This book examines the relationship between producers and users. On the one hand, media content producers are subject to numerous motives, controls and constraints dictated by the economic, political, organizational, technical, social, cultural and ideological contexts in which they operate. On the other hand, each audience member chooses and interprets media content differently, depending on gender and other psychological, social and cultural factors.

To convey such critical knowledge about the media, I have divided this book into two parts. The first part reviews a number of theoretical models that examine mass media production processes and audience attitudes from different perspectives. These models uncover the workings of the mass media and the constraints operating on them. This part, however, does not include a detailed study of the theoretical elements and the main arguments of these models, or a strictly chronological account of the theoretical models covered. Instead, it attempts to present to readers the general concepts of these theoretical perspectives, thus providing the necessary tools for the empirical media analysis in the second part of the book. This empirical analysis focuses on the content of different forms of communication produced by certain media, such as television and print, and also examines how certain audiences respond to this content. But let us first look at several concepts used throughout this book.

MASS MEDIA CONCEPTS

While many ideas and theoretical notions will be introduced in each chapter, I believe it is necessary at this early stage to present some general concepts and provide an idea of the book's overall perspective.

Communication

Communication between individuals or groups is an essential element of social organization in any society. After all, as Williams noted (1976), to communicate is to "make common," or "impart" information to other people. The need to communicate directly or indirectly with others, either through speech, gesture or writing, is as fundamental as the need for shelter and, to a certain extent, food. The term "communication" means exchange. As such, the expansion and multiplication of different forms of communication is a product of the collective and individual development of people in societies that have preceded ours. According to Siegelaub, communication, or exchanges between people, has increased in quantity and quality over centuries to become "at the heart of the advancement of society, one of the principle marks of social progress, the basis of true liberation, whether national, regional, local or individual" (Siegelaub, 1983: 14).

Communication is not something abstract or general, but a link between real people that occurs at a specific point in space and time. Communication, then, is influenced by various factors such as the channels through which it flows, the time and place in which it is produced, and the various technical means by which it takes place. These factors also include the characteristics of the people involved, such as their economic and political status, culture, gender and will or reluctance to communicate. The type of communication used depends on which factors are present, and which ones take precedence over others.

If, for instance, we consider the factor of time in the study of forms of communication, we see that in the eighteenth century the only existing form of long-distance communication was writing. As for gender, this book will repeatedly show that the content of mass media products intended for male and female audiences is influenced by the different characteristics and preferences of these two types of audiences. Forms of communication are therefore influenced not only by technological factors, but also by the social, economic, political and cultural conditions in which they are developed.

Given this context, the decision to choose one form of communication over another is made in response to certain needs that have arisen in history. For example, one form may have been developed to stimulate the economy of a society, or to help meet certain political needs (such as maintaining social order) or some other social needs. This is why it is important not only to look at the various forms of communication that have been developed over time and how they have been used, but also to examine who produced them and for what purpose.

We can distinguish between two fundamental forms of communication: the so-called "natural" forms, which include oral and non-verbal communication, and those that are produced by technological means or by the media. *In this book, the notion of communication refers to the forms or types of communication that are produced by different mass media.* For example, television produces a different type of communication than literature does, even though their content may sometimes be quite similar (e.g., the content of a soap opera is sometimes like that of a Harlequin Romance). In the chapters to follow, we will take a critical look at the different types of communication and media in our society, the social factors that contributed to their development, and the impact they have on audiences.

Mass Media

The media are communication tools that are used to convey messages or information between people. These messages are said to be *mediated* in that they reach receivers via some intermediary agent (a technology, a person, etc.) that may or may not alter its meaning. Some of the media in our society have developed into *mass media* capable of reaching a large number of people at the same time. But the fact that a medium can reach so many people all at once does not necessarily mean that it is a mass medium. So what distinguishes the mass media from other types of media?

Masses have specific characteristics that distinguish them from other groups of people. But how is addressing a mass audience different from addressing a crowd? The problem is more than simply a matter of semantics. The information and messages broadcast in the media are often produced according to the audiences for which they are intended. In this respect, the concept of mass poses a particular problem. According to Gustave le Bon (1895), crowds are different from mass audiences in that the former adhere to a collective identity that incites its members to behave according to certain common objectives (in Beaud, 1984). Crowds gather together when people want to express their approval, joy or opposition. A speaker addressing a crowd is able to determine why it has assembled and adapt his or her speech according to its needs and expectations.

Given the very nature of their distribution, Williams (1976b) contends that the *mass media* attempt to reach a large number of people who are not necessarily gathered together. In fact, the people involved are usually relatively isolated from one another. People read books, consult newspapers, listen to the radio, or watch television in various places (e.g., at home, at work, in their car) and for different reasons. In contrast to crowds, mass audiences are not assembled in any one location. As a result, the composition of a mass audience does not enable one to make suppositions about the common features of its members. Since the social conditions in which mass audiences receive messages are different from those in which crowds assemble, the content of these messages must also be produced in a different manner.

This distinction between crowds and masses is an important one, since it has led researchers to modify the way they view the effects of the media. In the case of a public discourse, the extent of a speech's impact on a crowd is considered to be proportional to the number of people in the crowd. Because mass audiences are far more scattered than crowds, they are not subject to the social pressure of their peers in the same way that crowd members are. For example, public speakers will often urge people to respond immediately to the interaction they produce among the crowd members. Conversely, since television viewers are isolated in their respective households, they will not feel the influence from their peers until several hours or even days after the communication occurs, when they will engage in conversation with fellow viewers in the absence of the communicator. In contrast to public speakers who can immediately gauge what an audience wants to hear, producers of mass media content are hard-pressed to predict how their message will be interpreted if they do not know the characteristics of the individuals who make up their audience.

As we will see in greater detail in the chapters to follow, control over the production of mass media content is in the hands of a few small groups. Thus, the notion of mass media refers to the ability to steer the social action of majorities towards points of view supported by the minorities who control the production process. This is done by choosing the information and messages that are sent to audiences. For producers, mass audiences are seen only as abstract units who fulfil one of the following four criteria (Williams, 1982a): a) they represent audiences that are completely abstract, devoid of specific features; b) they are composed of humans belonging to a society; c) they are composed of social beings with certain specific characteristics; or d) they represent groups of individuals with unspecified features. Williams has contended that mass media producers never perceive mass audiences as consisting of individuals with distinct characteristics.

With the development of more and more sophisticated tools for measuring audiences, it becomes easier for the producers to learn the characteristics of their viewers more precisely. Neilson Ratings that result from individualized audimeters and BBM (The Bureau of Broadcast Measurement) questionnaires procure invaluable data on audiences. Still, these methods of measurement are not infallible. On the one hand, the audimeter will count any individual sitting in front of the television even if the person is not watching but reading the newspaper. On the other hand, people are not always entirely honest when filling out questionnaires because they may be ashamed to admit that they watch certain shows. However, in this "quick-zapping" era, these tools of measurement are indispensable to the producers in order to control audiences as much as possible and guarantee a certain number of viewers to the advertisers.

Throughout this book we will see that the power struggle for control over the mass media is a complex one, considering the economic, political, ideological and cultural stakes involved. Thus, even though the mass media grew out of an oral culture, they are not a mere extension of oral communication.

In light of these considerations, *this book uses the term mass media in its broad meaning, that is, to refer to those media which allow for a broad transmission, or diffusion of content*. This definition includes some media, for instance certain literary genres, that are not usually recognized as mass media. I have included these because they involve mass audiences.

Social Construction of the Mass Media

In the analysis to follow, I will refer to the *social construction of the media*. This term refers to the fact that mass media content is not a simple reflection of reality, but a product that is intended to achieve a specific goal. The success of such products depends on whether they appear to be "natural," when in reality they are carefully constructed by producers on the basis of decisions made at different levels with regard to certain specific goals. The mass media therefore *construct reality* into their products in a similar way that, from the time we are born, we construct our own vision of the world around us, and give the world meaning based on our observations and experiences. When these same observations and experiences are prefabricated for us by the media, it is possible to see that they contribute to the construction of our own reality.

However, audiences are not empty boxes waiting to be filled. *They interpret or negotiate the meaning presented in the media*. In order to better understand the mass media, it is necessary to know how they interact with us. The outcome of this interaction is our own *interpretation* of mass media content according to our needs and concerns, the events in our daily lives, our racial and sexual attitudes, as well as our familial and cultural environment. Media content is thus said to be *mediated* by the characteristics of audiences; in other words, the impact of the media is not direct, but is "negotiated" through these characteristics.

As mentioned above, the media are also influenced by factors external to the production process. For example, we must not forget that media production is a commercial undertaking from which producers must make a profit. Therefore, it is necessary to examine *sources of control,* and the effect they can have over the production process with respect to the ideological messages and social values conveyed, for example, attitudes regarding women, the authorities, patriotism, consumption, etc. We must find out if the media are at the vanguard of ideas, or if they are simply in the business of reproducing reality by imitating ideas and activities that already exist in our society.

It is important to look at this issue, since the effects of mass media also have social and political implications. Even though they are not generally known for creating new ideas and values, the mass media help legitimize and reinforce existing ones. As a result, the media have an impact on the nature of family life and the use of leisure time. Moreover, it is a well-known fact that the election of a national leader is largely dependent on the image he or she projects in the media. Here too, we must look at how different mass media manipulate certain values and political events.

Finally, the form of a mass medium also has an influence on its content. It is therefore important to understand the hidden aspects of the relationship between form and content. Different types of media produce different forms of communication; furthermore, a medium can adopt various forms to transmit content.[1] For example, while the same family values may be conveyed in various media, the forms of communication used—print, television or new mass technologies—will be distinct. We can ask whether the same types of content conveyed in different forms of communication affect audiences in the same way.

The purpose of this book is to provide readers with a critical tool to study the organization of mass media production, the values and ideologies present in mass media content, and the contribution of audiences through their interpretation. My objective is to present a number of critical perspectives to help readers better understand the features of media practices that are prevalent in our society—practices that are not readily apparent to the uninformed observer. There are, of course, other perspectives available to study the media, and Chapter 2 will provide a short survey of some of these. My objective is not to debunk these perspectives, but to point out some of their limitations, and also those of critical perspectives.

Readers will note that I have not resorted to any single author to criticize others. Instead, I put forward concepts developed by several researchers, whose perspectives sometimes contradict and sometimes concur with one another. One of the virtues of this approach is to suggest that there are no *absolute truths* in the study of communication and the mass media. There are, instead, various phenomena that can be explained in different

---

[1] The print medium includes novels, newspapers, etc.

ways depending on the approaches used. The advantages of the critical perspective used in this book is that it will help readers understand the forms of power and control that influence mass media production and consumption. And, as will be emphasized throughout, this understanding suggests ways to resist, oppose or negotiate these representations of power. Careful readers will be able to discern these distinctions, which will be used to qualify or criticize the views of every researcher discussed in this book.

The two parts of this book, theoretical and empirical, attempt to distinguish between real facts and value judgments, establish the validity of certain sources, determine the accuracy of assertions, detect biases, reveal inferences, and acknowledge the strengths of arguments. To this end, I have developed a theoretical model that takes into account the conditions of media production and consumption. This model borrows a number of concepts from certain dominant approaches in communication studies, but primarily from critical theory and feminist analyses of the mass media. The second part, which consists of a study of specific forms of communication, will apply the analytical concepts developed in the first part.

First, I will present a concrete analysis of the development of two mass media that produce different forms of communication: print and radio. This historical survey will familiarize readers with the production conditions of these two media and the basic factors that have influenced their development. An immediate introduction to the empirical conditions of production will help readers understand the analysis that develops in the chapters to follow.

PART 1

MASS MEDIA AND SOCIETY: THEORETICAL APPROACHES

INTRODUCTION TO PART 1

This first part of the book consists of a theoretical analysis of the mass media. Its aim is to develop a conceptual framework to help the reader explore the underlying features of the mass media, particularly with respect to their role in society. As mentioned in the General Introduction to this book, knowing about the workings of various media enables us to understand not only the mass media in general, but also other social phenomena, since media content is often a reflection of social experience. By drawing on analytical features from the different theoretical models, we will construct a critical approach so as to better understand these phenomena. It should be noted that the critical model is just one of many approaches that deal with the mass media. I have chosen this model because it will help us review various aspects of the organization of the media, their production of content—the actual production process and the messages conveyed—and their audiences.

In short, this part provides insight into a number of contemporary debates in the field of mass media studies about the workings of the media, their role and their impact on our society. As mentioned in the General Introduction, Chapter 1 consists of a historical review of the development of two media: print and radio. Chapter 2 takes a careful look at analyses made from an administrative point of view: the psychological and functionalist models. Understanding these models will help us examine different aspects of the relationship between media and audiences. Chapters 3 and 4 present critical perspectives of the mass media. These theories examine the economic, political and social conditions under which the media operate, particularly with respect to production of content. Finally, Chapters 5 and 6 look at feminist points of view regarding the mass media. These last two chapters focus on the different experiences that men and women have with the media in their roles as workers and as audiences, as well as on the different ways they are portrayed in media content.

THE COMING OF THE MASS MEDIA: PRINT AND RADIO BROADCAST

INTRODUCTION

The mass media are a relatively new phenomenon. They are a product of modern society, as are the forms of communication they produce. The coming of these new forms of communication has brought about change—sometimes long and painful—in social and cultural practices. To examine the different processes involved in such change, we will look at the development of two forms of communication—print and radio broadcast— and the economic, political and social conditions that have influenced their growth. We will then discuss the impact of their emergence on society. It is my hope that this historical perspective of the development of print and radio broadcast will help readers understand the concepts presented in the chapters to follow.

The mass media emerged out of a long historical process that began with a type of communication that is unique to human beings: oral communication. Until the twelfth century, this direct and instantaneous form of communication was the means used to transmit information and messages within small communities in Western societies. With time, however, oral communication began to change. Though it was still a means of sharing experiences, ideas and knowledge, it was increasingly used to communicate with people of other cultures living in other places.

In oral cultures, public discourse was used as a direct link between message producers—or their representatives—and the audiences they addressed. Even after the book was invented, this feature of oral cultures persisted, since literacy was not widespread, and facilities and economic resources were insufficient to ensure the mass distribution of books.

Oral communication, however, has its limitations: it only lasts as long as it takes one to speak, and it only reaches those within earshot. As a result, people began to feel the need to preserve certain accounts or messages. To achieve longer-lasting and more far-reaching communication, various technical means were used: texts were engraved on rock or carved on wood, messages were written on wax tablets or parchment, and notices were inscribed on city walls, etc.

The fifteenth century saw the invention of a technology that would have a profound impact on all existing forms of communication: the printing press. When printing first appeared, it was by no means a mass medium. Books, which were first printed in the same format as manuscripts, were rare and their distribution was difficult, due in part to production problems. While improved printing techniques meant that books became less rare, distribution problems remained. As we will see shortly, the distribution and production of books created numerous complications which were often difficult to resolve.

Unlike commercial radio and television, print was not born as a mass medium. If a mass medium is defined as a communication technology that guarantees the creation and utilization of a product by the masses, then books could not have been considered a mass medium before printing technology made it possible to publish and distribute them in the millions. It was not until centuries later that such mass distribution was achieved. In contrast, radio had the potential for mass communication from the time of its inception. The speed of its commercial implementation was the only factor determining the size of the mass audience it reached. Let us now consider the beginnings of these two media.

THE COMING OF PRINT

As mentioned above, the emergence of a new form of communication can have a considerable impact on many long-standing social or cultural practices in a society. In the case of printing, the adaptation process was a particularly long and painful one, since it entailed a change in people's way of thinking as they shifted from an oral to a written culture. For example, although a handful of people already knew how to write, a larger part of society would have to become literate. To understand all the aspects of this transition, we will begin by examining the changes brought about by the first efforts to spread literacy to an oral society, and then look at the conditions under which printing developed.

The Manuscript

Before the twelfth century, social, legal and political practices in Western societies were primarily dependent on the word of the persons concerned or their witnesses. According to Clanchy (1979), because very few people knew how to write and read, it would have been too expensive to hire a copyist to record daily transactions in writing. Moreover, at the time, writing was not part of people's mentality. Under these conditions, it would have been far too easy to misrepresent and falsify handwritten records. For this reason, societies relied on oral communication, using the accounts of trustworthy impartial observers (intermediaries). Practices in oral cultures were so firmly rooted in people's minds that, when the print medium was invented more than two centuries later, the *reading* of printed books, which were then published in small numbers, was done *orally*. A person thus read aloud for a group, which might easily have included many illiterate persons. That some individuals were literate did not exclude them from participating in book readings. Since oral cultures were primarily socially oriented, people, both literate and not, preferred to read in a social setting than by themselves.

The population's mistrust of written texts abated with time as more people began to learn to read, if not write. Back in the twelfth century, reading and writing were separate abilities. Given that writing techniques are more difficult to learn than reading, more people could read, at least at a basic level, than could write. Efforts to spread literacy intensified in the thirteenth century as governments established guidelines on validating documents, which required the authentification of styles and signatures.

The transition from oral administrative and legal practices to ones such as bookkeeping and writing notarial deeds—which are now considered "normal" administrative procedures—occurred over many centuries. But the spread of writing—which gave those who knew how to write increasing control over those who did not—seemed to happen rapidly, at least among specific social groups. Thus writing, as a form of communication, first spread among the clergy, and in monasteries, the courts and small groups of people who controlled certain aspects of society.

The transition from oral culture in medieval societies to mass media culture in modern society was mediated by a long period of written culture. Clanchy (1979) has stated that the first signs of the transition from oral to written culture—and its consequences—appeared around the twelfth century when the production and preservation of registers attained levels never before seen. It appears that archival practices grew out of the desire to increase government efficiency, not the inverse. Since the practice of writing was well suited to new commercial activities, the need to preserve written archives developed primarily for commercial reasons, not for the sake of literary creativity. However, the use of writing by public and commercial administrations was not enough to bring about significant change in the mentality of an entire population used to oral practices. In short, society in general did not have a so-called literary mentality.

According to Clanchy (1979), it took several centuries for literacy to spread among the masses. This process occurred in two stages. First, as described above, there was a transition from oral practices to the use of writing for administrative and business purposes. It was not until the second phase, which took place around the thirteenth century, that a literary mentality began to take root. Writing habits were first developed among the ruling classes, who had the financial and political means to utilize writing techniques, and were later imposed by law on other social classes. Thus, even in the early stages of the transition between oral and written culture, we can see that the change in the form of communication was not only related to economic factors, such as commercial needs, but also to political factors, such as legislation that allowed the state to use the new technology to wield even greater control over the masses. By making it easier to detect deviant activities, the standardization of official documents and the growing use of statistical reports were efficient means of regulating certain practices among the population.

It was not until later, during the second phase of the spread of literacy, that written communication was imposed by legislation requiring that certain fundamental rules be followed: dating business documents, signing letters, etc. However, even these basic rules were not readily accepted by the population.

In oral cultures, legislative, commercial and social communication was ensured by the wisdom of elders, who, for instance, remembered the approximate date of a birth, a transaction, etc. by referring to periods of drought, of plenty, and so on. Moreover, people were often identified from memory by a neighbour or a parent. Clanchy (1979) has noted that in the twelfth century a person's word carried much more legal weight than any written document, even if registers already existed. When a distinctive mark (i.e., a "signature") was required to identify someone, an engraving in a knife handle or piece of wax, or even a drawing, would suffice. Written documents such as registers were not preserved or given legal value until a century later.

It should come as no surprise that people were distrustful when a law was passed declaring that written documents could establish a person's identity. How, for example, could one be sure that a letter was actually written by the same person who signed it, or that the name had not been forged, or that the person who supposedly wrote it was to be trusted? It is difficult for us, living at the end of the twentieth century, to understand such attitudes. But what these attitudes show is that the transition from oral to written culture, or vice versa, entails not only a change in the form of communication used, but also a complete change in people's mentality, and in social and cultural practices that had been in existence for centuries.[1]

One might think that once written and especially printing practices were entrenched, writing documents by hand would have appeared as an outdated production process for disseminating knowledge. However, this was not the case, even after printing began to be used. In fact, booksellers stocked only a small quantity of books, both printed and handwritten, rarely more than ten at a time (Febvre and Martin, 1976). The copyists working in monasteries and in the first universities were enough to meet the small market demand. It would appear that the lack of enthusiasm for books was due in part to economic conditions. Citing the financial statements of a few fourteenth- and fifteenth-century businesses, Febvre and Martin (1976) noted that the cost of parchment, though slightly higher than that of paper, remained competitive for a long time. Moreover, regular-edition sizes of manuscripts did not require large quantities of sheep or calf skin. Therefore, given that printing was not necessarily more economical than other production processes, printed book sales remained low.

The development of the book as a mass medium could not occur until after a sufficient demand was created and an efficient distribution system established. But first, mass production techniques had to be created. It was also necessary to supervise points of distribution in several large cities, and to hire staff to ensure that the merchandise reached its destination after shipment. This is why, according to Febvre and Martin (1976), the book publishing trade was rapidly taken over by wealthy merchants who knew how to organize efficient distribution networks. Thus merchants played a pivotal role in the introduction of the printed book in medieval Europe.

---

[1] They also show that television did not institute an oral culture in our mass-media society, as had been predicted by some pessimists. Indeed, all serious transactions are still conducted in writing.

The Printed Book

In *The Coming of the Book* (1976), which is still considered a classic study of print history, Febvre and Martin examine the conditions under which the book emerged, and the effects it had on different segments of European society between the period of the manuscript and the early stages of the mass production and printing of books. We will focus on three closely related areas, namely the development of printing in relation to other book-making techniques, the people involved in the production process, and the reading public. By examining the development of the printed book in Europe, we will be able to discuss the contradictions involved in the spread and the use of a new form of communication. Such contradictions are brought about by the economic, political, social and cultural conditions in which the new form is developed.

Although, for our purposes, it is not necessary to analyze the technological development of printing in detail, it is important to emphasize a few factors that had a large impact on the printing industry. Clearly, printing was closely related to other industries, particularly the paper industry. When printing first appeared, paper—which was then made from a mixture of cotton and linen fabrics—was rare and expensive. It was not until an inexpensive papermaking technique was developed using wood that the printing industry began to boom.

This technological change, as Febvre and Martin (1976) are quick to point out, only occurred after a long process of trial and error. Given certain economic and political forces, book manufacturing techniques developed into a specific form of production. Thus, technically speaking, the printed book underwent several transformations before attaining its current form: in the fifteenth century books consisted of handwritten reproductions; the first book made with printed letters appeared only a century later. Production techniques were also influenced by economic factors: for example, illustrations were more abundant in times of economic boom. But the development of any new form of communication, such as the printed book, is a complex process involving more than technical elements alone.

The invention of printing had an important economic impact on the book industry, since it significantly modified the existing occupational structure. The emerging industry saw the creation of jobs related to the new printing techniques, new types of producers knowledgeable in production methods, new types of shops and distribution networks to sell books, and a new clientele to purchase them. Furthermore, in order to survive, the printing industry needed new content producers, that is, authors. As we shall see shortly, the first authors experienced an uncertain status.

The first specialized occupation to appear in the wake of the invention of printing was that of printer. In the beginning, this was a poorly paid occupation. Thus, to improve their economic situation, printers tried to secure large contracts, which often meant travelling from town to town. In general, printers were financed by powerful enterprises, especially banks. As a result, these enterprises assumed economic control over the development of the printing trade, which soon blossomed into a real industry. Since bankers reserved the right to select which books to publish, they quickly extended their control to the contents of books. The decision to open bookshops also gave them economic influence over book sales. As a result, for many years bankers were regarded as booksellers, not as publishers. In this chapter, however, the terms "bookseller" and "publisher" are used indiscriminately. It was only later that the occupation of publisher became distinct from that of banker, without any loss of prestige. Since booksellers had financial and economic control over the printing industry, authors would approach them in the hopes of selling their manuscripts.

The profession of author, which was born as a result of printing, underwent several transformations over the centuries. With the supply of unpublished ancient texts dwindling at the start of the sixteenth century, publishers began to search for original titles. Authors seized the opportunity and submitted their texts. But they usually did not consider *selling* them. The concept of selling the fruits of one's intellect was not common practice then; in fact, it was considered corrupt. Authors made a living through a patronage system, which consisted of finding a patron—usually a rich nobleman fond of letters—to whom they sent their manuscripts with a flattering letter. In return for their gifts, authors were given a sum of money. Another way of obtaining money from the nobility was to print "at the beginning or end of the book, letters or laudatory verses to a powerful patron," a practice that "was usually recompensed" (Febvre and Martin, 1976: 160). Though this practice may seem astonishing to us now, since it is a different form of submission from what we know today, it was considered more honourable than to sell one's manuscript to a bookseller.

By the end of the seventeenth century, however, more and more authors were selling their texts to booksellers in return for a number of printed copies or a sum of money. While some prestigious authors, such as Boileau and La Bruyère, refused to partake in this practice, others, including Corneille, Lafontaine and Molière, willingly sold their manuscripts in order to survive. In general, authors from a humble background had no choice but to follow this practice because authors' rights were not protected at the time. And once they sold their manuscripts to booksellers, authors no longer had any control over publication.

The practice of selling one's texts sometimes resulted in exploitation. Since authors were given a fixed sum of money prior to the publication of their manuscript, the reward was often disproportionate to the book's success. Little-known authors generally received less money than what their manuscript was worth, while prestigious authors sometimes reaped more than what their work was worth. By the end of the sixteenth century, some authors began to print books on their own to avoid being exploited.

Little by little, the concept of copyright as the legal protection of "literary property" began to take shape. As Eisenstein points out: "The new forms of authorship and literary property rights undermined older concepts of collective authority in a manner that encompassed . . . texts relating to [different areas such as] philosophy, science . . . law," as well as religion (1983: 85). The first property right was given by the Venitian government to a printer in 1469, and the first publication copyright by the same government to Titian in 1567 (Eisenstein, 1979: 193, 231n2). Febvre and Martin (1976) have noted that other steps in this direction were taken when booksellers agreed to reprint a book only with the author's consent. Then, in 1709, the Copyright Act passed by the English court recognized authors as the sole holders of *copyrights* for a maximum of 20 years. This Act was not reinforced before the 1770s, however (Altick, 1957: 53–4). France waited until the end of the eighteenth century—after a long, fierce battle led by Diderot—before introducing legislation that would form the foundation of present copyright laws.

Thus, the new occupation—which is now a recognized profession—developed through a process of conflict that was influenced by the economic conditions of the trade and political intervention by the state.

Febvre and Martin (1976) have also written that state intervention was not limited to the writing profession, but extended to manual trades such as that of typographer. Although typographers were cultivated people who knew Latin and could read Greek, they were not well paid. And despite their many wage claims, as well as strikes, their income was only slightly higher than that of masons. In spite of the state's numerous attempts to undermine the creation of brotherhoods or guilds, typographers fought hard to create and maintain associations to help secure a certain degree of freedom over their work. This freedom enabled them to secretly print banned books, which they sold on the black market to supplement their wages. Since the state would ultimately benefit from improving typographers' working conditions, their work became regulated by royal decree as early as the end of the fifteenth century. The legislation met many of the typographers' demands by providing an official description of their tasks, restricting the number of apprentices—who often worked for free—and foreign workers employed, and by giving typographers more days off in addition to Sundays and holidays.

As we can see, the economic conditions under which the printed book emerged were closely linked to the role played by the state in the development of the industry. We shall take a closer look at how the interaction between economic and political factors affected the publication and distribution of books.

For a long time, copyists, and then printers, favoured ancient texts, particularly Latin and Greek classics, and the Bible. But when the supply of unpublished classical texts dried up, there was a demand for new works to be published. A number of men of letters, working in printing shops as proofreaders, became interested in taking advantage of this opportunity. Already familiar with the workings of the printing industry, it seemed natural for many of them to try their fortune as authors. Meanwhile, conflicts over what types of texts to print were beginning to arise.

At the same time, the process of text illustration was also undergoing a series of transformations. While in previous centuries bishops and the nobility preferred to publish religious texts with illustrations of biblical scenes, thirteenth-century bankers gave priority to secular texts, intended for their own personal use, containing illustrations of rural scenes. According to Febvre and Martin (1976), this change marked the transition of illustration as an instrument of religious propaganda to illustration simply for aesthetic purposes. But since the new types of illustrations were expensive, they appeared primarily in times of economic prosperity. Moreover, books containing such illustrations were always reserved for the well-to-do.

Publication policies in Europe, unlike those in the Far East, were not aimed at serving public interests. In fact, while the ruling and commercial classes in medieval Europe used the manuscript for their own political and economic benefit, the Asian elite appeared to use printing primarily to educate the population. For example, the following is a decree enacted by King Sejong of Korea in 1403:

> "To govern it is necessary to spread knowledge of the laws and the books so as to satisfy reason and to reform men's evil nature; in this way peace and order may be maintained. . . . I want letters to be made from copper to be used for printing so that more books will be made available. This would produce benefits too extensive to measure. It is not fitting that people should bear the cost of such work, which will be borne by the Treasury" (in Febvre and Martin, 1976: 76).

Thus, while printing in the Far East was used to democratize knowledge, European states never encouraged the development of printing to serve the people. In fact, political and religious authorities were afraid that democratizing knowledge via the printing of books in vernacular languages would undermine their control over the population. Without support from the state, the book trade had to adapt quickly to existing commercial practices. Given that depletion of book inventories was usually a slow process and that shipping to other markets was an onerous task, independent artisans would go bankrupt if they had difficulty selling one edition. For the most part, the only economically viable publishing businesses were run by merchants who were linked with a distribution network, sold a variety of books and had the liquidity required to continue operations while waiting for revenues from the sale of their products. This is why the trade fell in the hands of some bankers, who later became booksellers/publishers.

With the eventual support of the state, powerful merchants took control of the printing industry. The state granted certain producers monopoly status, claiming this was necessary to protect the burgeoning industry. Otherwise, it seems, the printing business would have fallen victim to speculators, which in turn would have hindered the technological development of printing. As an example, Febvre and Martin (1976) mention how fourteenth- and fifteenth-century papermakers were granted monopoly status so they could be guaranteed sufficient supplies of raw material (i.e., rags) to meet the paper production needs of publishers:

> "To ensure supplies and prevent the rag collectors demanding exorbitant prices, papermakers appealed to the State to grant them monopolies in rag collection. . . . In the 1450s, the papermakers of Genoa complained they were under the thumb of the rag merchants and sought to prosecute them" (Febvre and Martin, 1976: 35).

At first, state intervention in the distribution of books was aimed at protecting publishers against suppliers of counterfeit copies, which were inferior both in quality and in price. But the appearance of counterfeit books simply led publishers to lower their standards of quality. In reality, by giving publishers a privileged status, the state was able to tighten its control over the content of printed books. This is why the French court gave preference to printers located in Paris at the expense of less docile printers in the provinces.

Book and pamphlet publication was constantly monitored by the state, as well as by the Roman Catholic Church and the Protestant Church. However, offending publishers generally received only light sentences or token fines. As Eisenstein remarks, "Even the censorship edicts issued by archbishops and popes for the 1480s down through 1515 hail invention as divinely inspired and elaborate on its advantages before going on to note the need to curtail its abuses" (1979: 317). The fact was that, before the Protestant Revolt in England, churchmen considered the invention of print as an asset to both churchmen and laymen. However, in 1520, Imperial and papal edicts "aimed at arresting the spread of Protestant heresy" (1979: 347).

While the churches' primary targets were authors, attempts at secular control, especially by the King of France, were mainly aimed at publishers. Thus in the seventeenth and eighteenth centuries, following the Revocation of the Edict of Nantes, many French publishers, particularly less influential ones, were forced to seek refuge abroad, where a new type of polemical literature emerged, spearheaded by what Febvre and Martin call "printer-journalists" (1976: 156).

Thus, instead of extending the state's power, censorship laws had the opposite effect: they weakened the government. In order to counter the publication of polemical pamphlets and books, Jean Baptiste Colbert, chief minister to Louis XIV, imposed censorship laws in the mid-1660s. While these measures, which remained in effect until 1686, threatened the survival of provincial publishers in France, they were a boon to clandestine publishers located in Holland, who distributed their books throughout Europe via underground networks. As a result, peddling was one of the most important means of distribution of censored literature, and a highly profitable occupation in mid-sixteenth century France.

Government censorship of printed literature was but one political factor which influenced the development of the book. Another closely related factor was the Reformation. Febvre and Martin (1976) contend that the distribution of printed books played a pivotal role in the emergence of the Reformation, and that, reciprocally, the growing desire by people to know more about the movement spawned an increase in the publication and distribution of books, pamphlets and other types of literature.

Reformers took advantage of printing to disseminate their ideas to an audience more widely scattered than if they had used any other form of communication. As a result, there emerged a host of underground networks to distribute state-banned literature. Some networks were established by pedlars, who hid Reformation literature under the merchandise, clothes or fruit which they officially sold.

The resistance by Reformers forced the state to pass tougher laws. Censorship thus became so severe that publishers and distributers were only permitted to sell religious books. As one would expect, these laws were not always applied evenly and, with time, publishers and distributers found ways of getting around them. For example, Febvre and Martin (1976) reported that door-to-door distribution was highly effective since pedlars with no fixed address were quite elusive. In this way, new ideas were communicated to a growing number of peasants. However, politics was not the only motive for breaking censorship laws: for small book publishers and distributers the distribution of banned literature was an economic necessity.

As we can see, European society in the sixteenth century could no longer be considered as having an oral culture: it had developed a literary mentality. We will now focus on the impact of the book on reading publics of the time.

In *The Gutenberg Galaxy* (1962), which is a study of the development of printing, McLuhan compares the effects of oral and written culture on the creation of our perceptions, for, as he states in his book, perceptions determine the type of society in which we live. According to McLuhan, oral culture allowed the senses to interact so that both auditory and tactile perceptions became the most developed. Under these conditions, members of a community became dependent on one another. Conversely, in written culture, every experience is reduced to a single sense, that of vision, at the expense of all others. The isolation of visual perception brought about "the self-amputation of the body" and fostered a uniform and linear view of the world. Thus, McLuhan insisted in his book, the emergence of printing not only radically changed the reading public's mentality, but also had a direct effect on the cultural forms they support, as well as an indirect impact on the economic, political and social structures of society. In short, people moved away from a community identity founded on an oral culture to a type of society fostering an individual identity based on the need for intimacy and private ownership, and engendered by the isolation created by the emergence of printing.

The work of Febvre and Martin concurs only partly with McLuhan's assertions. While Febvre and Martin (1976) acknowledged that the printed book had an impact on the popular culture of pre-modern societies, they pointed out that this effect may be analyzed as two consecutive and contradictory events. It appears that the production of books first had a unifying effect, particularly among intellectual communities. This was largely due to the fact that the language used in books, when they first appeared in Europe, was Latin, which at the time was considered the universal language.

Later, in an attempt to increase their profits, merchants, printers and publishers began producing books in popular languages in order to increase their readership. Authors thus began writing vernacular-language texts intended for the masses, who did not know Latin. It would appear that this change undermined Latin as the sole language of printing, and fostered the emergence of various national languages at the expense of the universal language. It is in this sense that Febvre and Martin (1976) claimed that the printed book contributed to the fall of a universal culture—which, it must be said, was exclusively an elite culture—and promoted diverse national cultures, which were more accessible to the masses.

The impact on audiences of any new form of communication, such as print, is never uniform. According to Goody and Watt (1963), even if some research such as that conducted by Febvre and Martin seems to show that the impact of printing was the same everywhere, the emergence of a new form of communication that requires the learning of specific abilities cannot influence different social classes in the same manner. For instance, artisans, peasants and manual labourers, most of whom were illiterate, could not benefit from the development of printing in the same way as the intellectual community did. This was particularly the case given that, as we saw earlier, it was relatively easy for the elite and the ruling classes to control not only the production of, but also access to, the printed book.

On the other hand, the coming of print should also be associated with a certain form of democracy, say some authors. According to Altick, in England, "the history of [the] mass reading audience is, in fact, the history of English democracy seen from a new angle" (1963: 3). He also stated that the notion of democracy should not be restricted to the social, political and economic spheres, but should be linked to "the unqualified freedom of all men and women to enjoy the fruits of a country's culture, among which books have a place of high, if not supreme, importance" (1963: 7). The "new way of escape and relaxation" offered by mass-produced books and newspapers procured by the workers condemned to "the regimentation of industrial society with its consequent crushing of individuality" provides a "means of engaging their minds and imagination" (1963: 4). Audiences may choose among the abundance of printed material available, though the range of choices may be limited for some groups.

In short, we can see that the development of a new form of communication is influenced by a variety of factors existing in the societies where it emerges. Some economic factors, such as the "profitability" of production and distribution industries, are mediated by political intervention, which in turn has an impact on the development of the new technology, as well as on its users. Cultural and social factors associated with users also have an effect on other aspects of the technology's development. This type of interaction between the diverse factors associated with the emergence of a new form of communication can also be observed in the development of "oral" mass media, or those media that involve the use of the human voice.

THE COMING OF ORAL MASS MEDIA

Oral media have brought about significant change in the development of long-distance communication. What was most fascinating about these media when they first appeared was that they made instantaneous long-distance communication possible. Before the telephone the only way of achieving long-distance communication was to send written messages. Regardless of whether a message was handwritten (such as a letter), printed or even telegraphed, it took anywhere from a few hours to several months to reach its destination. Conversely, messages transmitted by telephone or radio arrive instantaneously. But can the same be said about radio broadcasts that were, and are still, pre-recorded, and therefore not really simultaneous? First, it should be noted that when radio broadcasting began, pre-recorded programmes did not exist. And, later on, even if certain shows were pre-recorded, their transmission remained instantaneous. Instantaneity is therefore an intrinsic characteristic of this medium of long-distance oral communication. This characteristic also generated new oral cultural practices in Western societies.

As was mentioned above, the development of a new form of communication as a result of the invention of a new medium can induce social change on many levels. While oral communication by itself cannot be considered as a new form, long-distance and mass oral communication—which became possible with the telephone and radio—was a new phenomenon. And although the telephone cannot be considered as a mass medium, we will see that, for many years prior to the commercialization of radio in the 1920s, certain telephone activities closely resembled what have been traditionally viewed as radio activities.

The Telephone

When the telephone was first developed, it provided a means of transmitting group activities. For instance, in 1879 the telephone was used to broadcast religious Mass to the sick who could not get to church, and to the bourgeois population vacationing in the countryside where there were no churches. This type of broadcast, however, only lasted for a few years, as parish priests became concerned about its growing popularity and began to question its legitimacy. Nevertheless, the telephone was used to transmit other types of social activities, entertainment being the most popular.

Many concerts, recitals and poetry readings were transmitted over telephone lines, to the delight of operators, particularly in smaller towns. Martin (1991) points out that one of the most successful programmes, called *Sunday Evening Musicales*, broadcast concerts on Sundays to subscribers of the telephone systems in Kingston and Belleville, Ontario. When organizers were short of performers, they asked Bell employees to perform. Despite its success among subscribers, Bell disapproved of this activity. Company managers claimed the broadcasts damaged telephone lines and were an abuse of the company's property, which was intended to serve more serious purposes, that is, business communication. After a few months, the activity was removed from the telephone lines.

Telephone transmission was also used for other types of social activities. The most well known were developed in Hungary and the United states, and consisted of the broadcast of a "speaking newspaper" by organizations that could afford to rent telephone lines specifically for this purpose. The most important of these broadcasts, which began in 1893 and continued for over 18 years, was organized by *Telefon-Hirmondo Telephone Newspaper* in Budapest, Hungary. All day long the paper broadcast updated news bulletins on its system. The broadcasts ended when radio finally became commercialized in Hungary. Another similar service was provided by the *Telephone Herald* in Newark, New Jersey. For five cents a day, the telephonic newspaper provided subscribers with continuous news programming between 8 a.m. and 10 p.m. However, after only one year the local telephone company refused to renew the rental contract for the lines used for the broadcasts.

Many other types of programmes were broadcast over the telephone before the coming of radio. While most were very modest in scope, they demonstrate that there was a genuine interest among certain social groups for this type of long-distance transmission (Martin, 1991). It is not surprising that when radio was finally commercialized it enjoyed almost immediate success.

Radio Broadcast Throughout the World

As we saw previously, long-distance information and entertainment broadcasting began with the telephone. However, this type of transmission cannot be considered as mass communication, since it was limited to a few small groups who could afford the telephone. In fact, telephone transmission was a very selective form of communication, as opposed to mass communication.

The first mass transmission via radio was achieved in 1907 by a group of amateurs. Pool (1981), however, claims that radio did not become a reality until World War I, where it was considered a precious tool to be used only for transmitting important messages only between specific points. After the war, radio was commercialized due to pressure from certain segments of the business community. Soon, commercial radio stations began to spring up in Canada and the United States.

According to Pool (1981), depending on the political and social context of the country involved, commercial radio developed in one of three philosophical directions: "propaganda radio," "elite radio" and "democratic radio." Each of these development paths was directly linked to the ideology and culture of the country where radio broadcasting became commercialized.

Propaganda radio was first developed in the 1920s in the Soviet Union, and was later adopted in Nazi Germany during the period preceding World War II. Programming on propaganda radio was entirely censored by the "authorities," that is, by the government. In the Soviet Union, this form of control over broadcasting occurred with the emergence of commercial radio in the early 1920s. Since radio made it possible to reach a large number of people at the same time, the Soviet authorities, who were still sensitive to the events of the Bolshevik Revolution, believed that the new technology was too powerful to be allowed to operate outside the control of a state agency, which would ensure that broadcasters followed the "party line." At that time there were few radio receivers in the country, so the government built a network of wired loudspeakers to organize "collective listenings" of radio broadcasts in the streets and the workplace. These listenings were another means of censorship, since people—at least those who could not afford their own radio receivers—were able to listen only to government-sanctioned messages. As the name "propaganda radio" implies, only propaganda and information programming was acceptable; there was very little room for light broadcasting such as music and drama. In Germany, at the end of the 1930s, radio was developed along a similar model by Hitler.

Since there was no place for "alternatives" to official radio programming, resisting listeners had to find other ways of organizing. One of the characteristics of radio waves is that they know no boundaries. With short-wave radio receivers, people can listen to messages transmitted from other countries. But in the early days of radio only a few people possessed short-wave radio receivers. More recently, researchers have claimed that most households in totalitarian countries such as China and the ex-Soviet Union owned this type of radio receiver. According to Pool (1981), on some nights about one-sixth of the Soviet population listened to short-wave radio programming, which was, and still is, considered completely unnecessary in democratic countries.

Although radio censorship has never been exercised to the same extent in England, this is not to say that radio was allowed to develop in a haphazard manner. As soon as commercial radio began, state institutions controlled broadcasting by allowing only government-approved programmes to be aired. Pool refers to this type of controlled development as "elite radio." Although elite-radio programming was not restricted to propaganda, a government committee established that "the control of such a potential power over public opinion and the life of the nation ought to remain with the state" (Pool, 1981: 179). Louis-Philip of France had had the same reaction towards the coming of the telegraph.

This broadcasting policy was a "logical" extension of the transmission policy historically adopted by Great Britain. From the Middle Ages on, control over information transmission had been the exclusive privilege of the postal service. For example, the British postal service, which has since become nationalized, took over telegraph services in 1869 and telephone services in 1912. Thus, when radio arrived on the scene, it seemed logical that it be placed under state control.

State control over radio, however, was not achieved overnight. In 1922, during the early stages of commercialization, radio was in the hands of a private organization, the British Broadcasting Company (not to be mistaken for the British Broadcasting Corporation (BBC)). The following year, a commission of inquiry was created to investigate the company's operations. In its report, the commission recommended that while radio should be placed under government control, it should be under the auspices of a different organization than the postal service. Thus the BBC was founded in 1927 as an independent public corporation. Since the BBC was, and still is, funded by permit fees, advertising was not allowed. Under these conditions, the BBC immediately became, and still is, an elite radio station that broadcasts in a number of areas, namely drama, music, politics and science. Pool (1981) noted that programming was developed in accordance with the government's educational objectives, and that broadcasters transmitted content which they believed was informative.

However, there was one area in which the BBC was not an authority: news broadcasting. Unlike newspapers, which enjoyed a certain freedom because they were privately operated, the BBC had severe news broadcasting restrictions imposed on it by the state: the station was not permitted to transmit news bulletins longer than 2,400 words. These restrictions were not removed until 1938 when government agencies realized that news broadcasts could be received from neighbouring countries with less conservative programming policies. Moreover, it had become apparent that radio was not in direct competition with newspapers, and could actually be used to promote them.

Nevertheless, the restriction over news broadcasting—which seemed to contradict the very principle of a journalistic operation—became the BBC's key to success. The station specialized in international news broadcasting, and soon acquired a worldwide reputation unparalleled by any other broadcaster. During World War II, for example, the BBC broadcast news from both sides of the front line. It was the same story during the Vietnam War, where, unlike American stations, the BBC became the station *that could be trusted*. Since the war was unpopular in the United States, it seems that American stations originally did not inform their audiences of the true situation. According to Pool (1981), people who wanted to know the truth tuned in to the BBC, which forced American stations to reveal the true nature of the war. The pressure did not come only from the BBC, however, since several resistance movements had begun to force the American federal government, and the media industry, to reveal the truth.

The third direction of radio development identified by Pool is that which occurred in the United States and Canada: "democratic radio." This type of programming was geared to providing audiences with the shows they wanted to hear.

In the United States, and everywhere else for that matter, commercial radio began in the 1920s by providing entertainment programming. Commercial stations were financed by private companies such as Westinghouse, Marconi, and General Electric, and were linked to the AT&T system, the American equivalent to Bell Canada. In the beginning, AT&T attempted to establish a broadcasting system like the one used for the telephone. It sought to transmit radio communications, without necessarily being involved in their production, by building radio stations in every city. It hoped to sell air time to whomever was interested in buying it. Their customers were mainly patrons of the arts who wanted to promote their own artistic interests, or charitable organizations who supported public education. However, AT&T's plans failed, which confirmed the belief that advertisement was the most reliable way of making radio profitable.

In the beginning there was little legislation restricting the use of airwaves by private companies. In contrast to the previous two cases, democratic radio stations seemed to have complete political freedom over programming, at least until the 1930s. Paradoxically, this freedom came at a cost. Since stations did not receive funding from the state, they encountered a host of financial problems.

To finance operations, stations considered a number of options: a 2% tax on radio receiver sales; funds solicited from radio audiences; voluntary contributions from the public; and an annual tax levy on radio. None of these measures was adopted either in the United States or Canada. Pool (1981) contends that, as early as the start of the 1920s, stations turned to advertisement to finance operations. Stations asked sponsors to attach their name to a performer of their choice. As a result, sponsors were indirectly responsible for programming. This practice was so profitable, Martin (1989) tells us, that programming quickly became a hostage of the sponsors. To counter this trend, the government passed financing legislation in 1927. But since the practice of commercial sponsorship was already so well entrenched, "the decision about how broadcasting was to be financed had been made, not through informed discussion . . . but rather through default by business leaders interested in making profits . . . " (Sterling and Kittross cited in Martin, 1989: 53).

This mode of financing resulted in a type of radio programming that was almost diametrically opposed to "elite radio." Indeed, this format encouraged commercial radio stations to broadcast shows (vaudeville, easy-listening music, etc.) that would appeal to various types of audiences. During the early years, programming was not subject to fixed schedules, since unexpected events—e.g., bad weather or technical problems—would often upset broadcasters' plans. Performers who were willing to work for free were invited to do their numbers at a specific time. Despite such chaotic conditions, audiences grew rapidly. In 1923, 556 radio stations were operating in the United States, compared with 34 in Canada. Since transmission power was much stronger in the United States than in Canada, stations from south of the border were more popular, not only among Americans, but also with Canadian audiences. Despite their cost, in 1926 one in every 20 households owned a radio receiver. In the words of Sterling and Kittross, radio had truly become a "national craze" (cited in Martin, 1989). In order to satisfy a constantly growing public, programme contents were gradually diversified.

Yet, radio listeners had very little opportunity to express their opinion on the broadcasted content. The programming of public broadcasting channels like CBC was sometimes submitted to royal commissions, task forces or the scrutiny of their board of commissioners. But clearly, the content could not be considered as reflecting the opinion of the Canadian masses. The only way for listeners to show their approval or dissatisfaction was to refuse to listen to a particular programme. It was only in 1954 that a Bureau of Audience Research was created and that radio listeners had some means of exerting some influence on programming (Eaman, 1992).

Pool's categorization of the three types of radio has, like most exercises of this kind, some drawbacks. It is very difficult, for instance, to associate the Canadian case with any of these categories, since programming on both elite channels and commercial channels in Canada is subject to legislation, in contrast to the "democratic" system of the United States.

The first appearance of a formal inquiry to determine the extent to which the state should intervene in Canadian radio broadcasting was in 1929 with the Royal Commission on Radio Broadcasting chaired by Sir John Aird. The Aird Commission recommended "the nationalisation" of the radio system (Raboy, 1992: 157). However, because of a matter of jurisdiction between Canada and the Dominion, it was only in 1932 that the Canadian Radio Broadcasting Act created a national public system called the Canadian Radio Broadcasting Commission (CRBC). The CRBC "set out to create a national radio service in English and in French: a single service, using both languages alternately, so that the same programs were broadcast in both English and French" (Raboy, 1992: 157). It was only in 1941 that two parallel systems, French and English, were created. The most important factor forcing this division, according to Raboy, was "the absolute, militant refusal of anglophone communities in the Maritimes, Ontario, and Western Canada to accept the presence of French on the air" (1992: 158). The two solitudes were then reproduced on airwaves!

The Production of Radio Programme Content

The emergence of radio brought about the creation of new occupations. The most obvious was certainly that of speaker or announcer. Qualifications for this position varied depending on the type of station: the more prestigious the station, the more qualified the announcers. For example, the BBC hired only university graduates, while American and Canadian stations were less demanding. There was, however, general agreement on the notion that a radio announcer's primary role was to speak with "dignity," "professional sense" and "authority," apparently to give this new mass medium more credibility.

It appears that the concern to establish a certain credibility prevented station managers and owners from hiring female announcers. At that time, the only socially recognized roles for women were that of mother and housewife; women's participation in public life was considered inappropriate. Socially acquired "feminine" characteristics, including kindness, submission and obedience, did not command the kind of authority that radio broadcasters sought in regular announcers. Moreover, women's voices were said to have a nasal quality and too high a pitch. Nevertheless, a large number of women were hired on a part-time basis to host daytime shows on "women's subjects." Women therefore had little opportunity to express opinions about political or social issues. A number of male radio experts, nevertheless, believed that "some of the women announcers have better sense than some of the men announcers" (cited in Martin, 1989: 55). Are we to believe, then, that to be on radio it was better to be a man than to have common sense?

Male announcers were mostly responsible for programmes related to politics or news, or those dealing with current affairs. According to Martin (1989), during the 1920s, in Canada and the United States, men were relatively free to talk about any issue they wanted. But with advertising becoming the main source of financing, radio stations gradually had to pay heed to public opinion. As a result, programme financing and the ideological values of the station owners became a means of censorship. Eventually, the political content of programming became more tightly controlled.

CONCLUSION

This historical overview shows that the development of a specific form of communication created by the emergence of a medium is a complex social process that is influenced by many social conditions. The various factors involved in the process do not act independently of one another, but instead are interrelated in various ways.

While a new medium can have a considerable impact on long-standing social practices, people do not spontaneously accept the intrusion of a new form of communication on their social habits. In fact, new social practices or activities only emerge from a long, gradual process of adjustment and modification which is influenced by political and economic forces. What is the interaction between these various factors? What is the impact of each factor on the development process of a new form of communication? What measures of control, if any, are taken, and how do they affect access to the new form of communication? Do political, economic or cultural factors put restrictions, explicit or implicit, on the development process?

In the chapters to follow, we will examine a number of theoretical models to help find answers to these questions. By looking at the specific aspects considered in each model, we will discover how they may be used to explain the workings of the mass media.

MAINSTREAM MODELS IN MASS COMMUNICATION RESEARCH

INTRODUCTION

After World War II, the growth of mass communication—first with radio and later, television—and the concentration of ownership of the mass media among independent broadcasters in the United States and Canada led to the development of theoretical models explaining the impact of this new type of communication on populations. Almost overnight, researchers in several disciplines became interested in studying media content and how it influences audiences.

In the United States, the first attempts at theorizing about the mass media had psychological-behaviourist underpinnings. These models addressed the following question: what impact do the media have on the behaviour of people who use them? Research was focused on the media/audience relationship, which was assumed to be direct and unidirectional. After criticism from American sociologists, the psychological approach was quickly replaced by a model based on functionalist theoretical principles, which enjoyed considerable popularity at the time. With this new approach, research no longer looked at how the media influence audiences, but rather at how audiences use media content to meet their social and psychological needs. The two models, which were both developed in the United States, had a large number of proponents. Because they have had significant influence on communication studies, these approaches are collectively called the dominant paradigm. Though it is not within the scope of this book to undertake an in-depth analysis of each of them, we will examine certain *elements* that are relevant to the subjects in the chapters that follow.

In Canada, two theorists, Harold Innis and Marshall McLuhan, have had a strong impact on communication studies. Although their approaches are different in many respects, they agree on at least one point, namely that means of communication have a large impact on the development of new social forms. In this chapter, we will look at some aspects of these two approaches that attempt to explain mass media communication.

THE AMERICAN MODELS

The following are three examples of media events, transmitted via three different mass media, that influenced the behaviour of their intended audiences.

1. The Vietnam War: Experts in media studies all agree that the media played a significant role in the outcome of the Vietnam War. The information broadcast through the mass media caused public opinion to shift from support for American involvement in the conflict at the beginning of the war, to pressure for the withdrawal of American troops from Vietnam. Having learned from this experience, the American government imposed unprecedented censorship measures during the Gulf War on all information emanating from the front.

2. The American Revolution: Historians who have studied the content of the print media at the time of the revolution have concluded that a number of pamphlets and colonial weeklies influenced the outcome of the conflict. Not only did the print media keep the colonial population informed of events and ideas, but they also mobilized support for the Declaration of Independence. Historians contend that radical supporters of the independence movement carefully planned their use of propaganda.

3. The Martian Invasion: The most convincing evidence of the influence of the media on populations can be found in the entertainment world. On October 30, 1938, the CBS radio network, under the direction of Orson Welles, "broadcast a terrifying and realistic report of an invasion from Mars taking place near Princeton, New Jersey" (Agee, Ault and Emery, 1988: 40). The form of communication used was a broadcast imitating a regular news bulletin. The programme had a remarkable impact on its audience: believing that monsters had invaded their neighbourhood, many listeners immediately fled their homes before the end of the show when the broadcasters revealed the hoax.

These three events clearly show that the mass media have a considerable impact on audiences. But is this not the role of the media, namely to influence the people who use them? This is the type of question American researchers addressed in the 1940s when they developed models that involved a common general approach which is now considered as the *dominant paradigm*, and which still influences a large number of communication researchers.

A Psychological Theory: The hypodermic model

The psychological approach, also called the hypodermic[1] model, was developed by H.D. Lasswell, a law professor at Yale University, who was interested in studying the propaganda communicated through the media during World War II. Lasswell began his analysis with the principle that mass communication, regardless of its form, is something that

---

[1] Referring to a needle injected beneath the skin.

someone does to another person. In the case of the media, the communicator (i.e., the medium) does "something" to an audience, not the inverse. Lasswell analyzed this process by developing an analytical framework based on the following query: "Who, says what, in which channel, to whom, with what effect?" (Agee, Ault and Emery, 1988: 43). To answer these questions, Lasswell looked at the media, their content and audiences, as well as the effects of the media on audiences. Since the hypodermic model is based on a stimulus/response theory, it views audiences as masses composed of identical, passive, isolated individuals who react the same way to stimuli transmitted through the media. It is obvious that Lasswell's analysis of the effects of the media did not take into consideration any of the social factors that can influence audiences, such as its size, or the effect of peer pressure on the persons studied. From this perspective, masses are seen as groups of "atomized" persons with the following characteristics:

- they are presumed to be in a situation of psychological isolation;
- when they interact with others, they do so in an impersonal manner;
- they are not under pressure to conform to social norms (DeFleur and Ball-Rokeach, 1989: 157).

The concept of atomized individuals—the cornerstone of the hypodermic model—reduces the role of each audience member to that of passive message receiver. The link between a mass medium and its audience is seen as direct and unilateral, such that only message contents can modify behaviour. The hypodermic model is based on observations of a mass medium which, as we saw earlier, was first marketed in the early 1920s, namely radio. In the same way that a hypodermic needle injects medicine, it was believed that the reception of a radio broadcast could slowly impregnate the mind of audience members, where the message would gradually be ingrained. From this perspective, society appears as nothing more than an amorphous social organization in which interpersonal relations are absolutely insignificant. According to Gitlin, in such a society, "mass communications 'inject' ideas, attitudes, and dispositions towards behaviour into passive, atomized, extremely vulnerable individuals" (Gitlin, 1979: 210).

As this model is rooted in behaviourism, resistance to media messages is seen as an adverse force that must be eliminated. If resistance is detected, the injected dose is reinforced by increasing the intensity, frequency and omnipresence of the message so as to achieve the intended results. The effect of the message will thus regain its original strength. From this point of view, the efficiency of communication seems to be reflected in a linear relationship between communication which supports an option and that which opposes it.

Although this approach may appear a little eccentric today, it took on a different meaning in the historical context from which it emerged. The experience of the two world wars showed how propaganda was a powerful weapon of persuasion. It was first believed that people were helpless in the face of the almost omnipotent mass media, and that all that was needed to create an immediate impact was to transmit a message with enough insistence and emotional intensity. Researchers simply ignored results of studies using this approach that were not consistent with the hypodermic, or psychological, model. What is more, the method of analysis sometimes produced skewed results. For example, even though studies were conducted on one medium at a time, researchers generalized their findings to other media. A number of researchers who felt ill at ease about this practice sought to develop a new model that would take into account other aspects of the functioning of the media. Sociologists, for example, put media messages back into the social contexts in which people receive them. Thus a group of scholars, headed by American sociologist P.F. Lazarsfeld, developed a framework founded on functionalist principles.

Functionalist Models

The idea of drawing an analogy between equilibrium in societies and homeostasis in organisms is at the root of the functionalist analysis of social interaction. This sociological approach, which was developed in the eighteenth and nineteenth centuries by Constant, Tocqueville, Lamennais, Bentham, Spencer, and others, views social evolution as a natural process which constantly tends towards stability. With time, social systems that have proven to be viable are those endowed with an inherent structure that automatically maintains a state of constant equilibrium between social groups. In this context, state intervention is generally considered useless, if not intrusive, to the process of social evolution.

For functionalists, a society's stability is founded on a consensus reflecting an equilibrium between the interdependence of individuals, on the one hand, and their different personal needs on the other. By assuming that power is equitably distributed in a society, functionalists suggest various models to explain the relationship between social consensus and the functioning of that society. For some, equilibrium of the system is achieved through carefully planned state intervention. Consensus is viewed as tenuous, such that abandonment or modification of these social measures would lead to instability. Under these conditions, institutions are maintained through conservative policies that ensure total respect for the laws and conventions on which they are founded. For other functionalists, pressure for change is an indication of social disequilibrium, which may be caused, for example, by scientific discoveries or new lifestyles. The ensuing social change is the mechanism through which social consensus is re-established. Drawing on Darwin's concept of natural selection, these functionalists believe that all social systems, regardless of their political or ideological orientation, have the necessary properties to adapt to new situations. Under these conditions, intervention in society's dynamics is considered inappropriate unless it is obvious that natural processes are unable to re-establish social stability by themselves.

The functionalist approach, which dominated the social sciences in North America for much of the twentieth century, and which is still used in some scientific circles, has had an important influence on the interpretation of the impact of the mass media on society. Lazarsfeld borrowed considerably from functionalist theory to develop his own theoretical model of the media.

The "Two-Step Flow" Theory

The "Two-Step Flow" Theory, developed in *Personal Influence*, written by Katz and Lazarsfeld, severely criticizes the simplistic nature of the hypodermic theory. The authors summarized their critique as follows: " . . . the omnipotent media, on one hand, sending forth the message, and the atomized masses, on the other, waiting to receive it—and nothing in between" (Katz and Lazarsfeld, 1955: 20). In response to the hypodermic model developed by the Lasswell school, Lazarsfeld and his colleagues developed an approach in which the reactions of media users play a prominent role.

This approach was based on a study conducted by Lazarsfeld, Berelson, and Gaudet (1944) during the 1940 American presidential campaign between Wendell Wilkie and the incumbent Franklin D. Roosevelt. The study was the first large-scale methodological analysis of the impact of the media on public opinion. Every month, between June and November, 600 people in Erie County, Ohio, were asked a series of questions about the sources which influenced their political views, and about their opinion changes, if applicable. The principal media sources studied were newspapers, magazines and radio, as television was not widely available at the time.

According to the authors of the study, the results showed that the mass media were particularly efficient in reinforcing opinions people already had, at least latently. People who changed their opinion usually did so in the first days of the campaign. Thereafter, their decisions became reinforced, ruling out the possibility of future reversal. These results contradicted most of the hypotheses the researchers initially put forth concerning the sensitivity of public opinion regarding the mass media. While the remainder of the electoral campaign was not without information significant enough to influence individuals, public opinion changes did not occur. At first glance, it seemed as though a filter had been placed between the media and audiences which kept opinions stable.

The study of Erie County voters was founded on the hypothesis that with urbanization, interpersonal relations had become less influential than the media (DeFleur and Ball-Rokeach, 1989). For this reason, the initial research protocol of the study did not take into consideration the effect of peer influence. Nevertheless, in the course of their investigation, Lazarsfeld, Berelson and Gaudet observed that their subjects had taken part in discussions with peers more often than they had read newspapers or listened to the radio. This observation led to a reformulation of the theories that focused only on the direct contact between the media and audiences. What was the nature of this change?

The authors of the Erie County study observed that, while it is true that information transmitted through the media may be known by a large number of people, this does not necessarily mean they all receive it first-hand. Instead, the study showed that a mediator existed between the media and a significant number of people who became aware of the message. For example, in the context of the 1930s and 1940s, the written press could not reach many people living in rural areas, where few people knew how to read. These people, nevertheless, formed their opinions on the basis of the same political information reported in the press. For example, people who did not read newspapers or listen to the radio were aware of many of the issues raised in Roosevelt's speeches. How could this be, if the media had only a direct effect on people? The answer is that people founded their opinions on information which they obtained *indirectly* from the press. The study of Erie County voters, therefore, led researchers to abandon the notion that the media essentially have a direct impact on the masses. A new hypothesis was therefore needed.

It became obvious to Katz and Lazarsfeld (1955) that the impact of a mass medium extended beyond its immediate audience. The only plausible hypothesis, they argued, was that information is disseminated through the mass media in a *two-step flow* process. Persuasive messages first have a direct impact on a few "opinion leaders," who in turn have the power to shape the attitudes of people in their immediate entourage. Opinion leaders almost always act as mediators between the media and the masses. These mediators are more receptive to information communicated about certain social problems, to which they are particularly sensitive. With this information, mediators form an opinion which they quickly spread to people in their entourage. The effect is even more persuasive if the intended receivers of the message are already aware of some of the information held by the mediator. In this situation, the mediator's role is to confirm the impression that the information is accurate. In short, the effect of the mass media occurs in two steps: first, the message makes its impression on opinion leaders, and, second, on mass audiences through the personal influence of these leaders. This is why the model has been termed the *two-step flow* process.

Katz and Lazarsfeld (1955) thus added a new element to media research: that of the social context. But, if the media's impact is not felt directly, how does one study their influence on the process involved in maintaining social consensus, a process necessary for stability in society? The answer: by refusing to perceive media audiences as amorphous and nondescript masses, and by considering them in their specific environment, where they are not only subject to the media's influence, but also to that of their peers. This important new element of media analysis led these researchers to give less importance to the notion that the media have a direct influence on mass audiences.

For Lazarsfeld and his school, the mass media rarely bring about attitude changes, a view that challenges the hypodermic theory. In general terms, they believe that the effect of the media is that it reinforces beliefs or opinions that people seek to confirm. Functionalist researchers also doubt that the media have the ability to engender long-term changes in attitudes.

While it is difficult for the mass media to change existing opinions or attitudes in the short run, or the long run, Klapper (1968) believed they can shape opinions about new issues, or issues about which people have no prior opinion. Klapper reached this conclusion on the basis of a study of the presidential election of Fidel Castro in Cuba. Before Castro came to power, few Americans knew who he was. But a few months later, a majority of Americans had formed a relatively detailed opinion about his political leanings and his actions. According to Klapper (1968), the speed with which people became aware of Castro can be seen as the result of the media's actions. "It is not difficult to see why the mass media are extremely effective in creating opinion on new issues. In such a situation the audiences have no existing opinions . . . and opinion leaders are not yet ready to lead . . . " or in other words, influence their surroundings (cited in Gitlin, 1979: 217). It would follow, then, according to this model, that Castro's present image cannot be easily changed, since the topic of Castro is no longer new. The model suggests that the actual ability of the mass media to shape attitudes on new issues should not be confused with their often-presumed ability to change attitudes that are deeply rooted in people's lifestyles.

In short, functionalist principles have helped Lazarsfeld and his colleagues focus on the influence of people on the media, instead of the opposite, as the object of analysis. To maintain social consensus, it is necessary, in their view, to understand the functioning of the flow of media communications, not the production of media content. What do people do to the media? This question became the focal point of subsequent studies conducted by this school.

The Theory of Gratifying Uses For some researchers, Katz in particular, the inability of the media to change deeply rooted social attitudes seemed to suggest that a further revision of theoretical assumptions was needed to re-examine the impact of the media. The observation that the media reinforce already existing opinions and beliefs, instead of shaping new ones, led to the hypothesis that the media do not cause opinion changes, but uphold existing ones. According to Katz and Lazarsfeld (1955), the mass media provide audiences with a handy means of instilling and reinforcing cultural values. Far from being controlled by elite groups, the media are, in a sense, "held hostage" by audiences. In other words, if audience members are not satisfied with the contents of a medium, they will cease to use it. According to this new perspective, the media satisfy the social and psychological needs of audiences, and people will use a medium only if its content is "gratifying."

What are the implications of this assertion? First, since everyone enjoys the same control over the media, it follows that the model assumes that all users have equal opportunities to wield their personal influence over the *functioning* of the media. As rightful members of society, each of us is capable of resisting social pressures which run counter to our individual needs. In other words, users decide whether a medium will survive or not. Thus, under these conditions, the media must be aware of the attitudes of the people they address in order to attract them.

Audiences are therefore viewed as groups of people having diverse needs. In this respect, this approach is quite different from the hypodermic model, which views audiences as passive entities. According to the gratifying uses model, it is necessary to examine the social characteristics of audiences by subdividing them into homogeneous units on the basis of age, sex, economic status, profession, etc. But ultimately, according to this line of thinking, each receiver may be considered unique. According to Elliott (1974), this notion is a departure from the "personal influence" theory, and marks a return to the concept of atomized individuals who are insensitive to peer pressure. However, contrary to the hypodermic model, the gratifying uses theory does not assume that individual responses are homogeneous. The hypodermic model assumes that, although the intensity with which a message is received might vary slightly depending on the individual, the impact of a message is the same across the board. To assess the global impact, then, all that is needed is to generalize the results collected from small laboratory samples to entire mass audiences. In contrast, according to the gratifying uses model, a message can have antagonistic effects if audience members have different expectations from a medium.

Although the gratifying uses theory was developed to challenge observations made under the hypodermic model, it was nevertheless inspired by Lasswell's approach that audiences are seen as reacting directly to impulses conveyed through media content. The major difference between the two models, however, is that under the gratifying uses model, users are not perceived as unconditionally "hooked" to an irresistible source of stimulation, which continually sets off a reflex to focus on a particular message. Instead, users continue to use a medium only if its content provides reinforcement of previously held ideas, or gratification. The cultural content of different media is therefore determined by the social needs of audiences.

The functionalist approach developed in the gratifying uses model does not require that the media meet every human need. However, the media must satisfy at least certain needs that would otherwise not be met. Such needs may range from an unconscious desire for social contact to the conscious need for a specific piece of information. A medium is therefore listened to or read insofar as users can assign it a function. Listening and reading habits are essentially explained in terms of what users feel is best for themselves, either to justify "established behavioural patterns, or to adapt to environmental changes" (McQuail and Gurevitch, 1974: 288–9). People subjectively get satisfaction from using the media. Thus, for instance, audience members are able to define how television meets their individual needs (Breton and Proulx, 1993).

Katz, Blumler and Gurevitch (1974) singled out five basic assumptions of the gratifying uses model.

1. People who get their information from media sources are actively involved in establishing their content, form and uses. This assumption runs counter to the concept of passive audiences in the hypodermic model.

2. The mass media do not have a significant impact on behaviour. People get information from sources that correspond to their own, previously established ideology. Behaviour patterns are therefore determined prior to choosing a mass medium.

3. The mass media are not the only means through which an audience meets its needs. The impact of a medium is dependent on other competing sources of social satisfaction.

4. People are sufficiently aware of the use they make of the media that, methodologically speaking, one can rely on their verbal accounts to uncover the true motives behind their listening and reading choices. Little attention is given to other factors that may unconsciously influence their choices.

5. Value judgments concerning the cultural significance of the mass media must be suspended when examining audience orientations.

In short, the gratifying uses model suggests that the media have little impact on individuals. In fact, they may even have the opposite effect; that is, they may foster social stability by protecting existing social structures against dissatisfaction, or marginal satisfaction, which could cause instability. This is the point of view taken by McQuail,

Blumler and Brown (1972), who have argued that the media meet four different types of needs: a) they alleviate ordinary stress through diversion; b) they compensate for inadequate interpersonal relations; c) they help people in their search for a personal identity; and d) they provide social surveillance through public denunciations.[2]

Using this approach, it is impossible to predict the impact of the media without knowing what determines audience preferences. Since people are free to use the mass media of their choice, information presented in a medium must comply with at least a few of the users' needs, otherwise it will be completely rejected. But what types of social conditions engender needs that the mass media can satisfy? The functionalist research group composed of Katz, Blumler and Gurevitch (1974: 27) drew up a list of five conditions:

1. The social context gives rise to tensions or conflicts which can only be eased through mass media consumption.

2. The social context creates an awareness of problems, solutions for which must be addressed by the mass media.

3. The social context reduces the possibility of satisfying certain needs, which the media try to compensate for, or "complement," by their content.

4. The social context fosters certain values that are confirmed and reinforced through consumption of congruent media material, in other words, material that is consistent with the new values.

5. Social adaptation requires knowledge of a part of the material presented in the media. As a result, the development of media content must be closely monitored so that it bolsters adherence to social groups.

Katz, Blumler and Gurevitch (1974) proposed that the gratifying uses approach is best suited for the study of the mass media because it looks at the impact of the media from the public's point of view. They argued that an analysis made from the producer's point of view only engenders an elitist or intellectual perception of the social impact of the media. But social impact is primarily dependent on popular culture, given that regular media users find what they are looking for. In this way, media studies should focus on the culture of media users, instead of the culture of media producers.

An important criticism of reinforcement theories is that one can always find a way of linking a reinforcement to any behaviour under study. In some cases, people do what they do simply because they enjoy it. In others, behaviour that on the surface may appear to be adverse can be explained by the fact that it may be avoiding a greater ill. This is how gratifying uses theorists explain, for example, why people go to the dentist. The success of a medium is accounted for in a similar way, that is, it must be satisfying a need. If a specific need is not clearly identifiable, it is possible that it is so subtle that it is not yet measurable. Katz, Blumler and Gurevitch (1974) have given examples of a wide variety of needs, including the need for relaxation, the need for leisure time, and the need for time with one's family.

The gratifying uses theory has served as a pretext for the absence of regulation over media content, since, as some would have it, regardless of the content imposed by media

---

[2] See also Beaud, 1984, p. 65.

producers, it is audiences who will have the last word. Under these conditions, the media should be left alone, and the "natural" selection process be allowed to take its course in establishing conventions of media usage that will reflect the social equilibrium. This argument has drawn criticism of the dominant paradigm by proponents of other theoretical models.

Critique of Functionalist Models

Lazarsfeld and his colleagues developed a functionalist model as a critical response to Lasswell's theory of the media's impact on audiences by introducing concepts to help researchers understand what people do to the media. Their goal, therefore, was to shed some light on the public's influence on the media. As Gitlin (1979) and Hall (1982) have remarked, Lazarsfeld and his team were funded by various firms that sought ways of attracting certain audiences for their sponsors. In this context, commercial objectives prevailed over—if not dominated—theoretical ones, a fact which explains the model's failings.

The shortcomings of Katz and Lazarsfeld's model, which was highlighted in this chapter, are due to methodological as much as theoretical considerations. The favoured method used by these researchers to measure the influence of the media on people was before/after testing, which consists of asking people about their changes of opinion on a particular issue (the dependent variable), and the channel through which they believe this change took place (the independent variable). However, the use of dependent and independent variables with respect to specific situations excludes consideration of details that could be important in the interpretation of results. In effect, although Lazarsfeld and his colleagues considered the social status of their respondents, their method, which consisted of examining attitudes independently of one another, did not enable them to view their subjects in relation to the political and ideological structures of society. For example, simply knowing that someone is a lawyer is not enough to know about their views, their political involvement in the community, and so on. These factors all have a bearing on people's opinions. As Gitlin has pointed out, a "multiplication of categories is not necessarily a clarification of reality. Confusing the two is the occupational hazard of the positivist tradition" (1979: 222). Another methodological failing of this model is the attempt to extrapolate the results of a limited study to a general theory.

This method supports a theoretical model that led functionalists to acquire data that helped them discover *how* opinion changes occur, instead of *why*. This sort of approach was necessary to meet the administrative objectives of their financial backers, since the goal of the research was to provide certain firms with information on how audiences select their media. With this information, firms would be better able to adjust their programming to their audiences' needs. However, this approach completely disregards such notions as power, hierarchy and ideology, and their role in the functioning of the media.

For example, by asserting that people's opinions are indirectly influenced by opinion leaders who regularly use the mass media, instead of being directly influenced by the media themselves, functionalists casually dismiss the important role of broadcast and cable television networks. Yet the expansion of broadcast networks was organized according to specific economic, political and ideological conditions that affect the types of audiences targeted. As Gitlin said, they were analyzing the process of idea changes "through the wrong end of the telescope" (1979: 217). Such studies should instead begin by addressing the questions: who can use the media? And, what media are at their disposal?

Gitlin (1979) has also stated that the results of Katz and Lazarsfeld's study were based on interviews with people who were conscious of having changed their opinion. This consciousness undermines the importance of factors that might be involved in a long-term opinion change, and means that subjects focused only on the sudden awareness of an opinion change about a specific event. Moreover, their conclusions imply that "power" and "influence" are interchangeable concepts, and that their effect can be observed in the decision-making process. The researchers disregard the effect of ideology and social values with respect to the process of opinion changes, as well as the power relations between the various parties concerned. For example, the results make no mention of the beliefs and values that guide the subjects they questioned, or of the institutional power relations within the political and cultural structures of their community. Hall observes that "larger historical shifts, questions of political process and formation before and beyond the ballot-box, issues of social and political power, of social structure and economic relations, were simply absent, not by chance, but because they were *theoretically outside the frame of reference*" (1982: 59). Thus, according to Hall, even though the approach used by these researchers was empirically sophisticated, their ideological and political presuppositions were too specific and did not enable them to examine what was beyond the frame of reference of their study. Let us turn to an analysis of the consequences of such specificity on the fundamental concept of this model.

The cornerstone of Katz and Lazarsfeld's (1955) model is the idea that the influence of the mass media is limited to the reinforcement of opinions. Given this fact, the researchers have deduced that it cannot be argued that the media have a significant impact on society. But as Gitlin has suggested, "'reinforcement' can be understood as the crucial solidifying of attitude into *ideology*, a relatively enduring configuration of consciousness which importantly determines how people may perceive and respond to new situations" (1979: 216). Functionalists therefore ignore the link between opinion and action, since their approach overlooks such notions as ideology and consciousness. Yet the reinforcement of an opinion can make a person change certain habits.

Not only did these researchers give inadequate consideration to the notion of *reinforcement* of opinions, they completely overlooked the absence of opinion changes. This oversight is another indication of the inability of this model to explain the institutional power of the mass media to change public policies, mobilize support for government policies, and condition public support for such institutional changes. In addition, these functionalist models are unable to address such questions as: what are the sources of the institutional power of the media (Gitlin, 1979)?

Thus, according to Gitlin (1979), by taking the notion of power for granted—with respect to the media and audiences alike—the functionalist model, which claims to be a theoretical tool for understanding the role of people in the flow of media products, only reveals the *nature* of the channels through which these products flow.

Finally, the functionalist models are guilty of certain striking discrepancies between theory and empirical results. For example, Gitlin (1979: 219) has discussed the fact that

Katz and Lazarsfeld reported that more than half of their subjects had admitted to changing their opinions without discussing the matter with people in their entourage. This fact is actually significant enough to discredit their two-step flow theory. However, the authors only mention this in passing, without taking it into consideration in their analysis of the results.

This type of shortcoming has led Beaud (1984) to argue that, because one can always identify a need which the media can meet, it is impossible to really confirm the model. Of course, it is possible to know if a particular need is or is not a motivating factor behind the use of the media. But in a case where a need is not identifiable, this would only indicate that the researchers have been unable to identify the real motive for the use of the media. According to Beaud, empirical confirmation of the gratifying uses theory is not very useful, for instance, to fully understand the impact of the media. Beaud (1984) has claimed that such empiricism leads one to believe that a conclusion is reached on the basis of facts, while in reality the conclusion serves as the starting point of research, and is tautologically supported by carefully selected facts.

THE CANADIAN SCHOOL OF COMMUNICATION MODEL

Some researchers refer to the models developed by Harold Innis and Marshall McLuhan, the two pioneers in communication studies in Canada, as the "Canadian School of Communication." The models developed by each of these researchers are too complex to be surveyed in their entirety here. Rather, we will concentrate on the basic concepts for which they are well known in communication studies. Although Innis was not specifically interested in the mass media, his model has influenced many media experts. Salter (1983) has noted that Innis' influence on numerous Canadian researchers in the field is undeniable. She adds that these authors share an interest in the question of bias as defined by Innis, namely the bias expressed through a specific technological or economic organization of communication systems.

The theory developed by Innis, called the bidimensional communication bias model, is based on the hypothesis that a communication medium has an important influence on the spatial and temporal dissemination of knowledge—in other words, its relationship to time and space determines how important a particular means of communication is in the development of a civilization. In this way, time and space constitute the *biases* of a means of communication. We will thus look at Innis' model in terms of the notion of *bias*.

Communication Bias

Harold Innis was the first Canadian to be interested in the relationship between communication and political organizations. As a professor of economics at the University of Toronto, he was concerned with finding ways of making the Canadian economy function over a vast territory. For Innis, the means of communication and transportation are essential to maintaining a vibrant economy from coast to coast. Consequently, he became interested in how forms of communication contribute to the development of different political and economic organizations.

Innis' interests in communication led him to conduct a historical study beginning at Egyptian civilization and extending to the 1940s. In 1950, the results of his research were published in a work entitled *Empire and Communication,* in which he constructed a model to explain how a change in forms of communication can lead to the fall of monopolies of knowledge and the loss of material knowledge. Because this analysis covered such a long period, Innis had to reduce the number of elements in it. He acknowledged that this restricted the application of his model, but admitted that his interest was in only two dimensions: the period of time during which a political organization exists, and the territory it occupies during this period. Thus, Innis was only concerned with two sources of influence on the means of communication: time and space.

According to Innis, parchment, clay and stone are media that have a *bias for time* because they are heavy—and consequently difficult to move—and also durable (1950: 7). These two characteristics make it easier to transmit knowledge *through the ages,* and therefore favour decentralized and hierarchical political institutions. These media were particularly well suited to monopolies of religious knowledge. On the other hand, papyrus and paper are media that have a *bias for space* because they are light—and thus easier to transport—and less durable. These media make it easier to transmit knowledge through space, and favour centralization of knowledge and, therefore, of power, since they can be used to send knowledge to the core of people who hold power. They are well suited to systems of government where power is founded on a restricted hierarchy, and to large administrative empires that must do transactions over vast territories. As an example, let us consider how Innis himself applied his concepts to Chinese civilization.

> The monopoly of knowledge built up under ecclesiastical control in relation to time and based on the medium of parchment was undermined by the competition of paper. The *bias of paper* as a medium was evident in China with its bureaucratic administration developed in relation to the *demands of space.* A bureaucratic administration supported by a complex alphabetical script written with a brush implied limited possibilities of linking an oral and a written tradition and facilitated the spread of Buddhism, with its emphasis on the production of charms and statues among the lower classes. . . . Hence Buddhism spread with great rapidity in China but eventually, failing to overwhelm the political bureaucracy, spread to Japan.

> The spread of Buddhism and writing and printing in China was accompanied by an expansion of the paper industry and by its migration to the West through the Mohammedans. Paper *responded to the invitation* of the monopoly of knowledge based on parchment and reflected in monasticism with its emphasis on the concept of *time* and through competition hastened the development of political bureaucracy with its emphasis on the concept of *space* (1950: 171–2; my emphasis).

We can see that Innis attempted to explain the rise and fall of political and economic empires through time by linking them to major changes, in both time and space, of communication technologies. For Innis, the monopoly of knowledge, which was developed over the ages by ecclesiastical institutions, such as Buddhist monasteries, was based on parchment as a communication medium. Since large parchment rolls were difficult to transport, knowledge in ecclesiastical institutions was very decentralized and thus necessitated a complex hierarchy to control it. In the Roman Catholic Church, for example, the hierarchy consisted of several levels, starting with the Pope, then cardinals, archbishops, bishops, parish priests and ordinary priests.[3]

As for paper, it fostered the development of political institutions. In the example above, Innis viewed paper as being responsible for the development of a highly centralized and slightly hierarchical bureaucratic administration, suggesting that paper responded to the "invitation" of parchment. Since parchment was too heavy to be transported throughout the vast empire, it thus "invited" paper to replace it. However, because of the complexity of the Chinese alphabet, China's administration had little contact with the uneducated population. This proved to be a boon to the expansion of Buddhism, which used statues to spread the good word. Nevertheless, paper helped political monopoly overcome religious monopoly by shifting emphasis from time to space. Moreover, the ease with which political knowledge inscribed on paper could be moved about from one place to the next enabled certain political institutions to spread over vast territories and thus form empires administered from the "mother land."

In his two-dimensional model, Innis clearly emphasized the technological characteristics of the media as factors capable of influencing different forms of political and religious governments. But this aspect of Innis' analysis puts a limit on the scope of his model, since he did not give serious consideration to some of the factors that influence these forms of monopoly and power, for example, economic, ideological and social conditions. As a result, Innis assumed that communication is readily achieved in both time and space, between centres of power and peripheral institutions. For example, he did not talk about Chinese cultural traditions, the Chinese economy or even the political system in existence before the coming of paper. Instead, he assumed that his readers would have prior knowledge of these facts, which says nothing about how this knowledge relates to his model.

In the same breath, Innis suggested that the two media biases—time and space—are mutually exclusive and independent of each other. For example, he stated that large political organizations, such as empires, existed only because they were able to take advantage of the media situated at the crossroads of the dimensions of time and space, and that they lasted for long periods because they were able to overcome the bias favoured by each medium. In other words, conditions favourable to the development of an empire are met if the empire expands at a time when the transition from one medium to another (e.g., from parchment to paper) is timely and that the bias of one medium (time, in the case of parchment) favouring decentralization is neutralized by the bias of another medium (space, in the case of paper) favouring centralization. Thus, Innis acknowledged that the simultaneous effect of time and space is a factor in change, but he emphasized that these two dimensions act independently of one another, each one being biased by its own specific medium. What is not clear, however, is why a medium should favour only one dimension. That is, why should the biases of time and space be mutually exclusive and independent of each

---

[3] With today's modern communication technologies (the telephone, fax machines, e-mail, etc), long-distance communication is easy to achieve and one can imagine that the Roman Catholic Church hierarchy could be reduced and limited to the Pope, his bishops, who would act as his regional representatives, and priests, who would minister to the faithful, and whose instructions could come directly from the bishopric, without the need of parish priests.

other? In fact, in the first chapter we saw how Febvre and Martin (1976) argued that one of the consequences of print was to make writings permanent. Since printed material can also be easily transported, print thus has a bias for both time and space.

Innis made another important oversight in his analysis of the transition process from one medium to another. In the example given above, Innis jumped from Buddhism (a religious monopoly) to bureaucratic administration (a political monopoly) without offering any explanation for this transition other than the effect of the media. In his analysis, political organizations and religious institutions seem to exist without any apparent opposition; the social contradictions and political struggles inherent in any organization, and which make up the social context of the development of these forms of power, are not considered. Should one not assume that these factors have as much influence as the forms of communication that a new medium allows?

Despite these shortcomings, Innis' model of communication bias has opened up important avenues in the field of communication studies. One of its contributions is that it has steered communication studies towards a historical approach, focusing on understanding the processes involved in the relationships between social and technological development. Another contribution is the introduction of the notion of political power to the analysis of the media. Innis, who conducted his research at the same time as Lazarsfeld and his colleagues, also brought a number of other factors into the study of communication, including some aspects of the political, economic and social context in which media development occurs. This contribution explains why many researchers, even those who do not agree with Innis' approach, apply some of the concepts of his model. One of these researchers was Marshall McLuhan.

Hot and Cool Media

Marshall McLuhan, another Canadian, has drawn a lot of attention over the years with his sensationalist theoretical assertions. In contrast to Innis' economically grounded approach, McLuhan developed a model that emphasized the "psychologizing" effect of the media on "human faculties." While Innis was interested in the use of the media by civilizations, McLuhan focused on the impact of the media on individuals. And while the former was interested in the forms of power in different civilizations, the latter looked at the power of the media. In *The Gutenberg Galaxy* and *Understanding Media*—his two most important studies—McLuhan developed a unidimensional approach which examines only the way the media shape social forms. This is the greatest weakness of his model.

Similarly to other researchers, McLuhan was influenced by his background training. From the beginning of his career as a professor of English at the University of Toronto, McLuhan was interested in the media. In 1955, he laid the foundation of his deterministic theory of the mass media in a short article[4] entitled *A Historical Approach to Media*, in which he applied Darwin's evolutionist doctrine to the study of the media. He perceived means of communication such as the mass media, as "species" capable of "struggling,"

---

[4] This article went almost unnoticed by the scientific community.

"adapting," and "surviving," that is, as living entities possessing the power to create and to change. In this context, his model was founded on the hypothesis that the media have a deterministic impact on the equilibrium of the human senses.

> Improvements in the means of communication are usually based on a shift from one sense to another and this involves a rapid refocusing of all previous experience. [Therefore] any change in the means of communication will produce a chain of revolutionary consequences at every level of culture and politics . . . (1955: 110).

As such, means of communication are "our extended faculties, senses, tools," and therefore influence our individual perceptions and the form of our society. This model was to be continuously refined in McLuhan's subsequent studies.

The Gutenberg Galaxy is, in my opinion, the most interesting of McLuhan's books because in it he showed that, despite his deterministic approach, he had not abandoned his interest in civilizations affected by the development of printing. The book provides an analysis of the impact of the spread of literacy following the introduction of books in different cultures. It also looks at the changes in cultural forms that occurred as a result of this new medium. This psychosociological study begins with the hypothesis that print created a new equilibrium among human senses, and that this equilibrium gave rise to a culture that is different from any other that preceded it: written culture.

Why did this happen? According to McLuhan (1962), oral culture allowed our senses to interact so that both our auditory and tactile perceptions became the most developed. Under these conditions, people became dependent on one another. This had an influence on social conditions at all levels: it had a direct impact on cultural forms, and an indirect effect on political and economic structures. The emergence of written culture, which favoured other senses, had an important impact on oral society. In written culture, every experience was reduced to a single sense, that of vision. This situation led to "the self-amputation of the body" and caused people to adopt a uniform and linear view of the world. According to McLuhan, since *oral* culture bolstered the interdependence of people, it strengthened community life. Conversely, *written* culture created a society based on private ownership, since it fostered individualism and the need for intimacy. In short, the medium that we use most *determines* the form of society—i.e., the economic, political and social structures—in which we live.

McLuhan denied his use of a deterministic approach by saying that he was simply examining the interaction between different historical phenomena. In a sense, he was right. The problem is that he analyzed this interrelation using a deterministic model. For example, he looked at the interaction between two cultures: one *determined* by a medium that favoured a specific perception, and another *determined* by a medium that created a different perceptual equilibrium. Thus, in this analysis, the form of the medium would *determine* the type of equilibrium occurring between the human senses, which, in turn, would *determine* the form a society takes.

In *Understanding Media* (1964), McLuhan's determinism becomes even more evident. It is in this book that he introduced the now-famous slogan "the medium is the message." This assertion implies that it is neither the content nor the characteristics of users that have an impact on societies, but the form of the medium that controls the range and form of human interactions and behaviour. Why did McLuhan focus on the technology instead of the content? The reason, according to him, was that a medium does not influence people's opinions or their conceptions of the world; instead, its effects are to "alter sense ratios or patterns of perception *steadily and without resistance*" (1964: 18; my emphasis).

To prove his hypothesis, McLuhan identified two types of media: "hot" media and "cool" media. This terminology does not refer to temperature or emotional intensity, but to the *degree of participation*. Hot media are those that require low participation from users, since they foster detachment. Conversely, cool media are those that require strong user participation, since they urge users to engage themselves completely in their use. Radio, for example, is defined as a hot medium, since listening does not require complete involvement from the user. One can drive, cook or do a number of other things and listen to radio at the same time, without missing part of the message. Conversely, television is a cool medium, since it requires more user participation: one cannot drive and watch television without missing images or being a menace on the road. Moreover, because of its form, television is more captivating and less rational than radio. In short, to use McLuhan's own language, in contrast to radio, the use of television involves the interaction of several human senses.

McLuhan propounded that it is the form, not the content, of the medium that interacts with audience attitudes. Regardless of the content of radio programmes, audiences will remain more removed and rational than television viewers, who will be more captive. A new form of medium therefore changes the way people perceive social activities, the activities they engage in, and the way they engage in these activities. Viewed in this light, it is easier to understand the slogan "the medium is the message." But this does not necessarily mean that we should agree with it, since it overlooks many important factors.

How did McLuhan come up with this slogan? He considered that the purely technical and physical properties of the media are the only determinants of social change. All of his writings are faithful to his first theoretical assertions, namely that technology has its own force, so powerful that it can change people's perceptions and, consequently, the whole of social life, without giving people any choice but to follow the path cleared by the new medium.

Should we reject McLuhan's model because of its determinism? Not necessarily. The model can be useful in analyzing specific technological aspects of the media. In fact, when studying the media, it is important, among other things, to take the technological characteristics of a medium into consideration so as to distinguish between technological impacts, on the one hand, and social, political and economic impacts, on the other. Combined with other theoretical approaches, McLuhan's model can add an interesting dimension to media research. However, one must be careful, since McLuhan's theoretical "vision" underestimates the significance of many important aspects of the media. For instance, in our society, the dominant class is more familiar with governing than with being dominated, even by a medium. Therefore, one can safely assume that a society will favour the development of media that support the dominant ideology. McLuhan's strict determinism prevented him from considering the complex processes underlying the emergence and organization of new media in society. Removing the media from the historical and social context from which they emerge led him to develop a model in which the media are represented as living beings that have their own direct effect on society, and where, consequently, class, cultural and gender differences and power relations disappear.

McLuhan's assertion that events or social processes, including all types of social conflicts, can be explained in terms of the equilibrium of human senses must be refuted. An analysis of social change resulting from the coming of a new medium, or any other reason, will not be valid unless it takes into account the economic, political and social conditions in which the change occurs. In other words, one must examine power relations and the social contradictions brought about by the change. To ignore these important elements can only lead to a biased analysis in which everything is reduced to a single factor of change. In such cases, theory is reduced to a set of beliefs.

CONCLUSION

The models that reflect the dominant paradigm used in mass communication studies highlight a number of factors that must be considered in media analysis. While the hypodermic model, or the psychological approach, looked at the *impact of the media* on audiences, the functionalist approach focused on the *influence of audiences* on the media. As for the Canadian school, it has concentrated on the impact of the technical characteristics of the media on societies. Innis introduced the concept of temporal and spatial *biases* of the means of communication, and their effect on civilizations, while McLuhan put forth the concept of *hot* and *cool* media and their impact on the human senses.

Some of the concepts developed in these models may prove to be useful in the study of the media when placed in a more critical context. For example, one cannot deny that the media influence audiences, that audiences themselves have a certain impact on media content, or that the technological properties of the media also have a certain effect on our society. However, these different assertions become even more helpful when combined, that is, if one recognizes that the relationship between the media and audiences is a highly complex and interactive one. To understand this relationship fully, research must not only be able to analyze the types of audiences involved, or media content and its sources, but also social structures.

None of the models discussed in this chapter offers a global perspective of media research that takes into consideration the interaction of all these factors. Because of their determinism, the models have serious shortcomings that cast a shadow of doubt on their usefulness. Nevertheless, each of these approaches can still be of use if readers are aware of their limitations, or if they are applied in conjunction with a more complete model. This is exactly the purpose of the next few chapters, where we will discuss the fundamental concepts of critical theories of the mass media. One of the inherent characteristics of these theories is that the media are viewed from a more global perspective, that is, they are seen as social organizations, forming an integral part of society.

POWER, CONTROL AND RESISTANCE IN MASS MEDIA

INTRODUCTION

In the first two chapters we saw how mass media are related to many spheres of our society. Thus, in order to have a complete picture of the role they play, it is important to analyze all aspects of their connections with society. The first part of Chapter 2 described this relationship as unidirectional, focusing on two aspects: a) the influence of the media on people (the psychological model), and b) the impact of people on the media (the functionalist approach). By looking at the two Canadian models developed by Innis and McLuhan, the second part of Chapter 2 emphasized the technological impact of media on audiences.

In short, the models belonging to the dominant paradigm have developed a number of concepts to explain the relationship between mass media and their audiences from two angles. The greatest failing of these models, however, is that they analyze the media independently of the overall social context. McLuhan, in particular, never gave serious consideration to the economic, political, cultural and social conditions in which media are produced and used. This chapter attempts to make up for these shortcomings by discussing approaches in which media are viewed as an integral part of the broader social context. These models link the development, production and use of media to the social, economic and political conditions in which they evolve. Together, these approaches are known as the *critical school of communication*.

Why have these approaches earned the label "critical"? These theoretical frameworks all have one thing in common: they are based on Marxist concepts, that is, the notions developed by Karl Marx which view class conflicts as the foundation of our social system. The Marxist approach thus provides the fundamental elements of the "critical school" of media analysis. It is therefore important to begin this chapter by explaining the Marxist concepts that are necessary to understand the concepts used in critical approaches. The second part of the chapter will look at the emergence of the "critical school," and then conclude with an analysis of a few critical models.

CAPITALIST SOCIETY:
SOCIAL CLASSES, IDEOLOGY AND RESISTANCE

The approach now known as Marxism was developed in the nineteenth century—well before the coming of mass media as we know them today—by Karl Marx and his friend Frederick Engels. The two men, both Germans, were interested in the economic conditions created by the industrialization of European society. Marx was an intellectual who had received his doctoral degree in law and philosophy in 1841, and was particularly interested in philosophy and economics. He was first exposed to socialist thought while in France for a few years, before having to flee to England for political reasons, where he spent the rest of his life. Engels, who was born of rich parents, was more pragmatic than his colleague. After completing his studies in philosophy, he spent many years in England overseeing the operations of his family-owned textile factories. Although the two men published many works together, and their writings—even those published individually—were the fruit of their discussions, Marx is generally considered to be the father of Marxist analysis of capitalist society.

For Marx, the main difference between human beings and animals was that humans have the faculty of imagination. He believed that human beings are free to create, but only within the limits of the means available in society. Thus, a person is free to make choices, but he or she must also deal with the social and personal consequences of these choices. People have a certain control over the activities they engage in, but these activities are themselves both free and restricted by their creativity and history. Marx therefore saw that peoples' activities were influenced by social and individual freedom and restrictions. However, he believed that these social restrictions could be overcome if individuals were conscious of them and creative enough to find the means to triumph over them. Thus, by developing their consciousness, individuals could have better control over their activities, while respecting socially acceptable limits. "Men make their own history, but they do not make it just as they please; they do not make it under circumstances chosen by themselves, but under circumstances directly encountered, given and transmitted from the past. The tradition of all the dead generations weighs like a nightmare on the brain of the living" (Marx, 1969: 15). This was the premise upon which Marx based his approach.

The first questions Marx addressed were: how do people manage to feed and shelter themselves in a capitalist industrial society? What social relations have brought about the activities that enable people to feed and house themselves? Although these may seem like simple questions, they address complex and sometimes contradictory issues. To answer these questions, Marx developed a theory which he called *historical materialism*: materialism because the approach focused on the economic system of society; historical because this system changes over time, and from one society to the next.

In his analysis, Marx explained that over the course of history there have existed various modes of organization of material life in society. For example, early societies had a lifestyle based on "primitive communism," a system where all members of the community shared the use of available goods. There was no such thing as private property. In ancient Greece, the economic system was based on "slavery," where a number of individuals owned other people who worked for them without pay. In this system, however, owners were obligated to provide their slaves with room and board. "Feudal" society was founded on an economic system in which a small group of lords possessed most of the land, and a large group of serfs were subjected to certain obligations set by the lords. Serfs spent most of their time cultivating the lords' land and were obligated to rent their own plot of land that they cultivated for their personal use. Feudalism was followed by our current economic system, "capitalism," which will be discussed in detail in the following pages.

Marx hoped that capitalism would be followed by a final stage of economic development, that of socialism, where all members of society, not just a small group of wealthy people, would share the wealth produced by society. He thought it was outrageous that a few people—those who had the good fortune of being born wealthy—had the privilege of dividing among themselves most of society's wealth. Marx believed that since all human beings are equal, everyone had the right to an equal share of the wealth. The socialist system envisioned by Marx was therefore founded on the principles of equality and liberty of individuals, but has never been successfully implemented, even in so-called "Marxist" societies.

To help develop a true "socialist" society, Marx and Engels became involved in the workers' struggle, for they believed that the workers themselves would bring about liberation. The two decided to help workers acquire the means of organizing themselves politically so as to obtain power. The *Communist Manifesto* was the first of many pamphlets they wrote to steer workers towards a better future. The objective of the *Manifesto*—as it is commonly called—was to give German workers living in Germany, as well as those who had emigrated to North America, England and elsewhere in Europe, the means to organize their liberation. The pamphlet had an impact internationally, and has become one of the most widely read books in the world.

The *Manifesto* was introduced to workers for the first time in 1847 at the World Congress of the Communist League (the name given by workers to their organization). In it, Marx and Engels predicted what impact technological development would have on labour relations by drawing on concepts from the approach they had begun developing. We will now turn to a discussion of the main elements of Marxist analysis.

Canadian, European and other Western societies are based on capitalism. The main characteristic of this economic system is that it is based on private property. In other words, a small group of people, known as capitalists, own and control society's natural resources (water, forests, mines, etc.) and enterprises (factories, industries, transportation networks, media, etc.), while the vast majority of people, who do not have the financial means to own such operations, must sell their ability to work to owners when the latter feel they can make a profit by using their labour.

Marx did not believe that the capitalist economic system was bad in itself. In fact, he looked favourably on capitalism to the extent that it enables societies to attain new levels of civilization, in which they enjoy more wealth, produce an incredible amount of material goods, and achieve great scientific and technological progress. The Marxist ideal was to use the large profits generated by such societies to increase the wealth of the collectivity instead of a small group of capitalists. Capitalism, so Marx hoped, would give way to a socialist system where all members of society would benefit from these great social and economic benefits.

Because the capitalist production system is guided by the principle of business profitability, it has led to various forms of exploitation, involving certain contradictions. For example, is it not contradictory that millions of people die of hunger while society spends billions of dollars stockpiling weapons of destruction; that people believe they are free because they have enough to live on, while most of them must sell their ability to work for a subsistence salary; that people see themselves as autonomous and whole individuals while, in our society more than any other, they depend on others for their livelihood? How long could any of us live if we were to rely solely on our own means? Put more concretely, how could any of us live in a city if we could not count on other citizens to respect the rules of urban life? Finally, is it not contradictory that industrialized capitalist societies face the problem of being buried in their own garbage?

How does the theory of historical materialism explain these contradictions? In our capitalist society, the average person must work for someone else in order to earn wages to live modestly. Of course, it is possible for people to survive with no salary, but not without having to ask themselves at the end of every month, "How will I make ends meet?" Social welfare is a creation of modern-day society. In the days when Marx developed his theory, there was no social safety net to assist the poor and the unemployed. In fact, it is the wealth of capitalist society that has made it possible to create social security for the underprivileged. But, then again, capitalist society could not survive without workers, since they are the ones who generate profits.

How do workers generate profits? Marx argued that workers earn less in daily wages than the value of the commodities they produce in a day. Moreover, these commodities belong to the capitalists who own the enterprise. They, in turn, sell the commodities and keep the money, which they use to make profits. The accumulated profits are then converted into capital. A simple example will help clarify these concepts. Let us say that every day a worker produces $500.00 in commodities, for which he or she earns $100 in wages. If, over and above the worker's wages, the owners pay $250 in general production costs per employee, they are left with a surplus of $150. If the capitalists own a medium-sized business, with 50 employees, the total surplus value is $7,500 ($150 × 50 employees). This surplus value constitutes the owners' profit for the day. The accumulation of daily profits is called capital. It follows that the less employees earn in wages, the more capitalists make in profits and capital. Moreover, since workers depend on capitalists for work, and capitalists depend on clients for sales, it is less risky for capitalists to increase profits by refusing to pay employees higher wages than by raising the price of goods. Thus, workers and capitalists have opposing interests; they are engaged in an *antagonistic relation*.

The relations between workers and capitalists are called the *relations of production*. For Marx they constituted *relations of exploitation*. Why? Because the surplus value that workers produce ($7,500 in our example) belongs to the capitalists instead of being shared proportionally by all members of the collectivity. Concretely, this means that the majority of people work for their entire lives just to attain a modest living standard (not to mention those who cannot find work), while a small group of people profit from the surplus produced by the workers' labour. According to Marx, this exploitation is due to the fact that capitalist society is founded on a *social class system*, in which different classes have opposing interests.

Which social classes did Marx identify? The two main ones discussed by Marx are the *working class* (the dominated class, or proletariat), which does not own the means of production (excluding personal goods such as houses, cars, clothes, etc.), and the *capitalist class* (the dominant or ruling class, or bourgeoisie), which has economic power and owns the factories, plants or other means of production that require workers to function. The entire capitalist system of production is based on the antagonism between these two classes which results from the fact that a small group of people (the capitalists) control most of the means of production, while workers must sell their labour for a period of time to earn enough money to survive. Thus, workers sell their labour power to capitalists, who need it to keep their factories operating or, more specifically, to *produce* commodities and accumulate money, or capital. Marx defined labour power as "the aggregate of those mental and physical capabilities existing in a human being, which he exercises whenever he produces a use-value of any description" (Marx, 1967: 167). He also noted that labour power is a commodity that workers must *sell* to capitalists to obtain the financial means to live. These *relations of production* are the foundation of the economic structure of our society.

To better understand the concept of relations of production let us consider a concrete example. A seamstress (a proletarian), who does not have the capital necessary to buy industrial sewing machines (the means of production), must sell her labour power to a factory owner (a capitalist). In exchange, the capitalist pays her wages, an amount that is socially determined. In other words, wages are a sum of money that society deems sufficient to obtain subsistence for a particular category of worker. The seamstress produces clothes (a commodity) which the factory owner sells in various places for a profit (capital). This relation between the worker and the capitalist is an example of the *relations of production*.

Of course, as the cost of living increases, the seamstress tries to obtain higher wages, while the owner tries to secure more capital. The relations of production between the seamstress and the capitalist are therefore antagonistic: they involve two parties belonging to two classes with different, even opposing, interests. In short, the *capitalist mode of production* is based on class differences, which result in class struggles.

Marx identified a third class, called the *middle class*, which is composed of neither capitalists nor workers. Since the middle class was quite small in the nineteenth century, Marx did not discuss it at great length. At the time, this class consisted of "the small manufacturer, the shopkeeper, the artisan, the peasants" (Marx, 1973: 46). In large part, it has been replaced by the middle class we know today, which is made up of salaried professionals, civil servants, and other workers whose salaries enable them to have a better standard of living than the proletariat, but which are still insufficient to purchase the means of production (factories, industries, media, etc.).

According to Marx, the *economic system* created by the capitalist mode of production must be supported by a *political system* and an *ideological system*. He claimed that a capitalist economic system cannot exist if it is not legitimated by a political system. Thus, the political system of a society is highly influenced by the economic structures it must maintain: political intervention must be geared to foster economic development. For example, it is legal in our society to have a monopoly of natural resources such as waterways, forests and mines; this is not the case in native and communal societies. It is also legal for strong, rich companies to crush a smaller competitor, and in the process ruin its owner's and workers' livelihood. In fact, in times of economic recession, "soup kitchens" are sometimes frequented by people whose small businesses were ruined by firms with strong financial backing. *Our political system allows such things to happen.*

However, for this type of system to exist, the majority of people must believe in its legitimacy. According to Marx (1969), achieving this consensus is possible because the classes who monopolize the material means of production also monopolize the means of production of ideas. Marx claimed that capitalist economic structures have developed a capitalist ideological system in our society. Thus, the ruling classes control not only the means of production, but also the means of transmitting information—media, schools, etc.—which they use to establish a system of ideas, or ideology, to support their economic and political activities. This control, however, is not wielded in a haphazard way, or without opposition.

Marx did not claim that the economy determined every aspect of people's lives. Even though the dominated classes do not control many aspects of power in a capitalist society, he believed they have the power to protest, resist, rebel and even revolt, and therefore bring about radical change in society. In the *Manifesto*, Marx and Engels claimed that "the proletariat alone is a really revolutionary class" (1973: 46). Resistance may be expressed by individuals acting alone—for example, employees who sabotage machinery (a common occurrence on factory assembly lines)—or, more efficiently, by workers who unite to fight for better working conditions, increased autonomy and creative input in their work, and better social security (e.g., unemployment insurance, pension programmes, and education and health services).

But the struggle between capitalists and workers is not only fought on the economic front, but also on the ideological front. Capitalists tend to legitimate the present situation by portraying it as normal and natural, as always existing, and as the only viable system. From the Marxist viewpoint, the media is one area in which the struggle regarding the legitimation of social inequalities is fought. This struggle, however, is unequal, since the biggest media operations with the largest broadcasting budgets are themselves owned by capitalists, or by government agencies who support the ruling classes. In the following sections, we shall see how each social class attempts to influence the conditions of media production.

MASS PRODUCTION AND LIBERATION: THE FRANKFURT SCHOOL VIEWPOINT

This analysis will focus on the concepts of the Frankfurt School theory that will help explain modern Marxist analysis. Since many of the ideas put forth in the Frankfurt School's research have been adopted by later generations of critical theorists of communication and mass media, it is important to review the main characteristics of this body of research. It was in the 1920s, in Germany, that a significant school of thought began to emerge among researchers at the University of Frankfurt. They were to develop one of the most important perspectives of critical theory of culture.

In his book *The Dialectical Imagination* (1977), Martin Jay asserts that the members of the Frankfurt School were highly critical of quantitative studies, which at the time constituted the bulk of research in the United States. This is not to say that they rejected concrete analyses as such.[1] Their main objection to most North American research was that the researchers refused to analyze mass media within the *social context*, that is, they limited their work to studying the effects of media on audiences and vice versa, instead of examining how communication is a socially *constructed* phenomenon. By considering communication phenomena as social constructions, the Frankfurt school uncovered some previously ignored aspects of media. What concepts did these critical researchers introduce?

It is no small task to summarize the extensive and varied body of work that is commonly referred to as the Frankfurt School. By looking at the themes addressed by this school, one discovers a tendency to use an antisystematic approach that resulted from their willingness to refuse indoctrination or uncritical thought. It is not without reason that the sum of the work of the Frankfurt School is known as *critical theory*.

In contrast to the determinism of some early twentieth-century Marxist theorists, who claimed that all social change resulted from economic conditions, Frankfurt School researchers posited that people could respond to their social environment. They assumed that this power is primarily achieved through "genuine" cultural activities, as opposed to ones produced by the culture industry. According to critical theorists, the culture industry is "anticultural" since its only objective is to make cultural production profitable. The objective of profitability destroys the cultural element of the industry's products, which can no longer be seen as culture. In fact, they are the exact opposite of "real," or elite culture.

How did Frankfurt School researchers justify their refusal to consider culture industry products as authentic culture? The reason for their stand may be partly explained by the fact that this industry allows *mass* distribution of its products. This "massification" leads to the transformation of *culture* into *culture industry* among audiences. In this context, audiences lose all contact with authentic works based on tradition. Individuals are reduced to purchasing *cultural products* that do not stimulate consciousness or critical thought. The culture industry therefore contributes to the *alienation* of individuals by "massifying" their thoughts and thus reducing their level of consciousness.[2]

According to the Frankfurt School, all classical art—including the more anarchist genres—is a force, as well as the creative reflection, of human protest against institutional pressures. Culture must provide individuals with a means of transcending ordinary life; it must move them to aspire to harmony in their physical and social environments, and to a certain happiness. Thus the Frankfurt School strongly condemned the industrialization of culture, that is, the standardization and production of culture for the sole purpose of profitability. For them, "popular" culture is an ideological notion. They claimed it is a "phony"

---

[1] For instance, Goebbels made use of such media as radio and cinema. And, before having to leave the United States because of his critical thinking, Adorno collaborated with Lazarsfeld on empirical research into popular music and the listening of radio music.

[2] However, it should be noted that Marcuse was more optimistic than his colleagues regarding the possibilities of revolutionary change, but he believed that they would be created by marginal groups (e.g., students, cultural minorities, Third World countries), instead of the underprivileged classes in Western societies.

industrialized culture, lacking spontaneity and consciousness (Jay, 1973: 216). Popular culture is also materialistic, since its only purpose is to generate profits. Messages disseminated through this barbaric culture can only lead to conformity and resignation, and thus cannot bring about protest, social change, or the liberation of oppressed groups.

From the viewpoint of the Frankfurt School, one of the main criteria for judging the value of a work of art is whether or not it has been produced with a specific market in mind. As Jay (1973: 216) remarks, a genuine work of art is "formalistically" seen as "purposiveness without purpose," whereas an industrial work of art is considered to be "purposivelessness for purposes" dictated by the market and guided by profit. For members of the School, authentic culture must be rooted in concrete socio-historical situations. Thus, only original works of art may be considered authentic. Reproductions are seen as barbaric and meaningless, and as pure commodity.

Since the mainly functionalist currents of thought prevailed in the United States after World War I, the Frankfurt School went largely unnoticed. Nevertheless, most critical theorists of media phenomena acknowledge the School's enormous contribution in analyzing and explaining the process of "commoditization of culture."

However, many critics accused researchers at the Frankfurt School of elitism. Jay argues that, because of their classical training, the members of the School were critical of any artistic work that was not rooted in academic tradition. For example, Adorno always refused to see jazz as "authentic" music. In his words, jazz "does not transcend alienation, it strengthens it. Jazz is commodity in the strictest sense" (cited in Jay, 1973: 186). Their bleak vision of culture, combined with the fact that they were Jewish intellectuals working during the time of Nazi Germany, largely explains the pessimism of their research. The growing industrialization of culture, the expansion of mass-reproduction processes of works of art, and the oppression of Jews gave the researchers little reason to hope that an "authentic" culture could even exist.

The contribution of the Frankfurt School to media analysis has been significant. As we saw earlier, Marxist theory considered that economic and political factors had a direct and indirect influence on society's development, but failed to include culture as an important social force capable of effecting change in social structures. The Frankfurt School showed that cultural activities were an integral part of the social system, and that the massification of these activities, made possible by industrialization, was congruent with the economy of our capitalist society. These notions were adopted and further developed by numerous contemporary models in communication and mass media studies, some of which will be examined in the last section of this chapter.

THE POWER RELATIONS IN THE ORGANIZATION OF MASS MEDIA

To examine the power relations at work in the organization of mass media, researchers using the critical theory of communication built a model around the concept of the *mode of production*, that is, the way in which various forms of communication are produced in capitalist society. More specifically, the approach involves an *analysis of the context* in which messages are produced and exchanged. Critical approaches all have one point in common: they each recognize that the mechanisms of production and exchange of media messages are the same as the mechanisms of production and exchange of human activities in general, which were examined in the first section of this chapter. Thus, having *control of the media* is an asset to the ruling classes, both financially and in terms of their ability to spread their opinions. It is for this reason that critical theory began analyzing the power relations behind the different forms of control of communication production. The critical model assumes that, by explaining the types of control wielded over the media in our society, it is possible to understand why and how certain forms of communication are produced at the expense of others.

Even today, the idea prevails that communication is merely a form of technical exchange. This train of thought is now largely associated with the functionalist school of communication studies, which we discussed in the last chapter. Functionalists still believe that with the development of the various means of communication, such as the increased sophistication of satellites and the growing number of television channels available, there is a proportionate increase in opportunities for individuals to interact and, consequently, to participate in democratic life.

Marxist theorists have criticized this simplistic and utopian view of the development of communication technologies, and have underscored the importance of the economic and social component of the production process of media, and of their contents. These considerations explain not only the production and sale of media products, but also the means used to diffuse ideas and opinions. The last sections of this chapter will examine how certain researchers link media development and production of content with the power relations established by the economic and social conditions in society. First, let us begin by answering the following questions: how does access to production and use of a medium influence the forms of control wielded over this medium? What means are available to resist these forms of control?

Forms of Control of and Accessibility to Mass Media

Raymond Williams (1980, 1974) has developed a model to study the relationship between accessibility to media and control of content production. A British researcher who taught literature at Cambridge University, Williams[3] developed his model in response to certain approaches put forth by other theorists, which he believed were too limited in scope. To better criticize these theories, Williams (1980) divided them into three categories.

The first category includes psychological and functionalist models, which, as we saw in the previous chapter, essentially view the media as a means of transmission; in other words, their only function is the passing of information and messages between senders and receivers. In this context, transmission does not appear to be affected by external factors, that is, messages reach their intended audiences unchanged. Audiences are seen as accept-

---

[3] Williams (1974) is the founder of the Cultural Studies model which has been adopted by numerous critical theorists. In this model, Williams developed the notion of "flow" used in many mass media studies.

ing these messages at face value, and are therefore viewed as groups of undifferentiated, or slightly differentiated, individuals with more or less the same characteristics. The models in this category, which Williams (1980: 51) calls "bourgeois" and Gitlin calls (1979: 224) "administrative," ignore any differences that may exist with respect to media production and usage as well as the "biases" that may affect content during the mediation process.

In the second category of theoretical viewpoints identified by Williams, the different forms of media are themselves responsible for producing different types of communication. For example, "natural" ("face-to-face") means of communication produce a form of communication that is different from the one that emerges from "technological" (mass media) means of communication. A variant of this category is the model put forth by McLuhan. As we saw earlier, McLuhan recognized the existence of technological differences between the means of communication, but succumbed to a technological determinism: that the effects of a medium are determined by its technical properties (Williams, 1980: 52). For Williams, this position is inadmissible. He has argued that, by establishing a difference between ordinary, face-to-face language and mass media, McLuhan ignored the fact that the media also use ordinary language in their content. In fact, the media use ordinary language in various ways and audiences receive these contents under different social conditions. Thus, authors such as McLuhan failed to consider an important variable, namely the social context in which the media are developed and received.

The last category of models criticized by Williams consists of Marxist analyses, in which authors refuse to include the means of communication (including mass media) as part of the conditions of the process of formation of society. Researchers whose work falls in this category view media as second-order processes that develop only after the "decisive" social relationships of society have already been established (Williams, 1980: 52–3). This point of view ignores the fact that, in our society, mass media are not only producers of content, but are themselves produced in particular contexts and thus have a growing influence on social relations.

These three theoretical positions, which dominate the field of communication studies, have engendered mainly empirical and historical analyses of audiences or of the technological development of new media. Few of them have examined the development of communication and media within their social and historical contexts, which is precisely what Williams attempts to do in his approach.

Williams establishes the link between media production and society by looking at the media as a means of production of content. In this approach, the media, as well as their content, are produced socially and materially. In other words, they do not develop by themselves, and must be considered as *social constructions*. Media are conceived by people with specific intentions, and are organized in ways to help meet their goals. The same production process is applicable to media content. Thus, the link between media production and social production is due to the fact that means of communication have historically been a central element of all forms of social activities and organizations. As we saw in the introduction, media are also closely related to people's social activities, and are a vital component of social relations.

By looking at media within the context in which they are developed, Williams attempts to explain the issues of accessibility to media and control of media production.

To do this, it is useful to distinguish between two essential modes of communication. The first is *human* modes of communication, which are dependent on "immediate human physical resources" (i.e., direct spoken language and non-verbal communication, also known as "body language"); these are central to society and inevitably result from social conditions. The second is *mechanical* modes of communication, which are *constructed*—in other words, they are developed by certain groups of people—and consist of non-human, or technological, material (Williams, 1980: 54–5).

By considering the media as a means of production of content, it is possible to define the role played by technology with respect to media accessibility and control. For example, we may ask if a technology such as television is more easily accessible than print. In order to appreciate these distinctions, Williams (1980) puts forth a typology that accounts for differences in media accessibility and control of content production. He identifies three main categories of effects media have on communication. The media may be said to be:

- amplificatory: ranging from the megaphone to those media such as radio and television that make direct transmission possible;
- durative: ranging from works of art such as paintings, to technologies like records and videocassettes that make it possible to preserve oral cultural activities;
- alternative: this category refers to the use of objects such as signs, writing, graphics or symbols as means of reproducing cultural activities; these means were already used in ancient civilizations.

This typology is essentially based on the different types of social relationships involved in the communicative process. Thus, the first two types of media (amplificatory and durative) can be differentiated from the third (alternative), since the skills involved in using the former—speaking, hearing, gesturing, observing and interpreting—are already developed in primary social communication situations such as face-to-face contact. This means that the use of media does not require specially acquired skills or social differentiation. If power relations emerge around the production or use of media, one can assume that these *differences are based on who controls the access to these means of communication*. This question is of particular interest to the ruling classes.

Let us consider an example. In theory, we all have the ability to produce content that can be broadcast on television, since this activity entails speaking on one or many subjects. The problem is gaining access to the means of production, namely the technologies that make broadcasting possible. Consider, for instance, a labourer who wishes to produce a television programme to show in great detail, and with evidence, how workers are exploited by capitalists. If the labourer wants to have the programme aired by a private station, he or she will have to submit a project proposal to the station owners, or their representatives.[4] The project will therefore be judged by those whose interests are to legitimate the system that enables them to make profits. Thus, even if the labourer has the

---

[4] According to the critical model, administrators who represent the owner's interests are vested with the same antagonistic powers with respect to other workers.

skills required to produce the programme, there is little chance the project will be approved by private stations. As for state-run networks, they should in principle allow this taxpayer to use this means of broadcasting, since they are publicly financed and thus theoretically owned by the community. However, these networks are managed by people whose interests are the same as those of the ruling classes, and who therefore must work to keep the status quo. One may then conclude that the labourer in our example does not have any more access to the CBC than he or she does to private stations.

As we saw in the first section of this chapter, an economic system requires the support of political and ideological systems to ensure its survival. Because media can be used to disseminate ideas, they are of great interest to the ruling classes. Accordingly, these classes systematically apply various forms of control over media, as well as restrictions on their accessibility. According to Williams, (1980: 56) beyond the question of simple class differentiation, there is a direct and important relationship between the economic and political power required for media amplification and duration, on the one hand, and the amount of capital required for their installation and use, on the other. For example, only those people with the economic power to possess television networks, or the political power to use them as they wish, can control content production. Who has not seen regular television programming interrupted by a message from the prime minister? Moreover, the greater the area over which a medium is capable of broadcasting, the easier it is for private industry or government institutions to monopolize it, since the technological means required for its proper functioning are so expensive. Thus, it is easier to establish a capitalist monopoly in radio broadcasting than in the use of megaphones. However, the problem of control and accessibility goes deeper than this first level of technological differentiation.

We have seen how amplificatory media are easier to use since they require few skills. We have also seen how access to these media can be restricted by the ruling classes, which have the financial means to monopolize their development. However, there is a third level at which restriction can be achieved, that of content production. For example, in the case of amplificatory media, only a limited number of voices can physically and technologically produce content that can be selected for radio or television amplification. A similar type of selection occurs with respect to content preservation (or duration) on records, cassettes, or other similar technical means. It is in this sense that Williams (1980) argues that amplificatory and durative media can also be considered as alternative media, that is, as containing material that is not produced spontaneously, but *constructed so that it has a particular meaning*. Let us consider in greater detail the implications of this assertion.

On the surface, the direct transmission and reception of television content involves only the speech and gestures of the people who transmit this content. However, most television stations have specialists whose job is to transform content in certain ways and according to specific rules. This editing and writing process has a qualitative and determining effect. Thus, material that appears to be directly transmitted and received has in fact been written and re-written, cut and transformed to become content approved by people responsible for production, and who are themselves accountable to station owners or their representatives. The process entails much more than editing and selection: it is a response to the demands of a group of administrators. These modifications are done for the purpose of giving content new meaning,[5] which in the end can be quite different from its original meaning. How is this work carried out, and what are its consequences?

Let us consider an example. Most people know that during the Gulf War the flow of information was entirely controlled by state agencies, namely the allied, and particularly American, armed forces. Even though the CBC (whose budget had just been seriously cut back by the federal government) and many private stations, for that matter, used only correspondents without cameras, an enormous amount of information was televised about the war. For some Québécois announcers, the conflict became known as "*La guerre en direct*" ("The live TV war"). But did this information paint an accurate picture of reality? As one television announcer remarked, "there was so much information that people had to block some of it out" (G.M. Boivin, *Télé-Service*, Radio-Québec, March 21, 1991). Thus, viewers themselves were involved in negotiating a certain amount of content. Moreover, given the economic conditions in which the news reporters operated in the Gulf, the content of the news bulletins was manipulated at different levels, which leads us to question the "objectivity" of the information broadcast.

Messages were first *manipulated* at the source by the armed forces. Then, the CBC and its competitors had to buy pictures from American networks, whose correspondents had already made an initial selection of images *they believed were important*. Canadian reporters stationed in the Middle East then interpreted these pictures, and made a second selection, retaining only what *they thought was important*. At the end of this chain, bureau chiefs—who play the role of mediator between audiences and administrators—in Canada had the last word, and kept only those images which *they judged to be interesting* for their audiences. They could even scrap entire stories, if they so desired. During this conflict, censorship by both the armed forces and American networks—who wanted to keep exclusives for themselves—was such that stories coming from the Middle East were sometimes outdated. In some cases, bureau chiefs would call their journalists stationed in the Gulf to inform them of the most recent developments and ask them to redo their stories, resulting in reports that were sheer interpretation (J.F. Lépine, *Enjeux*, Radio Canada, March 7, 1991). At this stage of the reporting process, one may wonder whether such stories were in fact information.

Williams therefore argues that television and other types of direct-transmission media (for example, radio and film) must be viewed as alternative media as opposed to amplificatory media, which only reproduce reality as it is. On a more technical level, Williams (1980) gives the example of how an ordinary camera can give a different meaning to a confrontation between police and demonstrators simply by changing camera angles. A camera located behind police officers, for example, would focus on demonstrators, reducing the role of the police. The effect would be the exact opposite if the camera were behind the demonstrators, and more or less neutral if the camera showed both parties equally.

---

[5] Hall notes that the *signification*, or meaning, of things is a *social product*. The meaning of events is a site of *struggle* where the groups who control the dissemination of ideas can make their point of view legitimate and credible. This leads Hall to claim that the adoption of ideological systems by society is the result of relations of power in that society which can be described as the "politics of signification" (Hall, 1982: 70).

Thus, cameramen show what they want to show, journalists say what they want to say and administrators broadcast what they want to broadcast. Although the final product received by television viewers may appear to be realistic, it is in actual fact a *social construction*.

In this context, it is important for different social groups to take possession of the means of production of media content. The mode of "naturalization" of this type of media content is so powerful in passing off images as reality that one must repeatedly analyze the production process to uncover the power relations behind the organization of the media and the real activities they are engaged in.

Economics and Politics as Factors in Media Production: Resistance to Forms of Control

Although there are *different* Marxist analyses of the media, they all have one point in common: each attempts to explain how and why certain forms of communication have developed in society at the expense of others. The reason for this convergence is that historical materialism, the fundamental principle of these theories, provides a number of concepts that can be used to analyze the mechanisms behind the organization of media with respect to both their production and use. In this section we shall see how the concepts of *class, dominant ideology, state system* and *resistance* are used to develop an understanding of various aspects of media that were completely ignored by theories in the dominant paradigm. On the whole, Marxist theories address the following questions:

- How do the economic, political, ideological and cultural forces in society influence the development of mass media?
- How do forms of communication produced by mass media reflect and influence society?
- How are the media that are developed by the ruling classes integrated into our society's economic system?
- How do the dominated classes integrate their own activities in this media system?

Inside the Media To answer these questions, Marxist theorists suggest an approach that analyzes the media in light of the historical conditions surrounding their development. For them, it is not enough to answer the above questions by stating who did what, through what channel, to which public and to what effect. These answers mask the social differences that are inherent in capitalist societies. Moreover, they do not shed light on the latent elements involved in the production of content or use of media, and thus confirm the legitimacy of the existing media system. For example, the functionalist approach argues that the audiences' role is restricted to accepting or rejecting media content. But, according to Marxist theorists, audiences also *interpret* this content, that is, they give it a meaning that suits them. It is therefore important to study the mechanisms of power and control behind the organization of media.

The model put forth by Armand Mattelart (1979, 1983) provides some useful concepts for this type of analysis. Like Williams, Mattelart considers media as *producers* of forms of communication and content. It follows that in order to study the various aspects of the production of communication, it is necessary to analyze not only the production technology (radio, television, and so on), but also the methods used to produce messages, information, or entertainment programmes. It is also important to examine the power relations that exist between the people involved in the production process, that is, between owners and different levels of employees, and between producers and audiences.

In other words, the Marxist analysis of media production explains how these factors have come together to interact with one another. For example, the theory is helpful in showing how the internal management of media such as television, radio, cinema and the press is carried out not only in step with technological progress, as suggested in some models examined earlier, but also in response to certain economic or political conditions and ideological struggles.

To illustrate these concepts, let us consider the example of television networks. Some of the characteristics that define television networks are related to the technique employed; for instance, television differs from radio because it involves pictures. Television, however, is more than a technique. In other words, Marxists do not believe McLuhan's assertion that "the medium is the message." Each television network (which all utilize the same means of communication) has its own approach to broadcasting that is dictated by its owners, or more precisely, by the members of the board of directors selected by the owners. For example, state-run television networks, which are publicly funded, can decide to have more educational or informative programmes than private networks, which need funding from sponsors to operate. Thus, private broadcasters will have programmes that are likely to attract large audiences, who will tune in and see the sponsors' commercials. So it is clear that the way in which a medium is financed plays a role in the type of content it produces. Moreover, networks establish their own specific policies concerning employee/employer relations, with rules that determine the working conditions of employees, as well as the degree of autonomy and the level of creativity they may have. These are but a few examples of the economic and political conditions underlying the operations of different television networks.

World Market Domination Now that we have analyzed the conditions under which media production is organized, the next step is to examine the funding of media content. Media are playing an increasingly important role in the capitalist mode of production. In fact, media products—films, records, books, television programmes, etc.—make up a large share of the capitalist market. Flichy's (1980) research is particularly helpful in identifying the economic conditions specific to the circulation of media products in our society.

Media products can be divided into two large categories according to their mode of financing: a) cultural commodities, and b) flow culture:

1. *A cultural commodity* consists of a product such as a record, film or book that is sold on the market for a specific purpose. Their production is influenced as much by the creativity of the artists who produce them as by the need to satisfy a large audience.

For example, authors generally write books not to satisfy an audience, but because they have something to say. Under these circumstances, the specific market value, or popularity, of the cultural commodity (e.g., a book) is not known at the time of production. Thus, it is possible to assert that, in the recording, film and publishing industries, only one in ten products will be profitable.

2. *Flow culture* consists of content produced by media such as radio and television. In this category, production is, first and foremost, guided by the need to attract the largest audience possible. It is the producers' way of combating product obsolescence, which happens almost overnight as new products appear every day. This category encompasses both cultural and informative media products. Flow culture is usually financed through advertisement (press, radio and television) and by the state (radio and television).

As was mentioned above, each category is based on the specific economics of producing media products. Cultural commodities such as records, books and films, are financed by audiences who purchase them over short or long periods of time. In the case of the record industry, companies ensure they remain profitable by introducing new products such as compact discs and cassettes, and by internationalizing contents. As for the film industry, the main source of financing, screening revenues, is declining (Flichy, 1980). The drop is due to—and compensated by—the growing video-rental market. As a result, the financial success of blockbusters, which have a worldwide distribution, has become increasingly dependent on enormous advertising budgets. Some movies incur more in advertising costs than production costs—four times as much in the case of the last *Rocky* movie.

In contrast to cultural commodities, flow culture (i.e., radio and television products) is characterized by instantaneous consumption. A viewer can only watch one television channel at a time; for this viewer, the contents of the dozens of other channels available simply disappear at the same time as they are shown—except for cases of video taping. Thus, it is possible to say that contents are, in themselves, less important to television networks than the viewing potential they represent. In the case of the Québécois television series *Les Filles de Caleb*, which attracted up to 3,500,000 viewers, one can imagine how this time slot was problematic for other networks, especially those who had counted on the success of their shows in the same slot. *Les Filles de Caleb* was so popular in Québec that it took viewers from other networks.

Although these two types of media product are consumed differently, what they have in common is that their production and distribution are now concentrated in the hands of large, global media corporations. Moreover, the majority of the largest of these corporations are based in English-speaking countries, which accounts for the global dominance of English-language media culture: everything from wire service news reports to popular music to film and TV drama. In 1994, 19 of the world's top 25 media corporations were based at least partly in either the U.S. or Britain, and had a total revenue of almost U.S. $107 billion (Variety, 1995: 28). The growing size of these coporations results from the pressure to expand and consolidate markets which, in turn, generates a constant process of takeovers, mergers and joint ventures to capitalize on the economies of scale that greater size normally brings. This is what allows them to stay ahead of the competition in the quest for profit.

Take, for example, Time Warner, the world's largest media corporation with a revenue of almost U.S. $16 billion in 1994. Time Warner resulted from an earlier merger of Time Inc., the publisher of *Time* and other mass market magazines, and Warner Communications Inc. whose most well-known asset was the Warner Bros. film studio. Today, Time Warner is a global conglomerate with interests in magazine and book publishing, cable TV systems, the HBO cable channel, and film and music production. In another example, in July, 1995, the Walt Disney Co. announced its acquisition of Capital Cities/ABC, a deal that resulted on paper in a media corporation whose 1994 revenues would have topped U.S. $16 billion, replacing Time Warner in the No.1 spot. Time Warner, however, subsequently reached an agreement in principle to take over Turner Broadcasting System (1994 revenues in excess of U.S. $2.8 billion) whose flagship operation is the global news network CNN. It has taken almost a year for the U.S. Federal Commerce Commission to permit such an important merger, imposing only mild restrictions to protect consumers against the abuses which such a monopoly might produce (*Le Monde*, 24 July, 1996).

Central to this constant process of expansion and consolidation is the organizational tendency towards vertical and horizontal integration. Vertical integration refers to a corporation's control of each level of an overall production process, thereby reducing its dependency on others to perform necessary functions. For example, Québécor, which publishes *Le Journal de Montréal*, Québec's largest circulation daily newspaper, also controls one of North America's major printing operations. Horizontal integration refers to a corporation's control of the production and distribution of different but complementary products or services. The Walt Disney Co., for example, has diversified into areas such as theme parks and the licensing of products and services such as toys, clothing and retail outlets associated with its world-famous cartoon characters. As a result of both forms of integration, most media corporations are now multi-media conglomerates characterized by cross-media ownership in different areas such as print, broadcasting, cable systems and channels, TV and film production, and telecommunications. The 1994 Canadian takeover of Maclean Hunter Ltd. by Rogers Communications Inc., for example, created a multi-media conglomerate which, at the time, had interests ranging from the Sun chain of daily newspapers to a cellular telephone network.[6] The rate of this kind of takeover may even increase in the next few years, as the federal government recently announced that cable and television companies will soon be allowed to encroach on each other's services, making it legal for telephone companies to provide cable services and for cable companies to sell telephone services.

One of the consequences of this pattern of corporate concentration is that the global market is dominated by Western, particularly American, media content. In the early 1980s, for example, it was estimated that the U.S. accounted for about 75% of the world's total exports of TV programming (cited in Hoskins and Mirus, 1988: 499). The obverse of this was that while other countries, even other developed ones such as those in

---

[6] Rogers later sold the Sun newspapers in the summer of 1996.

Western Europe, imported significant amounts of (mainly American) programming, the U.S. itself imported a mere 2% of its overall TV programming, the lowest of any country (Varis, 1984). In another example, in the case of news, the American news agencies, Associated Press (AP) and United Press International (UPI), followed by the British agency Reuters, produce far more information than alternative news agencies based in less developed countries. In 1987, AP's and UPI's combined daily output of information was over 30,000,000 words, as compared to 25,000 words for the Caribbean News Agency and 20,000 for the Pan African News Agency (cited in Roach, 1990: 290).

The unevenness of this relationship, which some critical theorists refer to as "media imperialism" (Boyd-Barrett, 1977), led to the call for a New World Information and Communications Order (NWICO) in the 1970s and 1980s on the part of many Third World countries seeking to redress the imbalance and develop their own communications media independently of Western dominance. The NWICO movement met strong resistance, particularly from the U.S., which saw it as a threat to the political and economic interests of American media corporations. The initiative behind the NWICO movement, however, has not been completely extinguished despite the fact that pressure remains strong on developing countries to deregulate their communications industries to allow Western media corporations to exploit growing Third World markets (Roach, 1990).

The logic behind all of these processes associated with globalization is that of the capitalist market and the need to generate ever-greater levels of consumption and profit. The consumer, or media audience, is the target of a constant promotional strategy, particularly in the case of flow culture, where media revenue comes primarily from advertising rather than directly from the viewer or listener. As a result, certain theorists argue that what commercial radio and television actually sell to advertisers is not so much air-time for advertisements as their projected audiences in the form of potential consumers. It is the audience, rather than the programming itself, which is the primary "commodity" that is the main source of media income and profit. In a way, this argument is similar to the functionalist position, which claims that viewers have a large influence over media. We will see in subsequent chapters that this phenomenon is more complex than it might first appear to be.

To ensure that their products remain profitable, some media industries have attempted to harmonize their markets. High-definition television is a good case in point. But harmonization is not easily achieved: even if all producers want products to be standardized, there will be fierce competition to determine what that standard should be. Officially, the battle is being fought between private corporations, but the issue has become so important that the state is now intervening. This leads us to a discussion of the political conditions surrounding media development.

State Intervention Earlier we saw that, according to Marxist theory, the role of the state with respect to the media is generally to ensure the perpetuation of the economic system, or of the dominant ideology. The next chapter will provide a detailed explanation of the role of ideology in the media. But for now, let us simply note that state intervention in media operations is seen both as legitimate and as legitimating the various systems in society. It has the power to influence ideas concerning the objectivity of messages, freedom of the press, public opinion, or any practice concerning the organization of media.

In every country the state plays a role in the operation of radio and television. This can vary from total control of air waves or content to the management of Hertzian waves, as in the United States.

In the early days of radio, European standards were biased in favour of long waves, while in the United States medium waves were favoured. According to Flichy (1980), there are two reasons for the situation in Europe. From a political standpoint, long waves made it possible to centralize broadcasting throughout entire nations. From an economic standpoint, since the use of long waves requires different-sized radio receivers than those used in the United States, European manufacturers were able to avoid competition from America.

Standards regarding colour television have also been subject to political pressures, which are, in turn, based on economic pressures. Flichy (1980) notes that, at the national level, political intervention in the form of standards is motivated by economic reasons, that is, by the state's willingness to take measures to prevent foreign invasion of the marketplace. Thus, in 1953, the United States adopted a set of norms which were later copied by Japan, whose economy at the time was highly dependent on America's. A few years after, the French imposed a different set of standards in order to protect their market. Later, the Soviet Union adopted the French measures within the context of a strategic political alliance. Finally, Germany developed another system, which was quickly adopted by England, followed by most European states.

Nevertheless, the state's involvement in radio and television broadcasting was often implicit, especially in Europe, and was guided by a fear of the media's use of the power of propaganda. For example, following the liberation of France in 1945, General de Gaulle, who had experienced the power of the airwaves firsthand in London, re-established the state's monopoly in radio and television to limit the power of journalists. The private sector, however, was allowed to consolidate its control over the manufacturing of technical equipment.

In short, over and above the political aspect related to media (that is, the state's desire to control the power structures and content of media), the economic conditions of media production are the driving force, and are aimed at conquering the large market of communications goods and services. The internationalization of media content has made media products more exportable. Nevertheless, economic and political control of different aspects of the organization of media has led to certain contradictions. What are these contradictions? Why have they emerged?

CONCLUSION

The concept of class, as defined in the first section of this chapter, provides a number of helpful elements to explain the influence that class differences have on people's lives. The concept rejects the propositions made by the dominant approaches, which claim that reality is as it appears, and that relations between various social groups are transparent, that is, no underlying forms of power or control exist. The concept also questions the notion that the relation between media producers and users is based on such principles as equality and objectivity.

A study that takes into consideration class differences in society can only contradict what Mattelart (1979) has called the "Sacred Truth," which states that individuals are free to contribute equally to the organization of the media. In fact, the theory of historical materialism has shown that people belonging to different social classes have different forms of powers, and that the ruling classes not only have economic and political power in society, but also control the production of ideas and values. Applying the notion of class differences to the analysis of the media sheds light on the notion of coercion that is involved when a particular class imposes certain media content on other classes: the class with economic and ideological control can *impose* its own vision of reality through media content. If, for example, we look at fiction television programmes like soap operas and situation comedies, we see that the vast majority of them are about the lives of the ruling classes (*Dallas, Dynasty*, etc.) or of the middle classes (*Seinfeld, Home Improvement*, etc.). If we recognize the success of these shows, we can ask how those viewers who do not belong to these classes can relate to their content. In the next chapters we will take a closer look at a number of studies on this subject. In the meantime, however, we can ask why television period pieces, such as *Anne of Green Gables* and *Les Filles de Caleb* in Québec, which are essentially about the lives of the underprivileged classes, have attracted large audiences.

Applying the notion of class to the study of audiences sheds light not only on the power relations with respect to content production—for instance, who controls broadcasting—but also on the role of users in the organization of the media. Therefore, the notion of class enables us to analyze how the dominated classes manage to integrate media content into their reality, which brings us to the notion of resistance.

As Marx underlined in most of his works, the concept of dominated class necessarily implies resistance. That is, members of the dominated classes are not passive: they react in various ways to pressures from other classes. With respect to the media, the dominated classes—in other words, those classes that apparently have no power over the organization of the media—not only have the choice not to listen to or watch those shows which they do not like, but also have the power to negotiate the meaning of their content. That is, they can make their own interpretations of this content, which, taken to an extreme, can actually be the opposite of the meanings intended by media producers. Later on we will examine some specific cases of resistance. Nevertheless, it is important to mention this aspect of the media at this stage of our analysis. To understand the complex notion of resistance, it is necessary to situate audiences within their social and cultural environment, which is the objective of the next chapter.

IDEOLOGY, CULTURE AND OPPOSITION IN MASS MEDIA

INTRODUCTION

In Chapter 3 we made the link between the forms of communication produced by the mass media and the economic and political conditions surrounding these media and the social system in which they develop. We saw that this link has influenced not only the organization of the media, but also the production of their content and, to a certain extent, the audiences they attract. In particular, we focused on the materialist features of this issue. According to Marx, the materialist aspects of social phenomena are related to the ideology that underlies the society in which they occur. Moreover, we will recall that the members of the Frankfurt School underlined the importance of examining the cultural component of communication. In reality, all these aspects of the media are intertwined, and sometimes even indistinguishable. Nevertheless, to have a full understanding of the media, it is necessary to examine the specific role of each of these aspects independently.

Having looked at the economic and political conditions surrounding the media, we will now focus on the *ideology* and *culture* conveyed by the media. In the introduction we claimed that the mass media are, in many ways, an important part of people's everyday lives. Who does not listen to the radio or watch television in the morning? Who does not read a newspaper or a book on the way to work? Who does not watch television in the evening? Who has never been to a movie, concert, or a play? It is clear that in order to understand the relationship between the mass media and their audiences, it is important to examine it within the context of the social and cultural activities people engage in.

In our study of the economics and politics of the mass media, we focused on the *production process* of the media from the perspective of the roles played by media administrators and producers, and the economic and political conditions in which they develop. In this chapter, we will concentrate on the *process of use* of the mass media, so our interests will be turned towards examining the content of the mass media and their audiences in relation to their ideological and cultural organization. We will begin by establishing a distinction between *ideology* and *culture*. This will be followed by a study of various *types of ideologies* and different *forms of culture*, as well as the way they are conveyed by the media. Finally, we will examine the *role of audiences* in the process of media use, and the distinctive features of the unequal, yet interactive, exchanges between audiences and the dominant classes, which control the media.

IDEOLOGY AND CULTURE: INTERRELATED CONCEPTS

The distinction that we make here between ideology and culture is not universal, and is strictly theoretical. These two notions are complex and involve a variety of closely related factors that are difficult to distinguish in practice. Nevertheless, for the purpose of analyzing the media, it is important to make a distinction between these two notions. Thus, for each term, we will provide a *definition that applies to our analysis specifically*, and which will be used throughout this book.

Ideology

In the last chapter, we saw that societies like ours are founded on a political and economic capitalist regime, with features that are equally applicable to the administration and production of the mass media. We also saw that every regime must legitimate itself. To achieve this, it will present itself as being grounded in history, that is, as having emerged out of a process of "natural" evolution. Moreover, in order to survive it must show its vision of society as being the best, while downplaying other systems. This justification is achieved by means of a system of ideas, or ideology, developed by the ruling classes, and which extends across all of society. Since ideas are now largely disseminated through the mass media, the issue of ideology is at the heart of mass media analysis. Thus, in order to develop a critical perspective of the influence of the media on our society, it is important to answer the following question: what ideology is communicated through media content?

Here, *ideology is defined as* a system of ideas, principles and mental representations that serve to guide a set of social practices. In capitalist society, this system of ideas, or ideology, is controlled by the same small groups of people, the capitalists, who have economic and political power. Thus, society is said to have a *dominant ideology* (or bourgeois ideology) that keeps it on a specific course, which is to reproduce social relations that exist in the capitalist mode of production. This is why it is important to understand the expression "bourgeois ideology of communication," which consists of the forms of ideology that the ruling classes would wish to become the "cement" holding the social class system of our society together.

For example, the ideas and principles associated with the notions of freedom of the press, freedom of expression and professional ethic are ideological forms that relate specifically to the field of information and communication. However, the *journalistic ideology* applies as much to objectivity, freedom of the press and forming public opinion as to establishing this ideology as the only possible way of perceiving and practicing journalism. These practices may include what is described as tracking down a lead, writing and editing, and the impact of photography and photomontage, as much as journalism itself.

As Mattelart and Piemme (1980) remark, these practices, or modes of production, reflect a form of social relation with the receiver of information. In our society, the form of this social relation is based on the relations of production, in other words, class conflicts.

Even though the dominant ideology tends to reproduce the capitalist mode of production, Mattelart and Piemme (1980) claim that popular groups may engage in spontaneous forms of resistance to exploitation, which are related to equally spontaneous forms of class consciousness. *Ideological struggles*, however, are different from economic struggles in that the former are not limited to class conflicts. They can occur between individuals with similar economic interests, but who have different ideas, or definitions, about what is an acceptable society. The study of ideology cannot be limited to that of the dominant ideology, but must include an analysis of the ideologies that struggle against dominance. In fact, one of the strengths of the capitalist ideology, and one of the reasons for its survival, is that it has been able to accommodate oppositional ideologies, either by integrating them into its own system of ideas, or by rejecting them on the basis of a social consensus.

Let us look at an example of the appropriation of an oppositional ideology by the dominant ideology. Ten years ago the ecological movement was considered as an oppositional organization, and was the object of constant ridicule. Individuals who supported ecological ideas were mockingly called "tree huggers," and few people, especially those in positions of power, took their message seriously. However, with time and with the evidence of damage caused by pollution, ecological ideas became so widespread that a growing number of companies used them to increase profits. Who has not seen the green recycling symbol on products such as garbage bags and disposable baby diapers—which are actually not entirely bio-degradable—or on packages of tissues or toilet paper—which have always been bio-degradable? In fact, the ecological idea of bio-degradable products has become so popular that manufacturers believe that the simple act of including this term on product labels will increase sales.

Other industries have even gone so far as to modify their products. For example, laundry detergent companies were forced to produce phosphate-free soap to increase their share of the market. On the political front, environmental-protection legislation has been adopted at various levels of government to satisfy the growing number of people who support the ecological ideology. For instance, the federal government considers the population of non-smokers large enough to institute a regulation forbidding smoking in all its buildings, despite the opposition of smokers. At the municipal level, cities like Toronto and Montréal require that restaurants of a certain size have a non-smoking section, and a growing number of cities have been forced to establish programmes to collect recyclable products. As for the media's role in this movement, more and more television programmes (and newspaper articles) are devoted to discussing such issues as the "horrors" of pollution and the means of combatting it, and the importance of a well-balanced lifestyle to prevent certain types of disease. From a news standpoint, ecological catastrophes often make the headlines. These examples show how certain aspects of the dominant ideological system can be "adjusted" to respond to resistance from "fringe" groups, and how such ideological changes affect other social spheres, such as the economy and politics.

The appropriation and integration of alternative and oppositional viewpoints, meanings and values into the dominant ideology is part of a broader political process that critical theorists call *hegemony.* The term is taken from the writings of the Italian Marxist Antonio Gramsci (1891–1937) who distinguished between domination and hegemony as modes of organizing and exercising power. Domination refers to the direct, overt exercise of power in the form of constraint or coercion, as when the police arrest a suspected criminal and the courts imprison him or her upon conviction. Hegemony, on the other hand, denotes the exercise of power in the form of social, cultural and intellectual leadership or direction. Hegemony, in other words, is more about power in the form of persuasion, inducement and incitement rather than limitation or prohibition.

Gramsci recognized that no social formation—especially one in transition from one mode of production to another—has a simple, polarized class structure consisting of just two naturally unified, mutually exclusive classes. For Gramsci, the class structure consisted of a more complex arrangement of different classes and class fractions organized in shifting relationships of contradictory and complementary interests and goals. The ruling class, then, is comprised of an alliance or "bloc" of different elements whose political and economic unity has to be constantly forged and re-formed in the face of opposition from subordinate classes and other social groups. In order to retain its dominant position, this ruling bloc must secure consent from the ruled for its actions and initiatives, which entails the exercise of hegemony. The dominance of the dominant class, in other words, comes with no foregone guarantees: it has to be won and re-won on a continuous basis.

Hegemony operates on all levels of the social formation, but at the ideological level it consists of countering the resonance and appeal of alternative and oppositional ideologies by addressing, accommodating, incorporating and even sometimes conceding to the viewpoints contained in these ideologies. Rather than suppressing oppositional and alternative meanings, hegemony works by negotiating with those involved to construct a sense of common ground and purpose. In this way, hegemony entails the attempt to recast oppositional and alternative ideas as non-antagonistic with dominant ideology. Hegemony does not eliminate ideological differences so much as domesticate them, defusing the oppositional ideology of its antagonistic potential.

This involves two related processes. The first is the construction of semantic boundaries within which a certain amount of ideological difference can co-exist and be regarded as acceptable or normal, even desirable. These boundaries circumscribe the field of legitimate differences of opinion while at the same time stigmatizing ideas and meanings that fall outside as bizarre, comical, foolish, dangerous, etc. The second process is to articulate dominant ideas and viewpoints at the expense of alternative and oppositional ones within those boundaries. *Articulation* involves both expression and connection, and in this respect it is central to both hegemony and the process of signification in general. In the process of communication we construct meanings, or what linguists call "signifieds," by means of connecting and combining together different signifiers (words, visual images, or other means of representation). This combinatory process results in a chain of equivalences in which something is defined by being represented as equal to—of the same value or meaning as—something else (Hall, 1985). In a similar fashion, the ruling class or bloc exercises hegemony by connecting its own values and ideas to, and combining them with, those of subordinate classes and groups. For example, in its opposition to the ban on the use of strike-breakers introduced by the former NDP government in Ontario, business argued in the media that the ban would discourage investment and result in fewer jobs for workers. In this way, it opposed government policy not by expressing a concern over what would happen to profits, but over what would happen to workers. Business articulated its opposition in terms of the interests of others, and in so doing remained mute about the effect of the ban on its own direct interests (Knight & O'Connor, 1995). In this way, it claimed to speak in a universal voice, representing the broader interests of society as opposed to the narrower interests of its own privileged position.

Oppositional ideologies, however, are integrated into the dominant ideology only when it is profitable *economically* and *politically*. Otherwise, they are completely dismissed. For example, the pacifist ideology has historically been rejected in favour of the war ideology, which is more profitable—economically for industrialized countries and politically for our government systems. In this respect, the recent Gulf War was but a repeat performance of other conflicts in Vietnam, Lebanon, Afghanistan, etc., where pacifist groups unsuccessfully pleaded for peace. In all these cases, pacifist messages were brushed aside on the basis of moral and numerical arguments. Through the mass media, governments everywhere argued that the Gulf War should be viewed as a battle against "evil," and that their involvement was supported by the "majority." But did the information transmitted through the media paint an accurate picture of reality? Was it not a reflection of the dominant ideology, presented as the only viable option? How else can one explain that a majority of people accepted the idea that so much destruction was "necessary," except to say that the media are dominated by the ideology of those in power? How can one convince a "majority" if not by constantly conveying a system of very specific ideas about what is good and evil, good being "our" ideas, and evil those that oppose them?

Of course, some news bulletins and interviews presented different opinions, such as short news reports on peace demonstrations, and interviews with experts who supported certain elements of the Arab viewpoint. But these voices were drowned out in the torrent of information emanating from official sources. In fact, because the presence of these dissenting opinions served to confirm the media's objectivity, their impact was implicitly reduced.

These observations have important consequences with respect to the analysis of the relationship between ideology, the means of communication and society. Indeed, an analysis of the issue of ideology from the two perspectives of dominance and opposition calls for a study of the confrontations between classes and diverse social groups, and the opposition between dominant ideology and oppositional ideology. Now we must ask whether these confrontations also exist at the level of culture.

Culture

Although the concept of culture is often equated with that of ideology, there are significant differences in terms of our analysis. Whereas ideology is limited to a system of ideas and general principles that guide social practices, *culture is considered as a system of practices guided by values and ideas.* These practices are closely related to people's day-to-day activities, and have an influence on education in addition to work and leisure. The notion of culture affects all aspects of ordinary life and, as such, serves to distinguish between people, groups, classes and societies. Thus, while ideology is considered in more abstract terms as a system of ideas guiding the actions and activities of an entire society or of smaller groups (e.g., journalists, ecologists, pacifists, feminists), culture is viewed as having a more concrete effect on people's everyday lives. In this context, culture is understood not only as a form of artistic expression, but also as a set of ordinary practices engaged in by a group of people. Therefore, the concept refers equally to creating a work of art as it does to cooking, dressing, responding to a joke, perceiving religion, etc. Siegelaub's definition of culture seems to fit this point of view. For him, culture is "the specific 'way' a historically-determined group or class creates, reproduces and develops its material and social existence" (Siegelaub, 1983: 12).

Siegelaub thus considers culture to be a way not only of creating material goods, but also, at a more abstract level, of consciously or unconsciously influencing beliefs, values, feelings, ideas, ordinary habits, as well as body and verbal language, and thus communication. Culture is "a way of life, a way of doing things . . . a sort of social personality" (Siegelaub, 1983: 13). In short, culture creates comfort zones within our vast, unknown universe, and helps people find some familiarity in the infinite number of situations they encounter in a day.

Since culture is closely related to everyday life, it can vary from one group of people to the next, or differ depending on the media through which it is expressed. These variations may be observed between ethnic groups or social classes, and come under the designation of *popular culture*, as opposed to *dominant culture*, which refers to the culture of the ruling classes. Finally, *mass culture* refers to culture that is disseminated through various mass media. We will now examine these three types in greater detail.

FORMS OF CULTURE

A number of critical approaches in communication studies make a distinction between dominant culture (or elite culture), popular culture and mass culture, but still consider them to be dependent on one another. As we shall see, different forms of culture do influence one another, with some borrowing certain activities and practices from others. In this section we will address the following questions: What social mechanisms enable such an exchange to occur? What is the impact of this exchange on each type of culture?

One of the features of our modern society is that it offers the possibility of multiple social contacts, or communication, between people belonging to different groups, classes, neighbourhoods, regions and even nations. Though these exchanges greatly enhance the quality of social life, they also bring about new types of confrontations, new forms of dependence and autonomy, as well as new ideas. This communication affects every individual in society, since, with the development of many forms of communication, it occurs in all directions, with consequences for all social groups. Nevertheless, we should not forget that communication technologies are mediated by technical means developed by a particular social class—the capitalist class—whose interests are to use these means of communication to impose its own ideas and culture. But what exactly is this dominant culture?

Dominant Culture

Dominant culture is that culture which is powerful enough to impose its norms, values and ideas on the cultural practices of an entire society, in terms of both the activities of everyday life and artistic creation. Dominant culture thus emanates from the dominant classes, but is not limited to them, since it may be influenced by the conflictual relations between different social groups. Earlier we saw that people with control of the economic and political apparatus also have the power to impose their ideas. This power applies to their culture as well, although it encounters resistance from other cultures. In fact, within the dynamics of cultures opposing one another, the dominant classes face the challenge of establishing themselves as *the* standard of what culture should be.

Let us consider an example. Historically, the notion of culture propagated by the dominant classes has been one of exclusive creation: a painter creates a painting, an author produces a classic literary work, a playwright creates a play, a composer writes a symphony, etc. Renoir, Dickens, Shaw and Beethoven are artists who created "real" culture. Thus it may be said that "classicality" is the main characteristic of dominant culture. This culture tends to spread across all capitalist Western countries (European countries, the United States, Canada, etc.), which are considered to be the most "civilized." In this context, a play created by amateurs from working-class neighbourhoods cannot be considered to be "culture" by the bourgeoisie. It may be viewed as entertainment by the general population. But as culture? Never. This example reflects the ideal of what dominant culture is in theory. In reality, however, there is an interrelation between dominant and popular cultures: the former appropriates some activities of the latter and, conversely, the latter re-appropriates the products of the former by transforming and interpreting them. Is opposition to the dominant culture the *raison d'être* of popular culture?

Popular Culture

Popular culture is that culture which is understood by a majority of people in a society (the dominated classes *vis-à-vis* the dominant classes) or in a social group (the majority *vis-à-vis* minority ethnic groups), and which constitutes their forms of expression. This culture provides an opportunity for people to internalize and express their experiences. It therefore has a *liberating quality*. Since it is a culture of the majority, it stands in opposition to the dominant culture, which views itself as an elite culture. In fact, the dominant classes have historically considered popular culture to be anticulture, a vulgar expression of the poor taste of the dominated classes or groups. Whether it is folklore and square dancing, as it was many years ago, or jazz and romantic novels, some years later, or popular theatre and "heavy metal" music more recently, these forms of popular culture have all been rejected by the ruling classes as the vulgar expression of the dull and wretched life of the proletariat or popular groups. How can this rejection be explained? Is it related to economic conditions? If so, how?

Mattelart (1983) has claimed that popular culture is actually a unified system of responses by dominated classes and groups to the culture the ruling classes attempt to impose on them. Popular culture is therefore an equilibrium between two extremes, reaction and liberation. In reaction to their situation of being dominated, popular groups some-times become involved in conservative activities, which serves only to confirm the domi-nant culture and ultimately results in more oppression of these groups. Consider, for example, the role that the British working classes played in keeping Margaret Thatcher in power for so long, which clearly had negative consequences on workers' daily lives. The working classes' political support for Thatcher was linked to their perception of her as a "woman of the people." Thatcher carefully nurtured this image by repeating she was the daughter of a small, working-class grocer, and had been raised on popular culture. For the working classes, this appeal based on a common cultural background was stronger than Thatcher's conservative policies, which in effect redistributed society's wealth to the more privileged.[1] A similar situation occurred in Québec during the 1988 federal elec-tion, when Québec's working classes helped re-elect Brian Mulroney, the "boy from Baie Comeau," despite his conservative politics.

One of the reasons why popular culture wavers between liberation and conservatism is that it is essentially a culture of the present, one of opposition to the daily exploitation of the dominated classes, a culture of people who struggle day in, day out to eke out a liv-ing, or who are trapped inside the large, impersonal institutions (schools, bureaucracies, etc.) of capitalist society. It is therefore a culture of ordinary life. It corresponds to the ways in which the dominated classes get things done; it is a way of re-appropriating the social and cultural spaces built by the dominant classes, and with which the other classes cannot identify. Thus, popular culture is important because it is a form of protest against and appropriation of the dominant culture. In this context, it may be defined as a form of opposition to the dominant culture. "It does not exist in itself. It is constituted at the same time in its dependence to and its reaction against the dominant culture of yesterday and of today" (Mattelart, 1983: 24).

Let us consider a concrete example. Artists who are considered to be classics (for example, Shakespeare, Wilde and Rembrandt) are generally unknown to and unappreciat-ed by the dominated classes. But why is an author like Québec's Michel Tremblay so popular? In the early seventies, Michel Tremblay appropriated two artistic forms of the dominant culture, literature and theatre, and transformed them by incorporating the expe-riences of the working classes and giving voice to their viewpoints. The work of Michel Tremblay was thus considered to be popular culture. Inside the well-protected borders of elite culture, his work was seen as vulgar, even anticultural. Nevertheless, it was reappro-priated by the elites, who turned it into a lesson to show the working classes that they must improve their education and culture. In this new light it achieved such a resounding success that the "cultural elite" were forced to adopt it in their repertory of real culture. Today, Michel Tremblay's work generates interest among all classes.

This example can be extended to other domains of popular culture, like cooking, for instance. Thanks to immigrants from various countries, Canadians have become familiar

---

[1] It should be noted that during her first years in power, Thatcher had promised to buy the apartments of some tenants at a price lower than that of the market. Therefore, there was a material basis at the time for the working classes' support of her government. Nevertheless, even after this programme was eliminated, she remained pop-ular among the working classes. As a matter of fact, in the end, Thatcher was forced to step down by her own colleagues.

with and gained an appreciation of some of the world's most exotic cuisine. Who has never eaten, or at least heard of, sushi? Similarly, some of the most "popular" dishes have spread to all social classes in our society. How many bourgeois have never eaten a hot dog? Another area where popular and dominant cultures have mutually influenced each other is the media. Mass media such as radio and television were originally viewed as transmitters of banalities. In the last chapter, we saw how members of the Frankfurt School accused these media of having one objective, profitability, and were thus anticultural and antiliberation. Today, "elite" cultural activities such as operas, classical concerts and plays are regularly broadcast on these media. Moreover, political parties in power often use the media for the purposes of propaganda, which leads us to our next topic of discussion: mass culture.

Mass Culture

The difference between popular culture and mass culture varies according to the country in which they are studied. In the United States, the *melting pot* has made it such that popular culture has traditionally been identified with mass culture. Why? In a way, *mass culture* has borrowed from popular culture. As one American researcher said:

> American advertising shows many characteristics of the folk culture of other societies: repetition, a plain style, hyperbole and talk talk, folk verse, and folk music. . . . How do the expressions of our peculiar folk culture come to us? They no longer sprout from the earth, from the village, from the farm, or even from the neighbourhood or the city. They come to us primarily from enormous centralized self-consciously creative (an overused word, for the overuse of which advertising agencies are in no small part responsible) organizations. They come from advertising agencies, from networks of newspapers, radio, and television . . . (D.J. Boorstin, cited in Mattelart and Mattelart, 1992: 146).

In contrast to the United States, the tradition in European countries such as France has been to preserve dominant culture as the cultural standard. According to Mattelart and Mattelart (1992), in Europe, "culture" refers to original, authentic, classical works, and is therefore completely distinct from mass culture.

In this study, we make a distinction between mass culture and popular culture, the former being the culture that is capable of reaching the masses, defined as a very large number of people who do not necessarily have specific affinities or common goals. Thus, mass culture is based on the technical means that make the mass transmission of cultural products possible. As such, it is directly related to mass media. Like popular culture, it is possible to say that mass culture is opposed to elite culture, although they are not independent of each other. In fact, mass culture could, in a way, be considered a form of popular culture that is communicated through the media.

In essence, mass culture is a culture of the industrial age. It is founded on the mass production of both the written and spoken word, and on their dissemination as a commodity, in other words, for generating profit. Mass culture is therefore a culture of industrialization, and is omnipresent in our society. In fact, Ewen and Ewen (1982) have claimed that the ability of the mass media (e.g., print, radio and television) to form reality and then to reproduce it repeatedly has led audiences to accept such creations as reality. How is this substitution possible? Ewen and Ewen have argued that with the division of labour, industrialization, as developed by capitalism, has helped establish attitudes based on individualism which have led to the abandonment of community life. People, particularly in urban centres, have found themselves living and working under conditions that facilitate the reception of mass culture, a culture which has the "advantage" of being consumed in people's living rooms or dark theatres.

Why has individualism brought about conditions that are favourable to the reception of mass culture? The answer is that this culture is intended for the masses, and that the masses, as we saw in the introduction of this book, consist of large groups of people who have little or no contact with one another.

> The masses are always the others, whom we don't know, and can't know. Yet now, in our kind of society, we see these others regularly, in their myriad variations; stand, physically, beside them. They are here, and we are here with them. And that we are with them is of course the whole point. To other people, we also are masses. Masses are other people. . . . In an urban industrial society there are many opportunities for such ways of seeing. (Williams, 1958: 299–300).

The urban industrial environment has created conditions that are favourable to mass culture by breaking traditional links of dependence that existed in a community, and replacing them with a new system of standardization and dependence based on mass commodity production. Mass media productions have the same power to standardize and mobilize. However, people must give meaning to this massive flow of images and words. This is why it is important to have a critical imagination that transcends the symbols projected in the media so as to uncover their real message.

Democracy, according to Ewen and Ewen (1982), is being able to interpret the world, including that which is projected by the mass media, in a critical manner. One must be all the more vigilant because the media project prefabricated representations that are ready for consumption, having rejected all others. This is why the study of mass culture must be combined with the study of *ideological power*. Only then is it possible to uncover how oppositional ideologies manage to counter the dominant ideology and break through the wall of mass culture. However, one must be careful not to go to the opposite extreme and assume that all action undertaken by oppositional groups is successful. Otherwise, one could end up concluding (incorrectly) that such groups are autonomous and operate in complete independence of the dynamics of capitalism. This, of course, happens only in the movies.

According to Mattelart and Mattelart (1992), two obstacles hinder the emergence, in the mass media, of new cultures emanating from oppositional ideological groups: a) the "sacralization" of a certain view of professionalism, which states that professionals are the only ones who possess the know-how of media broadcasting; b) the "cumbersome heritage" of a culture of militant and oppositional communication that labels all media production by these groups as folklore. Nevertheless, mass culture is more than a response to capitalism. But, among those elements that support mass culture, which ones are based on a logic other than that of profitability?

To answer this question, it is necessary to consider not only the production of mass culture, but also the way in which it is consumed. As we will see in greater detail in the second part of this book, audiences use the media not only because they are there, or because they are alienated by their daily lives. Research (Mattelart and Mattelart, 1992) has shown that people have a good sense of the present, a desire to take advantage of life, to have a good time. Like popular culture, mass culture satisfies audiences in the here and now. Thus, there is a certain logic of pleasure—the pleasure of relaxing by oneself, with one's family, or in a group—that must be integrated into the analysis of mass culture produced by the media. For this reason, there appears to be more than one way for audiences to approach mass culture produced by the media.

As was seen earlier, audiences *negotiate* the meaning of media content; in other words, the meaning that was intended at the time of production is modified, even reversed, upon reception. According to Hall (1980), this *negotiation* can occur in one of three ways: according to the dominant code, the negotiated code or the oppositional code. The *dominant* code is adopted by viewers who perceive the meaning of the content exactly as it was intended by its producers, whose responsibility is to reproduce the dominant values. The *negotiated* code is that used by people who clearly understand the producers' intentions conveyed through messages, but who interpret them with a mixture of acceptance and opposition depending on the specific situation. For example, people like the idea of war if it is waged against Saddam Hussein, but not if it is against the United States, or if it leads to compulsory enlistment. Finally, the *oppositional code* is that used by people who completely reject all aspects of the media's messages, and who interpret them in a way that is completely opposite to what was meant. For example, a message urging people to adopt a healthy diet would be interpreted to mean that it is healthy to eat food accompanied by large servings of natural products such as butter or cream. The different audience's backgrounds and the variety of content are generally responsible for these differences in content negotiation. This question will be discussed in greater detail in Chapter 6.

Regardless of the way media content is negotiated, communication is always an exchange linking people in their daily lives. It has already been noted that a communication can reach a larger and more dispersed audience by using various technical means such as the mass media. Mediated communication is therefore the means *par excellence* of spreading a certain form of popular culture, which under these conditions becomes mass culture. Is this type of communication suitable to dominant culture as well? If so, is the dissemination of popular culture different from that of dominant culture?

It is possible to think that dominant culture is the antithesis of the mass culture that is disseminated by those media that seek to satisfy the largest audience possible. For example, the general manager of a Québec television station, TVA, claimed that, since the goal of his station was to reach as wide an audience as possible, its programming had a more popular orientation than stations that are either more elitist or more educational, like Radio Canada (the French section of the CBC) or Radio-Québec (*Forces*, 12, 1991: 50). But are there real differences in content from one station to the next?

One might argue that the answer to this question is no, for several reasons. First, most media are the property of capitalists, whose primary goal is to make a profit. Capitalists are therefore interested in producing content that will attract the largest audiences possible in order to find sponsors more easily. But the content that attracts large audiences is popular in nature. Since mass culture is directly related to mass media, and the latter are managed in a way to generate profit, one can claim that mass culture is influenced primarily by the economic conditions of the stations through which it is broadcast. For example, a publicly funded television network like the CBC can afford to broadcast shows intended only for the elite. However, as the CBC becomes less and less financed by the state, it must rely increasingly on sponsors to finance its programming, and consequently its orientation will increasingly resemble that of private stations. Thus there is a difference in the broadcasting of dominant culture and popular culture through the media.

However, even if dominant and popular content is different to begin with, who is to say that the dominated classes will not interpret them in their own way so as to integrate them into their existence? Moreover, as we saw in the previous chapter, those media that want to make money are forced to standardize their content to be able to export them to other countries. This is how a television series such as *Dallas* became the most watched television programme in many countries, including France and Japan. This leads us to a discussion of the movement involving the globalization of media products.

INTERNATIONAL CULTURE: EXPORTATION OF MEDIA CONTENT

As we mentioned in the last chapter, the internationalization of culture is achieved essentially through exports by multinational firms. For these mostly American companies, achieving large-scale production and reproducing American culture in new territories is imperative. With the appearance of various communication techniques (radio, television, tape recorders, etc.) and telecommunications satellites, cultural commodities have themselves become profitable to export to international markets.

The increasing sophistication of modern mass communication techniques has enabled firms to assume this new role fully. From the promotion of the Real (American) culture to the proliferation of advertising, there has been an all-out effort to promote a consumer society and the Western model of development. Radio, television, video recording and the massive transfer of information from large press agencies (also based in Western countries) have all contributed to the phenomenon of multinationalization.

Multinationals have always presented their vision as the only valid one. For over 30 years they have zealously played the role of broadcasting agent for American culture.[2] For Mattelart (1979), this internationalization of large corporations must be studied along with the expanding role of the information industry and the media in the economies of so-called "developed" countries. Even *mass telecommunications* have become an important factor in the process of industrial concentration, while at the same time enabling the

---

[2] It should be noted that even American multinationals that have been purchased by Japanese multinationals (for example, Sony Corporation, which has bought Columbia Pictures) continue to broadcast American productions. Only time will tell whether this situation will change as the Japanese grow more anxious to spread their own culture.

development of programmes and content. Since spreading the "good word" requires that cultural products be exported in large quantities, it is necessary to produce "industrial-size" cultural commodities with content that is easy to export.

This has led to a kind of reinforcement of mass culture, which Mattelart has described as follows: "Destined to become the universal culture which encourages the expansion of Empire and by the same stroke contributes to the enslavement of each country's national consciousness . . . " (Mattelart, 1979: 3). The improvement of production techniques and processes has also made it possible to take into account the specific characteristics of different audiences (e.g., age categories). As a result, economic profitability increases as "ideological profitability" increases. With products adapted to each audience, the efficiency of messages transmitted through the media is optimized.

Production standards are theoretically based on the "needs" of consumers as identified by market research. But what multinationals attempt to sell is nothing short of what can be described as the most widely marketable product, aimed at reaching the largest audiences possible, while satisfying at least a small part of their needs. In short, the goal is to sell new cultural products on a worldwide scale. One of the interesting features of the internationalization of mass culture is that the capitalist economy which supports the media industry has managed to appropriate popular culture, transforming it from a process of resistance and liberation that it once was—and still is within each community—to one of dominance within the standardized mass culture. The last 30 years have seen a major increase in the export of all sorts of cultural products, mostly from the United States. In all countries open to international broadcasting, popular cultural practices (lifestyles, music, cinema, etc.) are now, consciously or unconsciously, subjugated to the "American style." If theatre is an exception to the rule, it is because it cannot be easily exported through the mass media. But, if theatre cannot be readily transformed into mass culture, what kind of cultural products can be exported?

Let us look at a concrete example. When it comes to culture and leisure, North Americans have managed to universalize their model of the organization of the media. They have imposed genres, areas of interest, programming styles, ways of producing information and spending leisure time upon the "free world." One of the first forms of mass culture to be exported were children's programmes. In most cases, programmes and television series for children are created by large foundations (the largest, e.g. the Ford Foundation and the Rockefeller Foundation, have billions of dollars in capital and several hundred million dollars in annual budgets).

The internationally acclaimed *Sesame Street* is probably the most striking example of this kind of programme. The show was first created by an association consisting of several foundations and the American government (the *Children's Television Workshop*) whose aims were: "To find the best way of using electronic technology, especially television, as a medium for teaching children" (cited in Mattelart, 1979: 161). Top experts were called upon to produce a show intended to reflect the values of American society. The results were staggering: four years after its creation in New York, *Sesame Street* was being distributed to 90 countries.

Many private corporations participated in this educational show. Mobil Oil financed the handbooks distributed to parents, RCA donated colour television sets, General Foods paid for the teacher's guide, and Xerox made a large contribution to the Spanish and Portuguese translations of the programmes. This philanthropic movement marks a change in the attitude of the corporate world towards mass cultural activities, inspired by "a need to polish up their image" by participating in educational and cultural activities (Mattelart, 1979: 165). Beyond developing cultural products, major corporations are ultimately motivated by their use as marketing tools and publicity gadgets that allow them to create spin-offs of all types (books, cassettes, toys, videos, T-shirts, to name but a few). Profit figures bear witness to this fact. For these multinational companies, mass culture has become an area of investment just like any other, and is engaged in for the sole purpose of profit.

The internationalization of mass culture is not limited to children's programmes. In fact, mostly other genres are promoted, such as television drama (soap operas and serials) whose potential for universality grows when produced on an industrial scale. These products are exported throughout the world, and have become popular in a wide variety of countries such as Brazil, France and Japan. Is such wide diffusion of culture an indication that the mass media are a process of democratic communication?

ARE MASS MEDIA DEMOCRATIC?

Since the end of the sixties the term "communication" has been in fashion. The reasons for this are many, and can be categorized into two major trends which, curiously enough, represent opposing views of mass communication: a) the utopian trend views the means of communication as themselves responsible for the liberation of the entire world; b) the decentralized trend believes that this liberation will be carried out through the appropriation of the media by small groups.

Proponents of the first category support the fine-tuning of various means of communication as much for the purposes of economic development as for the improvement of possibilities of ideological control. In this category of thought are utopians like McLuhan (who dreamt of the emergence of a global village where technological progress in the field of communication would bring about greater harmony), and most proponents of functionalist approaches in communication studies. The second category is made up of partisans of "the right to communication" and decentralization, which would enable all classes and social groups to have access to media production, against the will of the ruling classes which have controlled it for a long time. Thus, there exists a movement to consolidate counter-reactionary power for the purpose of breathing new life into the social environment by re-appropriating the mass media. But is this really a democratic movement?

Paul Beaud (1984) repositioned the debate between these two viewpoints by questioning the "democratic" role played by the mass media in a society like ours. To what extent can the media be the grounds for new social negotiation, or for liberation? Does access to the media, as a means of participation in social change, constitute a real victory in terms of the right to free speech in the public space?

Beaud has remained sceptical and does not believe at all in the media's attempt to democratize power. According to him, studies that claim that the decentralization of information is the road to liberation are founded on a simplistic perception of the mass media: on the one hand, monolithic and all-powerful, and, on the other, a means of primitive democracy rediscovered through dialogue, thanks to the "soft" technologies of decentralized information (Beaud, 1984: 208).

But reality is much more complex. The fact is, television is not only an instrument of power, but also an instrument of mystification. Through the media, a well-meaning elite can talk about power and pretend there is a real public debate by televising a few minutes of news stories. According to Beaud, this information is disseminated from the place where power is exercised, and where it will find social support. On television, politics is usually reduced to a daily, ritual act (Beaud, 1984). In other words, the media broadcast only information approved by the ruling classes. They project a reality that is authorized by the dominant ideology, which is supported by the classes that control media networks.

In fact, the effect of the media is to conceal where the real centres of power lie, and thus help keep this power within a closed circle of economic and political interests. How can the unsuspecting viewer see the influence that those with political and economic power have on daily programming? The mystification is so successful that the media are accused of having contradictory effects, that is, of sometimes manipulating information, and at other times making it accessible.

In reality, the mass media do not communicate opposition. On the contrary, the mass culture which they produce cuts people off from their cultural roots. In this context, mass culture stands opposite popular culture in that the former discourages opposition and resistance instead of encouraging it. For this reason, mass culture has instilled the idea of the need for "alternative" communication. People must be given the means to exchange openly. Beaud (1984) has argued that, since people like television only, they should be given access to video technology. Tongue in cheek, Beaud has added that this way everyone can become a broadcaster.

Since video is more accessible in terms of content production than a medium like television, it could become the panacea for a whole sector of community involvement that is developing around sociocultural activities and audiovisual communication. However, Beaud (1984) accused intellectuals of taking this sector by storm, since they believe that a new relationship with the media is emerging. For example, he warned that, by allowing live broadcasts of municipal council meetings, a few small towns in Québec will be overrun by battalions of new communication ideologists, who will come to witness the renaissance of direct democracy and popular culture.

Beaud has been highly critical of this decentralization movement, whose aim is to transform negative technical effects into positive ones. First, he has attacked the notion of democracy that these groups of intellectuals espouse. He has described their view as a short-sighted vision that would limit opposition to the operations of local media (Beaud, 1984). These groups portray their vision as democratic since it is inspired by the spontaneous involvement and cultural politicization of the masses, and uses less expensive and more accessible media such as video. Proponents of video technology knock television production material because it is cumbersome, and promote the use of video because the equipment is light and inexpensive, and makes simultaneous sound and image recording and spontaneous retransmissions possible, etc. Can democracy be reduced to having one's voice heard and to the emergence of new communication technologies?

Let us consider an example. In Québec, because of certain particular conditions, the phenomenon of community radio and television has been especially widespread. The growing interest in sociocultural issues, combined with the rapid development of the administrative apparatus, has led to an acceleration of the modernization of Québec society. In this context, the professional middle classes has viewed communication as a means of wielding their new-found influence. For these classes, the "alternative" media are seen as the means of access to speech, which they equate with power. Local and community television stations have shown a certain fascination with speech, debate and public discussion. Speech, in this case, is associated with live programmes and the appearance on television of individuals who are generally excluded from this medium.

Beaud (1984) is critical of studies that give the impression that having an audience's ear is the same as having power, and that fail to take into account the capitalist logic of production and the class contradictions that exist in communication, as in all other spheres of society. The problem, he has argued, is that making one's voice heard often means holding the floor at the expense of others, even though one may claim to give it back to them. Nowhere has rhetoric become such a weapon of the privileged than in Québec. However, the silent majority remain just that: silent.

In fact, community projects in the field of communication have all had a common denominator: wherever they occurred, they were extensions, on a local scale, of power structures existing at the national level. The decentralization of the media—be it radio or television—cannot bring about a transformation of social relations. In fact, to give all classes and social groups equal access to the media would require changing the relations of power in society, in other words, transforming the economic and political structures. Communication is still, first and foremost, an industry with markets to conquer. The new services provided by cable distribution, the channels available on pay television, home multimedia systems, and so on, are developed for a high-income clientele. Thus, the more sophisticated mass media technology becomes, the less accessible it is to everyone, and therefore the less democratic it is.

CONCLUSION

We began this chapter by making a distinction between ideology and culture. We saw that, although they are interrelated, they are still distinct from one another. Ideology operates at an abstract level by guiding people's experiences, whereas culture is more concrete in that it provides people with reference points that create comfort zones and provide familiarity to help people find their way though the myriad of possibilities they encounter.

On the basis of these definitions, we identified different types of ideologies. One of these, the dominant ideology, is conveyed by all aspects of social organization, more specifically the mass media, and is characterized by its ability to accommodate or reject other ideologies opposed to certain dominant ideas.

There are also different types of cultures. Dominant culture, or elite culture, is the one that is imposed on all of society as the cultural *standard*. It is opposed by popular cultures, from which it nevertheless borrows a certain number of activities. We also examined mass culture, which is essentially an industrial culture with a strong leaning towards individualism. Since mass culture is founded on the notion of profitability, it must represent the culture of the majority, while at the same time conveying the dominant ideology. It is important to recall that, according to critical theories, these concepts are all interrelated.

In the last two chapters, our analysis of the critical theory of the mass media has shown that it is helpful to study the phenomenon of media as a whole, that is, as an indivisible entity encompassing the economic, political, ideological and cultural conditions of the society in which they operate. Although it was necessary for the purpose of analysis to make theoretical distinctions between these elements, it must be emphasized that, in practice, these distinctions are impossible to apply since the elements are all interdependent.

Chapter 4 has shown that the mass media cannot be analyzed without being placed within the economic and political context of the society in which they develop, and are used. Thus, we have seen that the general characteristics of society are reflected in the organization of the media. As with capitalist production, media production is influenced by the economic and political conditions in which it occurs. Moreover, since the media are used to convey symbols and values, and are closely related to our everyday experiences, it is important to examine the types of ideologies and culture that are communicated in their content, which is itself influenced by the economic and political conditions in which it is produced. Therefore, it is clear that all these elements are linked and that the mass media do not exist *in a vacuum*. They are, instead, the result of the social conditions of a specific type of society, at a particular time and place. There is, however, a social reality that has not yet been addressed, namely gender differentiation. In the next two chapters we will address the following question: do people's experiences with the media differ based on their gender?

POWER RELATIONS AND SEXUAL DISCRIMINATION IN MEDIA PRODUCTION

The women of today are in a fair way to dethrone the myth of femininity; they are beginning to affirm their independence in concrete ways; but they do not easily succeed in living completely the life of a human being. Reared by women within a feminine world, their normal destiny is marriage, which still means practically subordination to man; for masculine prestige is far from extinction, resting still upon solid economic and social foundations. We must therefore study the traditional destiny of woman with some care. . . . I shall seek to describe how woman undergoes her apprenticeship, how she experiences her situation, in what kind of universe she is confined, what modes of escape are vouchsafed her. Then only—with so much understood—shall we be able to comprehend the problems of women, the heirs of a burdensome past, who are striving to build a new future (de Beauvoir, 1953: XXX).

INTRODUCTION

This quote from Simone de Beauvoir which, remarkably, still applies today, accurately sums up the general situation of women in a society such as ours. Although women make up more than half of the world's population, they are still a minority in, and often completely absent from, positions of power. The situation is such that women were completely ignored in most social studies until the advent of an approach whose specific aim is to examine the impact of gender differentiation in our society: the feminist approach. As Marx was concerned with the question of how people manage to feed and house themselves in industrial society, feminists are interested in understanding how the majority of women find themselves in a dominated position and in subordinate occupations in this society. Whereas Marx was concerned with capitalist society, feminists are concerned with patriarchal society.

The objective of the first four chapters of this book was to develop a general critical approach for analyzing the mass media in our society. Thus, we emphasized several aspects that must be considered, and showed that each of these revealed new elements that must be explained to understand the organization of the mass media. This approach draws on several types of analyses with a common focus, that of an abstract, asexual subject, or, more specifically, a male subject referred to as *Man*, he, him, etc. However, contrary to what most researchers think, Women were not created in the image of Men. Their place in society, their activities and ideas are often divergent, or even opposed.

In the next two chapters, we will concentrate on an aspect of media analysis that has long been neglected, namely gender differentiation with respect to not only stereotypes conveyed in content, but also discrimination in the production of content and in the construction of audiences. We will see that men and women have very different life experiences, and that this divergence is equally reflected in their use of the mass media. Consider, for example, the question of media consumption, where men and women do not necessarily engage in the same types of activities, and when they do they are not necessarily drawn to the same content. Thus, a man and a woman may agree to watch television together, but may not want to watch the same programme; similarly, they may agree to spend an evening together reading, but may not like to read the same kind of literature. Is this distinction between female and male activities limited to mass media consumption? In other words, is it also present in the production process of the media? Do men and women occupy positions with the same degree of power over the organization of the media? If not, what differences are there, and what impact do they have on the management of the media?

To help answer these questions, this chapter will focus on the *production of content* in the mass media. However, in order to understand the *relations of production* involved in the development of mass media content, it is important to first study, on a more general level, the *roots of differentiation* between the social experiences of each sex, and then examine how these experiences are expressed in the social practices of women and men. We will then see *how* these distinctions are reproduced in the production process of the media by looking at the power relations between male and female workers. But in order to understand the specific nature of these relations we must first study the general characteristics of the production process of the mass media.

MEDIA INDUSTRIES: CAPITALIST PRODUCTION

In Chapters 3 and 4, we saw that the mass media are an integral part of capitalist society and, as such, display the same characteristics: the media are the property of a small group of capitalists whose objectives are not only to make money, but to reproduce the dominant ideology of society. This small group of administrators thus controls the internal organization of the media, including the production of content and the audiences targeted.

Are media industries different from other capitalist industries? In general, the *production of media content* follows the same capitalist rules that apply to other industries, although they may differ in certain aspects. Like most capitalist industries, the media industry is an important part of the accumulation of capital by our society's dominant classes. Thus, in order to make profits, it must go beyond simply meeting already existing needs: it must create new ones so as to satisfy the economic and political systems in place. Like all other industries, it uses advertising to create a demand for the products it puts on the market. One need only recall the publicity surrounding the premieres of *Anne of Green Gables* and *He Shoots, He Scores*, or any other big-budget programme. The production of cultural commodities entails considerable risk, a fact that has consequences on the production process of media content and on the relations of production within this process.

In order to minimize the risks involved, the production of large media enterprises is generally based on a *process of collective labour*. This is more than a series of production stages. It consists of a process of *integrated labour* in which a coordinator, called the *producer*, is responsible for the final product. The process includes other occupations, ranging from the artist who designs the cultural aspect of the product to the distributor who finds ways to distribute it. To illustrate this process, we will examine two specific cases: the production of records and popular novels.

To produce popular records, the process of collective labour must integrate a composer, a singer, an arranger, musicians, a sound engineer, an artistic director, etc. The job of the producer (generally a representative of the record company) is to coordinate all these tasks with the goal of achieving the desired product. In a similar manner, the production of popular novels involves as team that consists of a producer (or editor) who coordinates the work of a writer, research assistants (in some cases), critical readers, proofreaders, translators (if necessary), graphic designers, data processors, etc.

The bigger the media industry, the more complex the production process and the more closely the process reproduces the dominant model of capitalist industry. Within this process there are many types of jobs that involve some degree of autonomy, power and control over the final product. In all cases, however, the product does not belong to any of the workers, not even the artist, who nevertheless usually receives royalties. The artist may sometimes have some control over production, but it is the producer who ultimately decides what form the product will take. In all production processes, this control decreases as one moves down the job hierarchy until it becomes only symbolic, as in the case of subordinate workers, which includes freelancers. The majority of non-permanent occupations, including freelance positions, are occupied by women who cannot find steady work, or who refuse it so that they may take care of their children, a task that has been socially assigned to them.

As we mentioned earlier, cultural products are high-risk commodities. For this reason, some of the production work is done on a freelance basis, since contract workers represent smaller financial risks. According to Miège (1979), employers require that a pool of workers be available to work at their beck and call. Because of their precarious situation, freelancers have little power or control over their labour. The integrated production process is therefore founded on the same relations of production as those of other capitalist industries. Moreover, we will recall that in all capitalist enterprises, the relations of production are based on contradictory interests that lead to class conflicts between employers and employees. As we will see shortly, these conflicts can also result from sexual discrimination. But first let us examine in greater detail the relations of production in media industries.

The means of production of the media—such as television and radio networks, record companies and publishing houses—and the commodities they produce are not the property of workers. As Rinehart (1987) points out, this situation leads to working conditions identical to those of any capitalist enterprise: the owners, or the managers who represent them, control the production process and decide what kind of labour the employees will do during the workday. For employees, their labour becomes instrumental, a means of earning a living. In this context, labour relations are reduced to economic relations in which media owners need workers to make profits, and employees need work to make a living. Moreover, since making a profit is the ultimate goal of owners, the production process is not organized according to the needs, interests and skills of workers, but is aimed at making the enterprise productive and profitable. Thus, one can say that workers are *alienated* from their work in the sense that they have no real control over the means of production, the products themselves, or the division of labour within the production process. How can workers be made to accept such alienation, and how can their productivity be maximized?

In all capitalist enterprises, specific mechanisms have been developed by employers to ensure that employees abandon bad work habits and submit to the demands of regular and constant production. According to Foucault (1982), three mechanisms in particular are used. The first two are applied by external means, and the last consists of a form of internal control or self-discipline. Through these mechanisms, workers are submitted to a training process where they are forced to learn company rules, and are conditioned to respect them. Workers are subjected to a hierarchy in which those at the bottom must fulfil the wishes of those in the upper echelons. Workers are also conditioned to develop a form of self-discipline that will unconsciously lead them to act in the interests of the enterprise.

These mechanisms, which capitalists have developed to make production more efficient, are not without their difficulties. In the mass media, as in any other enterprise, the relations of production between the different classes, even in the most regulated cases, have their share of contradictions, conflicts, resistance and struggles. It is these dynamics, which are created by the interaction of dominance and struggle, that bring about change. Are these dynamics limited to class differences? Do they extend to the relations between workers of the opposite sex? It is impossible to answer these questions without examining the process through which males and females become integrated into society, referred to as the *socialization* of individuals. What exactly does socialization mean?

SOCIALIZATION OF INDIVIDUALS

Socialization is the term that sociologists use to refer to the learning process by which individuals develop their identity and acquire the knowledge, skills and motivations for participating in social life. Socialization is a lifelong process that consists of *mechanisms* of social learning. These mechanisms are applied through agents that operate within certain social *milieus*. Socialization is very important, since it represents the link between the individual and society. It is of particular interest to us here because, in a modern society like ours, most of the socialization of individuals is done via the mass media. This aspect of the socialization process will be addressed in another section of this chapter.

For now, let us examine in greater detail how the various elements of the socialization process operate.

In order for people to integrate into a society or community, they must first learn and then internalize the sociocultural features of their environment. Thus, throughout their lives, individuals acquire new knowledge that will help them deal with new situations. Through these new experiences, to which their personalities adapt, individuals develop a social conscience—a moral order or a form of self-discipline—that will dictate the "normal" way of behaving. This knowledge will also enable them to integrate into their environment, in other words, to assimilate enough common elements to live in anonymity.

How does a person acquire the social skills required to live in anonymity? Through *mechanisms of socialization*. The necessary knowledge is partly transmitted by parents and partly acquired by observing others in the community, or watching imaginary characters in cultural productions from the mass media. Some types of mechanisms, such as punishment/reward, are used to ensure that the child's acquisition of knowledge meets specific goals. Who, as a child, was never punished or rewarded? It should be noted that this mechanism is not limited to childhood: for example, society sends "criminals" to prison to punish them and show them how to adopt "better" behaviour; society grants scholarships to "good" students to reward them for their hard work and to encourage them to continue.

This leads us to the topic of the *values* conveyed by the process of socialization. It is during this process that we learn what is "right" and what is "wrong," what we "ought" to do and "ought not" to do, and so on. It is also through these values that the process of socialization occurs *along gender lines*. Thus we learn such things as: which toys are "good" for girls, but not for boys? What signs of affection are appropriate for girls, but not for boys? Is it appropriate for a man to take care of the house and children while his wife works outside the home? Should women be openly encouraged to practice non-traditional trades, such as garbage collector, bus driver, mechanic, technician, etc.? Because socialization is the process through which people learn to adapt to society, these are very important questions since they reflect the prevalent values and ideas in our society. Social values may be instilled by external means such as parents, friends, the media, etc., or may be acquired by the "internalization of others," which consists of acting according to what we think others think of us. This internalization is so powerful that even in private, people will often unconsciously act as if others were watching them.

The mechanisms of socialization are applied via *agents of socialization*. The *milieu* will determine the extent to which learning is formal. The *objective* will be more or less specific depending on whether learning is intended simply to train an individual so that he or she may be accepted into an association, or, more particularly, to educate someone to obtain a diploma. *Age* is another agent of socialization. Since the process of socialization lasts a lifetime and varies according to the individual's age, researchers have divided this process into three stages: a) primary; b) adult; and c) resocialization. *Primary* socialization occurs during childhood, the period when an individual acquires skills in various areas: language, self-control, general knowledge, moral standards and social-role awareness. Since learning begins in childhood, messages are received by highly vulnerable individuals who have no preconceived ideas or opinions and who are therefore more easily influenced. Following childhood, the *adult* stage of socialization reinforces previously learned attitudes and, with time, introduces individuals to new expectations based on gender. During this stage, people learn the different roles that society assigns to women and men. The last stage, that of *resocialization*, varies in impact from one individual to the next. Resocialization is often triggered by an unexpected event that renders obsolete part of the knowledge a person has acquired, making it necessary to learn new knowledge. This stage may or may not be difficult, depending on whether the adjustments to be made are radical or slight.

Let us consider the example of a male worker employed as a welder in a small boat-repair factory. He works alongside other skilled workers in a completely male setting imbued with a working-class culture. Many studies have shown that this type of culture is often sexist, racist and even male chauvinistic (see Mackie, 1983). However, due to an economic recession, the factory has to lay off its junior employees, including our worker. Since he is young, he decides to enroll in university in a bachelor's programme in organizational communication. After graduating, he finds a job in a government agency where he is responsible for applying an affirmative action programme for women, visible minorities and the handicapped. The worker thus finds himself in a situation requiring completely new skills, not only in terms of the intellectual knowledge he has acquired in university, but also with respect to his experience with people. He will need to be *resocialized*, first as a member of a new social class—he now belongs to a professional middle class—and then as an individual who must be sensitive to and understanding of social differences. He will have to relearn a language and an attitude that are non-sexist, non-racist and non-discriminatory. He will even have to learn to dress differently because of his new surroundings, which brings us to a discussion of the last aspect of the socialization process, the *membership milieus* and *reference milieus*.

Membership milieus are important, as these are where agents of socialization and socialized individuals are integrated economically, politically, socially and ecologically. For example, individuals are socialized differently depending on whether they belong to a rural community or live in a city, whether they are members of a visible minority or not, whether they are men or women, or whether they belong to the working classes or the bourgeoisie. But individuals also borrow ideas and patterns of behaviour from other, reference milieus. An example would be the school system they belong to. The values of school systems are those of the dominant classes; thus, in working-class neighbourhoods children are in a paradoxical situation because they do not have the financial means to adopt the model they are taught. Another example is the fact that adults borrow values and models from the dominant classes, believing this will improve their children's chances of succeeding. Finally, a person can also acquire values conveyed by Canadian television, which itself borrows from American television. The media, in all but a few exceptions, are reference milieus with unclear goals. As we will see in greater detail in the next chapter, the television content of programmes such as soap operas and serials carry informal values and messages that users receive by the thousands during viewing hours. These values are also transmitted through popular literature, cinema, etc. So it is not an exaggeration to assert that we are literally bombarded with messages and values that can influence our social experiences.

In short, the concept of socialization consists of a process of education in the broadest sense of the word, that is, where human beings constantly learn new things from the time they are born until their deaths. This process is the very essence of the socialization of individuals: it is through their education that they learn how to respond to different situations. This education begins in the family, and carries on in school. But it does not end there. Individuals continue to learn through their experiences with their friends, or with the use of the media. Thus, we can see that socialization can be intentional, especially in the family or in school. For example, the manners we learned from our parents or the knowledge we were taught in school were intentionally instilled in us to facilitate our integration into society. But when it is done in an informal manner, socialization may also be unintentional. For instance, the knowledge acquired through the media or the habits (good or bad) picked up from a group of friends are communicated unintentionally.

It is therefore through all these elements of the socialization process that individuals become socially constructed as rich or poor, as white or black, as women or men, etc. Beyond physical characteristics, how do individuals learn to become *feminine* or *masculine*? This is the question that feminist analyses have addressed, and which we will examine in the following section.

SOCIAL CONSTRUCTION OF MASCULINITY AND FEMININITY

Feminist analyses have brought a new dimension to studies in the social sciences, including sociology and communication. They have shown that men and women do not necessarily have the same experiences, and that it is therefore often useful to distinguish between the sexes when conducting research on society. Where does the social differentiation of the sexes originate? Some sociological feminist analyses have suggested that the discrepancies in the experiences of males and females are largely due to the fact that girls and boys are socialized differently.

The French author Simone de Beauvoir had a determining influence on early feminist analyses. Her work *The Second Sex* (1953), which constitutes a comprehensive analysis of the situation of women in society at the time, is still frequently used by researchers interested in understanding the position of women and men in today's society. In her study, de Beauvoir rebels against what she calls the "*destin figé*" ("fixed destiny") of women: a destiny that is fixed by the bourgeoisie which has established a gender hierarchy that confines women to an inferior position and a subordinate role. She contends that the chances of every individual, man or woman, should not be defined in terms of happiness, but in terms of freedom. One's existence can be justified only if it opens the door to endless future opportunities; one can be free only if one's actions continually bring about new freedoms. In her book, de Beauvoir firmly maintains that existence and freedom should be the same for both sexes. But she notes that such equality for opportunity has been invalidated by the *myth of femininity*—developed by patriarchal society—which confines women to a set of stereotypes that limit their existence and freedom. In other words, the origin of the *notion of femininity*, as we know it, is not "natural" or "biological." "One is not born, but rather becomes, a woman" (de Beauvoir, 1953: 267). How does one become a woman? That is the question addressed by feminist research.

It was not until the end of the sixties that a group of sociologists began to ask questions about the way social science research was conducted. Based on their experience, these sociologists observed that men and women do not necessarily have the same attitudes regarding social phenomena, and that their experiences and their activities not only differed, but were sometimes in opposition. Thus, they began to conduct research first on women alone, and then on the differences between the two sexes. These researchers became aware that such sex differences in personal experiences were *socially constructed*, and that they originated in childhood, at the beginning of the socialization process.

At this point, it is important to note that there exist different feminist approaches. Moreover, not only do they not all address the same issues, but when they do, they often have different, sometimes even contradictory, results. Nevertheless, feminist analyses all have one point in common: they recognize that there is a difference between the experiences of women and men, and that scientific research should take this fact into account. Since the first studies appeared, the feminist discipline has changed considerably and has also become diversified. In the beginning, feminist studies had a tendency to consider women as a homogenous group, with every member having the same needs and desires.[1] This is what some feminists have denounced as the enslavement to women's solidarity. With time, however, feminist studies have become more sophisticated. Today, some of the more serious analyses take into consideration that, despite the fact that they are of the same sex, women from different classes and cultures may have radically different experiences. And, in some cases, the activities of men and women belonging to the same class and culture may be more alike than those of women from different classes and cultures. The most important and positive aspect of contemporary feminist studies is that they continue to focus their analyses on real social practices—such as sexual discrimination in the workplace, or sexist images in media content—instead of researching abstract concepts, or "universal" subjects with nonspecific characteristics, such as Men and Women. The fundamental question of all scientific feminist research is: what are the causes (social, political, economic and ideological) of the differentiation between the experiences of women and men?

These causes begin to take root during childhood. Feminist researchers have noticed that, in order to adapt to our society, children must be conscious of the existence of different social expectations of boys and girls. Thus, they quickly learn to internalize stereotypes regarding behaviour (boys must be aggressive and girls gentle), chores (boys take out the garbage while girls do the dishes), physical appearance (boys wear pants, girls look prettier in skirts), peers (boys play with boys and girls with girls), etc. As children grow older, *they learn the typical roles assigned to each gender*.

These differences, which are learned during childhood, will be maintained throughout life and are often transformed into discrimination against women. For a long time, girls were refused access to higher education on the pretext that they should get married

---

[1] In fact, this is what the quote from Simone de Beauvoir at the beginning of this chapter implies. Even though her comments draw attention to a situation that still exists today, they could stand to be qualified.

and stay at home to raise a family. Women who did not get married had to settle for subordinate jobs. This discrimination is not limited to the family and school, but exists in all other spheres of society related to work and leisure. For example, on the eve of the twenty-first century, women in our society earn only 64% of men's wages, either because they are refused, or at least limited in their access to well-paid, steady jobs (such as technician, engineer, janitor and even garbage collector), or because, in cases where the two sexes are equally represented in an occupation, women receive lower wages than men. Table 5.1 shows the "progress" achieved in Canada in this regard during the decade between 1973 and 1982. We can see that the gap has not narrowed at all over this period: women's average gains increased by less than 5% compared with those of men. Women's occupations continue to be undervalued with respect to men's, and are therefore less well paid. For example, a nurse earns lower wages than an electronics technician, even though they have both received the same number of years of training; the wages of a chambermaid are lower than those of a janitor, even though their jobs require the same kinds of skills.

If we look at a category of media specialists such as writers, editors, journalists and the like, the situation seems to be slightly improving. Data for all wage-earners included in this category show that in 1985 women earned 65.3% of men's wages, and that in 1990 the gap had narrowed a little, with women earning 72.7% of men's wages. For full-time and permanent workers, women earned 71.7% of men's wages in 1985 and 79.4% in 1990 (Statistics Canada, April 1993). Why does this type of discrimination exist in our society?

TABLE 5.1 Comparison of wages in terms of dollars and percentages, 1973–1982

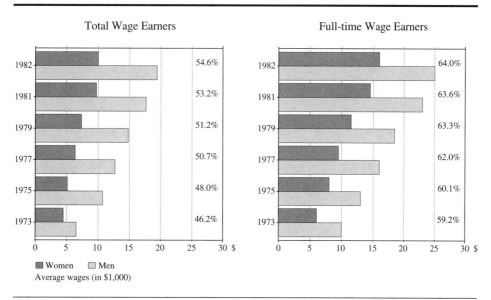

Adaptation of the table of the average gains of women and men. Council on the Status of Women, 1987 Annual Report.

In feminist analyses, discrimination against women is attributed to the fact that we live in a *patriarchal society* that is supported by a *patriarchal ideology*. In this patriarchal system, women's occupations, requiring women's so-called "natural" skills (cleaning, care-giving, etc.), are considered less important and less prestigious than men's occupations. What is a patriarchal society? What is a patriarchal ideology?

A patriarchal society is a society founded on male dominance. In this type of society, men occupy most, if not all, positions of power and assume the authority to control all social spheres, whether it is in the family (as head of the family), politics (as head of government), business (as head of a company), and so on. Since men have authority, they occupy positions of control where decisions are made concerning the organization of society. A patriarchal society is therefore one in which men make the decisions and women follow them. When women manage to occupy positions of power, they are always in a minority and generally have to suppress their experiences as women and adopt men's ideas and imitate their actions. Some researchers claim that women have a choice between "observing silence" or "being silenced."

The federal government committee that was set up to establish a law banning the sale of automatic weapons following the massacre at Montréal's École Polytechnique provides a good example of the silence imposed on women. The committee, composed of six males and one female, all members of the House of Commons, recommended measures rejecting a ban on these weapons because, according to the male members of the committee, this would inconvenience hunters. The female committee member was so angry at this attitude that she distanced herself from the report by not signing it. She later confirmed to the media that she was convinced that had the committee consisted of an equal number of women and men, its recommendations would have been quite different. The divergence of opinion between these men and this woman brings us to a discussion of ideology.

As we saw in the last chapter, a society's ideology serves to justify that society's dominant social practices. A patriarchal society is therefore supported by a patriarchal ideology, that is, a system of ideas that justifies the supremacy of men and upholds the institutions they govern. Thus it can be said that we live in a society that conveys a *patriarchal capitalist ideology*, a society where the ideology supports the class system and the dominance of men in positions of power—be they in financial enterprises or political institutions. Given that women represent half of society's population, we may ask whether there are as many female as there are male members of parliament or ministers, or chairmen and chief executive officers of large corporations. We will see in the next few pages and chapters that women and men are also unequally represented in the mass media, a fact that is reflected as much in media-related occupations as in content. For example, with respect to media content, men are more numerous, they generally have the best roles, etc. Some will argue that this situation has changed. But has it really?

It goes without saying that the emergence and development of the feminist movement has greatly contributed to the identification of the various forms of oppression from which women suffer, and has led to some progress. However, the observable gains have not been achieved without great pain, since women have had to overcome fierce resistance in all their struggles, regardless of where they occur or what the issue may be. The women's movement has emphasized the social inequalities between men and women, and has attacked the distribution of roles along gender lines, whether in the home, the workplace, or other social spheres. How do feminists explain the patriarchal system?

Feminists are not all in agreement on the answer to this question. Fox (1988) has identified three types of models that explain the existence of the patriarchal system: patriarchy as a form of collective male dominance over society; patriarchy as a self-contained, autonomous system; and patriarchy as a system based on gender differences. Let us now look at these three models in greater detail.

The model of *collective male dominance* considers male supremacy over society to be collective and historically invariable. It results from men's innate desire for power, which has remained constant over time. This male power is applied to a society with particular characteristics, that is, society is seen only as an aggregation of individuals acting according to rational objectives. The dominance of one sex (male) over the other (female) is explained biologically. The biological impossibility of men to bear children is replaced by an innate desire for power, or dominance, in other spheres. Thus the model considers patriarchy as a characteristic of our society, which is not the case in the second approach, which defines patriarchy as a self-contained system.

The *self-contained system* model contends that our society is based on a dual system of capitalism and patriarchy. Although they are equivalent in status, these two systems are not related and operate parallel to each other. Patriarchy is defined as a system of female oppression on the basis of the "domestic mode of production" in which gender relations replace class relations. Men own the means of production (house, furniture, other property, etc.), and therefore constitute the dominant classes, while women, whose sole possession is their labour power, constitute the dominated classes. In this system, marriage is considered a work contract, according to which women are required to do the domestic labour that is indispensable to society's proper functioning, thereby enabling men to appropriate women's labour without financial compensation.

Finally, the *gender/sex system* model, in which patriarchy is viewed as a system based on gender differences, is founded on psychosociological arguments. Here, patriarchy is defined as a system in which women are psychosociologically disposed to fulfilling their roles as mother and spouse, and men are disposed to supporting the family economically and dominating the public sphere. Male dominance is the result of men's painful separation from their mothers during childhood, an experience that enables them to acquire their own identity. The pain of separation is compensated for by men's desire for power and dominance, that is, the desire to feel superior to women. This is accompanied by a feeling of hostility towards their mothers, a feeling which is later transferred to other women. In short, this argument is similar to the first model, except that it is based on psychology instead of biology.

There are other ways to categorize the diverse feminist approaches to the question of the patriarchal system. Sandra Whitworth (1994), in her study of women's role in world politics, has also divided feminist models into three groups: the liberal, the radical and the postmodernist approaches. Her categories, as we will now see, differ significantly from Fox's.

The liberal model explains women's discrimination in three ways. First, in their infancy and teens, women are socialized to move away from activities socially known as masculine, such as playing with guns or military toys; then, girls are raised to be less ambitious than boys; finally, systemic barriers are built both by men with authority who refuse to promote women and by legislation which limits women's employment and training opportunities, and so on. The problem with the liberal approach, says Whitworth, is that it "accepts the prevailing power structures" in arguing that a greater inclusion of women in decision-making occupations would suffice to achieve equality between the sexes (1994: 76–7).

The radical model contains two different angles: biological and psychosociological. It corresponds more or less to Fox's two models of patriarchy: one as a form of collective male dominance and the other as a system based on gender differences. The idea is that "Men seek to control women through controlling their sexuality, their roles in reproduction and their roles in society more generally" (Whitworth, 1994: 78). So while the liberal model is concerned with women's activities, the radical approach concentrates on women's attitudes which are said to be inherently different, both biologically and psychosociologically. The positive aspect of the radical model, Whitworth argues, is that it recognizes that theories are not neutral and should be explicit about the biases they involve. The model, however, has several limitations, some of which Whitworth addresses herself. One serious drawback is that it places "nurturing, virtuous, natural" women in opposition to aggressive, arrogant, power-seeking men. Another drawback is that it presents an essentialist, universal view of women as mothering without consideration of time, place, culture, class, race or sexual orientation.

The postmodernist model "rejects the suggestion that subjects have an authentic core or essential identity" (Whitworth, 1994: 81). It first aims at the deconstruction of categories of *woman*, namely by rejecting the "naturalness" of particular feminine characteristics. The model may be useful in the sense that it assumes no universal notion of woman ("no single and generic 'woman' of a particular class, race, and sexual orientation"), but several different women. Meanings, including that of the concept of woman, are socially constructed and vary with time, place, people and the like. Thus, the model analyzes the ways knowledge and meanings about gender relations are organized. The problem is that postmodernists "locate the construction of those meanings almost exclusively in the play of an ambiguously defined power organized through discourse" (1994: 82). This means that power relations are constructed in the absence of individuals, who then have very little opportunity to challenge these meanings. Whitworth remarks, "postmodernists are equally postfeminist . . . for their analysis loses sight of the political imperatives that form Feminism: to uncover and to change inequalities between women and men" (1994: 82). In Graham Murdock's words, "to succumb [to postmodernism] is to relinquish our hope of developing a critical analysis of the contemporary world" (1993: 52).

Although each of these models contains factors that are applicable to our society, because of their limited perspective they appear to be extremist, even acrimonious, to some researchers. As Marjorie Ferguson has rightly pointed out, "work that focuses on texts and images at the expense of power and the structured and situational constraints of class, income, culture, and history risks reifying the text and providing only partial accounts" (1990: 217). Therefore, since all of these models are unsatisfactory, both Fox and Whitworth suggest, each in their own way, a critical feminist approach which considers patriarchal society as a complex phenomenon that must be analyzed carefully. It is unacceptable to reduce complex social relations to biological or psychological explanations. We recall that capitalist society is founded on specific structures that do not disappear when discussing other aspects of this society, such as patriarchy. It is therefore simplistic to present society as an aggregation of people with a collective will that is based on rational objectives, and to explain a system of power by simply referring to male desires. Instead, it is necessary to examine the underlying structures of the system.

A critical feminist analysis of patriarchal society brings many elements into consideration. It argues that the essence of male dominance resides not only in human beings, but also in social structures. The division between private and public spheres has historically institutionalized women's place in the home, and men's outside the home, in the public sphere. This situation has led to a depreciation of women's place in the labour market. Within social structures, biological sexual differences have been transformed into political gender differences, thereby defining women as unequal to men: weaker, less intelligent, less rational, and so on. To use the expression coined by Simone de Beauvoir, women are defined as the "Other." This political difference has repercussions at the ideological level in that it divides the world into private and public, work into feminine and masculine, milieus into family and work, and places these spheres under patriarchal control. The patriarchal system, however, has changed considerably over time, since the notions of gender and class differences on which it is founded are rooted in social practices, which themselves change over time.

Nevertheless, despite the improvements and the gains achieved, can we conclude that women's place in society has really changed? This question leads to a series of others: What is the role of women in media institutions? What image of women is conveyed by the mass media, whose content is claimed to reflect society?

WOMEN IN PATRIARCHAL CAPITALIST PRODUCTION PROCESSES

The critical feminist approach establishes a link between the capitalist and patriarchal systems on which our society is founded. The place of women in our society is considered to be the result of the interaction between elements belonging to the two systems. Women's contribution to society's economy is therefore made in the two spheres that link the two systems, the waged-labour and domestic spheres, according to the needs of capital. Thus, in order to absorb the fluctuations of the capitalist economy, and depending on the demands of industry, women are called upon either to stay in the home, or enter the labour market.

Let us consider an example. During World War II, while most men of working age were sent to the front, many industries, especially those that supplied materials used for weapons, needed a workforce to continue their operations. Thus, despite the stereotypes that existed at the time, these industries began hiring women as technicians, mechanics, etc. Even though women successfully performed these jobs until the end of the war, they were never recognized as having the physical power and "masculine" skills required for these types of jobs. Women therefore obtained these jobs by default, because of the short supply of men due to the war. When the soldiers returned from the front, women were laid off, even those who wanted to stay at their jobs, to make room for the men. Thus, in our patriarchal society, it is legal to lay off women whose work is satisfactory to make way for men. It is also considered "normal," in time of war, to take advantage of the availability of women—who are refused the opportunity to work in time of peace—to keep the economy going and ensure the accumulation of capital in industries that would otherwise be forced to close, or at least reduce their production considerably. After the war, when the economy returned to "normal," women were sent back home. During the 1950s, only women aged 18 and 19, and some married women or widows over the age of 45 were wage labourers. Moreover, the jobs of these women did not require high qualifications, and their wages were very low. A third of these women were employed on a full-time basis, and the others worked part-time or only sporadically when the economy needed them.

Thus, the pool of female workers is used to solve some of the problems of the capitalist economy. The advent of capitalism and of industrialization has led to the division of the labour force and segregation according to gender in the production process. As we saw in Table 5.1, men clearly have better positions than women and obtain higher wages. The ideology of women in the home has achieved its objective. If women consider themselves first as wives and mothers, they are less likely to demand interesting work and wages that can guarantee their autonomy. But, according to critical feminists, the contribution of women to the economy is not limited to paid work; it also includes domestic labour.

In the critical feminist approach, women's domestic labour is defined as the "invisible" labour that underlies the economic structure of our society. In a patriarchal capitalist economy, women are the pillar of the family, as they provide material, emotional and moral stability, as well as reproduce life. They are the ones who socialize children in compliance with the dominant social consensus, which is founded on the internalization of the dominant values that define the roles of men and women in a discriminatory fashion.

Despite its essential contribution, domestic labour is generally devalued and unappreciated both socially and culturally. Invisible labour is considered normal and natural, while its economic value is not recognized for the simple fact that it is not paid work. The media reinforce this devaluation of domestic labour by inculcating their programming with content that "glamorizes" the feminine condition, which involves staying in the home and devoting oneself to the family. Even today, regardless of the type and theme of their content, most programmes implicitly suggest that the tasks that women perform in the home are not work, but a duty as dictated by the "natural" role of women. These ways of seeing and doing meet the same objective, namely, of integrating women into their everyday lives and having them accept their destiny. This brings us to a discussion of how the sexes are portrayed in the media.

As we saw in the first section of this chapter, the mass media are a secondary source of socialization. They are, nevertheless, a very important source of learning due to their high visibility. For example, a study by Mackie (1983) showed that 98% of Canadian households own a radio and 96% a television set. Moreover, Canadians spend at least 23 hours a week watching television. If we add the millions of popular books sold and the many films people see, it becomes obvious that the media are an important source of socialization. It is essential, therefore, to study how men and women are portrayed in the media and how female and male audiences respond to these images. However, before studying gender differentiation in both media content and audiences, we will investigate the role played by women and men within the production process of media content. What is the role of women in media production? Do they occupy positions of power, or decision-making positions? Are there power relations in the organization of the media that lead to gender differentiation and sexual discrimination? If so, are they caused by economic, political, cultural, biological or other factors?

POWER RELATIONS IN THE PRODUCTION PROCESS OF MASS MEDIA

In Chapter 3 we saw that people's interests differ depending on the class they belong to, and that these interests are sometimes contradictory and even opposing. We also saw that these divergent interests can lead to conflicts that, in turn, can bring about important change. Let us now see whether such conflicts exist between groups of men versus women, and if so, how they are expressed in the production process of the mass media.

To study the roles played by women and men in the production process of the mass media, it is important to examine not only the notion of "gender," but also other related concepts. This is because the gender difference of workers in media industries does not exist independently of other aspects of production. The mass media are part of a capitalist production process which, as we saw in Chapter 3, consists of different classes brought together in a market and profit-driven economy, where they are often confronted with opposing interests. Workers thus belong to a production system founded on divergent class interests that can result in conflicts. Moreover, this capitalist system is also a patriarchal system founded on gender differences that can also lead to conflicts, or at least to sexual discrimination coupled with class conflicts. It is therefore impossible to study "gender" independently of other elements that characterize the patriarchal capitalist production process, including ideology and culture. However, the media are means of communication that change rapidly with time, and their use can vary from one milieu to the next. Thus, in order to understand the practices of those who control the media, we must consider such concepts as class, culture, milieu and time. First, we must ask whether there are gender hierarchies in the production process of the media. If so, how are they constructed, maintained, legitimated and defied in terms of employees' working conditions? For example, do media-industry employees of different sexes and different classes have the same degree of autonomy, the same wages and the same opportunities for mobility?

Why bring up the notion of class in a chapter dedicated to a discussion of gender differences? In the first sections of this chapter, we saw that, in our patriarchal society, men and women are labelled with stereotypes which are often socially harmful. Is it better for a man to be called aggressive than it is for a woman to be identified as submissive? Such stereotypes have genuine effects on the lives of men and women, which in a patriarchal society are usually expressed as discrimination against one of the sexes, namely women. Nevertheless, discrimination against women is not uniform and may take different forms depending on the classes to which women belong. As we will soon see in a concrete example, this situation is especially marked in the media industry, where certain occupations are performed in the public eye, and others behind the scenes. Thus, in order to identify the type of sexual discrimination that exists in the media, it is important to link this concept with that of class. Why does sexual discrimination take a different form on the basis of one's class?

Similarly to the notion of class, the concept of "gender" is related to the economics and politics of media institutions. Men and women are not equally represented in the economic and political spheres of the media. Whereas women are generally excluded from positions of power, they make up a large segment of those employed in subordinate jobs. The number of women in the production process of media industries varies considerably depending on the classes they come from and their place of work. Let us see how one study illustrated these differences.

A historical comparative analysis (Martin, 1989) between working-class operators employed in the private sphere and professional, middle-class radio announcers working in the public sphere showed that discrimination against women working in media industries can take different forms according to their class and place of work. The study revealed that women are more in demand for subordinate jobs such as that of operator, who must work in anonymity and submit to the demands of employers and clients. Employers exploit these women's so-called "natural" qualities, namely that of submission and gentleness associated with "femininity" while paying them low wages. Operators are conditioned to submit to a rigid discipline and have no authority. Moreover, women are paid lower wages and have fewer opportunities for mobility than male workers in jobs requiring similar skills. Under these conditions, women are considered ideal candidates to perform long-distance oral communication jobs.

Martin (1989) has noted that this was not always the case. When the telephone was first commercialized in the 1880s, companies initially hired young men as operators. However, the companies were quick to learn that these men were difficult to discipline and careless at performing their work; they also talked back to highly demanding clients, thus driving them away. As early as 1882, telephone companies began recruiting women, as they were known to be submissive. One can say, therefore, that the lure of profits was the main reason for hiring women as operators. From this moment on, and for years to come, the occupation of operator became a female "ghetto," that is, an occupation in which men were unable to make any sort of breakthrough, either because they were not considered submissive enough, or were not interested by the low wages. Thus, in the telephone industry, the occupation of operator was (and still is) more easily accessible to women who, by choice or obligation, consented to take a subordinate position where they worked in complete anonymity; where their opinions were not conveyed to mass audiences; where, in fact, they had no time or right to have any opinions at all; and where they possessed very little power.

Since radio is also a medium of long-distance oral communication, one might assume that the female voice would lend itself equally to radio as to the telephone. Martin's study, however, showed that, despite the similarities in the basic techniques used by the two media, women who attempted to break through as radio announcers found (and still find) themselves in a completely different situation than operators. First, the job of radio announcer was performed in public. Moreover, announcers were conferred a certain degree of authority which women were not granted at the time. While the majority of people recognized that the female voice was custom-made for the job of operator, women were ridiculed as radio announcers. As we saw in Chapter 1, the female voice was said to have a nasal quality, with too high a pitch. As a result, women were not welcomed in the public sphere. At the time, the patriarchal society was ready to accept women in certain subordinate occupations only, but not in positions of power, especially not in the media, which provided a forum to exercise such authority. Women were appreciated as long as they kept to their "natural" role in the privacy of their homes. Public life was for men. This kind of discrimination was the starting point of feminist questioning in the field of communication. Is this discrimination applied uniformly to all women, as some research would have us believe?

The extent of discrimination against women varies according to social class. Feminist studies are all agreed on one point: as women move up the job hierarchy, and thus attain positions of power, they are confronted with more and more resistance from employers and even their colleagues. Moreover, if a woman also happens to belong to a visible minority, it will be almost impossible for her to achieve a position of control. These discriminatory practices are also influenced by whether the job is performed in the public eye or behind the scenes. Women who wish to work in the mass media industry will meet more resistance if the jobs they are seeking are performed in public. But haven't the times changed? Surely such discrimination no longer exists. Are there not more women journalists today than in the past?

If we examine Table 5.2, taken from a study conducted by Dubois (1988) on the place of women in media industries, we can see that there is still a discrepancy between the number of women and men employed in this type of work. Moreover, not only is pay equity between the two groups far from a reality, discrimination against women worsens as the status of the position increases: the percentage of female managers is disproportionately low given that, in society as a whole, there are as many women as there are men. One would think that the situation in the state-funded media, such as the CBC and TVOntario, would be more equitable. Unfortunately, Table 5.3 shows that there is more discrimination in the state-funded than in the private media. Although the media industry is usually considered to be avant-gardist, the situation of women is worse here than in other types of industries. Whereas the number of women with paid jobs increased by 70% between 1970 and 1981, the proportion of female journalists increased by only 6% between 1972 and 1987. According to Dubois, this discrimination manifests itself not only in terms of the number of female journalists in the field, but in other areas of work as well. Indeed, the criteria applied to women are not the same as those applied to men when it comes to hiring (women must be pretty, etc.), job ranking (women's experience is not always recognized), and promotions (women are less often promoted to decision-making positions). In concrete terms, these discriminatory practices translate into the devaluation of female journalists in terms of assignment, salary and mobility.

To explain this discrimination, Beauchamp (1988) has established a link between the place of women in the production process of the mass media and the fact that these media

TABLE 5.2 **Media employees by occupation and sex in large centres and outer regions of Québec, 1987**

	Total		Managers		Journalists	
Media	M	F	M	F	M	F
Written (large centres)						
N	439	82	155	12	284	70
%	84	16	93	7	80	20
Written (outer regions)						
N	81	20	31	5	50	15
%	80	20	86	14	77	23
Electronic (large centres)						
N	227	61	81	13	146	48
%	79	21	86	14	75	25
Electronic (outer regions)						
N	175	48	58	9	117	39
%	78	22	87	13	75	25
Total (large centres)						
N	666	143	236	25	430	118
%	82	18	90	10	78	22
Total (outer regions)						
N	256	68	89	14	167	54
%	79	21	86	14	76	24

Source: Dubois, 1988: 118.

are owned by capitalists. Owners, the majority of whom are men, produce content that is geared to glorify economic and political power, as well as internationalization. Moreover, because media production is rooted in a patriarchal ideology, it is almost entirely in the hands of men at both the administrative and journalistic levels. The news is "male," asserts Beauchamp, and focuses on subjects that interest men: ideologies of power in politics, economics, sports, etc. Moreover, information is white, heterosexual and sexist. For the most part, women journalists must submit to this ideology if they do not want to be restricted to "women's shows."

Far from diminishing, this trend has intensified with the monopolization of media industries by a small group of capitalists. The more sophisticated the means of production, the more costly they become and the more necessary it is to find private funds to finance these industries. As a result, control of the media is concentrated in a small network of institutions under male dominance (Beauchamp, 1988). In this administrative and male-dominated milieu, women do not have much power. As in other areas, the jobs to which they do have access are low in status, with little power and poor remuneration. Nevertheless, female journalists have attempted to put up some resistance to this situation.

TABLE 5.3   Media employees by status and medium, Québec, 1987

Media	Total		Managers		Journalists	
	M	F	M	F	M	F
Private radio						
N	168	29	52	7	116	22
%	85	15	88	12	84	16
Public radio						
N	54	18	22	2	32	16
%	75	25	92	8	67	33
Private television						
N	95	38	29	8	66	30
%	71	29	78	22	69	31
Public television						
N	85	24	36	5	49	19
%	78	22	88	12	71	29
Private media						
N	139	41	58	7	81	35
%	77	23	89	11	70	30
Public media						
N	263	67	81	15	182	52
%	80	20	84	16	78	22

Source: Dubois, 1988: 117.

In 1984, given that women were overtly discriminated against in the media industry, the National Federation of Communication Workers created a "committee on the status of women," which looked at all employee categories in the field of communication. Beauchamp tells us that the committee's mandate was threefold: to bring attention to discriminatory articles in collective agreements, to identify and eliminate the problem of sexual harassment, and to institute an affirmative action programme to establish an equilibrium between the number of male and female employees in this sector. Was this committee successful in re-establishing this equilibrium? The answer is both yes and no, depending on the occupation and the place of work. In other words, the results were mixed.

While there was some improvement in the number of female journalists in certain media, in others it diminished. At Radio Canada, the French sector of the CBC, women represented 20% of journalists between 1980–81, but only 12% in 1984. As for announcers, during the same period, the ratio fell from three women for every seven announcers to two for every eleven. In 1985–86, the situation seemed to improve slightly, as 22.8% of journalists were women. However, only one in four foreign correspondents, one in seven national reporters, and three in twenty parliamentary columnists were women (Beauchamp, 1988: 225). Beauchamp notes that these positions have been traditionally reserved for men. There were even fewer women in decision-making positions. According to Beauchamp, one had to search with a fine-toothed comb to find them. Women, however, were best represented in subordinate positions: researchers and audio-visual librarians (90%) and script-assistants (95%).

The situation was not much better in the private sector: for instance, there was only one woman in the newsrooms of two Montreal-area radio stations, CKAC and CJMS. The situation was similar in Québec's newspaper industry: at Montréal's daily papers *La Presse* and *Le Devoir*, only 19 out of 129 and 6 out of 31 full-time journalists, respectively, were women; at Québec's *Le Soleil*, this proportion was 15 out of 105. What are the causes of this discrimination?

In "Women and the Media in Canada: A Progress Report," Gertrude J. Robinson (1992) unveiled some statistics for English Canada. In the 1980s, in CBC radio, women represented 28% of the staff and 39% of management (mostly office workers), while in private radio, the percentage decreased to 20% of FM radio workers and 4.5% of AM radio producers. In 1990, at the CBC, 34% were women while private industry scored a bare 14%. However, in both industries, men had the most prominent jobs: only 10% of women were seen on screen as experts; 23% as newsreaders; and 30% as voice-overs. In addition, most of the 28% of women who had management positions at the CBC were found at the bottom of the hierarchy of occupations (office, make-up, script, wardrobe, etc.). Finally, women with the same type of occupation as men continue to receive lower wages, varying between 67% and 97% of men's salaries, the average being 75% (1992: 261–2).

Journalism is a privileged means of reaching the public. A female journalist has a certain power to influence people, since what she says will be heard by mass audiences. As such, she must comply with the dominant ideology, or remain quiet. According to Beauchamp, in order to reflect this patriarchal ideology, the media hire only those anchorwomen and female journalists whose physical features correspond to a number of stereotypes that are socially ascribed to women. For instance, women in these positions must have a "feminine appearance," they cannot be too old, and they must have an attractive figure and a charming personality. But, once they are hired, do women enjoy some autonomy, or power?

According to Beauchamp, women have neither autonomy nor power. Whereas men are expected to have a personality that transcends the television screen, women are required to neutralize theirs, either by wearing stereotypical clothes or make-up, or by adopting "feminine" attitudes (smile, soft voice, etc.). Moreover, because their work is assessed by their male colleagues and employers, women are expected to meet male standards of journalism. Thus, according to Beauchamp (1988), the restriction of autonomy is achieved internally, out of the public eye.

Robinson (1992) expresses the same concern using different words. She states that while visible barriers are now prohibited by laws, "invisible" ones are built up based on actions rather than laws or regulations. "They are found in attitudes, biases, and presumptions that senior managers, who are frequently in their sixties, continue to harbour concerning women" (1992: 262).

In "Images of Power and Feminist Fallacy," Marjorie Ferguson (1990) comes to approximately the same conclusion as Beauchamp and Robinson about American women in media production organizations. She asserts that in the United States, although women have made some gains in absolute number in the labour force, these are "not necessarily in terms of relative powers in the media workforce" (1990: 221). In the television industry, between 1975 and 1985, the proportion of women employed in production increased from 26% to 35%, and those hired at top-level occupations almost doubled, from 14% to 27%. Yet, a study of more than 200 network correspondents shows that there were very few on-screen women at the top, and that one-third of television female news anchors earned only 60% of their male counterparts.

In the press, the proportion of female journalists doubled, from 20% to 40%, yet they are still very much underrepresented as editors: the highest percentage (18%) of female editors are found on papers with very small circulations (below 10,000), while those with more than 250,000 circulation score only 13%. Again, there is discrimination with respect to wages, which increases with the number of years a journalist has worked for a paper: the more years of service, the larger the wage difference between men and women (1990: 221).

We can see that although the number of female journalists and announcers has increased since the 1920s, women are still greatly underrepresented in all media industries. Moreover, they face the same types of hurdles that keep them from attaining important positions or international assignments. Thus, although the patriarchal system adopts different forms within the media industry, it still regulates the contribution of women in the area of media production.

CONCLUSION

This chapter introduced the elements of feminist scientific analysis related to the question of gender differences in people's experience. We saw that this difference is often expressed as sexual discrimination against women in society as a whole, and in the production process of capitalist enterprises such as the mass media. Why does this discrimination exist? Because the capitalist society in which we live is also a patriarchal society where power resides with men. In fact, capitalism and patriarchy are founded on specific rules that exclude women from most decision-making positions, even today.

In the patriarchal ideology, authority and competence are vested in men. Men are therefore placed in positions of power to control society, including the family, as well as political and economic systems. Meanwhile, women continue to be ascribed traditional qualities that qualify them as "naturally" suited for the role of housewife and mother; and paid work, if they have any, is considered an added bonus to the household. Viewed in this light, it is impossible to allow women access to positions of power, either because they do not have the required biological ability (*Women* are not qualified to manage), or because their labour is "unsteady" (they often take time off to have children or to take care of them). Thus, in a patriarchal capitalist society where men are considered to have the "natural" capacities for power and economics, a majority of women find themselves in subordinate positions. This situation is also true of the production process of media content. In the next chapter, we will see how the characteristics of patriarchal capitalist society influence the content of the mass media, as well as their consumption by audiences.

CAPITALISM AND PATRIARCHY AS CONCEPTS IN MEDIA CONSUMPTION ANALYSIS

INTRODUCTION

In the last chapter we saw that the discrepancies between women and men regarding their experiences are not based primarily on biological distinctions and cannot be explained as "natural," as some researchers implicitly argue. A critical analysis of communication phenomena must therefore consider *female* and *male* traits as socially constructed concepts; in other words, it is not sexual characteristics that cause men and women to behave differently. The patriarchal capitalist system reinforces the conditions that help create specific cultural categories for each sex, which in turn contribute to the maintainance of our current economic and political systems. For this reason, conceptualizing sexual roles in terms of the notions of universality and biology can serve only to overshadow all other social differences between individuals. Therefore, in order to identify the nature and origins of these social phenomena, all communication research on mass media content and audiences needs to consider the concepts of capitalism and patriarchy.

As was mentioned in Chapter 5, the interaction between the patriarchal and capitalist systems results in situations that influence the power relations in the production process of the mass media. This chapter will use the same link to examine media content, as well as audiences. Chapter 4 showed that media products convey the dominant ideology, namely the patriarchal capitalist ideology. How is this ideology reproduced in media content? Is the sexual discrimination that exists in the production process transmitted in media content? How do audiences respond to this content? Do female audiences respond differently than male audiences? To answer these questions, we will begin by looking at the *values* and the *ideas* conveyed in media products.

The ideas transmitted in media content are often developed on the basis of *stereotypes* approved by our society. One of the most enduring is that which presents the so-called "natural" roles of women as restricted to the private sphere, in other words, the family, which is the milieu *par excellence* for women to exhibit their "natural" qualities in their roles as wife, mother and maid. By maintaining women in these roles, the media content of large mass media corporations reinforces this stereotype. To achieve this, these enterprises have created a myth which, for decades, has been widely disseminated over the air waves, on television and movie screens, and in magazine and newspaper pages: *the myth of modernity.*

MODERNITY: A MYTH IN THE SERVICE OF CAPITAL

The *concept of modernity* is by all means not new. As early as the nineteenth century, Baudelaire claimed that modernity was characterized by "the ephemeral, the fugitive, the contingent" (cited in Frisby, 1985: 16). Some years later, Marx examined cultural manifestations that were based on the "new" and the "modern." Observers at the time were all agreed on the transitory nature of "newness" and its impact on society. According to Frisby (1988), this impact was seen as a challenge to linear progress, in that modernity would cause society and social relations to be in a state of flux and constant movement. As soon as the modern is conceived it becomes outdated and must be replaced. The modern escapes deterioration, since it is replaced just as it comes into use. The modern is sought after before it is created, but is discarded as soon as it exists. It is ephemeral and eternal at the same time, for it continually eludes us. Fashion is the best example of these contradictions. Designers present their line of winter fashion in June, and summer fashion in September. Thus, just when clothes are being designed—even before they are worn, as they are not yet in season—they are out of style. As soon as they are bought, they are no longer fashionable. Is it not true that rich women change their wardrobe with each new season? When clothes are out of style for the bourgeoisie, they are put on the market as "ready-to-wear," for *modernity is an invention of capital.* The concept of modernity could not exist but in a society that produces mass commodities that must be sold as soon as possible to generate profits. This concept must also rest on a class system in which certain classes produce the commodities that the other classes consume. How does the concept of modernity apply to the analysis of women?

In her analysis of modernity, Michèle Mattelart (1981) establishes the link between this concept and the patriarchal capitalist ideology by associating the notions of continuity and rupture in our society with femininity and modernity as conveyed in mass media content. She also associates the notion of family—society's place of choice for women's own fulfillment—with that of continuity, since the family, as invented by capitalism, represents security and the "ideal" refuge, as much in stable modern societies as in societies in crisis. The concept of femininity portrayed in media content constitutes another form of continuity, in that it perpetually confines women to the restricted space of the household. However, this concept of femininity is also associated with another notion, that of *modernity*, which represents the transitory. These two notions, which on the surface appear to be contradictory, are repeatedly used by the media to describe women. Let us now see how these notions are related to the concepts of capitalism and patriarchy.

Creation and History of the Modern Housewife

As early as the 1920s, around the time when mass media such as radio emerged, the American cultural industries began presenting a feminine ideal which was directly related to the new ideology of modernity. These American media industries went on to become multinational corporations, which, in the name of change and the evolution of women, have disseminated the *ideology of modernity* around the world. This concept of modernity plays an essential role in maintaining our patriarchal capitalist society, since it not only helps keep women in the traditional roles of wife and mother, to which they have been assigned by patriarchal society, but it also gives these roles a new significance by providing women with the complementary role of consumer, who will help increase the profits of capitalist industries. However, the *feminine ideal* has not always existed.

With the advent of media such as radio and, later, television and magazines, the "ideal" image of women began to change from the role of *producer* of domestic goods (food, clothes, etc.) to that of *consumer* of industrial commodities. It is through the ideology conveyed in media content that the feminine ideal, a key concept of this ideology, stimulated industrial commodity production. How was this achieved? In the name of this feminine ideal, women became the target of media messages. From the outset, these messages had two goals: first, on the patriarchal level, to encourage women to stay in the home by promoting resources that promised to improve their lot; second, on the capitalist level, to urge women to purchase domestic products obediently. Let us now see how the concept of modernity was used by the media industries to achieve these two goals.

The media used the concept of the feminine ideal to encourage women to consume commodities produced on a large-scale basis by capitalist industries. Media content (advertising and soap operas) used this concept to convince women to view the routine nature of their role as modern housewives as providing an outlet for creativity. The tendency was to discredit traditional and "homecraft" knowledge. New technologies were glorified and portrayed as promising to improve women's lives and guaranteeing women's fulfillment in the home. The household was opened up to the outside world, and became the repository for the "new," as well as the endless stream of constantly changing commodities which were promoted through the electronic media and women's magazines. The home became the ideal market for capitalist production. Industries hoped women would quickly get accustomed to market principles and to consuming. The role of women in the home was upgraded in accordance with the new criteria of rationalization and technology that translated into the concept of domestic *modernity*: the modern housewife was no longer a cook, she had become "a can-opener" (C. Frederick cited in Mattelart, 1986: 26).

Similarly, the role of mother was also given new importance. From all sides, women were offered the necessary commodities to make their families happy; they were even provided with a model, that of the *superwoman* endowed with the scientific know-how to release her from her intuitive and ancestral knowledge. There was no more need to rely on old wives' remedies. Products were advertised as having scientific authority, and were linked to the image of the *ideal mother* as containing all the requirements to ensure the nutritional and hygienic well-being of children, thereby cultivating guilty feelings among women for whom this ideal was out of reach.

The new feminine ideal, which was presented as both a brain wave and an integral part of modern life, was conveyed in all the media. In reality, this concept did not encompass anything new. The dominant image of women was still characterized by their most traditional roles, namely wife and mother. Over and over again, women were shown in these roles in the mass media. However, according to Judith Williamson, one of the most important aspects of these images of femininity in modern society "is not what they reveal, but what they conceal" (Williamson, 1986: 103). Even today, women continue to be shown as desiring a home, love or sex appeal, but their links to waged labour, as well as their belonging to a social class and their political views, are *hidden*. Even though women still have no voice in these spheres of society, they are portrayed as "free" and "happy" as long as this freedom relates to their personal life and their femininity, that is, as long as it corresponds to the image of the *new woman*.

It is important to recall that this "new" image of the modern housewife emerged in the United States in the political context of women obtaining the right to vote. This modernization of the traditional role of women was related to the political context of their emancipation, and was disseminated as the "good word" by radio and cinema, two media which were new at the time.

However, it was not until the end of World War II that this new feminine ideal underwent a phenomenal boom: the home was then portrayed as a domestic laboratory and consecrated as the "natural" place of the modern woman, thereby removing her from the working world. As we will see in greater detail in the next chapter, the media sustained this new ideology by creating content that portrayed women, first, as the "queen of the home" and, second, as a cheap, secondary labour force in the service of the fluctuations and the needs of the economy.

Even if the present situation of women on the labour market has improved considerably in comparison with the 1950s, it is interesting to note that in our "modern" society, female labour, however valued, has yet to be fully recognized socially. It is often portrayed as a supplement to the husband's income (which they will soon have if they are still single), or as compensation for love (to be given or received). The primary roles of women are still those of wife and mother, with all others considered as secondary. In case of divorce, our society finds it "unnatural" for a mother to give the father custody of the children; with regard to the father's ability to take care of his children, the burden of proof lies with him. In most families, it is the mother's duty to take the kids to the doctor when necessary, and attend parent meetings at school or daycare, etc. Even today, the media's image of women rarely suggests the possibility of couples sharing household tasks more evenly. Moreover, media content never alludes to the possible socialization of domestic labour in the direction of the organization of kibbutzim in Israel.[1] This approach is likely

---

[1] Kibbutzim are collective settlements located in Israel which are generally used for agricultural production. A kibbutz can consist of a few or many families. Regardless of the kibbutz' size, most members work the land, or are employed outside the settlement. During the day, various child experts belonging to the kibbutz raise the children while the parents are at work.

considered "unnatural" by the media, since it runs counter to the function of motherhood, which the patriarchal capitalist ideology has mystified by portraying it as a "natural" function. But how has the concept of modernity been renewed since the 1920s?

Obsolescence and Eternity in Modernity

As we saw in the previous section, the concept of modernity provides a basis for the production of material goods in industrial societies. The term *modern* is characterized in terms of objects that are always defined as being "at the cutting edge of. . . " and that are "indispensable," "durable" and "eternal." Yet these objects quickly become outdated and are replaced by other more modern objects. Mattelart (1981) calls this continuous process of renewal the *principle of planned obsolescence*: the technological aging of an object is associated with the appearance of a new object. According to this principle, new products are replaced by newer products even before the latter have deteriorated or become obsolete.

We know that this principle, which is supported by the media, satisfies the needs of the capitalist system that relies on production and consumption of commodities. According to Mattelart (1981), the principle does more than merely sustain the economy: it also serves an ideological purpose in that it helps to conceal, and even justify, the dominance of certain classes over others. She has claimed that the notion of the "latest craze" conceals this dominance by enabling the dominating classes to renew, over and over again, the traits of their elitism and purchasing power (Mattelart, 1981: 55). Concerned with the idea of being in style, women forget their real situation, in which they are subordinated to the economic, political and ideological power of men. In this context, the "latest" clothes compensate for wage discrimination or for being confined to the home; giving a woman new jewellery is taken as a sign of renewed affection that would otherwise be imperceptible. After the dominant classes have used up the modernity of *haute couture*, they allow these clothes to be mass produced. The dominated classes are thus given the power to consume the *modern*, which serves to help them forget their subordination. Who has never overcome frustration by buying some new object? In this way, Williamson (1986) argues that the family and femininity are the most lucrative markets of the capitalist economy. "The 'natural' phenomena of the family and sexuality throw back an image of a 'natural' economy, while the economy penetrates and indeed constructs these 'natural' and 'personal' areas through a mass of products—liberally offering us our own bodies as sites of difference . . . " (Williamson, 1986: 106). Like Mattelart, Williamson remarks that the myth of modernity gives the impression that, through consuming, people are given a choice.

This perpetual process of maintaining and reinforcing compulsive consumption does not, however, affect relations of dominance between men and women. In this respect, women's liberation from the myth of modernity and all that it implies is not going to happen in a hurry. For women, wage-earners or not, beauty and seduction are still the main assets approved by the patriarchal ideology. As Mattelart (1981) points out, media content upholds the vision in which a woman's security depends essentially on her value on the sexual market—a value that is closely related to her purchasing power. The more a woman has the means to buy little "extras" (jewellery, fashionable clothes, make-up, perfume, etc.) for herself, the more her future is secure. In this context, it is not at all surprising that women who are not young, pretty, slim, or fashionable are not generally seen in media content; neither are unemployed women. Since the late sixties, the preferred target of the media has been the working wife, for she is a woman with a disposable income. These women constitute a new market to be exploited as much through television shows as through advertising itself. For proof, one need only consider the success of such television series as *Designing Women*, *LA Law* and *Street Legal*.

Within the context of modernity, the media have greatly reinforced the image of the emancipation of feminine sexuality in television series, as well as in the advertising through which these shows are financed. In some respects, this image is linked to the politicization of sexuality as defended by the feminist movement's struggle for the transformation of the social position of women. In fact, however, the image is in itself contradictory: women are liberated from their traditional social role by their "enslavement" to modernity, which is grounded in the sexualization of situations that were once taboo.

The next chapter will show that the media tackle women's issues only from the perspective of women from the privileged classes, that is, well-educated professional women. For this reason, the media are accomplices in the integration of the process of women's liberation into the capitalist production system. This can be seen by the media's lack of sympathy for the problems and struggles of working-class women. The emancipation of women as portrayed in the mass media is a question of class, in that only women who have attained a certain social class—in other words, those who represent a certain potential for consumption—have the opportunity of being liberated. Moreover, the silence regarding women of other classes implicitly suggests that the "ideals" presented in media content are accessible to all women. This silence denies the very existence of the underprivileged classes by tacitly integrating them into the privileged classes. What are the elements of the concept of modernity that appear to eliminate class distinctions?

Elements of the Myth of Modernity

As we saw earlier, the myth of the modern woman as presented in the media does nothing for the economic emancipation of women, and instead serves to give a new "value" to the most traditional characteristics of women. By appropriating certain elements of the feminist ideology of women's liberation, media contents have trivialized this movement by associating it with capitalist consumption. The liberated woman portrayed in the media is an individual who gives herself a modern "look" which she can achieve by consuming certain types of commodities. But will purchasing products A, B and C make women feel free or liberated? How can a majority of women, even the most informed, be influenced by this idea?

It is a fact that modernity is a key notion that influences the social and cultural experiences of our society and provides the basis for making this type of society a universal model. Modernity transcends all spheres of our society and affects all of our activities. For this reason, it is important to define the elements that make up the myth of modernity.

The Modern as All-Powerful Modern objects are presented via advertising, which helps to market mass commodities. To achieve this, Williamson (1981) has claimed that advertising must create structures of meaning. Thus, the function of advertising is not limited to selling the virtues and attributes of a product, but it must also make these properties meaningful to audiences. The myth of modernity comes to the rescue of advertising by suggesting that all the qualities of the *modern object* are transferrable to whoever possesses it. With the object thus humanized, the person is given new vitality, feelings, personality and energy. A person's value is thus determined by the object he or she possesses. In this context, Mattelart (1981: 50) argues that the object is the fountain of love, of emotional and sexual fulfillment, of liberation, success and happiness. As Williamson says:

> But in our society, while the real distinctions between people are created by their role in the process of production, as workers, it is the *products* of their own work that are used, in the false categories invoked by advertising, to obscure the real structure of society by replacing class with the distinctions made by the consumption of particular goods. Thus instead of being identified by what they produce, people are made to identify themselves with what they consume. From this arises the false assumption that workers 'with two cars and a colour TV' are not part of the working class. We are made to feel that we can rise or fall in society through what we are able to buy, and this obscures the actual class basis which still underlies social position. The fundamental differences in our society are still class differences, but use of manufactured goods as means of *creating* classes or groups forms an overlay on them (Williamson, 1981: 13).

Thus the modern object as presented in advertising has the effect of obscuring the real social conditions in which we live.

Moreover, the *object becomes an agent of change*. Its purchase goes hand-in-hand with progress, individual growth and social evolution. Because of its technological nature, the object is synonymous with modernization, as well as the promotion of industrialized products, which foster modern thinking. For Mattelart (1981), this view of progress can only revive and aggravate the inequalities that exist within a country and its dependence on the outside world. In capitalist societies, development is "exogenous" in nature, that is, it tends to expand externally. It is a form of expansion based on the acquisition of goods, and is forward-looking in that it despises the past and belittles traditional knowledge and local cultural practices: nothing existed prior to eternal progress. Conversely, in many non-industrialized countries, development is rooted in the past. There, development is based on past experiences that foster "endogenous" conditions of progress, that is, conditions originating within a country's borders.

As Mattelart (1981) points out, these two models of development sometimes come into conflict with each other, for example, when multinational corporations attempt to introduce their products in countries with different models of social development. Let us look at a concrete example. A few years ago, the Nestlé company launched a publicity campaign, aimed at women in underdeveloped countries, to promote the use of powdered milk and bottle-feeding. The campaign was founded on a "modern" attitude that

Nestlé wanted to instill in women in the Third World, which satisfied the imperatives of capital; for these women represented a new potential market for Nestlé's products. However, this advertising strategy, which was based on the value of progress, had negative consequences on the health of nursing infants. Because of a lack of information in the ads, the powdered milk was not used properly by mothers and thus lost its nutritional value. Moreover, bottle-feeding, which replaced the practice of breast-feeding that prevailed in these countries, had the effect of removing an important source of maternal physical contact from the infants. Furthermore, the living conditions in these countries were such that the hygienic practices required to prepare the formula and sterilize the feeding bottles were completely inefficient (in Mattelart, 1981: 51–2). This particular "modern" object, which was portrayed in the publicity as being able to solve all the problems of both mothers and infants, was not well suited to the social context into which Nestlé wanted to integrate it. The object was therefore useless to the population for which it was intended. The true "power" of the modern object was thus revealed. *Therefore, above all, it is the social relations permitted within the social structures that have the power to liberate individuals.*

We have all seen how exotic images, which are inspired by other countries, are widely used in media advertising. Why? Williamson (1986) has argued that such exotic images create the illusion that what has vanished from our reality (the exotic, the charming and the primitive) still exists. Thus, "it is the *idea* of 'natural' and 'basic' cultures which seems to guarantee the permanence (and, ironically, the universality) of capitalist culture" (Williamson, 1986: 112), which is a contradiction in and of itself. Indeed, our society's value system refuses to legitimate other cultures, but at the same time attempts to naturalize our own structures in the image of the "natural life" that exists outside our system. Other cultures are therefore used to project classless images in which these "exotic" cultures, like women, are reduced to the function served by the commodity advertised.

The Modern as an Indivisible Whole Out of the myth of modernity there emerges an "abstract" and "generic" society which indiscriminately applies the characteristics and privileges of the dominant classes or Western culture to all other societies. The irony is that by transforming objects that originate in other cultures our society appropriates them.[2] This type of society silences the bitter existence of social inequalities and removes the limits of the social practices that define different social and cultural groups. The privileges of the dominant classes are displayed on the counter as if they are accessible to whomever truly desires them, independently of the social class one belongs to. This is what Mattelart (1981) calls the "democracy of desires." Conscious of the unequal budgets of target audiences, advertising levels out these inequalities by selling the idea that any segment of modernity encompasses all of modernity. Thus, a modern object offered at a

---

[2] A young woman can be admired for posing with a turban in a series of fashion pictures, but a Sikh dressed in this manner will be looked at with curiosity, if not suspicion. Similarly, a young bourgeois woman who shows up at a party wearing jeans will be considered "stylish," but a male labourer would not produce the same effect.

reasonable price carries the full promise of progress (Mattelart, 1981). A single object can transform an ordinary woman into a *modern woman*. But what is a modern woman?

The ideal of the *modern woman* is a woman who belongs to a rich, urban milieu in a highly industrialized country. According to Mattelart (1981), by highlighting the purchasing power and discrete charm of the triumphant bourgeois woman, this ideal is offered to all women as "eternal femininity": *women* are the same everywhere and at all times. This concept runs counter to the critical feminist ideology, whose fundamental principle is to take into consideration not only the differences between men and women, but also between different classes and cultures. The feminine ideal suppresses all social inequalities, as well as the disparities between industrialized and non-industrialized societies. Based on this logic, the cosmetics industry, for example, legitimates its international expansion by placing a permanent and universal value on the image of "beautiful white skin" (though tanned white skin is even more beautiful) and on the Western model of feminine beauty, which is presented as particularly desirable. The mass media is a privileged means of conveying the values of modernity. Media content (entertainment, information or advertising) reproduce the modern-woman stereotypes of beauty and efficiency. But are audiences fooled by this content? In other words, do they adopt the values and ideas conveyed in the media without resistance or opposition? This issue is addressed in the next section.

CAPITALISM AND PATRIARCHY AS CONCEPTS IN AUDIENCE ANALYSIS

We have just looked at some of the more important aspects that guide the production of media content. We will now examine how audiences respond to it. In the models studied in Chapter 2, we saw that some researchers studied the effect of the media on audiences, while others examined how the social, economic and cultural characteristics of media users affect the way they receive messages. In Chapter 4, we saw that Hall (1980) argued that audiences negotiate the meaning of media contents, which would imply the existence of differentiated audiences. Does this differentiation exist along gender lines as well? None of the models mentioned above made the distinction between the sexual differences of audiences. Do female audiences receive messages in the same way as male audiences? Do they have the same preferences in terms of mass media consumption? Feminist approaches are unique in the sense that they make such a distinction in their analysis of audiences. We will now examine these approaches.

Female Television Audiences

Most feminist studies have shown that the heads of large television networks are aware that women are major consumers of television, and that it is in their best interests to orient programming according to what they think is appropriate for this clientele. In a study of audiences, Virginia Nightingale (1990) examined programming formats to look at how several television networks in Australia (1987) attempted to attract women viewers. One particular channel intended to target a clientele of women aged 18–39 by featuring the following comedy series starting at the 7:30 p.m. time slot:

- *Cheers*, which takes place in a bar;
- *Rafferty's Rules*, which tells the story of a suburban male magistrate;
- *Her Dad*, which is about the life of a single father, his children and his infatuated secretary; and
- *The Big Chill*, a film about the crisis of male identity;
- *The Man who Loved Women*, a film about the confessions of a Casanova.

Thus, this television network thought it would be successful in attracting female viewers by providing programming that was essentially about men, or that predominantly featured male characters. It is obvious, as Nightingale (1990) points out, that the broadcasting strategy of this and another station in the study was based on a narrow definition of women, one in which they are seen as depending on and living for men, the Other. This strategy was therefore not based on a practical knowledge of the real desires of female viewers, but on what the network thought *should* interest them. The objective of broadcasting these shows, which were intended for housewives and mothers, was to improve overall ratings, and, with this in mind, they targeted these women's husbands and children as well.

This strategy confirms that programming decisions made by television network managers, mostly men, are guided by the dominant ideology, namely the patriarchal capitalist ideology, which encourages male capitalists to believe that since male activities arouse broad interests, shows that highlight these activities will generate more profit than ones that show women's activities. For these managers, the "family" context defines women, their interests and concerns, as well as their subordinate status within the family. Moreover, these men are convinced that women themselves choose to be subordinated to patriarchal power because of their love for their husbands and children. Since male managers are not aware of the desires of female viewers, Nightingale (1990) argues, they construct women as they would like them to be in accord with the dominant ideology. What content do women really want to see on television?

A study of British audiences (Stoessl, 1987) has shown that during the winter months, women in Britain watch 35 hours of television a week, as opposed to 27 for men. This difference in television viewing time reflects the fact that women spend more time at home during the day than men. But what do women watch for so many hours?

The study revealed that, in general, the choice of what programme to watch is made by consensus through a two-stage decision-making process. The first stage consists of deciding whether to watch television or do something else. It seems that this decision is not highly influenced by what is on: 90% of viewers are rather indifferent to the contents of programming. Then it is time to decide what to watch. This decision, which depends on the size of the family, will be made within the domestic context of family relationships. Who, among the father, mother or children, decides what to watch?

A study (Morley, cited in Stoessl, 1987) of 20 working-class South London households showed that when women are in a family situation they have little control over the choice of programmes viewed, and rarely watch programmes that interest them. Another study (Hobson, 1990) has even shown that, in households where the power relations between spouses are clearly defined by male supremacy, men have such control over the choice of programmes viewed that they will turn the set off, without giving any explanation, if they come home and find their wives watching soap operas.

For most women, Stoessl (1990) remarks, the pleasure resides in watching their favourite programmes or serials when the rest of the family is out. However, women indulge in this only if they feel free enough of their domestic responsibilities, that is, if they believe they have completed them. It appears that women often feel guilty about their enjoyment of watching television during the day. Women are therefore in a paradoxical situation in which they obtain pleasure from watching shows they like, such as serials and soap operas, but which they also find dumb and not well acted. Many women also realize that these programmes convey the patriarchal ideology in which women are in subordinate positions—a situation with which many women can identify. This paradox places women in a situation where they find it difficult to defend their preferences when the family is deciding what to watch, especially when they believe that their husband's choice is much more worthwhile. Thus, women watch the programmes they like when they are alone or with friends, and when they have the time to do so. In short, female audiences do not really choose when they watch television. Because our society does not value romance as highly as it does violence, women generally hide their media preferences. They prefer to miss their favourite programmes than to be ridiculed for admitting that they enjoy them. They can also record them on video and watch them later, when the other members of the family are out.

Several studies have shown that the television genre that female viewers enjoy the most is the soap opera. These studies have attempted to determine not only the reason why soaps are so popular among women, but also the contradictions this genre may bring about in the lives of many women. How can this fascination be explained? In the next few sections we will examine the arguments presented through the construction of two major feminist models regarding this question: the French model and the model developed by English and American researchers.

The French Feminist Model: Soap Operas, "Temporal" Pleasure and Resistance

The French feminist model, essentially developed by Michèle Mattelart (1981, 1986), questions the act of consumption itself by explaining the contradictions it brings about in audiences in relation to ideology, class and sex. This model links the pleasure experienced by female television viewers with the *temporality of women*. This temporality is characterized by the traditional functions of the domestic woman (namely wife and mother) and is grounded in what Mattelart calls the *myth of permanence*. Mattelart challenges the very act of consumption by questioning the monolithic nature of the dominant ideology, which cultivates class and gender differences. As we saw in earlier chapters, the media convey the values and ideas that correspond to the interests of the ruling classes. For example, the television media convey the patriarchal capitalist ideology through programming. Using this observation as a starting point, Mattelart asks whether audiences passively internalize all aspects of the dominant ideology, or if there is room for the interpretation of content by audiences on the basis of class or gender.

To answer these questions, we must examine the act of watching and consuming media content, using the following question as a point of reference: is the act of consuming mediated by the personal background of audiences members or by the history of a group or class? In other words, should the notions of class, gender and culture be taken into consideration in an analysis of media audiences? For example, how do the dominated classes respond to the capitalist ideology conveyed in television, popular novels, magazines, and so on? How do women react to the patriarchal ideology disseminated through media content? Do they internalize television programmes and novels without reacting, or do they resist certain ideas?

Research conducted by Mattelart (1981) on female audiences in Chile confirms Hall's (1980) concept of negotiated meaning by showing that audiences do not necessarily internalize messages in the way that their senders (media directors and producers) intend. The way in which messages are received by certain groups or classes can negate the internal logic of media content, and even lead to opposite interpretations.

Indeed, these studies showed that female viewers in Chile engaged in "a roundabout process of consumption" (Mattelart, 1986: 15). Despite their enjoyment, these women watched their television soap operas with a critical eye, particularly the illusory aspect of the social mobility as presented in these programmes. The women interpreted these contents with a keen awareness of social class differences. Conscious of their class background, these working-class women were also aware that the characters in the soap operas always belonged to the bourgeoisie or to the upper-middle classes. They also knew that it would be impossible to move from their own social class to that of the characters depicted in these television programmes, and that instead there was a chasm separating these classes due to their fundamentally different interests.

However, it is disturbing to see that these programmes should provide pleasure for such critically aware female viewers. This situation leads us to the following question: given that television soap operas transmit values that are alienating for women and that the most critical of these female viewers are aware of this, how can we explain the contradiction that resides in their enjoyment of these programmes?

Mattelart attempts to explain this phenomenon by evoking the notion that men and women have different perceptions of time. How can this *temporal divergence* be explained? The ancestral mythical image of women developed in patriarchal societies is associated with the immutable and cyclical nature of fertility and life-giving elements (such as water and fire), and is therefore linked to such notions as continuity, perpetuation and timelessness. What Mattelart is referring to here is the *temporality of women* that transcends all "upheavals, crises and chaos" (Mattelart, 1986: 36). This temporality, *which is imposed on women by the patriarchal system*, unifies past, present and future, and perpetuates the eternal and traditional female roles: housekeeper, wife and mother. The temporality of women flows through time in a cycle unique to women, the rhythm of which is presented as "natural," repetitive, eternal and therefore permanent. The temporality of women, according to Mattelart, is grounded in the *myth of permanence*.

Mattelart (1986) argues that soap opera storylines reflect both the temporality of women and the myth of permanence, since the themes, images and meanings of these stories cultivate the patriarchal ideology, which created and has reproduced the temporality of women. Let us now examine how the feminine notion of time is portrayed in television soap operas. It seems that, because they are broadcast daily over long periods of time, these programmes would imply the cycle of repetition, eternity and permanence. They are therefore grounded in the psychic and unconscious psychosociological structures of female audiences that have always had to respect the constraints and the strict framework of the temporality of women. According to this logic, the reason why women derive so much pleasure from consuming soap operas is that they identify with the image of women they present, for this image has been perpetuated, and unconsciously internalized from time immemorial. Whatever social changes may occur, women eternally remain mothers and wives in the service of others.

In no way should this proposition be taken to mean that female audiences, who take pleasure in watching content in which women are exploited, support the patriarchal ideology that has created "the ancestral mythical image of women." According to Mattelart, the proposition instead suggests that these audiences have submitted to an ideology that has contributed to the development of different perceptions of time on the part of women and men because of the role and place that women are assigned in patriarchal societies. Mattelart argues that even modern women, especially those who stay in the home, have not yet managed to escape from the temporal shackles, a scenario which soap operas exploit for the purpose of pleasing them, and which have the effect of reproducing the taboos and stereotypes attached to the image of women in our society. In what follows, we will see that the North American and English model addresses this contradiction from a different perspective.

The North American and English Model: Soap Operas, "Illicit" Pleasure and Resistance

The feminist model developed by North American and English researchers brings to light a certain form of resistance among women to the ridicule aimed at their programme choices. This model suggests that women take advantage of the absence of other family members, who often denigrate their choices, to watch their favourite programmes alone or sometimes in the company of friends. This ritual assumes the same characteristics as that of an illicit carnival, in which the denigrated programmes take centre stage. It would appear that women who gather together in front of the television take advantage of such occasions to share opinions and discuss their problems—one of the most important being their exploitation within the family. This model therefore sees soap operas as an integral part of women's culture. They provide women with a locus for resistance and empowerment where they can both express their pleasure and complain about their exploitation.

For these pragmatic and political reasons, North American and English feminist studies of television have focused on the programmes that principally interest women, namely soap operas. This emphasis is understandable, since it allows feminists to shed light on the complex issue of women's enjoyment of programmes that are generally denigrated by society as a whole. In fact, for a number of feminist researchers, the fact that women take pleasure in watching soap operas represents a *form of resistance*. These researchers have attempted to analyze how women's images on television are used by viewers as a response to their social position. They are also interested in the political meaning of women's enjoyment in watching these shows, which play on their emotions and their ability to consume.

A study of American female audiences conducted by M.E. Brown (1990) has shown that, especially in the United States, the soap opera is viewed as an exclusively female genre. The social function of the soap opera is "to colonise women in the home as consumers" (Brown, 1990: 203). This is achieved by exploiting women's loneliness due to their exclusion from the economic production process and lack of recognition of their domestic labour. Soap operas play a vital role in maintaining the ideology that portrays women's place in the home as natural. However, in keeping with the model of French feminists, this North American study also recognizes that women derive pleasure from watching these shows. Brown admits that the contradictions brought about by women's enjoyment of television soaps—after all, women are critical viewers—cannot be ignored.

The fact remains, however, that in the dominant discourse about soap operas, these programmes are described as rubbish. As a result, women find themselves in the uncomfortable position where their own pleasures are belittled. The irony is that both cultural institutions such as the popular press and feminists denigrate these programmes.

Brown (1990) criticizes this widespread contempt and claims that soap operas should be considered an integral part of women's culture: different than, but not inferior to, dominant culture. To the extent that women who consume these cultural forms are aware of other existing forms, they can be seen as engaging in feminine discourse. Brown applies the notion of the inherent power relations in linguistic practices, developed by Foucault in his numerous works, to explain the relation between media production and consumption. Foucault claimed that linguistic practices are governed by a set of rules which are invisible to the speakers involved. Such rules are founded on a "kind of 'cultural unconscious' which is not universal or archetypal, but is shaped by forces of constraint which determine what serves as truth and what is acceptable" (Brown, 1990: 205). According to these invisible rules, most people have learned through their socialization what language to use with the majority of people in order to be accepted.

The mass media operate in a similar way: the values conveyed in media products are based on unwritten, invisible rules where the constraint—which determines what is the only acceptable truth for the cultural unconscious—is moulded by the dominant patriarchal culture and the capitalist economy. For example, because the system of mass media consumption relies on attracting the largest audiences possible in order to be profitable, the media continually need "to win and rewin audiences to dominant values" (Brown, 1990: 205), since this is what the popular media's power is based on. This is especially true of private networks, which cannot afford to develop content that appeals to a selective audience only. Since the process of choosing content according to dominant values is based on the invisible rules of the majority, the selected programs are capable of meeting the needs of capital and of different social classes, even if the interests at stake—those of media managers and those of audiences—are contradictory.

However, all power relations carry within their structures the possibility of resistance. Foucault writes: "Every power relationship implies, at least *in potentia*, a strategy of struggle, in which the two forces are not superimposed, do not lose their specific nature, or do not finally become confused. Each constitutes for the other a kind of permanent limit, a point of possible reversal" (Foucault, 1982: 794). It would appear that the two elements involved in the relationship between the soap opera and the female audience can remain distinct. Thus, by developing an awareness of the limits of soap operas and by constructing their own limits, women can avoid the confusion where fiction and reality become indistinguishable. On the contrary, women can use certain elements of soap-opera fiction to define and articulate their oppression, and thus develop "feminine discourse." In such cases, Brown claims that to name is to resist. A study of female audiences in the workplace confirms this assertion.

A large proportion of mass media audiences consists of women who work outside the home. A study (Hobson, 1990) of the behaviour of women in the workplace revealed that female audiences are far from being passive media consumers. The study was conducted on a group of women living in London, England, who worked as telephone sales representatives for a pharmaceutical and feminine hygiene company. The study showed that the women enjoyed watching soap operas and that these programmes were an important part of workplace conversations. In this context, soap operas played many roles in their discussions. First, they helped reinforce team spirit by getting all female workers involved in these discussions, which on the surface appeared to have neutral subjects. The women talked a great deal about television shows such as *Moonlighting*, *Coronation Street* and *Dallas*, which were all very popular in England at the time. However, there were profound reasons for this popularity.

According to Hobson (1990), the topics addressed in these television programmes served as catalysts for more serious discussions by providing the women with opportunities to draw parallels with their own personal experiences, which were often too painful to talk about openly. It seems that this "therapeutic" effect was strong enough to entice women who were not avid soap opera viewers to begin watching them so they could participate more fully in these serious discussions. Thus, there was a circular effect: the soap operas triggered conversations among the women, and the conversations persuaded more women to watch the programmes. The results of this study refute theories that claim that female viewers of soap operas and serials are passive. On the contrary, these viewers used the issues tackled in these programmes as catalysts for more open and general discussions which extended to all aspects of their lives. Moreover, the effects of these programmes lasted well beyond the actual time of viewing: they were discussed for hours, even days, after being televised. Thus, these programmes had a liberating effect by helping women articulate their problems. But how do such contents contribute to the emancipation of women?

Brown (1990) argues that feminine discourse helps women to empower themselves and understand their subordination so that they can better resist it. The discourse involves female discussions where women can talk openly, where their values are appreciated, and where listeners share similar views of the world. Thus, women are able to recognize their "tenuous position in relation to dominant social and cultural practices . . . " (Brown, 1990: 206). Moreover, this kind of bonding can help women gain strength by their acknowledgement of the mutual and collective restrictions they face in their respective milieus.

Thus, women are better able to recognize the contradictions between their own pleasure and that of their husbands, which is related to the dominant discourse. According to Brown (1990), the boundaries which women form with their circles of friends and which are based on mutual preferences, establish an alliance among women founded on "relationships of pleasure." Thus, for members of this group, it is acceptable behaviour to watch soap operas. The group therefore represents "a locus of empowerment for their own brand of pleasure. The source of pleasure here is not only textual but is also contextual" (Brown, 1990: 207). In other words, pleasure is no longer limited to watching these programmes, but extends to talking about them as well. Female viewers are able to give new importance to their programmes, not individually or in isolation, but as a group in a familiar and domestic context: their home or that of their friends. However, now, the home is no longer simply the place of their domestic enslavement. Rather, it becomes a place where women reverse their roles by giving themselves the power to experience pleasure. The secret nature of these meetings adds an element of subversion to the resistance of these women.

It is in this sense that the relationship between television and women's culture becomes potentially political. The appropriation of soap operas by women, coupled with the fact that they enjoy these programmes, creates a political situation "in that in the process women take pleasure into their own hands. They nominate, value, and regulate their own pleasure" (Brown, 1990: 210). Thus, in the same way that consumers can use the products of the consumer society, female viewers can use television as a means of resistance while remaining within the dominant economic order.

The studies on audiences outlined in this chapter reveal certain aspects that are unexplored in other approaches. For example, they show the distinctive characteristics of female audiences by exposing the contradictions involving women's enjoyment of television programmes in which heroines are oppressed and exploited by their families and society. An interesting aspect of these feminist models is that, in contrast to the general approaches used in communication studies, and even in other feminist approaches, their authors refuse to ridicule the viewing practices of women or accuse them of lacking political and social consciousness. Instead, these researchers insist on the existence of *political interpretation* on the part of women with respect to soap operas, as well as forms of *resistance* that occur with respect to both these programmes and certain aspects of women's personal, family and social lives. In fact, female audiences sometimes become participants in their role as fans.

Female Fandom: From Spectators to Participants

The ways in which soap operas become a part of female culture, both as a source of plea-sure and as a focus for talking about everyday personal problems, clearly discount any notion of the "passive" TV viewer, silently and distractedly absorbing sounds and images in an uncritical, conformist way. Indeed, there are some women who have appropriated the content of these shows to an even greater extent than the oral culture established by those in Brown and Hobson's studies. These are the fans who, through participation in informal gatherings, local fan clubs, correspondence networks, and regional and national fan con-ventions, actively rewrite source material taken from TV drama in the form of stories, nov-els, poems, artwork, and songtapes. This material is circulated in self-published "fanzines" through the mail and at meetings such as fan conventions. In the manner of de Certeau (1984), Jenkins (1988) refers to this process of appropriation as textual "poaching": an impertinent, unauthorized use of someone else's property in accordance with one's own experiences, needs, fantasies and imagination. Fan writing blurs the boundaries between spectating and participating, consuming and producing, and reading and writing, and high-lights the way that all forms of cultural products are in some sense hybrids.

Fan writing is a predominantly female activity, and one that is also intensely social. In her ethnography of female fandom, Bacon-Smith (1992) shows how the fan communi-ty consists of different circles and levels that allow for varying degrees of fan participa-tion, from the occasional to the more committed, for whom the fan community acts almost as a surrogate family. For the fan writer, involvement is usually more extensive, and occurs through a gradual process of socialization. The fan community provides "mentors," established members who initiate new recruits by introducing them to net-works of fellow fans and the community's codes and practices.

The fan writer must learn how to deal with both the source material and the existing body of fan writing to which she will add her own contributions. The community acts as the social space in which the writers develop their stories through interaction and mutual exchange with fellow fans. New fiction is first developed through the process of a "talk-ing story" in which the writer talks about the rudiments of the plot to others, and gets their feedback and advice, which is then sifted through and selectively incorporated into the final product. The talking story is an inclusive, dialogical practice rather than a divi-sive, monological one; there are no strict distinctions between speaker and listener but a constant oscillation between them. Writers understand that their work is part of a broader, collective process, and they often draw on one another's work as inspiration for new pro-jects. The conventional narrative structure of linear time, with a beginning and definite ending is often suspended, and replaced with looser, more open-ended forms of narrative continuity that are closer in character to the endlessness of the soap opera serial than the action/drama series. This incorporates what Bacon-Smith (1992) calls a "story tree" in which a root story may branch out into all manner of coexisting, overlapping and even retrospective narratives by other writers.

Fan writing emanates from a particular process of fan viewing or reading of the source material which is also part of fan socialization. This reading occurs simultaneously on two levels, in what Bacon-Smith (1992) calls the macroflow and the microflow. The former refers to the viewer's overall sense or mapping of the source programme, the world view it encapsulates, the characters that populate it and the relationships that bind them together. The microflow denotes the fan's awareness of and appreciation for the details of the dramatic scene, for example, the mannerisms, gestures and recurrent turns of phrase that different characters employ. On both levels, what counts is less the structure of individual, episodic plots than the characters, their traits and relationships, and particularly the moral ambiguities and challenges that continually arise. These are the basis for the writer's own speculations and extrapolations from which new stories are made.

Similarly to the soap opera viewers discussed above, fans and especially fan writers run the constant risk of being ridiculed and denigrated by others outside the fan community, the "mundanes" as fans call them (Penley, 1992). Television drama is generally regarded by fans as uniformly low-brow in terms of the dominant cultural ideology, and fans are often stigmatized as bizarre because of their interests and tastes. This can be especially problematic for women with professional careers who deal with the public in their work, such as teachers, nurses and librarians, and who make up a good portion of the fan writing community (Penley, 1992). To deal with the risk of exposure, many use pseudonyms in their writing. Another strategy that they use to deal with their stigmatized identity is to maintain a sense of humour about their activities. Playfulness is a constant thread running through fan culture, and allows members to act on their experiences, interests and concerns under the guise of something that is generally deemed trivial (Bacon-Smith, 1992).

While television fandom occurs across a variety of different dramas, what is striking is that fan writers do not draw primarily from the soap opera genre that is normally associated with feminine culture, but from more action-oriented drama where the main protagonists are male. The single most prominent source of ideas for fan writing is the science fiction *Star Trek* series. A number of different interpretations have been given for this. Jenkins (1988) argues that science fiction, a typically masculine genre in which patriarchal roles and values prevail, offers a kind of challenge to female writers. *Star Trek* allows women writers to enter a ready-made world of action, conflict and technology outside the concerns of traditional feminine culture, where they can redefine the female characters in less stereotypically subservient ways, as dependent on men for their identities and survival, and recast them as strong, wilful and independent. For Jenkins, this reflects a "feminist vision" in which romance and the sharing of feelings and lifestyles still play a significant role, but do not result in women's subordination (1988: 98–9).

While Bacon-Smith (1992) accepts fan writing as a way in which some women deal with a masculine culture that limits and denigrates their concerns and experiences, she is critical of attempts to portray it in overtly political terms. She focuses on two sub-genres of writing which at one time were associated with some degree of controversy within the fan community. The first is known as "slash" fiction, which involves narratives about homoerotic relations between central male characters. Slash fiction is associated with a number of drama shows portraying a male partnership, such as the Crockett and Tubbs characters of *Miami Vice*, but the dominant form of this category of writing is about the Kirk and Spock characters in the original *Star Trek* series. The second, and closely related sub-genre, is known as "hurt-comfort," and again involves narratives about central male characters, one of whom is physically harmed, usually by a third character, and subsequently develops an even closer relationship with his partner/companion on whom he depends to alleviate his pain and suffering.

Bacon-Smith (1992) sees the popularity of these sub-genres as multifaceted. The absence of women from the narratives represents a kind of metaphorical distance that enables the writer to address more directly central moral and ethical issues. Moreover, in a masculine culture where closeness, affection and romance can be risky for women, the homoerotic focus allows women to write about sexual excitement without putting female characters at risk. Masculine culture lacks strong erotic female characters, which makes it difficult to construct plausible female characters whose sexual and romantic desires are realized in the context of egalitarian relationships with another. At the same time, Bacon-Smith argues, these writers are aware that they are writing about men, not simply women in disguise. "Men are the alien, the other"; thus, the purpose is to understand them, particularly their propensity for violence, and thereby change them "into people with whom women can coexist more comfortably" (1992: 247–8). Both homoerotic and hurt-comfort narratives are ultimately about stripping men of their masculine power, the source of their male individuality, and re-situating them in social relationships where the bond takes precedence over other aspects, and open communication is the key to its integrity and success.

Any system of power relations can only be maintained over time if the subordinates learn to see and understand the world through the eyes of those who dominate them, while at the same time seeing and understanding it from their viewpoint as subordinates. Culture that is produced in the interests of patriarchal ideology requires women to undertake a kind of interpretive transvestism in which they adopt the male point of view in order to make sense of what they see and hear. In this respect, ironically, women acquire a greater range and flexibility in their capacity to understand the world. This ability is put to use in fan writing, in reinterpreting and manipulating the masculine coded genre of science fiction in a way that allows a broad array of identifications and desires to come into play. As Penley (1992) put it, when women write slash fiction, the fantasy they enact enables them to identify with, to be Kirk or Spock, at the same time as having either or both as an object of desire. And in doing so, they and their readers evade, if not resist, the exclusionary, binary logic—the either/or conception of choice—that dominant ideologies strive to impose.

Yet, fan writing is only an indirect means of participating in the content of television programmes like soap operas and action-oriented dramas. Other types of programmes like game shows have the same liberating quality in giving women the opportunity to participate directly.

Female Audiences and Participants in Television Game Shows: "Subversive" Pleasure and Resistance

According to a number of American studies, game shows are another genre of television programmes that are greatly enjoyed by women. Moreover, these programmes involve the same contradictions and the same possibilities of opposition as soap operas. Here, however, women can be not only audiences but also participants in the show. John Fiske

(1990) uses the "carnivalesque" characteristic of quiz shows to explain the tactics of the resistance of female viewers. This resistance is not aimed directly at the repressive system, but takes advantage of its weaknesses. Since women do not have real power in a patriarchal society, they must use the means at their disposal to resist, that is, to explore the weaknesses of the dominant system.

Like soap operas, game shows are generally viewed as an inferior form of television. Fiske (1990), however, argues that the reasons for denigrating these shows are not based on a desire to ridicule the programmes themselves, nor their place in women's culture, but are based in the patriarchal ideology, the principles of which serve to discredit all that resists, threatens, or enables one to escape the system of patriarchal power. Are game shows, which play an active and pleasurable role in women's culture, a menace to this ideology?

Fiske (1990)—who views the quiz shows he studied as a cultural product of capitalism—claims that by providing a showcase for consumer goods they blur the distinctions between their content and advertising. The threat is due to the fact that, in these programmes, women play a role in which they excel, that of housewife and consumer. The content of these television game shows are inspired by three elements that are omnipresent in women's lives: consumerism, the family and romance.

Consumerism According to Fiske, "*The New Price is Right* is the consumerist quiz show par excellence" (Fiske, 1990: 135). The majority of contestants are women, and the skills required to participate in the programme are associated with what our society calls "women's knowledge": the ability to judge the price and value of commodities. In the show, the pricing of commodities is done through a series of games where the winner is the woman who makes the best estimate. However, if it is so obvious that *The New Price is Right* reproduces and reinforces women's essential role as domestic labourer, why is it so popular among female television viewers? If women are responsible for shopping for the family in everyday life, why do they choose to spend their leisure time participating in or watching a programme that reflects the same activities?

To answer these questions, we must first acknowledge the differences between the conditions of consumption as conveyed in this show and those in domestic labour. The most obvious difference is that consumption on *The New Price is Right* is made in public, while everyday consumption is essentially a private act, which is largely unrecognized and unacclaimed. The game show is characterized by the applause and cheering of the studio audience, which sometimes borders on hysteria. Moreover, the top contestant stands to win a prize. For Fiske, this situation has a carnivalesque dimension:

> . . . the carnival was the occasion when the repressions of everyday life could be lifted, when the voices of the oppressed could be heard at full volume, when society admitted to pleasures which it ordinarily repressed and denied. The essence of carnival was the inversion of the rules of everyday life, necessitated by the need to maintain the oppression of a populace that would otherwise refuse to submit to this social discipline. So the forces of carnival are opposed to those which work to repress and control the everyday life of the subordinate (Fiske, 1990: 136).

Fiske (1990) argues that this context offers the show's audience members two forms of liberation. First, they can express themselves noisily. Second, they can do so in public, which represents a form of escape from the demure respectability of "femininity" approved by our society. Most of the women who make up this audience come from the underprivileged classes and are thus subordinated economically, as well as politically and socially. Not only do they have little money, but this money generally comes from, and belongs to, their husbands. Traditionally, earning money for the family is the role of the husband, while spending and managing it is the role of the wife. In *The New Price is Right*, the husband's money is replaced by the wife's skills, which might win the family a prize. "The show symbolically liberates women from their economic constraints and in so doing liberates them from their husband's economic power . . . " (Fiske, 1990: 137).

But the difference in consumption is not limited to the distinction between the private and public spheres. It is also expressed in terms of the concepts of work and leisure. Shopping for the family is a task that confines women to their roles as housewife and mother. However, shopping for pleasure is a form of liberation from these roles. In women's culture, shopping for oneself is a liberating and recreational form of leisure, while doing it for the family is a form of subordinate labour. Fiske (1990) notes that *The New Price is Right* is a way of approaching consumption not from the point of view of domestic labour, but from that of leisure and liberation. This inversion is also carnivalesque in that it represents the pleasure for the subordinated in resisting and evading the forces that dominate them at the very moment the carnival takes place.[3]

The carnival, of course, involves subversive elements. It is characterized by "excess," by going too far. Thus by overstepping the bounds of established social norms, it reveals the arbitrary dimension of these norms and their function as social discipline. Excess is behaviour or pleasure that is out of control, while the norm, like a rule one must follow, is repressive. It represents the policing of social discipline to defend the interests of those who control power and establish the norms. Within these patriarchal norms, as Fiske emphasizes, "women's culture is usually characterised (by patriarchy) as 'excessive'" (1990: 138). In this context, the carnival of consumerism put on by certain televised game shows has a certain liberating quality for women. Do other types of game shows have the same effect?

The Family As mentioned above, the content of televised game shows is also inspired by the family. According to Fiske, the programme *Family Feud* is a good example of this category. The show opposes two competing families, each composed of four people, with women playing a central role. Whereas the form of knowledge required to play *The New Price is Right* is women's ability to manage the family's financial resources, the knowledge used in *Family Feud* is associated with their ability to manage the family's emotional resources. In this game, even if the family team can include both male and female members, women are often given the role of spokesperson. Here, their role on the human relations level, which is normally confined to the domestic sphere, becomes public.

---

[3] M.M. Bakhtine (1965) also tackles this question in *Rabelais and His World*, Cambridge: MIT.

Women "speak for their families in a way that has traditionally been the role of the male" (Fiske, 1990: 138).

Fiske sees the same kinds of contradictions in *Family Feud* as existing in *The New Price is Right*. The valorization and deprivatization of the emotional qualities of women and the inversion of male and female roles as public spokesperson constitute forms of pleasure for women who participate as viewers or players in this game show. Thus, if *The New Price is Right* exploits the traditional characteristics attributed to women, *Family Feud* emphasizes the inversion of roles, that is, making the private role of women public. This inversion is pleasurable for women, since it gives them an opportunity to distinguish themselves in public, an opportunity they are not often given. Let us now see if the last genre of television game shows, those inspired by romance, has the same liberating quality.

Romance The exploitation of romance is nowhere more obvious than in the Australian game show called *Perfect Match*. In this show, a "wooer" of either sex must choose a date among three members of the opposite sex participating in the programme. During the course of the game, each of those being wooed must answer three questions asked by the suitor, who can hear the answers, but cannot see the other participants. The home and studio audience, however, can see and hear all participants. Thus, the structure of the programme tends to equalize the relationships between women and men. In fact, each show is composed of two games, the first of which features a woman choosing a date from among three men, followed by the opposite scenario in the second. As Fiske (1990) points out, the roles of initiating the relationship, choosing a participant and of being selected at the end of the game are shared by members of both sexes. The winning couple in each game—that is, the wooer and the man (woman) she (he) chooses—earn a prize, including a short holiday in a luxurious hotel.

One of the more important aspects of the game is that women are free of the usual constraints associated with sexuality. Most often, women live their sexuality and pleasure within the framework of the couple, namely within the traditional boundaries of male sexuality. Of course, the "liberation" provided by the game is never complete. The programme would not be such a success if this were the case. The traditional forms of patriarchal control, such as soft romantic music and a backdrop of pink and blue hearts, are omnipresent. But these traits are so exaggerated that they become a "parody of traditional romantic values," a parody which, according to Fiske, "is a subversive form, for it exposes and mocks the essential features of . . . the patriarchal conventions of the romance narrative" (Fiske, 1990: 140).

The highlight of the show is the appearance in the studio of previous winning couples who talk about their dates. In general, it seems that women take advantage of this occasion to poke fun at the sexual prowess of men. As Fiske (1990) says, the couples who were far from perfect matches and whose dates were failures represent much of the appeal of this part of the show. The faults of both men and women are discussed openly and laughed at. The women, in particular, talk quite freely and enjoyably about men's "shortcomings." "What is important in this is that the women show no guilt at the 'failure' of the date. They are freed from the feminine responsibility to manage the emotional life of the couple (or family)" (Fiske, 1990: 140). This attitude constitutes a form of resistance, since women can take advantage of their subordinate sexual role, which patriarchal society has given them, to rid themselves of the responsibility for the failure of the date.

This study shows that it is important to highlight the tactics of resistance adopted by dominated groups. These tactics, which Fiske (1990: 141) compares with forms of guerilla warfare, do not directly oppose the repressive system, but instead "make guerilla raids upon it and seek out its weak points, the places where it can be turned against itself. . . . The art of everyday culture is the art of making do, an art at which women excel through many generations of oppression . . . "

CONCLUSION

In this chapter, we saw that television content conveys patriarchal capitalist values. In these shows, men are generally associated with the public sphere, work, production and earning money. Women, however, are usually associated with the private sphere, leisure, reproduction and spending money. Moreover, the primary role of women portrayed in the media is that of wife and mother within the nuclear family. Soap operas suggest that marriage is a woman's ultimate goal in terms of self-fulfilment. These types of content define femininity on the basis of such characteristics as romanticism, sensitivity, fragility and the capacity to devote oneself to others (the other members of the family), as well as the ability to manage the material resources of the household. These "feminine" qualities are also exploited in game shows via the concepts of romance, consumerism and the family, which provide a basis for games where women are brought into the limelight. Who watches these shows? And what impact do they have?

In this chapter, we saw that the phenomena of soap operas and game shows have mass appeal among female viewers. These programmes provide women with a means of escape, as well as a means of resistance and negotiation. For a majority of women, the pleasure of watching these programmes lies in the very contradictions they present: women with critical minds appreciate media content in which women are subordinated, and in which they are portrayed as enslaved to consumerism, romance and the family.

In short, at first glance these women viewers seem to enjoy observing themselves in a dominated position. However, feminist studies have demonstrated that, on the contrary, some women are not only aware of this situation, but use it as a basis to discuss, if not improve, their own position in everyday life. For example, many groups of women use the themes exploited in soap operas as catalysts for conversations about more personal problems. Women thus establish a certain solidarity among themselves which can help them take control of certain aspects of their lives. Women can also use game shows to show off their skills in public and to give themselves the "subversive" pleasure of reversing traditional values. Thus, some groups of women know how to exploit the weak points of the patriarchal system within the mass media to escape their traditional roles, at least temporarily.

CONCLUSION TO PART 1

In this first part of the book we presented a theoretical analysis of the mass media in our society. We developed a critical approach that establishes a link between the organization of the mass media and the society in which they operate. To achieve this, we examined the theoretical concepts of a number of other approaches, retaining the concepts that appear to be helpful in elucidating media phenomena.

The psychological approach showed that the mass media have a considerable impact on individuals and, conversely, the functionalist approach demonstrated that it is people who influence the media. Faced with this contradiction, we pursued our analysis by examining critical theories in the field of communication. These models demonstrated that we live in a capitalist society—with its own particular characteristics—based on a social class system. The models also showed that, in order to explain the inherent contradictions of the organization of the media, it is necessary to examine the media within their broader context, that is, as an integral part of society. It is not enough to look at the media in isolation; the conditions in which they operate must also be examined. For example, to analyze media audiences, it is necessary to consider them in relation to the conditions under which the content is produced. However, to avoid the contradictions inherent in certain analyses, such as the psychological and functionalist approaches, we must broaden the scope of analysis to include such factors as the economic, political, ideological and cultural conditions that influence the organization and functioning of the media.

In the first chapters of Part 1, we examined useful concepts for a general analysis of the media. Up to this point, however, our analysis had not yet considered an important aspect of the organization of the media: gender differentiation. In examining various feminist approaches, we saw that applying the concept of gender differentiation revealed a number of aspects of the media overlooked by other models. Feminist approaches have made it possible to establish that our society is based on a patriarchal system, and that in this type of society men and women have diverse experiences in relation to various aspects of the media that are rooted in different socialization processes of each sex. For example, is it possible to say that in our society boys and girls are exposed to the same learning process during childhood? Or that men and women face the same expectations in life?

With regard to the media, these differences are often expressed as sexual discrimination—usually against women—among media employees and among audience members, as well as in media content. As an example, most television programmes intended for women are broadcast in the afternoon because our patriarchal society cultivates the myth that women should stay at home, while in reality 50% of women are waged labourers. In this context, programmes intended for men have a wide appeal and are consequently broadcast during prime-time viewing hours. Because of this situation, women are forced to either videotape the shows they want to watch, or miss them completely if they cannot afford a video recorder.

Part 1 thus revealed certain hidden aspects of the organization of the mass media with respect to their integration into society. Part 2 will address more concrete questions concerning the phenomenon of the media. We will deal with empirical studies of some particular areas of the media by applying the various theoretical concepts developed in the first part of the book. We will then examine some specific forms of communication (for example, soap operas, comic strips and advertising) produced by various mass media, as well as their content and their audiences.

PART 2

COMMUNICATION AND SOCIETY: EMPIRICAL CASES

INTRODUCTION TO PART 2

In the first part of this book we identified the conditions under which the mass media operate, and developed a theoretical understanding of the organization, production and consumption of the mass media based on a critical approach. In this second part, we will look at empirical studies of a number of specific cases, focusing on the impact that different types of mass media (e.g., television, books, newspapers, etc.) have on Canadian society. Since each of these media produces a distinct form of communication, it is possible to ask whether they have different impacts on society. This is the question that the case studies will attempt to answer. Thus, while the first part focused primarily on the conditions of production and consumption of media content, the second will look at the content conveyed by different media, that is, the messages, values, and so on, which they contain. We will also see how certain types of content vary according to the form in which they are transmitted, and how these have distinct effects on audiences.

Specifically, Chapters 7 and 8 look at the "romanticism" conveyed on television and in popular literature, as well as the diverse effects it has on audiences. Chapters 9 and 10 present an analysis of two forms of content aimed at children and adults in society: comic strips and advertising. Finally, Chapter 11 studies news content in the print and audio media, and Chapter 12 focuses on the impact of certain new tools of communication (videotex, e-mail, videocassette recorders, interactive television, etc.) on society.

WHAT DOES CULTURAL TELEVISION REFLECT?

INTRODUCTION

As agents of socialization, the mass media ensure social cohesion, as well as produce and reproduce social consensus and the coexistence of different classes and social groups. To this end, the content of a medium such as television must satisfy the varied tastes and expectations of its audiences. Thus, the primary objective of television, for example, is to maintain high ratings. Despite this constraint, cultural programmes like soap operas and serials cannot be perceived as a response to economic conditions only, but also to the ideological and cultural interests of producers and audiences. These interests vary, however, depending on the type of television network. In principle, the mandate of state-run television, which is largely financed by public funding, is to maintain high cultural standards by "complementing" the programming of other networks, and by competing with them in areas where their production is considered unsatisfactory. As for private television networks, they sometimes reserve part of their programming for content they view as ideologically and culturally beneficial. Finally, whether it is meant to or not, advertising constitutes a vehicle for spreading mass culture as defined in Chapter 4. In short, mass media content is influenced by many social factors.

As was mentioned in previous chapters, the people who design, produce, select programme projects and allocate budget resources have a direct impact on television content. They are the ones who determine what topics will be covered and in what context they will be addressed. They also decide who will comment on a particular issue, the duration of this response and, in the case of television dramas, the nature of these comments. However, their ability to impose specific content is restricted by the public they seek to attract, since television must, to a certain extent, meet audience expectations. Some television content—such as series, soap operas, serials and game shows, which constitute television mass culture—enable audiences to escape their daily lives. As we saw earlier, this content reinforces values and ideas that already exist in society, while creating occasions for viewers to discuss and resist some of the very same ideas. These shows thus play a pivotal role in relation to social practices, which is why this chapter will be devoted to an analysis of diverse televised cultural content, the values and ideas it conveys, as well as its impact on different audiences. Finally, in order to make this discussion more concrete and to confirm the theoretical assertions of the previous chapters regarding media content and audiences, we will present a more detailed analysis of two soap operas with worldwide television audiences: *Dallas* and *Dynasty*.

IMAGES CONVEYED IN TELEVISION CONTENT

Not without reason, certain minority and feminist groups have protested over the years against the skewed vision of Canadian society presented in some television productions. If aliens were to come to Earth and spend a week watching television to become more familiar with Canadian society, they would be left with some strange impressions: that our society is primarily made up of men; that women are generally too foolish to do anything but swoon over clothes, make-up and cleaning products, etc.; that, with very few exceptions, only whites belong to the middle classes or the bourgeoisie; and that all adults are, are about to be, or absolutely want to get married.

Where would they get these ideas from? Part of the answer lies in other questions: How many television programmes shown on Canadian networks are uniquely devoted to blacks, Chinese, or other minorities? How many shows have at least a few characters belonging to one of these groups? Is the percentage of such characters in television programmes proportionate to their numbers in Canadian society? Not only is the answer to this last question no, but when these minorities are represented, it is usually as "tough nuts to crack," or as wretched or base characters who must be eliminated. However, minorities are not the only groups underrepresented in television content.

Women are also underrepresented in the mass media, though they are discriminated against in a different way. Although the number of women in cultural programmes is generally lower than that of men, their representation is skewed more in terms of their image. The theoretical models developed in communication and media studies often neglect to consider gender role discrimination in the media's portrayal of women. This is why feminist theories have focused their research on areas that can shed light on the causes and the effects of this discrimination. As we will see in the following sections, however, these approaches do not all deal with the same aspects of the problem. Some examine the image of exploited women in terms of their traditional role as mothers and wives, and as sex objects. Others are not only interested in these matters, but take their research one step further by proposing a critical analysis that situates the question of women's image in the media within the framework of industrial societies divided into social classes. While these approaches may differ, their subject matter remains the same: television and its various forms of communication which convey women's image.

It is immediately apparent, then, that television content reflects only part of our social reality. Within this biased reproduction of Canadian society, another deformation manifests in the proliferation of certain images (to the exclusion of others) that focus on two themes in particular: violence and sexual stereotypes. It is therefore not surprising that, among the numerous studies conducted on television images, several have been carried out on the effect of violence on children, and on the image of women. We will now address these two themes.

Television Violence

As was mentioned in the introduction to this book, children and teenagers spend more time watching television than they do on school work. This disturbing fact has led many researchers to study what these young people are watching and what effects these shows have on them. In Chapter 5, we saw that the socialization that occurs during childhood is crucial, since children are particularly vulnerable to the stimuli they receive during this time. Given this fact, many social groups (parent associations, groups working against violence towards women and children, etc.) have protested against the excessive number of violent scenes shown on television.

This situation has led many researchers to look at the effects of violence on children and teenagers, as well as on emotionally disturbed individuals. The results of their studies, mostly conducted in the United States, do not always agree. Some analyses contend that violent scenes on television can induce aggressive behaviour in young viewers. Others claim that it is not possible to conclude that television violence has negative repercussions on most children, though they acknowledge that some children, or certain groups of children, can be influenced. It would appear that the impact of violent television scenes largely depends on the form of violence broadcast. For example, a violent act that is punished will have little or no negative impact. Thus researchers are careful to qualify their statements when describing the effects of television violence on young people.

Subsequent, more in-depth studies conducted by Agee, Ault and Emery (1989) have shown that the effects of violent television content is more subtle. For example, they observed that violent content has an undeniable impact on young viewers of both sexes, but that these effects are contradictory, sometimes even opposed. Thus, some young viewers adopt aggressive behaviour while others feel victimized and fearful. This observation led Agee, Ault and Emery to believe that television violence has profound effects which are manifested in more subtle ways than simply aggressive behaviour. For example, they observed that children who watch many television shows with a violent content sometimes become desensitized to real violence. In this context, some psychologists have compared the effects of television violence on young viewers with that of smoking on lung cancer. The one is not necessarily the cause of the other, though there is an undeniable link between the two. However, some sociologists' interpretation of the impact of violence on children is more complex. They claim that the effect is often manifested in the short run and is not as direct as others have believed it to be. They maintain that children's living conditions have a greater effect on behaviour than the shows they watch. Children who live in poverty, who do not have enough to eat nor adequate clothing, and so on, are exposed to much more violent conditions both psychologically and physically than from occasionally watching violent programmes. Put differently, when scenes of television violence are received in a poor milieu, where people have difficulty feeding,

clothing and housing themselves adequately, they can have much more harmful consequences than when they are received in a privileged milieu.[1]

The findings of numerous studies on television violence underline the complexity of
this issue. In reality, these contradictory findings simply constitute a good excuse for governments and television producers who wish to ignore the results to continue to include
violent content. Thus, researchers working for American networks such as ABC, CBS and
NBC are always quick to point out that these studies do not furnish any convincing proof,
and that the question is still open to debate. In the same breath, the networks increase their
programming of violent content, even in cartoons, which, it should be noted, attract a
broad audience and are therefore highly profitable. Yet, cartoon violence can be the most
harmful, since it is often deceitful and insidious; in other words, the violence is not always
expressed in extreme and visible forms. It can range from an apparently benign act, such
as Daffy Duck being whacked on the head, to outright violent behaviour, such as science-
fiction heroes using highly sophisticated weapons to kill their enemies.

Violence, however, is not transmitted simply in the form of aggression. It may also
appear in scenes of explicit seduction, innuendos and lewd language, which are becoming
increasingly common on television. Take, for example, the series *He Shoots, He Scores*.
Some scenes were considered obscene, indecent and crude given that the programme's
main theme—hockey—attracted a large, young audience, especially in Québec. It was in
the seventies that American television began to incorporate "risqué" scenes in situation
comedies and dramas, such as *Three's Company*, *Charlie's Angels* and, later, *Miami
Vice*. Although certain parent associations complained that some girls had become pregnant because the shows set bad examples, most viewers readily accepted the programmes
as long as they were in good taste.

One of the most deceitful aspects of television violence is that a large part of it is
aimed at cultural minorities and women. Yet these groups are underrepresented in all
genres of cultural programmes, as are homosexuals and lesbians, who, when they appear
in these shows, are often portrayed in an unfavourable light. While violence against
minority groups is more explicit (minorities almost always play the role of manhandled
scapegoats and villains), violence against women is more subtle and occurs primarily in
terms of the stereotypical images in which they are usually portrayed. Let us now take a
closer look at the issue of women's image on television.

The Image of Women on Television

During the last 20 years, women's movements in Canada have worked towards changing
mentalities and modifying social relations between men and women. However, while
some mass media such as television have drawn on these changes, they still continue to
convey traditional stereotypes of women as sex objects, mothers and servants to other
family members. While many shows have removed women from the home and put them

---

[1] For a similar discussion on violence, see K. McDonnell (1994) *Kid Culture*, Toronto: Second Storey Press,
Chapter 6; and B. Hodge and D. Tripp (1986) *Children and Television*, London: Polity.

on the labour market (*Street Legal*, *North of 60*, etc.), very few have moved far enough to show images of two spouses *equally* sharing domestic chores and responsibility for the children's education. Instead, television programme contents have helped create the myth that women can successfully lead a rewarding career and have a model family. As we saw in the previous chapter, feminists have referred to this image as "superwoman," or the "new woman."

Much of the feminist research conducted in universities (studies on the media, film and culture) and by women's movements and the media themselves have analyzed and criticized the image of women on television, and have brought to light many relevant facts. For instance, in a modern society such as ours, television continues to reinforce established beliefs concerning women and their sexuality. Although television defines itself above all as an information and entertainment medium, its content conveys ideas and values that play a major role in the production and construction of the dominant images of women as wives, mothers and sex objects. Moreover, as we saw in the last chapter, although market research shows that the majority of Canadians who watch television are women, it is men who own and control the mass media. Consequently, it is men's values, ideas and viewpoints that dominate the production system and the images shown. For instance, most head programmers in television are men (Martin and Proulx, 1995).

Confronted with the insistent complaints of feminist movements about the sexual and domestic stereotypes associated with the image and portrayal of women on television, the networks have had to acknowledge the legitimacy of some of their demands and criticisms. These "adjustments," however, have not prevented the media from exploiting all of the commercial and ideological potential that the creation of the "new woman" or "superwoman" represents.

In what follows, we will explore *where* and *how* the "new woman," as well as the more traditional stereotypes of femininity (domesticity and motherhood) are portrayed on television. It is important to recall that women—new or traditional—are still sex objects, that is, something that can be sized up and appreciated like a commodity and assessed by its parts (the eyes, lips, breasts, hips, legs, etc.).

It should be noted that by increasing women's representation on programmes, television is giving them a greater role. However, much of this representation continues to degrade women and trivialize them. Several studies (Cantor and Pingree, 1983; Canadian Radio-Television and Telecommunications Report, 1982; Ferguson, 1985) have shown that women are still cast in supportive roles, their prime preoccupation being family and romance, not their profession. The female lawyers in *LA Law*, the newshound in *Murphy Brown*, the policewomen in *Hill Street Blues* and the architect in *Family Ties* are visible as mothers and wives, but barely as professionnals. Moreover, Ferguson (1990) remarks that the women who are most visible are those who hold and use power as wives, mothers, partners and who frequently "scheme or emote rather than employ logic in order to achieve their ends" (1990: 218). It seems astonishing that, despite the economic and social changes affecting women in the last 20 years in industrial society, the image of women on television has been altered very little and the sexual stereotypes have remained constant. From Lucy in the 1950s to Alexis Carrington in *Dynasty* and Blanche

Devereaux in *The Golden Girls*, 20 or more years later, women are still traditionally stereotyped as manipulative, dotty and helpless. "Thus, shifts in gender images and power relations on, for example, U.S. prime-time television are cosmetic at best," says Ferguson (1990: 218). "*Designing Women, Roseanne, Murphy Brown*, and *The Golden Girls* do offer portraits of female autonomy, confidence, competence, achievement—and dottiness. But the common characteristic of the women shown, in the office and the kitchen, is their ability to *manipulate*." "Is this a new form of female empowerment? Assuredly it is not," Ferguson states (1990: 218–9).

Other types of television programming also present women in secondary, unassuming and degrading roles. One need only think about the glamorous game show hostesses with their mechanical smiles, whose sole task is to escort participants. The principle host of most game shows, such as *The New Price Is Right*, is a man; the hostess's job is to serve him by performing small tasks or by simply posing next to the prize to make it look more "sexy" and "attractive." If not for their sex appeal, women are exploited for their "flighty" nature. For example, in Québec's French version of *Studs*, called *Coup de foudre*, the host's calm attitude gives an element of credibility to the show, while the hostess's carefree and scatterbrained attitude emphasizes the show's fun side. Could these hostesses not be given more intelligent tasks, or could they not be asked to provide a welcoming, instead of sexy or giddy, feel to game shows?

What about sports programming, an area dominated by male sports and male commentators? If there is such a thing as men's sacred ground in the media, it is sports. Sports coverage celebrates male values such as competition, endurance and physical ability, which are embraced by male audiences. In this context, insinuations denigrating female competitions often underlie sportscasters' comments. For example, women's tennis or skiing competitions are invariably described as inferior to men's. Or, when commentators are forced to recognize that the female competition is as good or even better than the men's, it is often accompanied by exclamations of surprise, incredulity or even denigration. For instance, it is not uncommon for a sportscaster to say that a female competitor is "surprisingly good for a girl," or that "this year the girls are as competitive as the men." The fact that male participants in sporting events are referred to as *men*, and female participants as *girls*, is a reflection of the importance of women in sports: as with "man" and "boy," the word "woman" represents a more serious and mature person than "girl." The reference to women as girls may be unconscious, but it nevertheless implies a difference in appreciation. More recently, sportscasters have been increasingly using the term "ladies" (as in "ladies' competition"). Although the term implies more seriousness than girl, it conjurs up an image of gentility and fragility that is not conveyed by the notion of woman. Finally, television sports programmes never show female teams playing certain traditionally male sports such as hockey. Since women's hockey is much less aggressive than men's, it is thought to be far less interesting and less serious. Women players do not have what a player on the Montréal Canadiens hockey team has called the "killer instinct." Do television shows exist that have a more equitable distribution between the sexes and minority groups? Let us see if soap operas, women's favourite programmes, are a case in point.

GENDER REPRESENTATION IN SOAP OPERAS

Soap operas draw on elements of everyday reality to create situations that are dramatized and integrated into long-term stories. Thus, *LA Law* suggests that women can succeed in the working world; *Sisters* offers solutions to family problems; *North of 60* analyzes the social problems in a native community; while *Beverly Hills, 90210* attempts to achieve the same thing among upper-middle-class high school students and young adults. There are many soap operas in Canadian and American programming, and they all address issues dealing with many aspects of people's lives.

Compared with the low popularity of documentaries or current affairs programmes, the craze for some soap operas is difficult to explain. (In Quebec, some have reached audiences of over 3,000,000 people.) It could be that, by fictionalizing moral dilemmas or social conflicts, these matters become more acceptable and interesting to audience members for whom they are a real-life concern. For example, the production of historical television soap operas in Québec is based on the notion that certain present-day social problems can be shown only if portrayed as temporally removed or exceptional situations. Recently, a soap opera called *Cormoran* addressed the issue of fascism in Québec by dramatizing the period preceding World War II. Before that, another soap opera entitled *Les belles histoires des pays d'en haut* denounced the state of perpetual indebtedness of the poor and the working classes by contextualizing the problem in nineteenth century Québec.

Soap operas are a relatively recent phenomenon related to the development of the "oral" mass media. Let us now take a brief look at their history and some of their characteristics.

Once Upon a Time . . . Radio: The Birth of Soap Operas

It was in the twenties, in the United States, that radio serials were born. Why were these melodramatic serials renamed *soap operas*? In their early days, these programmes were intended for female audiences; thus, soap (the housewife's product *par excellence*) manufacturers began to wage war on each other over advertising contracts during broadcasts. Within the framework of this new form of communication, commercial radio stations added a "sparkle" to household product advertising and thus reinforced women's roles as domestic labourers in the household. Since then, the term soap opera has been used to describe this type of show. Although they are broadcast in diverse formats, they are all based on either serial novels or comic operas. Soap operas are broadcast every afternoon or once a week for an entire season, or as a series (like *Anne of Green Gables*) lasting no more than a few weeks. In this book, the term *soap opera* is used to refer to all of these types of programmes, regardless of how they are transmitted, or whether they are on radio or television.

In Europe, commercial radio began to take off after World War II. Until then, radio had essentially been a public service devoted to broadcasting dominant culture and science. For example, at the time of its inception in 1933, Radio Luxembourg had an entirely "cultural" vocation. Over the decades, the station gradually added different variety shows and soap operas to its programming, which were financed by on-air advertising.

Most of the radio station's listeners were women. In order to take advantage of this female audience, Radio Luxembourg adopted a programming strategy that enabled it to "accompany" listeners in their homes and their everyday lives (Mattelart, 1981). Thus, radio—followed by all other mass media, especially television—became firmly established in the daily lives of women, that is, in their homes, where it extolled the merits of domesticity and private life.

The Classic Soap Opera Formula

Many studies (e.g. Dyer, 1987) show that soap operas not only address female audiences in particular, but that their content is constructed on the basis of women's experiences. This content is based on three elements: disequilibrium due to a particular problem, resolution of the problem, and re-establishment of the equilibrium. The initial situation is one of disorganization, and as the story unfolds audiences are shown the tensions existing between characters, and the contradictions inherent to the situations they are in. Over the course of a programme, these problems are resolved, one at a time, until the equilibrium is re-established.

Tania Modleski (1982) claims there are similarities between the narrative form characteristic of soap operas (namely the endless postponement of problem resolution and life's ups and downs) and women's domestic labour which, in turn, is related to the rhythm of their everyday lives. How is this so? The home is the scene of recurrent problems, which are resolved one at a time; it is also the setting of constant interruptions. In soap operas, the action is based on the identification of small problems and their resolution. The rhythm of soap operas thus reflects the constant state of distraction women face in the home due to their children, other adults, the telephone, cooking, cleaning, etc. Moreover, soap operas highlight the skills that are traditionally attributed to women, namely those used to deal with interpersonal relations and personal and domestic crises. In short, soap operas are constructed, or designed, to reflect certain aspects of the experiences of both women and men.

In *Love and Ideology in the Afternoon*, Laura S. Mumford (1995) discusses another interesting aspect of the soap opera genre: its redefinition of the public and private spheres through its treatment of the concept of privacy. The author argues that the way soap opera characters lead their lives makes privacy impossible, since everyone seems to have a right to intrude on someone else's personal affairs and feelings. "In effect," Mumford says, "there is no 'private' sphere in the soap opera community because there is no privacy" (1995: 49). The barriers which exist in real life between the private and the public spheres do not usually exist in soap operas, and when they do, they are regularly breached. Actually, the "ruling dynamic of soap opera," Mumford continues, is the exposure of people's private experiences and feelings to the audiences. In publicizing the private sphere the way they do, "soap operas also strip them [the programmes] of whatever political and social meaning they might have." This depoliticization encourages the spectators "to see a rigid separation between supposedly apolitical 'private' life and a 'public' sphere that is the proper site of political and social activity," Mumford argues (1995: 65).

Because the private sphere is socially associated with women and the public with men, this depoliticization might have some consequences on women spectators' understanding of society. However, Mumford states that regular viewers do not necessarily accept the patriarchal ideology expressed by the genre, and may even resist it in different ways. It seems that one of the pleasures involved in watching soap operas is to disagree with its sexual politics. It is important, then, "to recognize the extent to which resistance to and enjoyment of particular popular cultural artifacts such as soap operas are not mutually exclusive, but simultaneous" (1995: 118). A number of studies have been conducted on soap operas in Canada, particularly those produced in Québec. In the next section, we will turn our attention to these analyses.

The Construction of Québec Soap Operas

In their research on various aspects of Québec soap operas, Philippe Sohet and Jean-Pierre Désaulnier (1982) revealed some of the specific features of these programmes. For instance, the crisis which steers the subsequent events in soap operas may be any event or statement that provides fodder for discussion and that results in the expression of diverse opinions. These discussions generally occur between decent people, who never speak about inappropriate issues such as politics, inflation, unemployment (except on an individual basis) or other social problems. Soap opera themes revolve around family relationships, and more importantly, romantic affairs, and the numerous situations that threaten them. The topics are strictly of a private nature and centre on the individual and the family. Furthermore, every situation is "privatized." Joys, as well as hardships, are portrayed within either the family or one's circle of friends. Social advantages and problems are always looked at from the individual's viewpoint, or as resulting from coincidence. As Sohet and Désaulnier (1982) have pointed out, social problems do not exist since, for all intents and purposes, society itself does not exist. According to these researchers, Québec soap operas are adorned with every social stereotype in Canadian society, and respect the existing social hierarchy by keeping characters locked in the social ranks determined by their social function. Soap operas usually begin with a crisis, for which a solution is always within sight. In short, what is played out in soap operas is the process of re-establishing the social order. Endings always have a positive side, which enable female viewers to sigh with relief.

A study by Armande Saint-Jean (1989) shows that Québec soap operas portray women in diverse roles, some traditional, others more modern. Among the more modern roles, she mentions the policewoman with a sense of humour, the sprightly grandmother, the sassy teenage girl and the emancipated housewife. In short, women play all sorts of roles. The values presented by these characters, however, remain traditional. In the original French version of *He Shoots, He Scores* (*Lance et compte*), the female characters, who were confined to secondary roles, acted as foils for the male characters, particularly in bedroom scenes. In the programme *Des dames de coeur*, created by former Parti Québécois minister Lise Payette, while female characters were searching for more autonomy they were still portrayed in very traditional feminine roles. Women were betrayed by their husbands—like a legacy handed down from mother to daughter—and were sexually assaulted, but they still tried to be generous and, like all "real" women, forgave their husbands. Saint-Jean (1989) has remarked that, in these soap operas, a single woman who enjoys a successful career will complain about her lack of success at love, a married businesswoman longs for a child, and a mistress enjoys playing second fiddle. Thus, women are stereotypically portrayed as eternally unsatisfied and impossible to satisfy. Conversely, male characters know what they want out of life and are often happy with their fate.

In short, the construction of Québec soap operas reflects the stereotypes and dominant values that underlie Canadian society. As a result, they do not encourage social change, and instead help construct a moral consensus on how men and women must conduct their personal lives. For certain feminists, it is this moral consensus that outlines the code of behaviour that women feel they must follow in the private sphere, causing them to remain in their most traditional roles. Michèle Mattelart (1986) asserts that, by reproducing these "natural" roles, soap operas integrate women into the regulatory function which they perform in society, which enables the social system to remain in equilibrium. Thus, soap operas consecrate the division of the labour force and the segregation of sexual roles in the production process of capitalist societies. This impact is all the greater given that soap operas are not limited to local broadcasts, but are often imported and exported.

THE SOAP OPERA:
AN INTERNATIONAL CULTURAL PRODUCT

As we saw in Chapter 4, culture has become synonymous with capital expansion. The process of media internationalization was begun in the 1850s by French, British and German press agencies. In the 1920s, American advertising agencies began expanding their operations abroad. The twenties also marked the beginning of the internationalization of American film production under the form of co-productions. The same occurred with cartoon production in the 1930s. During World War II, a Spanish version of *Reader's Digest* was created for distribution in Latin America. In recent years, the process of internationalization has spread to a new branch of the media industry: cultural products such as television programmes, video tapes, films, magazines, etc. In capitalist countries, where this new market was first created, the cultural industry supports and disseminates a lifestyle based on the consumption and purchase of material goods. The industrialization of cultural commodities has led to the export and spread of a mode of economic development.

The result of the internationalization of media consumption is that the same products are seen on all screens around the world, or are displayed in every newspaper stand in all the world's major cities. These products, which originate in Western capitalist societies, invade developing and non-industrialized countries, and, as Michèle Mattelart (1981) has claimed, tend to impose a way of perceiving media programmes as well as programming. The television programmes exported to these countries convey ideas based on Western values of what is good and bad. In the last chapter, we saw that these values engender a universal image of the ideal woman, which can be found in various television programmes such as soap operas.

For Mattelart (1981), the soap opera is a particularly efficient form of television production for integrating women into their everyday lives. How is this done? First, soap operas are generally intended for a mainstream female audience. Moreover, they are present, in varying ways, in all capitalist countries; they are omnipresent on commercial television networks; they are an important vehicle for advertising, the contents of which are often related to the topics addressed in the day's programme; and, finally, they are an agent of audience segregation.

Some of these programmes are broadcast on a large scale so as to bring the "good news" to all women of the world. For example, in Latin America, a number of companies specialize in exporting Spanish-language soap operas. Thus, directors must comply with the requirements of these companies regarding content production. To reduce production costs and increase profits, directors must submit to the rules of serial production by resorting to stereotypes and exploiting trivial situations. These approaches appear to be very popular: in 1979, Televisa, Mexico's commercial television network, exported 24,000 hours of soap operas to the United States, South America, Central America and the West Indies. As there is a large Hispanic market in the United States, Mattelart (1981) reported that, by the end of 1976, Televisa was received in more than 13 million households in the United States, while Mexico's national television network reached only 5 million households.

But what "good news" is exported in soap operas? Usually, they are riddled with scenes of violence and sex—though not always explicit—mixed with scenes of various forms of bribe, rape, etc., all of which take place within a family context where women are totally subordinated to their spouses. Mattelart (1981) has contended that, in these programmes, social hardships such as poverty and violence are always presented as individual misfortunes. In these situations, the good must be rewarded and the bad punished. While we may agree with Hall's (1980) suggestion that contents are negotiated by viewers, it is also true that these types of messages cannot lead audiences to liberate society from violence; on the contrary, they foster violence. Nevertheless, not all soap operas contain physical violence. Among these, two of the most frequently watched were *Dallas* and *Dynasty*. In the next section we will discuss why these shows were so popular.

Dallas: A Cross-cultural Analysis

The programme *Dallas* portrayed the life of a rich Texan family, the Ewings, whose fortune was secured through the financial success of the grandfather's oil business. After the grandfather's death, the family business ended up in the hands of two of his sons, J.R. and Bobby—modern versions of Cain and Abel. During the programme's early years, their wives experienced nothing but misery, and it was only the grandmother's empathy that kept them on the Southfork Ranch, the sacred homestead where most of the family members lived. Later, however, the storyline was peppered with marriage, widowhood and divorce, which created a state of constant turmoil within the family. As a result, the premise of *Dallas* may be summed up as a series of interpersonal conflicts caused by the explosion of the original family core; thus, it corresponded to the classic soap opera scenario.

Even though this was a typically American product, the programme was successful almost everywhere in the world. Of all the countries where the programme was introduced, Japan was the only instance of failure (Liebes and Katz, 1988). Its popularity was as astonishing as the complexity of its storyline, in which each character had a serious conflict with just about all the other main characters. Traces of these conflicts were omnipresent, to the extent that understanding each new intrigue often required having a global view of the entire scenario.

How was this type of intrigue "interpreted" by audiences from different cultures? This was the question addressed in a study conducted by Elihu Katz and Tamar Liebes (1990) on a number of couples from the Jerusalem area who represented four cultural groups (Arabs, Jews recently arrived from Russia, Jews of Moroccan origin, and Jews living on kibbutzim), plus a group of white Americans from Los Angeles. All participants were under 40 years of age, and none were university-educated. The study showed unequivocally that all of these groups had the same general understanding of the programme content. Thus, the dramatic components of the show were sufficiently universal so as not to require long explanations in complex dialogues, at least for people belonging to the same social class.

If the general understanding of the show's intrigues seemed to be identical, their interpretation, however, could vary according to culture. Katz and Liebes (1990) identified three types of interpretations in their study: sociological and psychological decodings, which focus on the characters, and ideological decodings, which emphasize the show's production. Let us see what these differences mean concretely.

For Katz and Liebes (1990), *sociological decodings* are ones which identify characters according to their *place* within the family (the head of the family clan, the brother, the mother, etc.) and are used to analyze the characters as if they belonged to a real family. The more traditional groups such as the Arabs and Moroccans tended more towards these types of interpretations. *Psychological decodings* are ones in which the characters are referred to by name. The authors of the study identified two variants in this category. The Jewish kibbutz members used the characters' names and discussed their actions not in terms of social norms, but in terms of their personalities and psychological problems (a difficult childhood, for example). However, the Americans used the actual names of the actors playing a role and explained their actions on the basis of the actors' contract negotiations with producers (for example, when a character was written out of the show, it was because she asked for too much money). Finally, *ideological decodings*, which were most common among Russian subjects, placed the emphasis not on the characters, but on the *producers* who control them; thus, the story became secondary. In this case, people concentrated on the fact that producers manipulated viewers via the characters created by the show's authors. In other words, when Russian Jews watched this show, they put aside the story, the characters and the actors in order to focus on the way in which the content attempted to influence viewers.

Katz and Liebes (1990) divided these three perspectives into two large categories: *referential decodings* and *critical decodings*. The former includes the viewers who described scenarios and roles by referring to reality, thus comparing the actions of the characters with what goes on in real life. The latter focuses on the viewers who treated the programme as a construction based on a specific narrative formula which transmitted certain messages. Given that this type of interpretation takes into consideration the social construction of the soap opera, it is considered to be "critical." The referential perspective was used more often among Arab and Moroccan subjects, while the critical perspective was used frequently by Americans, Russian Jews and kibbutz members. A fairly obvious example of these two types of decodings lies in the respondents' answers to explain the presence of several children in the programme. Arab and Moroccan viewers explained this fact by referring primarily to the importance of children—the "foci of family integration" and "sources of happiness" (Katz and Liebes, 1990: 54)—as heirs. The other groups of viewers suggested that children in soap operas represent sources of conflict, which are useful for enlivening storylines, thus attracting more viewers and generating more profit.

The fact that respondents based their answers on more than the show's content to explain some of the programmes' features led Katz and Liebes (1990) to suggest that this type of programme invites viewers to reflect on their own situation. This viewpoint is similar to the findings of feminist studies which have revealed that women are not passive viewers, as they had long been described, but instead watch soap operas with a critical eye. From all appearances, *Dallas* was also an important source of discussion between peers, regardless of gender. Putting aside the Ewing family's wealth, the programme offered an occasion to discuss interpersonal problems experienced by people from different social classes. The authors of the study mention in passing that all the Russian emigrants were particularly skilled in perceiving that one of the show's implicit messages was to persuade audiences that the rich are unhappy or immoral, and that people from other social classes "are better off" (Katz and Liebes, 1990: 57). Thus, the programme conveyed the dominant ideology, justifying class differences by claiming that it takes all kinds—the rich and the poor—to make a society and that the poor are just as happy as the rich. Moreover, when questioned about the American lifestyle, the viewers concluded that their own lifestyle was superior to that of Americans, which was believed to be similar to that of the characters on *Dallas*. As we will see in the next section, this type of decoding seems to motivate many viewers to watch soap operas. It would appear that soap opera consumers enjoy watching these shows because they see that their situation is not so bad after all. It is this kind of reaction that led Michèle Mattelart (1986) to say that soap operas are catalysts which serve to make life easier for women (for men too, for that matter), as well as help them accept their fate. Thus, soap operas are seen as a means of maintaining the social consensus and preventing protest and resistance. Is this the reason why *Dallas* was so popular throughout the world?

According to Katz and Liebes (1990), the programme enjoyed widespread success, even if it was American, because it offered embellished images of the family, social success, sexuality and women's place that other cultural groups could either disagree or identify with. Moreover, the show provoked a broad range of discussion where people attempted to distinguish themselves vs. Americans. *Dallas* became a global success, despite its utterly American nature, by transforming itself into a topic for self-questioning, and for discussion within the family and even in public. This last observation confirms the assertions made by feminist researchers analyzed in the previous chapters concerning the effects of soap operas on audiences. As Méar et al. (1981) pointed out, the constitution of the soap opera universe enables one to look at certain realities with a critical eye.

All the cultural groups in the Katz and Liebes study engaged in these kinds of discussions in which a link was made between programme content and people's personal lives. However, Katz and Liebes (1990) note that this response was not related to the degree of viewer involvement. Regardless of whether viewers believed the story in general was real or not, their decodings led them to comment on reality because they believed the story had at least an element of truth, even if it was dramatized. These smatterings of reality were enough to enable viewers, even the more critical ones, to identify with the characters or with their experiences. In short, one's involvement in a story is unrelated to the perspective from which one watches a programme, be it either referential or critical. Consider, for example, a situation where viewers spend a good deal of time decoding a manipulative message. In this case, their involvement in the story takes on a different form depending on whether their goal is to resist the message (or its "appeal") or to experience the emotions of the characters in the programme.

Katz and Liebes (1990) found that, in general, viewers were excellent critics, a fact which supports the findings of feminist studies which claim that female viewers are critical *vis-à-vis* the programmes they watch, even those that appeal to them. Katz and Liebes observed that this critical perspective manifested particularly among people of less-educated groups, who had a tendency to criticize members of their own group, while people from better-educated groups directed few critical remarks at themselves. Some of the more severe criticisms were those expressed by Russian Jews concerning the directors of *Dallas*, whom they accused of engaging in cultural propaganda.

One of the main effects of the show, and at the same time one of the reasons for its popularity, is that it generated discussion that could be extended to other issues. According to Katz and Liebes (1990), these discussions took two forms: there were debates run by "group archivists" which enabled people who missed an episode to be updated or who had difficulty understanding segments of the show to receive explanations; and there were "debates over interpretation" which consisted of evaluating content from moral and aesthetic points of view. It is during this latter phase that viewers adapted the show's content to their own culture.

Katz and Liebes (1990) give two reasons for the popularity of *Dallas*: its *primordiality* and its *seriality*. *Primordiality* refers to the universality of family experiences and conflicts revolving around "sibling rivalry, primogeniture, beloved-but-barren wives, incestual relations, and the like" (Katz and Liebes, 1990: 58). *Seriality*, or *serial structure*, presents the content of the show in the form of "never-ending, always-suspenseful" situations (Katz and Liebes, 1990: 58). In this way, soap operas are very similar to certain forms of literature, as we will see in Chapter 9. The fact that viewers come to know the characters who nevertheless maintain an independent existence provides viewers with "an active and creative viewing experience:" they can watch them live, decode their lives and integrate them into their conversations.

The popularity of *Dallas* was also related to its impact on viewers. As was mentioned earlier, the programme was a source of conversation and discussion of topics that would probably not have been tackled otherwise. It had the effect of creating a link with other social questions, such as the division of domestic labour and relations between the rich and the poor. Nevertheless, some subjects were taboo. For example, politics, which was absent from the programme's content, was also avoided in viewer discussion. Thus, the main topics were limited to the family and social relations.

It is important not to generalize the results of this study to other groups. Indeed, the size of the sample and extent of cultural representation was *insignificant*. Moreover, the study took only one programme into consideration.[2] Since audience reception can be different for other types of content, we will now look at a study of *Dynasty*, another television soap opera with worldwide success.

Dynasty: **An Interclass Analysis**

The story of *Dynasty* centred on two families, the Carringtons and the Colbys. The Carrington family was a patriarchal clan headed by Blake, the divorced patriarch who lived with his second wife, Krystle. The Colby family was a matriarchal clan headed by Alexis, Blake's ex-wife. The scenario revolved around the personal and financial conflicts between the two clans. The content was purely American in style, lapsing into extravagant and extreme situations involving wealth, passion, hatred, etc.

The personalities of the two principal female characters were no exception to this rule of excess. Krystle, for example, represented the "perfect woman." Married to Blake Carrington, the fabulously wealthy main character, she was essentially positive, humane, sensitive and, on top of it all, the mother of two beautiful children. Conversely, Alexis was the "evil woman" incarnate. Divorced from Blake Carrington, she was manipulative, ambitious, cold and power-hungry. As a "sexy" woman, Alexis used her "sexual allure" to obtain financial gain and personal favours. The dichotomy between the heroines was so caricatural, and the context of such fabulous wealth so rare, it is difficult to conceive that such characters could exist in real life.

Andrea L. Press (1990) conducted a study of American female viewers whom she interviewed concerning the opposition between the programme's two heroines. Press believed that the unrealistic nature of the characters offered an interesting opportunity to evaluate the ability of female viewers to analyze television characters with respect to their own life experiences. For her study, 41 American women were questioned: 20 were from the working classes, that is, their husbands, or the women themselves—if they were divorced or widowed—were labourers (butchers, factory workers, hairdressers, etc.); and 21 were from the middle classes (i.e., professional and university-educated).

Questioned about the realism of the scenario, the working-class viewers admitted to believing that the lifestyle depicted in *Dynasty* probably corresponds with the lives of extremely rich people, and that somewhere there definitely existed women like Krystle and Alexis. In the same breath, these women claimed they did not like such programmes since they were too unrealistic, though this did not prevent them from watching these shows. Conversely, it appears that the other group of women viewed television above all as entertainment and television content as fiction which does not necessarily have to reflect reality. Thus, while they accorded a certain credibility to the scenario and its characters, middle-class viewers were a little more sceptical and admitted to taking the stories "with a grain of

---

[2] For an other discussion on *Dallas*, see I. Ang (1985) *Watching Dallas,* London: Methuen.

salt" (cited in Press, 1990: 165). At the same time, they still managed to identify with some of the two heroines' experiences. However, the differences in interpretation between the two classes of women do not end here.

Most middle-class women made a link between their economic situation and that of Krystle and Alexis, claiming that the only major difference between themselves and the two heroines was that the latter were wealthier. The middle-class women thus reinforced the biological feminist approach, which assumes that women form a homogeneous group without any class differentiation, and that all women play the roles of mother and wife and have the same feelings (love, hatred, jealousy, etc.). In contrast, none of the working-class viewers made this distinction. These viewers simply asserted that somewhere in the world there lived women who had such extreme lives, without alluding to the differences in social status between themselves and the two female leads. According to Press (1990), their silence can be explained in that there was such a great financial disparity between these two groups of women that the situation appeared to threaten them and they, rationally and consciously, could not or would not imagine such situations arising in real life.

Thus, from the viewpoint of content interpretation, working-class women were less critical than middle-class women. The former did not concentrate on any class differences between themselves and Krystle and Alexis, either in terms of financial situation, lifestyle, or any other aspect of economic status. Instead, they focused on the differences in "opportunities" between the two groups of women with respect to everyday activities.

Conversely, middle-class women concentrated on the differences between themselves and *Dynasty*'s two heroines. They often criticized the two characters, while at the same time referring to situations in the programme as a means of understanding their relationships in their own families or circles of friends. Their attitude was therefore paradoxical: on the one hand, they were critical of the character portrayals themselves, but, on the other, they continued to identify with many of the heroines' experiences. Some female researchers explain this paradox by arguing that this identification is a means for women to feel morally superior to Krystle and Alexis, who, despite being rich, are often caught up in family dramas. This attitude is similar to that of the cultural groups in the Katz and Liebes (1990) study of *Dallas*. Press agrees with this interpretation, claiming that certain situations increase the moral value of the lives of female viewers, thereby providing the necessary motivation to continue watching the programme.

In short, we can see that the impact of soap opera content on audience members differs depending on social class. Press's (1990) analysis shows that middle-class viewers identified more readily with the traditional values attributed to women by comparing the heroines' roles with their own roles within the family. They appeared to be divided between a feminist attitude, criticizing the female leads for their lack of personality, and an anti-feminist attitude, claiming these characters were not good mothers or wives, thus implying that women should assume full responsibility for the family's happiness.

The response of working-class women was simpler and more consistent. First, they were more sensitive to the values associated with the heroines' lifestyle. For example, they criticized scenarios which disapproved of the lifestyle of the female leads, whom they found attractive and pleasant. Press (1990) accounts for this attitude by arguing that, since working-class women have serious financial problems, they are forced to concentrate on the material aspects of life instead of issues of interpersonal relations.

Press sees these observations as supporting the dominant ideology: " . . . the mass media play an ideological role in society, reinforcing and encouraging general world-views and specific beliefs which help secure the position of those groups already in power" (Press, 1990: 158). For her, the response of working-class women serves the interests of the dominant classes because the programme gave the impression that women from all social classes, rich or poor, experienced the same interpersonal conflicts, which in the show were only aggravated by wealth. The two soap operas *Dallas* and *Dynasty* illustrate that one of the objectives of this type of programme is to show that not everyone can be happy at the same time, especially with regard to love. Thus, the dominant classes are able to take advantage of the consensus created by soap operas, which is that middle-class, and even working-class, women have a better quality of social life than women from the dominant classes, who are too rich and too powerful.

THE PROMOTION OF THE DOMINANT IDEOLOGY BY WAY OF THE FAMILY

The typical representation of the soap opera family is not that of a united clan. Modleski (1982) has argued that soap opera intrigues give the impression that the family is perpetually unstable; its evolution must be closely followed in order to understand the difficulties of each family member. She claims that female viewers are attracted to soap operas not only because mothers are almost always portrayed as positive characters, with whom women can identify, but also because of the tolerance traditionally shown by the female character, whose role it is to keep the family together. In this context, soap opera content appears to be developed to give female viewers the impression that they are wiser than soap heroines, which consequently makes them feel good about their own situations: even if their situations are far from perfect, things could be worse. According to this perspective, the viewer's response is to sympathize with the hardships of the good characters and to judge the bad seeds "fairly," without nevertheless identifying with any particular character.

Clearly, the concept of the family, as portrayed in soap operas, does not owe its success to the fact that it reproduces family life as experienced by viewers: few families are like the Ewings or the Carringtons. In this way, the soap opera family is a surrogate family. According to Modleski (1987), soap operas promote the family as a fundamental social value not by giving the example of the ideal family, but by providing one of a family in constant turmoil, where members are constantly asked to demonstrate comprehension and tolerance. Despite the social distortion they convey, soap operas help create the illusion of community for people who feel isolated. The need for this illusion is sufficiently strong to captivate audiences despite the immoral or socially unacceptable conduct of the programme's characters. This dependence, which is fed by the fear of solitude, provides the ideal groundwork to construct contents involving a series of extreme situations where producers can impose their values: tolerance of main characters, who usually represent good, or rejection of casual characters, who are often associated with evil. The problems experienced by family members are rarely, if ever, among those for which forgiveness does not help reinforce the family.

> As a rule, only those issues which can be tolerated and ultimately pardoned are introduced on soap operas. The list includes careers for women, abortions, premarital and extramarital sex, alcoholism, divorce, mental and even physical cruelty. An issue like homosexuality, which could explode the family structure rather than temporarily disrupt it, is simply ignored (Modleski, 1982: 93).

On television, the valorization of homosexual couples is rarely shown and is not commensurate with its occurrence in our society. Over the years, however, a number of Québec programmes have included homosexual characters. Still, if female homosexuality, which on the surface is less shocking, is presented as an innocuous condition in *Un signe de feu* or *Des dames de coeur*, male homosexuality is portrayed only by exceedingly obliging characters (*Jamais deux sans toi*) or ones who are burlesque or frivolous (*La p'tite vie*). These compensations are necessary to repair the "evil" which this deviant behaviour brings to the family, for as Modleski (1982) notes, despite being denaturalized, soap opera's content relieves real anxieties and satisfies real needs and desires.

Soap Operas as a Source of Confusion

As we saw earlier, for the sake of continuity, soap opera endings must always be temporary. As soon as a problem is solved on the surface, new elements emerge to make it appear more complex than ever. The suspected mistress, who turns out to be harmless to the couple's marriage, will reappear in the next episode as a "blackmailer," threatening to take advantage of old secrets. It will come out that the victim of this blackmail committed some unspeakable act to the villainess, who as a result will appear as the real victim, and so on.

Because they have no ending, Modleski has claimed that soap operas lead viewers nowhere, least of all "out of ignorance into true knowledge" (1982: 105). As opposed to cinema, where dramatic intensity occurs at the film's conclusion and the denouement brings coherence to the story, dramatic situations of soap operas give rise to new, increasingly complex intrigues, instead of winding down to a single conclusion. In the case of movies, screenplay writers often ask the audience to identify with one character for the duration of a film. In soap operas, the unfolding of parallel intrigues constitutes a series of relatively independent stories, offering different characters for audience members to identify with in rapid succession. For Modleski, the fact that movie-goers are mostly male and that soap opera viewers are mostly female is a reflection of a type of social deterrent to keep women from efficiently identifying with power:

> If, as Mulvey claims, the identification of the spectator with 'a male protagonist' results in the spectator's becoming 'the representative of power,' the multiple identification which occurs in soap opera results in the spectator's being divested of power. For the spectator is never permitted to identify with a character completing an entire action. Instead of giving us one 'powerful ideal ego . . . who can make things happen and control

events better than the subject/spectator can,' soap operas present us with numerous limited egos, each in conflict with the others, and continually thwarted in its attempts to control events because of inadequate knowledge of other people's plans, motivations, and schemes (Modleski, 1982: 91).

Although Modleski's remarks are part of a much larger debate—that of the psychoanalytical effects of cinematography—we can still make the following observations. On the one hand, in films it is easy to identify with main characters, who accomplish an action, that is, identify a problem, set goals, plan a strategy of problem resolution, and achieve a result which can be evaluated in relation to the objectives. On the other hand, soap operas involve complex intrigues, numerous characters and short, intertwined sequences, all of which make it difficult for the same kind of character identification to occur. Such complexity has led Modleski (1982) to describe soap operas not as conservative, contrary to popular belief, but as *liberal*, chiefly because of the maternal characters, who are ever-present and have a liberal status *par excellence*. Indeed, like every well-meaning liberal, these characters consider all sides of an issue and are incapable of finding definite solutions to crises. This is what characterizes soap operas; it is also why Modleski refers to these programmes as liberal: soap opera mothers act as a counterweight to the conservatism of the other characters.

Such open-endedness could result in an ego divided by limited or incomplete situations, where conflicts are never-ending, and new complications invariably coming about before a feeling of resolution can take root. Soap opera producers are careful about preserving a degree of imprecision with respect to story endings in order to create opportunities to recover intrigues if the needs of the scenario justify it. According to Modleski, this cautiousness conceals the impossibility of concluding all of a show's intrigues satisfactorily. The web of soap operas is sometimes so complex as to make the incoherence between the characters impossible to resolve.

CONCLUSION

In short, if one of the strengths of soap operas is to depict dramatic situations with a touch of realism, their *denouements* often lack credibility. For example, soaps tend to exaggerate the moral correctness of the masses. Heroes are regularly despised by their entourage because of false accusations brought against them. After repeated social humiliation, the truth surfaces and the character is completely vindicated. This kind of *denouement* implicitly suggests that, in the long run, innocent victims of the enraged masses do not suffer grave damage. In this way, soap operas can be seen as supporting the dominant ideology by preventing real situations from leading to a questioning of the status quo.

As Méar *et al.* (1981) have said, the soap opera vision of reality is deformed. In many ways, the personalities of soap opera characters do not reflect the diversity of people who make up Canadian society. For example, their representation never corresponds with the cultural diversity of society. With the exception of a few shows which have "token" black and Asian characters, soap opera content features white characters only. Moreover, these characters rarely come from the underprivileged classes. Despite the fact that 20% of people in society live below the poverty line (*Le Devoir*, May 1, 1991), the issue of poverty is hardly ever tackled, nor reflected in soap operas. It is therefore possible to argue that these programmes provide a skewed reflection of real-life social situations.

Finally, as was suggested at the beginning of this chapter, the content of soap operas can often be compared with that of popular literature, at least in terms of the themes covered. Nevertheless, given that novels must have an ending, it is difficult to imagine how the content structure of these two forms of communication can be the same. In order to have a better understanding of the similarities and differences between these two forms, the next chapter will present an analysis of popular novels and their readers.

CHAPTER 8

POPULAR LITERATURE: FROM HARLEQUINS TO DETECTIVE NOVELS

PROLOGUE

Mr. and Mrs. Peabody have decided to spend a quiet evening at home. In order to escape what has been an exceptionally trying day, and because they have nothing special to say to each other, they both decide to partake in the pleasure of reading. While Margaret devours Forbidden Love Under a Tropical Sun, *George relishes the adventures of Lou Dickrous. Margaret finds pleasure in Harlequin romance, that is, romance with a tinge of sexuality. Of course, she identifies with the heroine, and understands all too well the hero's insufferable attitude. If he is such a beast, it is because he loves her. She even convinces herself that George's indifference at supper does not necessarily mean he does not love her; instead he must be burning with a hidden, inner passion, which she must surely explore. As for George, he is reading about Lou Dickrous's third rape, his sixth mistress, who will shortly become his sixth female cadaver. Lou Dickrous has already manhandled a dozen or so women, and called his mother so she can come do a little cleaning. Lou Dickrous has still found time to travel around the world three times. He has cracked a major drug trafficking ring by gunning down every ring leader in Miami, Hong Kong and Vancouver. He has defused an enemy atomic bomb with a simple toothpick. And, on top of it all, he has uncovered the secret of how they get the caramel inside the Caramilk bar.*

INTRODUCTION

The popular literature which the Peabodys find so interesting is another form of communication that influences the socialization process. This type of "assembly-line" mass culture is devoured by thousands of people and livens up otherwise boring evenings. It is this ever-increasing, now worldwide, popularity of this genre that has sparked an interest among numerous researchers. Those, however, who prescribe to the dominant paradigm of communication studies do not appear to be interested in such "women's subjects," even though there are as many men who consume these types of books as there are women. According to the principles of the dominant approaches, there are no marked differences in the impact of the different genres of popular literature on male and female consumers.

Yet, as we saw in the previous chapter, soap operas—which use the same types of content as popular literature—affect female audiences in a particular way (delivering a liberating effect, among other things). Do popular novels have the same impact on readers? Or, on the contrary, are they more an agent of repression, whose sole effect is to keep men and women in the shackles of social stereotypes? To answer these questions, we must first look at the content of popular novels, as well as the conditions in which they are produced. Only then is it possible to study their impact on female and male readers.

Popular literature has gone through many changes over the last 20 years. In the fifties, sentimental novels abounded with virgin heroines and presented the heterosexual model as the only solution to all of women's problems. Feminine virginity in popular literature was to remain in vogue until the sexual liberation (much to the chagrin, to say the least, of seventies' feminists).

The seventies was a turning point in popular literature, with the emergence of the theme of rape. In most cases, rape was associated with an act of vengeance against a heroine who was invariably described as untamable and unrelenting in her will to win. This new, more spectacular, type of novel, which replaced the sentimental novel and its equally mushy heroine, was based on the assertion that deep down, women want to be raped: rape was seen as a way for them to live out their sexuality without having to assume any responsibility. Feminists are highly critical of this type of assertion. By concentrating on the effects of the novels instead of the reasons for their attraction, feminist researchers looked at various genres not only from a psychological perspective, which focuses on women's desire for self-fulfilment, but also from a sociological perspective. Essentially, romances are seen as an instrument of patriarchal indoctrination through which women come to see themselves as men's objects. In the eighties, feminist researchers began to analyze the phenomenal appeal that popular novels have for male and female readers, and the reasons behind it. In this chapter I will concentrate on two sexually stereotyped genres: romance and detective novels.

We will begin our study of popular literature with an analysis of the best known and the most widely sold example of this genre: Harlequin Romances. These are the most widely read books by women throughout the world. The following pages are devoted to several feminist analyses of the Harlequin phenomenon in an attempt to uncover the reasons for their popularity and the interpretations that women make of these novels. This is followed by an analysis of another genre of popular literature, detective novels, which, it would appear, are especially popular among male readers. We will end this chapter with a comparative analysis of the content and readers of these two genres.

HARLEQUIN ROMANCE: A RECIPE FOR SUCCESS

Harlequin Romances are produced according to a very specific formula to which each female author must adhere. The number of pages is determined by the publisher, and a "standard" plot is applied to each story. Moreover, heroes and heroines must never stray very far from the model dictated by the formula. For example, male protagonists generally have black hair and dark eyes. If, on a flight of fancy, an author decides the hero should have blond hair and blue eyes, these more "feminine" traits have to be compensated for by a dark tan so as to accentuate his virile appearance. Thus, it is possible to deviate from the formula on the condition that the effect remain the same. This section, then, deals with a study of the Harlequin formula. But in order to have a good understanding of the Harlequin concept, we will first consider the historical development of the conditions surrounding the production of these novels.

The Enterprise

Harlequin Enterprises Ltd. was founded in Manitoba in 1949. In its early days, the enterprise distributed detective novels and adventure stories throughout much of Canada. In 1958, Harlequin launched its first romance and, seven years later, it decided to devote its activities solely to this genre. The enterprise moved into the international market first by storming the American market in 1971, when it bought the largest publisher of romance novels (Mills and Boon), and later, in 1978, by moving into the French and Québec markets. Then, in the early eighties, in an effort to increase production, the enterprise decided to buy its chief American competitor, Simon and Shuster, while maintaining a distribution agreement for the United States with Simon and Shuster's owners. Today, the enterprise's Canadian operations are owned by Torstar Inc.,[1] and while Harlequin has its own sales force for distribution in Canada, it has distribution agreements with well-known corporations in other countries: Hachette in France, Axel Spring in the United Kingdom, and Mondadori in Italy (Lorinc, 1994).

By pursuing a policy of continued acquisition and relentless marketing,[2] Harlequin has become the world's largest publisher of romance novels and the true leader in the

---

[1] Torstar Corporation is a Toronto-based conglomerate comprising different enterprises involved in "information and entertainment communications," including the *Toronto Star*, Metroland Printing, Publishing and Distributing, Harlequin Enterprises, Miles Kimball (direct mail catalogues), Marshall Editions (non-fiction books), and Southam Inc.

[2] The current (1994) CEO of Harlequin, Brian Hickey, was recruited in the 1980s from the "company that makes Johnson's Wax" (Lorinc, 1994).

genre. As John Lorinc suggests, "Harlequin became synonymous with romance" and "is to books what Bata is to shoes—a recognized Canadian winner in the international bear-pits for mass-produced, brand-name consumer goods" (1994: 1). With a 35% share of worldwide mass-paperback sales, Harlequin exports books in 23 languages to more than 100 overseas countries and controls "four-fifths of the [romance] genre's sales" (Lorinc, 1994: 14; Margolis, 1991). Its three principal collections (Harlequin, Silhouette, and Mira) provide a steady stream of over 200 million low-priced books each year (see Table 8.1). In 1994, Harlequin Enterprises' operating profits were $70.7 million, up 13% from the previous year (Torstar Corporation Annual Report, 1994: 11). In 1992, the enterprise released 60 English titles each month in the United States and Canada, and 18 French titles each month in Québec (Torstar Corporation Annual Report, 1993: 15). In Canada, Harlequin books are distributed through more than 10,000 retail outlets and through direct mail sales (Milliot, 1993). Retail sales are made through independent distributors in the same way magazines are sold. However, despite the large number of retailers carrying Harlequin romances, direct-mail sales still account for 50% of total sales (Lorinc, 1994).

Perhaps the most interesting change in Harlequin's operations has been its move towards cross-media promotion and products. Recent deals have involved the enterprise in a variety of projects such as made-for-TV movies co-produced with Alliance Communications (with distribution made through CTV, CBS and Bertelsmann), partial stories in Sassy magazine, and even a setup for on-line reviews and reader-feedback services on the Internet (Anderson, 1994). Further, Harlequin is looking to expand its operations to cable-television, videocassette (Milliot, 1995), and CD-ROM publishing (Lorinc, 1994). In addition to product and market diversification, Harlequin is still aggressively pursuing its expansion in international markets. One of the most disquieting developments in Harlequin's recent corporate activities is its expansion into the sphere of education. In 1994, Torstar created the "Supplementary Education business segment" after purchasing Frank Shaffer Publishers Inc. (Torstar Corporation Interim Report, April 24, 1995). To what end will Harlequin use such a 'business segment'?

As we mentioned earlier, Harlequin Romances are translated into 23 languages and distributed to over 100 countries. Table 8.1 clearly illustrates the annual sales growth Harlequin has experienced in the past 20 years.

Harlequin is said to have approximately 1,500 "active authors" and receive over "20,000 unsolicited manuscripts and queries" each year (Torstar Corporation Annual Report, 1994: 14–5). The following is a sample of the many different collections of Harlequin Romances available on the market:

- *Harlequin Romance*, 192 pages, 4/month, $2.99;

- *Harlequin Presents*, 192 pages, 4/month, $2.99;

- *Harlequin Presents Plus*, 192 pages, 2/month, $2.99;

- *Harlequin Superromance*, 304 pages, 4/month, $3.75;

- *Harlequin American Romance*, 256 pages, 4/month, $3.50;

- *Harlequin Temptation*, 224 pages, 4/month, $2.99;
- *Harlequin Intrigue*, 256 pages, 4/month, $3.25;
- *Harlequin Historicals*, 304 pages, 4/month, $4.50; (from Harlequin Enterprises Ltd., 1995, publicity pamphlet).

TABLE 8.1 **Annual sales growth of Harlequin Enterprises (Canadian $ millions)**

	Worldwide	Canada	USA	Overseas
1980		15	105	
1986	206			
1987	204			
1988	202			
1989	190			
1990	194			
1991	193			
1992	205	20	201	197
1993	199	21	223	200
1994	188		242	
1995	180			

Source: Torstar Corporation Annual Reports and Milliot. 1995, 1994, 1993, figures have been rounded off

Harlequin Sales Data (Canadian dollars):

US Sales:	1994	$241.5m (+8.5%)
	1993	$222.6m (+11%)
	1992	$201.1m (+14%)
North America:	1993	$244m
	1992	$221m
Canadian Sales		
(5% of total, Margolis, 1991):	1993	$21m (calculated)
	1992	$20m (calculated)
Overseas sales:	1993	$200m
	1992	$197m

Source: Torstar Corporation Annual Reports 1992–1994

Books Sold:	1994	188,000,000
(declining)	1993	N/A
	1992	205,300,000
	1991	193,100,000
	1990	196,500,000
	1983	215,000,000 (Bettinotti)

Source: Torstar Corporation Annual Reports 1990–1994

Harlequin claims to reach 50.4 million readers worldwide: 15% of women 15 years of age or older read at least one per year, across all markets (Torstar Corporation Annual Report, 1994: 14–5). The following is a demographic profile of North American romance novel readers:

- most are women aged 15 and older
- 70% are under 49 years old
- 45% are college-educated
- 51% are employed
- 41% have an average family income of more than $25,000
- each reader spends up to $30 per month on romance fiction[3] (Margolis, 1991: 59).

In order to maintain high book sales, Harlequin Enterprises takes advertising very seriously. As a manager said: "getting the book into the hands of the reader has been the key to getting the reader hooked on, not just a single book but the entire category" (Jones, 1990). In addition to its catalogue, the enterprise advertises in the print and television media, and especially on radio, a medium that is "much more geared to a female audience and more likely to reach the target market than book reviews" (Milliot, 1994). All the same, modernity beckons. In recent years, the enterprise has redesigned its marketing strategies to give it a "more contemporary image," hitting the information superhighway and participating in romance forums on the Internet, CompuServe and other on-line systems (Torstar Corporation Annual Report, 1992). It also has created a database where people can find information on their favourite author.

In addition to all these marketing strategies, the enterprise does regular "test-market covers" and market research studies to make sure it targets the right group of people. This information is certainly used to advantage, since Harlequin invested as much as $5,000,000 in the ad/promotion campaign for the Silhouette Shadows collection (Schulafer 1993). While the enterprise does not spend as much on each collection, this nevertheless shows that it considers promotion to be an essential business expense.

The popularity of Harlequins is partially due to their attractive prices: a Harlequin sells for as little as $2.99. But this is certainly not their sole attraction. What is it that attracts female readers? Is it the characters? The scenarios? Or romance itself? Let us look at these different aspects in greater detail.

The Characters

Harlequin Enterprises claims that, since the beginning of the 1990s, they have modernized the image of their romances to better represent contemporary North America. Susan Spano tells us that: "in the last few years, the tone of commercial women's fiction

---

[3] Spano (1992) states that romance fiction consumers spend an "average" of $1200/year on romance novels. This presents a considerable contradiction when compared with Margolis' figure of $360/year but it is possible if the Spano consumer is a committed long-term buyer as opposed to Margolis' figure which represents the average sales per consumer—but Spano's figures do not provide the necessary information to explain the contradiction.

changed. Going, if not yet quite gone, are the preoccupations with glitz, glamour and sex that dominated commercial women's fiction in the '80s. . . . What women want is something more integral to their lives" (Spano, 1992: 31). Some authors have even introduced interracial couples (Englander et al. 1995). All the same, says Lorinc (1994), although Harlequin has attempted to modernize the plots of its romance and some characters of the early 80s, several stereotypes persist. What are the recurring characteristics?

In her exhaustive study of Harlequin Romances, Julia Bettinotti (1990) notes that the characters are always introduced into a story in the same way. The heroine appears as early as the first page, since the narrative of the story is expressed through her. Without fail, authors of Harlequin Romances write in the third person, from the heroine's point of view, thus relating her interpretation of events. Does the heroine have to be beautiful, and be "in style," as in soap operas?

It would appear that the answer is no. She must be pretty and self-effacing, and duller than her female rival; in short, she must be an "ordinary girl" (Bettinotti, 1990). It is the hero who will discover the heroine's real beauty, and who will reveal this beauty to the readers. If the heroine is not always beautiful, she is almost always young: in 34% of cases she is between the ages of 22 and 24. She is generally either English or American. In order to emphasize her image as a fragile and available woman—which is the characteristic of the woman idealized in the patriarchal ideology—the heroine is an orphan in 57% of cases, and single in 70%. Finally, if she has a job, it is typically a "feminine" job: secretary (27% of cases), governess (17%) or artist (16%).

As for the hero, he will not appear until 20 pages later, when he meets the heroine. According to Bettinotti, he can be spotted immediately, as his features are essentially the same in every novel, though his age may differ. The young hero is the very image of "masculine" beauty: he is tall, strong and tanned, and has black hair, dark eyes, a firm chin and an authoritarian mouth that denotes an unyielding character with a hint of arrogance. The strong features of this perfect male specimen is enough to make every woman fall to her knees. As Bettinotti (1990) notes, he is not simply virile, he is totally virile. As for the older hero, he is between the ages of 30 and 35 (40% of cases) and is usually English or Greek. He sometimes has both nationalities, which gives him an ambivalent nature. Thus he is sometimes an "angel" when his Anglo-Saxon character prevails, and sometimes a "demon" when he allows his Mediterranean or Arab side to show through. Like the heroine, he is often an orphan (37% of cases) and most often single (67%). Strangely enough, however, these characteristics do not make him any more vulnerable, as in the case of the heroine, but instead bolder and more determined. And it is usually for this reason that he is a landowner (40%) or president of a large corporation (26%).

Moreover, Bettinotti (1990) notes that Harlequin protagonists are always accompanied by supporting characters, namely male and female rivals (73%). The fact that they are only secondary characters, however, does not necessarily mean that they play a small role in the scenario. Nevertheless, their existence serves simply as a foil to the heroine and hero. In general, the fate of female (58%) and male (38%) rivals is to disappear without a trace. They are also often deserted by the hero (15%) or heroine (24%).

Finally, a few other minor characters enter into the world of Harlequins. They make only sporadic appearances and are introduced either as the heroine's friend and confidante (usually the most constant of this type of character), or as the children of the hero, who employs the heroine as governess, nurse or teacher. Invariably, a governess figures in every story: she is either a plump, jovial "nanny" whose role is to watch over the heroine, or a hostile, stuck-up "old hag" who is as tall as she is thin. All Harlequin characters, especially the hero and heroine, have a curious tendency to travel extensively, and their experiences appear sometimes to drag on or happen in a flash, depending on the occasion.

Space and Time

The heroine is a globetrotter, a frenetic traveller. The reasons for these trips, which are taken at lightning speed, are often incongruous, or unimportant. As Bettinotti (1990) points out, the trips must not interfere with the rapid development of the two main characters' storyline. The heroine journeys to many exotic places, each one a place more conducive to love, dreaming and escape than the last, yet a place that the characters only glance at, as if at a picture book.

The characters evolve within familiar places as well, such as the home, city streets and the office, in other words, places that are related "by cause and effect" to the characters and their vision of the world (Bettinotti, 1990). When the hero is a president of a corporation and the heroine his secretary, the two characters evolve in the same material world. In this situation, Bettinotti continues, their antagonism arises out of the clash between the female world and the male world. The heroine's trips tend to destabilize her situation. They take her far from her familiar, cosy and protective "home" to a strange and hostile "foreign place" which is the hero's home turf, but where she is vulnerable. Finally, the confrontation between these two worlds ceases on the last page of the novel when, at last, the heroine enters into the "wonderful" universe of the couple. This is where the Harlequin novel leaves her. What happens next is never known.

Time, on the other hand, is more flexible: it may be long or short; it may accelerate or slow down depending on the intrigue. A few lines may be enough to summarize a day, a month or a year; then again, numerous pages may be required to describe a brief moment of love or a short, but tough, confrontation. Time is not the object of the Harlequin novel. The real object is the story of the confrontations between a couple, two people who, at the beginning, appear ill-suited simply because of miscommunication, but who in the end become the ideal couple.

The Scenario

According to Bettinotti (1990), the Harlequin scenario is a series of facts linked together to depict a stereotypical structure. In other words, using a well-defined formula in which each situation is foreseen and has its own meaning and purpose, each Harlequin consists of a scenario based on every stereotype of the sentimental novel. Thus, the basic scenario of a Harlequin novel (i.e., *boy meets girl*) develops with the addition of stereotypical motifs (chance meetings, squabbles, etc.). Because these motifs can take endless forms, it is incorrect to assume that Harlequin Romances are all the same.

Bettinotti (1990) has come up with a list of five *stable* motifs, that is, ones that recur in each novel as the driving force behind the development of the scenario. These are the encounter, the confrontation, the seduction, the revelation of love and, finally, the marriage. In order to create variety, other *variable* motifs are added on. Let us now take a closer look at the five stable motifs.

The Encounter Bettinotti (1990) describes the encounter as *the* fundamental motif of every novel. It occurs at the beginning of the story and leads to a series of variable motifs, that is, situations which make for variation from one novel to the next. One such situation is the courtship (12%), which is characterized by a narrative in which the initial encounter is followed by other meetings and the marriage proposal which, of course, is always withheld until the last page. A male-employer/female-employee encounter (40%) is another motif that offers numerous possibilities, and is used almost as often as marriages of convenience. In 99% of cases, the heroine's lot is dependent on the hero who employs her as a governess, nurse or maid. A marriage of convenience is generally the fate of a poor heroine, who needs the money to help a sick parent. She sometimes agrees to marriage in order to exact vengeance on the insensitive hero, for vengeance is another variable motif that can provoke an encounter. Other variable motifs include the reconciliation of a separated or divorced couple, which generally occurs during divorce proceedings; cohabitation out of necessity, which unites a couple through some family association (e.g., the hero is the heroine's tutor, her brother-in-law or her father's friend). In the case of the motif of the imposter, the heroine assumes the identity of a person she is always helping out. The hero will be merciless when he discovers her deceit. Finally, trips, incidents and accidents of all sorts are also among the variable motifs of the encounter.

The Confrontation In Harlequin Romances, the storyline is always directed towards a confrontation. What variable motifs provoke such confrontation? Bettinotti (1990) claims that family rivalries are the most important of these motifs: for example, a father and son can both be attracted to the same heroine. There are also acts of deception, misunderstandings and wrongdoings. Wrongdoings are brought upon by female and male rivals, and cause the hero and the heroine to separate. Jealousy, which leads to squabbles of all kinds, is omnipresent in the Harlequin couple and is often provoked by a misunderstanding, generally on the hero's part. As for personality conflicts, these are based on the different experiences and incompatible behaviour of the two main characters. Finally, troubled marriages, the last variable motif used to set up the confrontation, often bring about antagonistic situations in which the hero and heroine confront each other.

The Seduction During the sixties, the seduction was described with sexual modesty and was limited to a few caresses and the chaste *happy ending kiss*. But over the last few years, the seduction scene has been liberated and become more physical and sexual. The one innocent kiss at the ending is gone; today, the characters' physical attraction is expressed in scenes of outright love-making. The hero is the only man capable of fulfilling the sexual desires and of satisfying the emotional needs of the heroine. In the eighties the motif of intellectual attraction was added, often motivated by a mutual professional undertaking.

The Revelation of Love The revelation of love between the hero and heroine usually comes about after a misunderstanding is cleared up and the facts are re-established. The mystery is solved, wrongdoings are fixed and the truth resurfaces. Suddenly, the hero's aggressive behaviour and cruelty can somehow be explained, and the two main characters can finally be reunited. With the male and female rivals eliminated, the hero and heroine confess their love for each other. Life is wonderful!

Marriage Marriage is the usual outcome of the relationship between the main characters. Bettinotti (1990) has asserted that almost half of Harlequin Romances conclude with a formal marriage proposal, while only a small percentage present common-law life as an alternative. Reconciliation occurs in 33% of separated couples. In some novels, the marriage ceremony is even included.

Confrontation and Marriage

Although, as a general rule, real-life confrontations often lead to disastrous consequences, in Harlequin novels they lead to marriage (Bettinotti, 1990). The heroine and hero are at odds because of their incompatible desires. She wants romantic love, he wants to satisfy his physical desires. She believes in love, he does not. She refuses sexual relations without love. In this confrontation, he is cruel, violent, vengeful and malevolent. She feels scared, frightened, panic-stricken as well as hateful, and sometimes submissive, bordering on enslavement. However, all this antagonism ceases following a confession of love and marriage proposal.

The Harlequin "Romance": A Modern Story?

Bettinotti (1990) and Dubino (1993) assert that there is no real difference in structure between eighteenth-century romance novels and Harlequin Romances. Feminine literature, which was denounced from its beginnings in the early 1700s, has evolved over the centuries within the context of a four-part union between the author, the heroine, the reader and the *world view* they share. Tacked on to the basic scenario of *boy meets girl* are the five stable motifs, invariably in the same order. Moreover, romance novels, the scenarios of which evolve according to a specific formula, invariably end in the same way, with love conquering all. This is unquestionably a point where romances differ from soap operas, whose intrigues are often more complex and always never-ending.

Another significant difference between soap operas and popular novels is that the narration of the latter is always in the third person, expressing the heroine's viewpoint. Bettinotti (1990) claims that this characteristic explains the popularity of Harlequins among female readers: it helps them identify with the heroine, an ordinary girl for whom, at a certain moment, joy triumphs over pain. By using the third person, the Harlequin novel invites female readers to enter the feminine world: a world where women genuinely live out their cultural specificity, where they feel socially inferior, earn less money and are less educated than men, and where they experience only confrontation with men, but nevertheless marry them. Some researchers (e.g., Bettinotti, 1990; Dubino, 1993) have highlighted some of the characteristics of Harlequin Romances that closely reflect the reality of women's everyday lives: the universal existence of male dominance over women; the relations of power within the economic system and the production process; the traditional female jobs (maid, secretary, governess, nurse, etc.), and so on. Other scholars, however, have argued that contemporary Harlequin Romances feature a more emancipated heroine "who is found in new social situations, economically independent, career-oriented, strong and aware of her sexuality" (Hudson, 1989: iii). As Hudson (1989) claims, the new heroine presents new possibilities for women. Thus, there seem to be paradoxical feminist perspectives concerning the extent to which female independence and traditional female stereotypes are conveyed in romances.

Paradoxes in Harlequins are also to be found in the plots. It is curious that, contrary to what goes on in real life—where struggles among couples are resolved by bruises and sometimes even death—Harlequin Romances, of which 65% entail confrontations illustrating disastrous relationships between the sexes, conclude with a "happy ending" symbolized by marriage. Hence, Bettinotti (1990) argues, the story cannot be logically explained in terms of the action, but rather as a coherent solution from a social perspective. Though marriage provides illogical, yet necessary, closure, it is never actualized. Female readers themselves accept marriage because it is one of the social norms. But the rate at which women consume these novels is proof enough that they never expect real-life marriages to have a happy ending: once they complete a novel, they begin another, thus unflaggingly repeating the same journey.

It would appear that it is not dreams, illusions or escape that inspire Harlequin Romances. On the contrary, they are born, developed and multiplied in a capitalist market, which nurtures and exploits a social and ideological context that ensures sales and profits. At this point, it is important to comment on Bettinotti's and Dubino's statement that Harlequins are not structurally different from eighteenth-century novels. If, as we saw in the first part of the book, the economic conditions surrounding mass media production have an impact on content, how can one claim that novels produced massively and according to a very rigid production framework are not significantly different from novels produced through a lengthy and individual creative process? While both types of novels are love stories with happy endings, the former are formula-based, allowing for little originality and produced in easy-to-read language, while the latter are literature studies of social conventions and characters, with subtle and often humorous language.

Harlequin texts, Bettinotti (1990) claims, are based on the fears, frustrations and hardships of being a woman in a man's world, and generally depict the same situations that are denounced in feminist analyses. Yet, it is dreams, illusions and escape that millions of female readers, who have devoured Harlequins for over 30 years, have been seeking. Feminist researchers have conducted studies on the reasons behind, and the effects of, the craze among female readers for Harlequin Romances. In the next section, we will review some of these studies, as well as their conclusions.

HARLEQUIN ROMANCE: ESCAPE FOR AS LITTLE AS $2.99

As we saw earlier, the contents of Harlequin Romances constitute a rigid form of communication, allowing for little originality in scenario presentation. This rigidity, however, does not mean that they are devoid of any elements worthy of analysis. A certain number of studies have looked at the values and ideas conveyed in this type of novel, the way in which they are communicated, and the impact they have on readers.

In the following sections we will examine three approaches, developed by three different researchers, for analyzing the forms of communication produced in Harlequin Romances and their effects on readers. All three models show that one of the constant features of these romances is escape.

Escape or Pornography?

In her study of Harlequin Romances, Ann Barr Snitow (1979) has recognized the phenomenal appeal that Harlequins hold for women, and that this mass appeal among female readers is enough to justify its categorization as mass media. Snitow (1979) has put forth a number of concepts to explain this appeal, emphasizing that her criticisms of various characteristics of Harlequin Romances do not extend to the women who read them. She has stated that one of the particular features of mass audiences is that they are capable of digesting cultural and social contradictions, while at the same time resisting what these contradictions imply. Thus, even though the content of this popular form of literature touches the inner reaches of the soul of certain readers, they still reject, sometimes unconsciously, certain aspects of Harlequin novels. For example, as we will soon see in greater detail, while female audiences accept the romantic aspects of scenarios and even, to some extent, male dominance over women, they reject acts of violence perpetrated on the heroine.

Although Snitow's research is somewhat dated and her approach more critical than Bettinotti's (1990), the two researchers have a similar outlook on Harlequin Romances. One of the main differences between Harlequins published in the seventies and those published in the eighties, however, is that in the earlier novels the heroine was always a virgin: as Snitow pointed out, "sex means marriage and marriage, promised at the end, means, finally, there can be sex" (1979: 144). Nevertheless, while attending to her business in between confrontations with the hero, the heroine remains in a constant state of anticipation of sex throughout the novel. The waiting, so titillating, adds to the excitement, for in "romanticized sexuality pleasure lies in the distance itself. Waiting, anticipation, anxiety—these represent the high point of sexual experience" (Snitow, 1979: 146).

As in soap operas, Harlequin Romances are conducive to conveying stereotypes entertained by the patriarchal capitalist ideology. For example, the virgin heroine hides her desires and considers the boorish hero as a potential husband despite appearances. Her character evolves in a world with no past or family, without reference to any specific ethnic or religious groups. There is no society or any cultural, economic or social context in Harlequins, only "surroundings." This has led Snitow to claim the following:

> The denatured quality of Harlequins is convenient for building an audience: anyone can identify. Or, rather, anyone can identify with the fantasy which places all the characters in an upper-class. . . . The realities of class—workers in dull jobs, poverty, real productive relations, social divisions of labor—are all, of course, entirely foreign to the world of the Harlequin (Snitow, 1979: 149).

But why are these novels so popular among women?

Snitow (1979) has argued that Harlequins fill a void created by women's social conditions. When women want excitement, patriarchal society offers them one option only: romance. When they imagine a companion for themselves, society offers them one and only one option: a male sexual companion. When women dream of success and of controlling their own aspirations, society offers them one option only: the power to attract men. And, finally, when women fantasize about sex, society offers them one option only: sexual taboos. For women, real self-fulfilment lies in social life, domesticity and sexuality. The world of romance is therefore a cultural milieu where women can feel at ease, since it agrees with "the prevailing cultural code: pleasure for women is men" (Snitow, 1979: 150).

In this context, Harlequin Romances largely overshadow complex social relations and, despite confrontations between the couple, provide a comforting outlet for exchanges between women and men, namely marriage. In 1979, the average marriage in the United States lasted five years and a rape took place every 12 minutes. Today, these numbers are even worse. Harlequins help eclipse all these contradictions and attenuate ambivalence. Men's brutal sexuality is magically converted into a love story, and the war between men and women, who cannot find common ground for communication, ends in a truce. "Stereotyped females are charged with an unlikely glamour, and women's daily routines are revitalized by the pretence that they hide an ongoing sexual drama" (Snitow, 1979: 150). Sexuality and sex are two central themes of Harlequin novels: they are ever-present, almost eternal. The present, a time of social confusion and disturbing ruptures between the sexes, does not exist.

Nevertheless, Snitow has claimed that Harlequins are not simply a means of escape for women, but are also specifically sexually liberating, a fact which appeals to a very large readership. Is this liberation in the form of pornography? Pornography signifies passivity, powerless abandonment and fantasy, and is often associated with pejorative masochism, as if passivity could never be pleasant. In a sexist society such as ours, Snitow has written:

> . . . pornography's critics are right—pornography is exploitation . . . we have two pornographies, one for men, one for women. They both have, hiding within them, those basic human expressions of abandonment I have described. The pornography for men

enacts this abandonment on women as objects. How different is the pornography for women, in which sex is bathed in romance, diffused, always implied rather than enacted at all! This pornography is the Harlequin romance (Snitow, 1979: 154).

What forms does pornography take in Harlequins?

Women consider sexuality as closely related to deep, personal emotions. Over and above their being socially and economically dependent on their partners, women are the ones who risk becoming pregnant. In Harlequin Romances, the heroine also has deep emotions and uncertainties about her sexuality. She is anxious about the hero's intentions, for her difficult economic situation means she is dependent on him. Thus, the scenes of waiting, fearing and speculating, intensified by romantic and sexually related situations "are as much a part of their functioning as pornography for women as are the more overtly sexual scenes" (Snitow, 1979: 157).

As for men, for social and psychological reasons, they are uncomfortable when confronted with romance and the need for security, which so often accompanies women's sexuality. Harlequins reproduce these differences between the sexes, and, despite the struggles between the heroine and the hero, the storyline combines the elements that can ultimately bring the heroine sexual satisfaction. Harlequins excel in creating a balance between romantic tension, domestic security and sexual arousal. As Snitow (1979: 158) has pointed out, the heroine "is in a constant fever of anti-erotic anxiety" so as to contain her sexual desire for the hero until she can dictate the terms of her own surrender. In the romantic narrative, "the heroine's task is 'converting rape into love-making' she must somehow teach the hero to take time, to pay attention, to feel, while herself remaining passive, undemanding, unthreatening" (Snitow, 1979: 158).

Thus, romance, Harlequin style, constitutes an important category of women's imagination. Snitow has criticized both the women's movement for taking only a slight interest in the phenomenon of women's consciousness, as well as certain women novelists who treat this type of literature with irony and cynicism. She writes:

> In spite of all the audience manipulations inherent in the Harlequin formula, the connection between writer and reader is tonally seamless; Harlequins are respectful, tactful, friendly towards their audience. The letters that pour in to their publishers speak above all of involvement, warmth, human values. The world that can make Harlequin romances appear warm is indeed a cold, cold place (Snitow, 1979: 160).

Snitow was one of the first female researchers to become interested in the phenomenon of popular literature, specifically in Harlequin Romances and how they have such an undeniably broad appeal among women. More recent research has focused on other aspects of this popular genre.

The Disappearing Act

Tania Modleski's (1980) study of Harlequin Romances focused on the reader's response to these novels. She suggests that reading such a novel may be compared to a disappearing act, to escaping into "the wonderful world of Harlequin Romances" (1980: 435). She has criticized researchers who attempt to show how these novels are a clear reflection of female "masochism" or a simple projection of the male dominant ideology. On the one hand, some researchers, like Germaine Greer, have claimed that the character traits created for the hero "have been invented by women cherishing the chains of their bondage" (cited in Modleski, 1980: 436). Modleski has argued that this position puts the blame entirely on women's shoulders by assuming they have the freedom to choose, a fact which is neither apparent in reality, nor in the popular literature women so enjoy. On the other hand, far from holding women responsible for creating such fantasies, other researchers, such as Susan Brownmiller, describe women as victims and as mirror images of the male ideology of rape.

Modleski places the truth between Greer and Brownmiller. To explain her position, she refers to the notion of masochism, which Thompson describes as a "form of adaptation to an unsatisfactory and circumscribed life" (cited in Modleski, 1980: 436). This notion of "adaptation," as she points out, implies a certain form of response on behalf of women, instead of "passive acceptance." She suggests that this response takes the form of varied and complex strategies used by female readers to adapt to the limited actions of Harlequin characters, and to convince themselves that these limitations are in fact opportunities. She identifies two basic enigmas in each Harlequin Romance: the hero's inexplicable behaviour and his realization that the heroine is an exceptional woman. Let us take a closer look at these two enigmas.

The first enigma revolves around the hero's behaviour. Why does he treat the heroine so badly, or with such contempt? Why is he so brutal? It would appear that the appeal of these novels lies less in the hero's character traits than in female readers' interpretation of his behaviour. As we have seen, Harlequins are most often based on the same scenario. Female readers are familiar with this formula and always know more about the intrigues than the heroine herself. So even if female readers are able to identify with the heroine to some extent, they can also attribute the hero's hostile behaviour to his being madly in love with the heroine, a fact he is incapable of admitting. "Male brutality comes to be seen as a manifestation, not of contempt, but of love" (Modleski, 1980: 439). Moreover, Harlequins perpetuate the ideological confusion that exists between male sexuality and male violence. The rapist's mentality is transformed into sexual desire which disguises the intention to dominate and hurt. Thus, according to Modleski (1980), romantic literature plays an important role in creating the myth that men's violence against women is in fact the awkward expression of their uncontrollable love, or simply a barrier they must put up in order to resist women's extraordinary charm.

As for the heroine, who knows less than her readers do, she must live with the confusion of not knowing whether the hero is friend or foe. Invariably, towards the end of the novel, she rebels and expresses her anger. In many cases, the hero does not realize the heroine's "infinite preciousness" until after she has left him, generally out of vengeance. It seems that for the heroine this disappearing act is the way she chooses to channel her anger and frustration. Modleski claims that this is a subversive act, since ultimately it is adapted to please the hero; in other words, this "cute" rebellion serves only to make women look more attractive.

In short, in this first enigma, female readers are faced with a dilemma: on the one hand, they identify with the heroine's frustration and anger; on the other, they desire a happy ending where the hero sees the heroine as an adorable creature, not a rebel. But one thing remains clear: these novels are a manifestation of women's anger and hostility. This is why Modleski considers Greer's notion, which holds that Harlequins are a reflection of only those women who cherish the chains of their own servitude, to be untenable. "What Marx said of religious suffering is equally true of 'romantic suffering': it is 'at the same time an *expression* of real suffering and a *protest* against real suffering'" (Modleski, 1980: 442–3).

The second enigma concerns the way in which the hero realizes that the heroine is different from all other women. The most striking difference between her and others is that her innocence means she is completely disinterested in the hero's material goods. In most novels, the heroine is a poor, young woman who will eventually marry the beautiful, rich, sensitive man. It is never possible to portray these young women as showing an interest in the hero's wealth and property. To underscore the heroine's innocence and selflessness, she is portrayed as unsure of the hero's feelings for her, and of her own feelings for the hero. This way, she cannot be accused of wanting to cheat or manipulate the hero. Her innocence is also accentuated by her youth.

According to Modleski (1980), the feminine ideal of innocence and self-sacrifice as depicted in Harlequin romances is not without contradiction and conflict for the heroine. First, while Harlequins emphasize the social, economic and aesthetic importance of having a wealthy husband, they also confirm that women cannot achieve these goals unless they deny how important they truly are. Second, given their profound knowledge of the Harlequin formula, female readers can both understand the hero's mood swings and identify emotionally with the heroine, who herself doesn't understand them. In this context, the reading process leads readers "to feelings of hypocrisy" (Modleski, 1980: 446). Finally, readers simultaneously empathize with the heroine's isolation and with the way the hero watches and judges her.

Despite the paradoxical situation of Harlequins, Modleski asserts that it is not the novels themselves that should be condemned, *but instead the social conditions that make them a necessity for certain readers*. In short, the contradictions women experience every day are responsible for the popularity of these novels.

> Moreover, the very fact that the novels must go to such extremes to neutralize women's anger and to make masculine hostility bearable testifies to the depths of women's discontent . . . The desire to perform a disappearing act suggests women's suppressed wish to stop being seen in the old ways and to begin looking at their lives in ways that are perhaps yet to be envisioned (Modleski, 1980: 448).

Thus, it is the values transmitted by our patriarchal society that are responsible for the immense popularity of Harlequin Romances among women. As Dubino points out, "romances help to reconcile women to their domestic role as houseworkers" (1993: 109). In addition, they "seem to respond to a need in women that patriarchal capitalism fails to address . . . Not finding what they want in the 'real' life, millions of women turn to romances in a vicarious attempt to compensate for the lack of attention and validation they get in their own lives" (1993: 107). Thus, Harlequin Romances appear to be a means of escape for women, a way of procuring pleasure, much like watching soap operas. Yet, these novels are a direct product of capitalist industry. In fact, "as obvious commodities," Dubino has reminded us, "romances helped to make publishers better capitalists" (1993: 107). Publishers' financial imperatives should be kept in mind. As Christian-Smith (1990) has pointed out, the corporate production of romance and the corporate link to political conservativism provide the mechanisms which allow themes suggesting that women are 'incomplete without a man' or 'destined for motherhood' to find their way into, and be perpetuated in, romance fiction. Thus, romance novels "become the site of ideological struggles for young women's hearts and minds" (Christian-Smith, 1990: 2). Let us now see whether Radway's analysis—the final study examined here—agrees with these assertions.

Illicit Pleasure: The Escape from Everyday Life

Although Janice Radway (1983) has recognized the pertinence of Snitow's and Modleski's research, she has nevertheless deplored the fact that they both focused on texts alone, without taking into consideration the context in which reading occurs, the choice readers make upon purchase and the reasons women read romances. Radway has claimed that to understand the real impact of Harlequins on female readers it is necessary, first and foremost, to unearth women's interpretation of their content and the meaning they ascribe to the actions of the main characters. She has contended that answering these questions will reveal what women get from reading these novels and how they integrate these repetitive romance readings into their everyday lives.

Radway (1983) explored these aspects of the Harlequin phenomenon by using a study consisting of interviews and questionnaires involving about 75 avid female readers of Harlequins who lived in the city of Smithton,[4] USA. The readers were married, middle-class women, and about half had high school diplomas. The majority (60%) of the women were between the ages of 25 and 44. Less than half (42%) had part-time, remunerated work. In 1983, 43% of these women had an annual family income ranging between $15,000 and $25,000, while 33% had an income between $25,000 and $50,000. The study showed that a large majority of these female readers (70%) read other types of books than Harlequins. Nevertheless, the women in the Smithton study devoured an incredible number of Harlequin novels: 50% of the respondents read between 40 and 60 Harlequins per month, and 40% read as many as 20 per month. Only a mass production system could supply so many books.

When asked why they read Harlequins, the majority of women in the study answered that it was for escape and relaxation. Reading transported them out of the present into

---

[4] Smithton, a pseudonym, is not the real name of the town in the study.

another world, thus enabling them to forget their daily worries. At the same time, they were aware that all these novels are, in fact, fairy tales with happy endings, and that they are not a true image of people and events in their everyday lives.

Thus, it would appear that the main reason for the appeal of Harlequins is precisely this unreality: the fantastic construction of storylines enables readers to escape completely from their everyday life, which does not always satisfy their desires. This form of escape implies both distancing oneself from the real world, which can be suffocating and burdensome, and transferring to another (more desirable) world, where events always conclude happily. But what do these middle-class women want to escape from? The answer was invariably the same: the pressures and tensions of their existence as wives and mothers. According to Radway (1983), this sort of escape amounts to a "declaration of independence," that is, temporary independence from their roles as wives and mothers. "By placing the barrier of the book between themselves and their families, these women reserve a special space and time for themselves alone" (Radway, 1983: 61). Indeed, these novels bring enormous pleasure, hope and immense satisfaction to female readers. These experiences are reminiscent of the soap opera consumers. Therefore, despite differences in terms of the forms of communication and content structure, it would appear that the act of consuming mass-produced romance has certain similar effects on female audiences regardless of the mass medium that produces it.[5]

But what aspects of the narrative in particular are able to ignite such positive feelings among female readers? Radway (1983) tells us that the answers of the women questioned reflected the contradictions experienced in their daily lives. On the one hand, the female readers abandoned themselves to the pleasure and hope of finding fulfilment in the arms of a gentle hero. This seems to support Dubino's claim that women read romances for the following reasons: they "reproduce female desire for the male sexual partner"; they allow women "to absent themselves temporarily from their workaday, routine world"; in reading romances, women "are doing something for *themselves*, and not for others"; and "romances recreate the magical stage of courtship. . . one of the most exciting and important times of [women's] lives" (1993: 108). On the other hand, Radway's readers were capable of articulating critical observations concerning the fact that many novels are about men who abuse and hurt the women they are supposed to love. Thus, despite their travels to the romantic world of Harlequin love, women remain conscious that reality is quite different from fiction. But, as Christian-Smith has reminded us, how critical can women be of romances which represent symbolic forms that "both shape and regulate definitions of femininity, class, race, sexuality and age"? (1990: 5).

Content analyses such as those conducted by Modleski (1980) and Snitow (1979) are based on the hypothesis that every Harlequin satisfies one formula only; therefore, they are all identical. Thus, an analysis of a randomly selected sample will invariably reveal the meaning conveyed in the genre as a whole. This type of analysis, however, overlooks the social conditions in which female readers receive these stories, conditions which create

---

[5] The Smithton women estimated that their consumption of Harlequins was distinct from their consumption of other forms of communication produced by the media, in terms of both quantity and quality.

variations in their perceptions. As Mattelart (1986) has said, it is a mistake to think that the influence of the dominant ideology is monolithic in nature. Such a view does not take into account the fact that audiences have personal histories and class backgrounds that can influence their interpretations. The Smithton readers did not believe all Harlequin novels to be identical, and neither did they appreciate all of them equally. They created distinctions and established criteria defining "good" and "bad" novels.

The novels that the readers identified as bad were those in which the hero abuses the heroine both physically and verbally, and where he is portrayed as fickle, in search of many conquests. Conversely, the most appreciated model was that of the traditional man/woman couple. For the Smithton readers, the fact that these conflict-ridden stories all end in marriage seemed to be unrealistic. These readers believed that men's macho behaviour is unforgivable and does not at all signify love. As Radway has noted, what women want is a hero who is "capable of soft, gentle gestures" (1983: 64). Women do not tolerate any novel where the heroine is seriously abused by the hero, regardless of whether the abuse consists of rape or brutality. They are offended by stories that include explicit sex scenes, which they label as "perversions," and avoid reading certain authors. Lastly, they do not appreciate detailed descriptions of male genitalia. For female readers, a good novel involves a bright, young, determined, sexually immature woman and a man who is incredibly masculine and capable of tenderness. They particularly appreciate novels that begin with a marriage of convenience, where the heroine thinks "she detests and is detested by her spouse" (Radway, 1983: 65).

It is important at this point to acknowledge that, as Hall (1980) has suggested, romance readings are decoded, that is, they are interpreted according to the *discontent*, as well as the satisfaction, of readers. It must be understood that the experience of certain readers does not conform exactly to the ideological statements that legitimize traditional marriages. On the contrary, the desires of female readers arise from the constant failures of the traditional marriage which has been unable to meet all of women's needs. For example, Radway (1983) has noted that female readers identify with a strong, independent heroine, and reject "an unusually cruel hero" whom they learn to hate, which is something they rarely allow themselves to do in their own lives. But once they have protested in their imagination, they are willing to accept the hero's explanation, and, like the heroine, forgive his cruelty, which in reality is an expression of love. When female readers close their books, they are momentarily liberated from their dissatisfactions, and reassured that men can learn to satisfy their needs for emotional intensity and security within the marriage. This reassuring effect, however, is only short-lived, since readers quickly feel the need to begin a new novel.

The results of Radway's (1983) analysis might help women understand that their attraction to Harlequins is related to their status as dependent women, and to their acceptance of the fact that love and marriage are their only means of self-fulfilment as women. Such awareness could lead women to search for other means of self-fulfilment in order to renew their self-worth.

This survey of the Harlequin phenomenon has helped reveal many of the characteristics of the novels themselves, as well as those of their readers. It has also helped us draw certain parallels with other forms of mass-produced romance, namely soap operas. We can also note that, although these two types of communication are based on different mass media, they sometimes have identical effects. Popular literature, however, is not limited to romance alone. The detective novel is another genre with wide appeal and a large readership. What types of male and female characters are found in these novels? What do they do? What audiences do they attract? These are the issues that are addressed in the following section.

DETECTIVE NOVELS: WOMEN DYING TO BE KILLED!

Anne Lemonde (1984) has claimed that, in contrast to Harlequin Romances, detective novels cannot be as readily associated with any one formula. Since they are constructed along varied and complex plots, there is not one genre, but many genres of detective novels. Moreover, these novels generally appeal to a male audience. Yet, the reasons for reading them appear to be similar to those for reading Harlequins. Indeed, aside from the desire for high-pitched emotions, the motives are comparable: distraction, change of scenery and escape from the familiar, tiresome and dull routine of everyday life. Even though detective novels are considered to be bad, or sub-standard literature, they appear to enjoy the same popularity as Harlequins.

Detective novels attract different readers than Harlequin Romances. It would be easy to think that this is related to the fact that most Harlequins are written by women, while the writing of detective novels is a male bastion. Yet some women have been, and continue to be, highly successful at writing detective stories. Who has not heard of Agatha Christie, P.D. James, Ann Perry, or Elizabeth Peters, to name but a few authors? Despite the large number of female detective-story writers, some researchers have noted that the gender difference in authors is not necessarily reflected in content, but rather according to the period in which the stories are written. In the following pages, we will study the characteristics of these novels.

In their study of detective novels, Gottlieb and Keitner (1979) observed that, during the 1970s, these novels had similar content in terms of form and style, regardless of the author's gender. For example, the image of women detectives reflected one of the following two options: they were beautiful in accordance with feminine stereotypes, but had so little talent as detectives that they needed a man's help to get the job done; or they were excellent detectives who lacked sex appeal and were often portrayed as old and eccentric (in Mackie, 1983). At that time, researchers usually referred to detective novels penned by women as "analytic detective" novels. Moreover, these female novelists wrote in a style that was as paternalistic as that of male authors. Nevertheless, during the seventies, some female authors (Amanda Cross, P.D. James, Margaret Truman, etc.) developed a "feminist" detective style featuring female detectives with rewarding and happy careers, and who were as good as, if not better than, their male counterparts. These women, however, rarely combined career with marriage. Nevertheless, irrespective of when they were penned, detective novels written by female authors have a style that is clearly less aggressive than that generally adopted by their male counterparts.

Detective novels can be divided into two categories: "analytic detective" fiction and "hard-boiled detective" fiction (Roth, 1994). The first is based on intellectual resolution of intrigues which appeal to the reader's intellect; in the second category, the intrigue unfolds through scenes of violence and eroticism, thus igniting sexual desires and violent instincts in the reader's subconscious. These two types of novels also differ in their cover illustrations. The covers of hard-boiled detective novels often depict half-naked women looking aggressive or offering themselves in submission, women dressed in leather or see-through clothing, or victimized women resigned to their fate. Paradoxically, the violence and eroticism so emphasized on covers are not always as graphic in the actual stories. Invariably, these elements fade away as the social order is re-established towards the end of the story, when the "good guys" win and the "bad guys" are punished. As Lemonde (1984) has remarked, after having quenched their thirst for violence, readers want to return to their peaceful, regular, normal world, at least until their drab and boring lives once again feed their desire to escape in a new direction.

Do women read detective novels? Lemonde (1984) has claimed that little is known about women's reading habits of these novels, though she suggests that this genre is reserved almost exclusively for men as readers, writers and heroes. This assertion, however, is not entirely accurate. A number of studies (Mackie, 1983; Fritz and Kaufman Henever, 1979) have shown that there does exist a female audience for this genre of literature. Lemonde's argument for the lack of female readership is that women find it difficult to identify with detective-novel characters, who are predominantly male. Although this hypothesis is true, there are motifs other than identification that can generate interest in reading popular literature novels. Thus, it is important, at this stage, to examine the main characteristics of detective-novel characters.

Heroes: Faster than a Speeding Bullet

While, as we saw earlier, the Harlequin Romance is the heroine's novel, the detective novel usually belongs to the hero. He is at centre stage, and provokes and dominates the action. The analytic detective novel generally revolves around the infallible hero, or what Fritz and Kaufman Henever (1979) refer to as the "classic sleuth." Sherlock Holmes and Hercule Poirot exemplify this infallible, yet paternalistic, character type. According to Lemonde (1984), the classic sleuth (whom she calls "*éminence grise*") is confident of his superiority, and thus believes women possess only "domestic intelligence" and are deprived of any ability to reason; in other words, he sees them as children of lesser intelligence. This male character usually operates in wealthy surroundings consisting of old houses, ancestral manors, luxurious hotels and wealthy neighbourhoods: hermetic, circumscribed and mysterious places, far removed from inner-city chaos. In most cases, he comes from well-to-do, bourgeois society, and is well aware of his class privileges. Consider, for example, Dorothy Sawyer's Peter Whimsey and Margery Allingham's Albert Campion. Still, some analytic detective heroes come from the underprivileged classes; however, they are respected by the wealthy classes for their efficiency and integrity. Such working-class heroes include Georges Simenon's Maigret and Ann Perry's Thomas Pitt.

The popular male heroes of hard-boiled detective novels are quite different: they are genuine "action heroes," or untouchable characters. According to Lemonde (1984), these virile characters are more prone to act than to use their brains. Spy novels have immortalized such heroes as George Smiley, James Bond and Simon Templar, while private eye novels have produced heroes the likes of Philip Marlowe, Sam Spade and Spenser. These novels are renowned for their fast-paced action and unexpected reversals. Moreover, women come in and out of the action as quickly as punches are thrown. Whereas the classic sleuth character has no time for women—he has pent-up emotions and is sexually repressed—the action hero is surrounded by female characters, each one associated with eroticism and violence. These women are abused, raped, struck and reduced to silence and servitude. Few of them are victorious or even alive at the end of the story. Finally, the urban action hero lives in a cosmopolitan world peopled with characters from all social classes with whom he can easily relate. In short, he knows how to fit in easily.

Of course, detective novels also feature "foils" or "antiheroes" who play the role of the victim or some other character whose discretion, ridicule or clumsiness serves to make the hero look good. Consider Watson's character in relation to Holmes. Some secondary characters, like Lugg (Albert Campion's butler), grew up in ghettos or shanty-towns, and are often outcasts, misfits or nonconformists. They come from a world in which violence is the only universal language (Lemonde, 1984). What about detective-novel heroines?

Heroines: In the Hero's Shadow, If Not at His Feet

Lemonde (1984) has written that women are not part of the essence of the detective-novel genre. In these novels, female characters are under the totalitarian rule of men. Indeed, male characters of all types (classic sleuth, action heroes, foils, antiheroes, victims, etc.) prevent women from getting involved and playing pivotal roles in the action. It is as if fiction could not go beyond reality.

Lemonde's comments paint a well-documented picture of the place women generally occupy in detective novels. Female characters usually have secondary roles and fit the stereotypes invented by men, who, in Lemonde's (1984) words, are anxious to secure and reinforce their grip on a world they already largely control. When the leading character is a woman, however, she is often old, or simply a spinster (the antiheroine *par excellence*), who unravels intrigues while she weeds her garden or knits her socks. One need only think of Agatha Christie's Miss Marple, Josephine Tey's Miss Pym, or Patricia Wentworth's Miss Silver.

However, as a general rule, in the shadows of the courageous hero there is a heroine: a "weak woman," a lying, irresponsible, rash chatterbox. She is a schemer; she sometimes even instigates crimes. She is a temptress, a devilish Eve who thinks only of plotting the hero's downfall. She is as beautiful as she is foolish: a mindless little thing in the hands of the hero, who is the master of the trigger and of the intrigues. She fulfils two types of functions. The *ornamental* function transforms her into an object-woman, a showpiece who behaves like a child; she plays the innocent virgin or the blond bombshell, generally liquidated shortly after she appears. Her *utilitarian* function is to act as a caretaker, secretary, witness, suspect, etc. In most cases the heroine is a victim. Sometimes she is murdered right at the beginning, and the remainder of the intrigue revolves around solving her murder. She may also be the object of conspiracies, which cause her to become hysterical or mad. In the hard-boiled detective novel, she is struck, beaten, raped, humiliated and subjugated.

Lemonde (1984) has noted that the detective novel can also feature the antithesis of the *femme fatale*: the "sheltering woman" (*"femme-refuge"*) personified by the wife or mother. In a world of violence, the sheltering woman appears as a symbol of security and calm for the tired hero. She is patient, understanding and supportive; in short, she loves him unconditionally. For the researcher, the sheltering woman is a reminder of women's sole reason for being: motherhood. On a more general level, she symbolizes an absent reality, namely the household. Instead of the mother or wife, the sheltering woman may also be a housekeeper, a maid, a nanny, or sometimes even a male servant. Nevertheless, this character means nothing to the lonely superhero: she simply has no real existence. She is often too emotional and can even jeopardize the hero's good work. As for analytic detective novels involving the classic sleuth hero, these storylines never include love affairs, for sexual relations could weaken the hero's deductive reasoning.

In short, this stream of characters with hierarchical and stereotyped functions reflects many social, economic and political inequalities. As such, Lemonde (1984) has claimed that these novels reproduce the dominating/dominated relationships inherent in the capitalist regime: rich/poor, powerful/weak, corrupt/decent, etc., and, of course, man/woman. However, such a comparison between social relations in imagined situations and real-life conditions must be looked at critically, since they suggest that modern societies are totally lacking in nuance, that they consist of black-and-white relationships in the fashion of detective novels.

A survey of the role of women in detective novels shows that they have essentially two functions: mother and prostitute. In Canadian society, these two roles stand opposite each other on the social-values spectrum. However, in this genre of literature, the mother is no more respected than the prostitute. The mother is ridiculed through stereotypes related to her uncontrollable emotions, and the prostitute through stereotypes related to her uncontrollable sexuality.

HARLEQUIN ROMANCES AND DETECTIVE NOVELS: A COMPARATIVE ANALYSIS

Although there are many differences, there are also certain similarities between the content, as well as the characters and readership, of Harlequin Romances and detective novels.

One of the most important differences is their content. Harlequins are all constructed according to the same basic scenario (*boy meets girl*) and the five stable motifs that underlie it (the encounter, the confrontation, the seduction, the revelation of love, and marriage) although, according to Hudson (1989), the plots, settings and outcomes are more varied than some researchers would have us believe. In contrast, detective novels are based on a myriad of aspects. Consequently, they cannot be said to encompass one genre, but many genres, each being completely different and attracting a different readership than the others.

This difference is reflected in character make-up as well. In Harlequins, the heroine (between the ages of 22 and 24) is the main character, and the stories are told in the third person, reflecting her point of view of the events occurring from the time of the encounter to the "happy ending" marriage. In the detective novel, the main character is a man, and the action is seen from his perspective. As opposed to Harlequin Romance heroines, who always end up getting married, a good, genuine detective marries only rarely. And when he is married, there is usually no apparent sexuality between him and his wife. If the main character happens to be female, she is often an old, asexual woman.

The difference between the two genres of literature can also be observed in their authors: Harlequin authors are almost exclusively women, while most detective novelists are men. Female detective novelists generally submit themselves to a male style, although in recent feminist detective novels the main character is often a very clever young woman.

With so many differences in content and authors, there must inevitably be differences in readership as well. Harlequins are intended for a specific clientele, namely women who avidly devour these novels. While some authors claim that detective novels are intended for all audiences, certain genres are more geared specifically to men. Female readers identify with Harlequin heroines and, it would appear, have difficulty relating to the essentially male characters of detective novels. Conversely, few men consume Harlequins, and those who enjoy reading detective novels appear to identify with their heroes.

People seem to read these two genres of literature for similar reasons: both men and women need to escape and distance themselves from the tedious and dull familiarity of their daily lives. However, the place they wish to escape to differs. In the case of Harlequin readers, they want to flee to a world of omnipresent sexuality and sexual tensions, a world of romantic sexuality based on the distance, waiting, anticipation and anxiety experienced by the heroine *vis-à-vis* the hero. Thus, even the most openly sexual scenes are implicit. The escape must feature a bright, determined and sexually immature young woman, and a man who is both very masculine and capable of tenderness. Female readers appreciate neither scenes of aggression, abuse, violence, nor rape. Conversely, readers of detective novels, especially hard-boiled detective fiction, are thrust into a world where escape ignites their violent and sexual instincts. At the time of reading these novels, the male hero is their model, while female characters, who always play secondary roles, are beaten, raped, humiliated and murdered.

There are, of course, other similarities between detective novels and Harlequin Romances, one of the more striking being the images of women and men they convey. These images constitute sexual and racist stereotypes that perpetuate long-standing values as well as preconceived ideas about women (as mothers or prostitutes), about men (as dominators and Casanovas) and about visible minorities (as idiots and rogues).

In both genres, the image of women is that of a dominated person. In Harlequins, they are not only socially inferior to men, they also earn less money and are less educated. Women have traditionally female jobs (maids, secretaries, governesses, nurses, etc.) and are submitted to the universal relationship of male dominance over women from all perspectives, but especially in terms of sexuality. Compared with the crude and sexually obsessed hero, women are patient, calm, maternal, innocent and sometimes even rebellious (though only a little). In detective novels, women are portrayed in two ways. First, women are weak, irresponsible and rash chatterboxes; they are scheming temptresses, *femmes fatales* or beautiful bimbos; and they perform either an ornamental or utilitarian function. They are crazy or hysterical victims, and are struck, beaten, raped, subjugated and often murdered. Second, there is the sheltering woman character for the tired hero: if his mother fails him, he can still turn to his maid, his housekeeper or his wife. As for the man, he is the very picture of virility, and of the dominance and power he exerts over women. And, above all, he is white. In both genres, he is a real man. It should be noted that both the classic sleuth characters of detective novels and the male heroes of Harlequins benefit from the prerogatives of the privileged classes. The former ignore women, even their wives; the latter mistreat women throughout the story, but end up marrying them.

Villains are often portrayed in an implicitly racist manner. If they are black, they are often described as being muscular, dressed in flashy clothes and having particular accents. They are stereotyped in roles either as idiots, who are villains in spite of themselves, or as wrongdoers or psychopaths with demonic or unstable personalities. Lastly, the racist connotation may be even more harmful given that these villains, of different race or colour, are always defeated by the good white hero at the end of the novel, unless they are completely forgotten, as is often the case with idiot villains.

In short, the two types of novels studied in this chapter feature a large number of social stereotypes. For some researchers, this seems to reflect certain social inequalities by their reproduction of the dominating/dominated relationships that exist in the capitalist regime: rich/poor; powerful/weak; fair/corrupt; whites/other races; men/women, etc. This assertion, however, sends us back to a dichotomous view of reality, an approach that critical study attempts to refine. It is indeed hazardous to compare social relations in society with relations created in sensational genres of literature such as detective and romance novels. As is the case in Harlequin romances, after waves of violence, sexuality and disorder, detective novels end with the social order being re-established. The good win, and the bad are punished. This, at times, can be far from reality!

CONCLUSION

In this chapter we studied two examples of popular literature which, despite some similarities in their portrayal of sexual stereotypes, reproduce two different worlds, or cultures: the sheltered culture of Harlequin Romance for female audiences, and the violent culture of police confrontations for male audiences. The readers of these two genres of literature are rarely interchangeable: very few men are interested in Harlequins, and the women who read detective novels do not appear to be any more attracted to sentimental novels than are men.

Nevertheless, readers of Harlequin and detective novels appear to have certain aspects in common. Although the contents of each genre are transmitted via different forms of communication and have distinct scenario structures, they are similar in that they appeal to similar kinds of imagination and the need for escape. Moreover, although they do not reflect real-life situations, they nevertheless convey traditional values and stereotypes supported by the dominant ideology.

EPILOGUE

The evening draws to a close as Mr. and Mrs. Peabody finish their respective novels. Margaret has just attended Laura's wedding: a lovely ceremony, and so romantic too. Will Laura find happiness in married life? Margaret does not know, and frankly does not particularly want to know. She prefers to think about the novel she will read tomorrow night to help her escape her daily life. As for George, having had his fix of violence, sexual aggression and high-pitched emotions, he has completed his novel with Lou Dickrous honoured with medals and commendations from his country's supreme leader, while the bad guys rot in jail or six feet under. Tomorrow, he will be able to forget his worries in another suspense novel. Everything is hunky-dory in the Peabody's world. A world where two cultures—that of woman and man—meet. Margaret will fall asleep awash in romance, and dream of the tenderness and sexuality that would help her express and share her feelings and emotions with her dearly beloved. George will fall asleep pumped up with violent and sexual energy, and dream of the intriguing, but dead, temptress. What a figure! The girl would have been great for a roll in the hay. But what a tart. Frankly, she got what she deserved: a slug right between the eyes. Two cultures existing side by side, like Margaret and George. With the lights out and their backs to each other, they fall asleep and travel to their own little dream worlds. But what are their children up to? They are devouring comic books.

COMICS: CHILDREN'S LITERATURE?

INTRODUCTION

Comics are another form of communication related to oral and written mass media. They are seen in movie theatres as animated film, as well as on television and in the printed media. They are as popular among young people as they are among adults. Who has never seen a *Mickey Mouse* film or read a *Donald Duck*, *Superman* or *Spider-Man* adventure? Comics are a mass culture product and, as such, can be found all over the world. Like all other media products, they transmit values and ideas that exist in society, but which are all the more concealed, as they are conveyed under the cover of laughter and innocence. In this chapter, we will examine the hidden side of comics, focusing primarily on the written forms, with some reference to the oral forms.

Because this children's literature—like adult literature—is produced by capitalist industries, we will look at the impact that the mode of production of comics has on content and audiences. We will pay particular attention to the ideology, values and images conveyed by comics, while at the same time evaluating their so-called "innocence." We will begin with a brief history of comics both here and abroad, particularly in English Canada, Québec and Europe, where they have become firmly established. However, we will conduct this study mainly by referring to studies of American comics, which enjoy worldwide distribution. The conclusion will consist of a critical analysis of research conducted on American comics.

COMICS: A WORLDWIDE PHENOMENON

Comics have existed for almost a century in both North America and Europe. In the early years the medium struggled through difficult times. However, after half a century in relative obscurity, comics began arousing a great deal of passion on both continents between 1947 and 1954. But they still had their critics: they were accused of propagating violence, foolishness and intellectual poverty. The Mothers of America, a highly reactionary association based in the United States, attacked them by referring to the theories of some psychoanalysts, who accused Superman of being a homosexual and Wonder Woman a lesbian, and who claimed that reading comic books could only lead America's youth to develop tendencies of paranoid megalomania, or delinquency. In the wake of these accusations in 1954, the American Congress established the Comics Code Authority, a censorship commission that in no time purged all of America's comics, in both newspapers as well as comic books (Sadoul, 1989).

In France, a press campaign spearheaded jointly by the Communist Party and Christian movements led to the *Loi de juillet 49*, which outlawed all American comics with the exception of those produced by Walt Disney which, as we will see, is a very revealing fact. In this case, the accusations were aimed at Flash Gordon's fiancée for being too skimpily dressed, Mandrake for his irrational magic, and Superman for his strength which supposedly disturbed young minds. As Sadoul (1989) claimed, the ghost of Bengal (a popular French superhero) was a menace to youth because he wore a mask, and justice should have nothing to hide in its fight against crime. Despite legal restrictions and censorship on both sides of the Atlantic, comics never ceased to expand and diversify over time; today they are officially recognized as a form of popular literature. Before looking at the global giants of comics, we will proceed with a brief analysis of comics produced in Canada and Europe.

Comics in English Canada

In a book entitled *Guardians of the North*, John Bell (1992) offers a survey of the development of comics in Canada. Comics first appeared in English Canada at the end of the nineteenth century in the form of strips in newspapers. It was only towards the end of the 1920s, however, that comics appeared regularly in Canadian newspapers, with Phil Nowlan and Dick Calkins' *Buck Rogers* and Harold Foster's *Tarzan*. This tendency towards ongoing strips increased in the Depression of the 1930s, during which two English-Canadian strips, *Men of the Mounted* and *Robin Hood* were created by *Toronto Telegram* journalist Ted McCall.

Comic books appeared at the same time. Originally, these books simply reproduced comic strips that had already been published in newspapers, but then they began to offer new material as early as the mid-1930s. It was during this period, more precisely in 1933, that the famous *Superman* was created by Canadians Jerry Siegel and Joe Shuster while they were still in high school. *Superman* did not gain quick recognition. On the contrary, until 1938 it was rejected by several publishers who thought its story too unrealistic to attract many readers. However, once published, Bell (1992) tells us, it had instant success with a young audience.

In December 1940, given war-time restrictions and the weakness of the Canadian dollar due to Canada's huge trade deficit with the United States, "the Mackenzie King government passed the War Exchange Conservation Act" to restrict the import of non-essential American products, which included American comic books read by thousands of Canadians. The impact of this boosted the English-Canadian comic book industry which had to satisfy the growing demand of comics fans. Bell points out that, "The deprivation experienced by Canadian comics fans was . . . short-lived. Four different Canadian publishers quickly recognized the opportunity that the comic-book ban represented.

Maple Leaf Publishing in Vancouver and three Toronto-based firms—Anglo-American, Hillborough Studios, and Bell Features and Publishing—all rushed to fill the void created by the exchange legislation" (Bell 1992: 3).

Bell has called the 1940s "the Golden Age of Canadian Comics." Among the new superheroes of the period were *Robin Hood and Company*, published in black and white like most Canadian comics, and *Better Comics* published in color and created by Vernon Miller, who introduced his famous Iron Man. Iron Man's character was very similar to that of his American cousin Sub-Mariner. In fact, according to Bell, these first Canadian superheroes adopted American cultural features and traits. However, other superheroes were created with Canadian attributes: Adrian Dingle's Nelvana of the Northern Light (1941) in *Triumph Comics*; Leo Backle's Johnny Canuck (1942) in *Dime Comics*; and Educational Projects of Montreal's Canada Jack (1943) in *Canadian Heroes* (Bell, 1992: 3–17).

These Canadian superheroes were short-lived, all disappearing before the end of World War II. They were replaced in the 1950s and 1960s by American comics based on "an outrageous melange of horror, crime, war, western, jungle, romance . . . " (Bell, 1992: 18). As Bell has pointed out:

> . . . what all Canadian comic-book readers of the 1950–1970 period had in common was a sense of alienation. For English Canadians, comics had become an American medium: the heroes were American, the settings were largely American, and even the alluring comic-book ads for toy soldiers and sea monkeys were American. Like U.S. television, comics seemed to contain an implicit message; Canada was a backwater bereft of heroes, bereft of guardians (Bell, 1992: 18–9).

The Canadian superheroes who did reappear in the 1970s were the heroes of the 1940s like Captain Canuck and Northern Light, but again they were short-lived. It was only in the 1980s that Richard Comely and George Freeman created a new version of Captain Canuck by redesigning his character to adapt it to the 1990's. Other satirical comics were started up and even survived the Captain. These included Geoffry and Scott Stirling's Captain Canada (1980); John Byrne's Alpha Flight (1983); and Mark Shainblum and Gabriel Morissette's Northguard (1984) (Bell, 1992: 27–36).

As we can see, English-Canadian comics had a tenuous existence. Legislation restricting the importing of American comic books had a beneficial effect on the Canadian comics industry, forcing Canadian creators to produce their own. However, English-Canadian comics were not the only ones threatened by competition from other countries. Québécois comics had to compete with the very lively productions coming from France.

Comics in Québec

A survey revealed that 301 comics appeared in the pages of Québec's five major newspapers between 1930 and 1950: 18 were Canadian (16 from Québec and two from outside Québec), 27 were French and 256 were American. During the American "comic-boom" between 1933 and 1939, nine Québec comics were created. Among these, three—Vic Martin's *L'Oncle Pacifique*, Tom Lucas's *Casimir* (1935–1945) and Christin's *La Mère Jasette* (1939–1951)—survived for roughly 10 years in the pages of the *Petit Journal*. According to Yves Lacroix (1986), these short-lived characters were characterized by their lack of control over time and their indifference to adventure (they had no plans). Character immobility was a dominant theme, and action tended to be manifested in words rather than behaviour. This immobility is said to date back to 1909, when American comics took the Québec market by storm.

In a sense, the history of Québec comics is the history of Albert Chartier, a prolific creator. Between 1935 and 1937, Chartier, in cooperation with René Boivin, published *Bouboule* in the paper *La Patrie*. It is interesting to note that this comic strip was discontinued because the character was said to be too sexy for his time (Samson, 1986). In 1938, Chartier was hired as an illustrator for the monthly magazine *Cancan*. From 1940 to 1942 he worked in New York City for Big Top Comic and Columbia Comic Corporation, where he perfected his technique and improved his productivity, which would enable him, upon his return to Québec in 1943, to establish the *Bulletin des agriculteurs du Québec*. It was in this newsletter that he created his most famous character, Onésime, and later (between 1951 and 1970) the strip called *Séraphin*, based on writer Claude-Henri Grignon's scenarios. Between 1964 and 1967 he created a daily bilingual comic strip for the *Toronto Telegram News Service*, called *Les Canadiens*. The goal of this strip, which appeared in 24 newspapers across Canada, was to promote francophone history and culture outside Québec.

According to Pomerleau (1986), Québec's consumers of comics can be divided into three categories: occasional buyers, who purchase only the most popular volumes; amateur collectors, who are more interested in comic strips; and serious collectors, who buy many volumes by their favourite artists. The most widely read comics in Québec are imported, mainly from Europe's French-speaking countries. *Tintin, Gaston Lagaffe, Spirou* and *Astérix* are quite popular among Québec audiences, for whom comics are not considered, first and foremost, as an imported product: Québécois are much less interested in their origin than in their content (Pomerleau, 1986). Thus, Québec's comic lovers tend to snub those produced here, and favour works from French-speaking European countries and translations of American comics. Because of the popularity and proliferation of foreign comics in both the Québécois and Canadian markets, we will dedicate the rest of this chapter to these types, with particular attention to those from the United States.

Comics In French-Speaking Europe

Many characters of the comics from Europe's French-speaking countries are well known not only to Québécois, but also to English Canadians, since many of their stories have been translated (e.g., Asterix, Tintin). It is not within the scope of this book to review the entire history of the production of comics in Europe. Instead, a short historical account of French-language comics will be outlined, especially those which have had popular appeal among Canadians.

La Bande des Pieds Nickelés, Zig, Puce and Bécassine are the comic characters who launched the age of French-language comics at the beginning of the century. Tintin, a character well known among youths the world over, appeared in 1929 in his first adventure called *Au Pays des Soviets* (*In the Land of Soviets*). Because of the story's notorious and primitive anticommunism, Hergé, the author, was forced to stop producing any more editions of the book until the profusion of pirate copies obligated him to allow bookstores to restock their shelves. *Tintin* went through difficult times in the beginning: it was not until the appearance in 1946 of the weekly magazine bearing his name that he achieved star status, not only in Europe, but all over the world, including China. The *Journal de Tintin*, a magazine dedicated to comics, launched the career of many authors during its long life. Jacobs made his debut in that journal with the series *Blake et Mortimer*, now considered a classic of French-language comics. In a similar manner, the magazine helped launch *Alix le Gaulois* and *Lefranc* (a reporter) created by Martin, *Ric Hochet* (a detective-journalist) invented by Duchâteau, and *Tibet* and *Michel Vaillant* (an automobile racer) created by Graton.

Another magazine specializing in comics, called the *Journal de Spirou*, was founded in 1938, featuring Spirou himself, a bellhop of great renown in French-language communities the world over, along with his bright companion Spip the squirrel. Although the comic strip *Spirou* was drawn by several artists, it was Franquin who, in 1946, would create Spirou's unparalleled, rich fantasy world involving new secondary characters: the Count of Champignac, Zorglub and the one and only Marsupilami. The *Journal de Spirou* was also the springboard for a new generation of comic strips: *Lucky Luke*, the lonesome cowboy created by Morris and Goscinny; *Buck Danny*, Charlier's fighter pilot; Peyo's *Les Schtroumpfs* (the original *Smurfs*); Franquin's *Gaston Lagaffe*; *Yoko Tsuno*, the young Japanese girl (trained as an electronics engineer) created by Leloup; and Cauvin's *Les Tuniques Bleues*.

Pilote is another magazine dedicated to comics. Created in 1959 by Goscinny, Uderzo and Charlier, the first issue included a strip—drawn by Uderzo and written by Goscinny—featuring a clever little man from Gaul named Astérix, who was to become one of the most popular comic book heroes worldwide. Over the years, *Pilote* magazine launched many comic strips, some of which proved to be more successful than others. In 1962, Goscinny collaborated with the artist Tabary to create the adventures of *Iznogoud*, the ignoble Arab. In 1963, *Pilote* introduced Greg's irreplaceable *Achille Talon*, Cabu's *Grand Duduche*, and the adventures of lieutenant *Blueberry*. Fred's poetic *Philémon* and Druillet's disquieting space adventurer *Loane Slone* first appeared in 1966 on the pages of this magazine, followed by Mézières' space and time travellers *Valérian et Laureline* in 1967. Gotlib launched *Superdupont* and *Rubriques à Brac* in 1970. F'Murr's *Génie des Alpages*, featuring a shepherd, a sheepdog and a flock of sheep in a humourous and nonsensical setting, began running in 1973. Finally, in 1975, Enki Bilal and Pierre Christin launched *Légendes d'aujourd'hui*, a series of volumes that are considered genuine works of art.

Although many other comics have been created in Europe's French-speaking countries, we have mentioned only the most popular ones distributed in Canada, through either French- or English-language newsstands and bookstores. Today, a large number of comic magazines are still sold in numerous locations, and are as popular as ever. In France, over a million copies of *Tintin*, *Spirou* and *Pilote* magazines are sold every year, and the adventures of their heroes are appreciated by both young and old.

The most distinct feature of French-language comics, especially on this side of the Atlantic, is their *hardcover volume* format. As Sadoul (1989) has noted, with the exception of a limited number of special de luxe issues, this format is unknown to the English-speaking world, and the few recent attempts to introduce it in North America have met with strong resistance from the reading public. The francophone comic book market is guided by a rule of twofold exploitation: a story first appears in a magazine, such as *Spirou* or *Tintin*, and is then published in volume format. This tradition is practically nonexistent in English-speaking countries, especially in the United States, where "comic books," small pocket-size "magazines," are the norm.

Comics in the United States

In the United States, "comic strips" and "comic books" have been the most popular formats for comics since the beginning of the century. A comic strip is a sequence of drawings appearing in daily newspapers. Between 1929 and 1938, the popularity of comics advanced by leaps and bounds under the comic-strip format, giving life to a host of heroes, including Popeye (1929), Mickey and Blondie (1930), Tarzan and Dick Tracy (1931), Flash Gordon and Mandrake (1934), The Phantom (1936) and Prince Valiant (1937). Then, interest in comic strips dropped until 1952, the year *Peanuts*, starring the infamous Charlie Brown, was created by Charles Schultz.

Comic books are small magazines featuring the adventures of a myriad of superheroes. The first issue of *Action Comics*, which appeared in 1938, introduced a timid journalist named Clark Kent, alias Superman. In 1939, the May issue of *Detective Comics* gave birth to Batman. It was in the 1940s, when a slew of superheroes such as The Human Torch (1939) and Captain Marvel (1940) appeared, that the comic book market really began to expand. In 1940, *DC Comics* invented a completely different concept: *All Star Comics* became an alliance of superheroes (who used to combat one another on the market, if not in actual stories) called the Justice Society of America. In these adventures, the scenario almost always revolved around war and the defense of America and democracy. Accordingly, this superhero alliance was dissolved at the same time that the war ended. In the meantime, in 1941, the female superhero Wonder Woman was created. Sadoul (1989) has pointed out that, despite being in love with her employer Trevor, Wonder Woman—an Amazon with incredible strength—was said to be a lesbian, because of her origin,[1] and to have sadomasochistic tendencies. Some claimed she loved humiliating men by putting them in chains, while others argued that she herself was tied up or put in chains far too often for someone with her Amazonian strength. In the 1960s, a new generation of superheroes was born, including The Fantastic Four, Spider-Man, The Hulk, The Avengers and Doctor Strange.

American superheroes have two things in common, regardless of their strength or origin (they are extra-terrestrials, the result of a scientific experiment gone awry, or dwellers of the deepest, darkest corners of the Earth). First, in ordinary life they are almost all average Americans, who are transformed into superheroes in dangerous situations only. Second, they always come to the rescue, in the nick of time, when a catastrophe (earth-

---

[1] Her character was born on an island in Amazonia, where only women lived.

quake, dam collapsing, super-villain attack, war, atomic bomb, etc.) threatens the small and the weak. They neutralize all the evils unleashed against America or the whole planet. It can be said that inside every American there is a Superman ready to make "good" triumph over "evil," life triumph over death, America triumph over the rest of the world.

There are, however, other heroes who uphold the fight for the same values, but who do not undergo any metamorphosis or have bulging muscles. Instead, they are characterized by their eccentricity. They invite readers to travel to the "wonderful" world of childhood; they are the Walt Disney characters. Disney advertising claims that inside each character there dwells an average American. The same advertising force has also introduced Mickey Mouse as the spiritual son of Walt Disney and his ambassador. Some Americans even consider Mickey to be the American ambassador to the world. Given the huge popularity of Walt Disney comics, not only here in North America but around the world, it is worthwhile to look at some of their characteristics. To have a better understanding of their impact on audiences, it is important to begin by examining the conditions in which the characters developed.

THE WONDERFUL WORLD OF DISNEY: DREAMS PRESENTED AS REALITY

Disney Productions is a huge multinational corporation which in 1988 had 32,000 salaried employees working principally in four sectors: amusement parks and resort centres; film and television production, distribution and broadcasting; real estate operations; and by-products (newspapers, publications, records, games, software and Disney character merchandising). The corporation's income is proportional to the breadth of its operations: in 1986, Disney reported two billion dollars in gross income; in 1987, first-quarter sales were 39% above the same period of the previous year. The corporation's financial success is based on a multimedia strategy designed and managed by administrators from large Hollywood production companies and big television networks. The animated cartoon division, which was computerized in the late 1980s, produces one animated feature film every 18 months on average. At any given time, Disney movie studios are working on more than a hundred film projects. Touchstone, the Disney group's "family viewing" production company, has become a world leader in videocassette commercialization, with sales bordering on one million dollars per quarter for the American market alone (Eudes, 1988).

The Worldwide Presence of Disney

Eudes (1988) has reported that Disney productions are transmitted by satellite to cable networks 24 hours a day, and reach every audience imaginable. The increasingly invasive presence of these productions on television screens around the world is the best means of promoting the company's various products. Among these is the merchandising of Disney characters, which generated more than $160 million in 1987. The movement is so widespread that boutiques specializing exclusively in Disney products are sprouting up all over the world, including Canada.

But it is the amusement parks—namely Disneyland in California, Disney World in Florida, Tokyo Disneyland in Japan, and Eurodisneyland in France—that profit the most from the showcasing of activities related to the movie and television sectors. Since 1985, the company's amusement parks have been modernized and expanded, through an annual $600 million capital infusion. The Disney strategy is to make the parks indistinguishable from the studios. New park attractions are inspired by techniques used on movie and video-production sets, and are designed by the most renowned filmmakers. Disney's first television broadcast was called *Disneyland TV Show*, a programme which actually preceded the 1955 opening of Disneyland. This programme—a weekly, one-hour broadcast on the American television network ABC—reached 90 million viewers, a record at the time. In France, Eurodisneyland adopted a similar strategy: every Saturday night the *Disney Channel* fills the television screens of FR3 viewers, a state-run television network. For some reason, however, Eurodisneyland has not been as successful as expected. It would appear that cultural differences are responsible for the lack of enthusiasm of the European public, especially the French.

The history of the Disney invasion of France is particularly revealing of the imperialistic force that the enterprise can engender through its advertising strategies. France, itself an imperialist country protective of its culture, was once astonishingly impervious to Disney's onslaught. The following anecdote dating back to 1971 is all the more startling, for it reveals Disney's capacity to penetrate a market that was hostile to American mass culture to begin with.

Michèle Mattelart (1976) has told how the release of the French version of the Disney movie *The Aristocats* was slated for Christmas 1971. On October 1st of that year, only 1% of the French population had heard of the famous felines. A month later, following a televised programme and a comic strip published in the newspaper *France-Soir*, the figure jumped to 19%. After the children's fair in mid-November, the advertising campaigns launched by various firms using Disney products (figurines, cereal-box building and colouring games, etc.) pushed this number to 40%. Finally, on December 1st, two months after the start of the publicity blitz, with the film not even released yet, 83% of the French population was familiar with the film's storyline.

This spectacular breakthrough was followed in 1975 by another event that illustrates the extent of the American colonization of the French public. When *Pinocchio* was released, two different cinematographic versions were shown in French movie theatres simultaneously: the Disney version, and a version made by a French director named Comencini. The American version was shown on 20 screens and attracted an audience of 482,000 viewers within a 10-week period, whereas the French version was projected on one screen only and took as many as 24 weeks to attract an audience of 47,200 people. This is how the "world of Disney" invaded the "world of the French," not only through cinema, but through other products as well, some of which can even be found on the breakfast table. Mattelart (1976) has claimed that Disney filters through every aspect of the relationships a child has with the world, life, people and things. Disney is more intrusive than school and surrounds us as a form of nature.

This influence is clearly measurable: Disney comics are reproduced in more than 5,000 newspapers, translated into more than 30 languages and broadcast in more than 100 countries. The characters are introduced into an endless number of households, and can be found not only on bookshelves or the breakfast table, but also on walls, pillows, bed sheets, and in the bathroom in various forms. "Disney has been exalted as the inviolable common cultural heritage of contemporary man . . . " In fact, "in more than one country Mickey Mouse is more popular than the national hero of the day" (Dorfman and Mattelart, 1975: 28). Disney characters are used for all sorts of purposes: everything from birth control campaigns in Third World countries to fundraisers for children's disaster relief. It is not surprising, then, that any attack against the image of Disney is construed as an offense to morality.

For Disney's advocates, these images represent "real" childhood, and their politicization should be forbidden. Entertainment is generally seen as an independent sphere, an enchanted world, in which children are portrayed as gentle and docile, unknowing of pain and hatred. It is sacred ground, one that is well exploited by Disney. As M. Mattelart (1976) has claimed, attacking Disney is tantamount to attacking this sacred ground and, consequently, childhood. According to this researcher, the defenders of the eternal, idyllic and problem-free childhood projected by Disney are not concerned that these ubiquitous messages obstruct other entertainment formulas, that is, other ways of imagining dreams and reality and of perceiving the child's relationship with these dreams and reality.

Moreover, commercial comics are a commodity produced by adults, who put adult ideas and thoughts into the mouths of infant characters, who thereby become "miniature adults." To be sure, this mass culture has a democratizing influence, but this effect has its drawback too: it produces communication that discourages self-determination; it is the self-colonization of the child's imagination. In the following sections, we will first analyze how comics are produced, and then look at the content of a number of comics marketed by Disney.

The Production of the World of Disney

Ariel Dorfman and Armand Mattelart (1975) conducted an exhaustive analysis of the Disney comic *Donald Duck*, in which they explored the underside of this "innocent" literature created for children. Given the phenomenal popularity of the world of Disney, the researchers decided to examine not only what is conveyed by the images, but also how Walt Disney built this empire. Their exploration of the production process of this capitalist enterprise was necessary, given that Disney products are distributed throughout the world.

As David Kunzle underlined in the preface to the Dorfman and Mattelart study: "The names of Presidents change; that of Disney remains" (Kunzle, 1975: 11). Sixty-seven years after the birth of Mickey Mouse, nearly 30 years after the death of the owner of the empire, Disney remains the most widely known American name in the world. How did Disney build his empire?

For Walt Disney, comics were not as important as movies and amusement parks, which are much more profitable activities. Disney would often create a new comic-strip hero named after one of his movies so that people would remember them longer. Yet, despite his preference for movies, his company, like any other multinational corporation, found that it was more profitable to decentralize and diversify operations. Thus, "franchises" were opened in many countries either to produce translations (more or less accurately) of existing works, or create new stories. How is the production of Disney comics organized?

Kunzle (1975) has claimed that the Disney production system is designed to prevent artists "from feeling any pride" for creating a particular work and from receiving any recognition. Once they sign a contract, the artists' work belongs to Disney and is marked as Disney's. Artists do not profit financially nor in terms of creativity. After 1926, Disney himself stopped drawing and writing dialogue. Yet it was he who was recognized as the greatest creator of children's, and even adults', fantasies. It was not until many years later that he was forced by the union representing American artists to include artists' names on their work. Disney, however, made sure his name appeared first and in bigger letters than the artists' so that he would still get credit for the work. Are any artists remembered for their work on Disney products?

One of the most prolific artists at Disney Productions was Carl Barks, the creator of Uncle Scrooge and many other children's favourite Disney characters. He created 300 of Disney's best stories, representing more than 7,000 pages of artwork, for which he was paid an average of $11.50 per page. Moreover, Barks did not have the right to sign his name on any page. In the meantime, Disney took all the credit for these creations, including the millions of dollars in profit each story raised. As for Barks, "his employers, trying carefully to keep him ignorant of the true extent of this astonishing commercial success, preserved him from individual fame and from his numerous fans who enquired in vain after his name" (Kunzle, 1975: 17). But who was the man, Disney?

Kunzle has told us that Walter Elias Disney was born in Chicago in 1901. At the age of four, his father, a carpenter and small building contractor, bought a farm in Missouri. After living for four years on the farm, the family returned to the city—Kansas City—where, according to his own memoires, he was forced to do hard, menial work and give his income to the household. Walt was also beaten regularly by his father. All the while, Disney's mother and younger sister were strangely absent from his memories. After becoming successful, Disney refused all ties with his family, including both parents and siblings, with the exception of his brother Roy, who was an "uncle father-figure." In fact, Roy became the financial manager of the Disney company and, until his marriage, shared a house with Walt. As we will see later, the absence of parents and family is a recurring theme in Disney's comics.

Walt's own marriage did not seem to involve any more affection or intimacy than he experienced in his family. After his brother's wedding, Walt found himself alone and in need of a "new room-mate" to share his house. So he married and had a daughter, who later claimed not to have had any sort of intimate relationship with her father. All the while, Disney openly admitted that women bored him and that the sole purpose of his relationships with women was to control them. The same could be said of his relationship to nature. He liked nature only as long as he could control or tame it. His personal garden, for instance, was highly structured. We will see that Disney's desire for dominance is also manifested in his comics. Let us now have a closer look at his work.

ARE DONALD AND MICKEY IMPOSTORS?

In their study of *Donald Duck*, Dorfman and Mattelart (1975) analyzed the ideas and values conveyed in various media products that are disseminated to millions of children. As we have just seen, Disney fabricates a universal mass culture, the characters of which form a big global "family" extending well beyond international borders, differences and ideologies. To mount an attack on this world, the authors have claimed, is tantamount to attacking the whole of civilization.

Yet this children's literature is an industrial product, a mass of texts created by adults on the basis of what they think children are, or ought to be, like. In these adult texts and drawings, childhood becomes a magical world immune to serious conflicts. Such is the dream childhood, the true nature of the young when described by grown-ups. Dorfman and Mattelart (1975) point out that this perception of childhood is a closed circuit: "Children have been conditioned by the magazines and the culture which spawned them" (Dorfman and Mattelart, 1975: 30). This idealized perception of childhood is projected in character-types that reappear in each Disney story. The most typical features of Disney comics may be summed up as follows: the complete absence of parents; the dominance of exploitative child characters over weaker ones; the submission to and discipline of dominated characters; and, lastly, the portrayal of female characters as asexual sexuated objects. Let us now look at these characteristics in greater detail.

The Invisible Adults: Father and Mother

In their analysis, Dorfman and Mattelart (1975) note that, oddly enough, parents are completely absent from Disney comics. There are uncles, nephews, cousins and great-uncles, but parents—those who conceived and gave birth to the characters—are conspicuously absent. Relationships between men and women, in which male characters dominate, do not extend beyond engagement: Daisy is Donald's eternal fiancée, and Minnie, Mickey's. Male dominance can also be observed among the child characters: twins and triplets (for example, Mickey's two nephews, and Donald's three nephews) are all male and have sprung from nowhere. In the words of Dorfman and Mattelart: "the last vestige of parenthood, male or female, has been eliminated" (1975: 34). Does this mean Disney comics are free of any sexual connotation?

On the contrary, the image of women in Disney productions is that of a lonely being and a pure and sexual object that is "solicited and postponed." Women, exemplified in Daisy and Minnie, are portrayed as submissive beings trapped in dominated positions. Alternately portrayed as beauty queens or servants, they are always subordinate to Donald or Mickey. These women must meet a particular code of "femininity," which says they must be seductive, flirtatious, domestic and passive. Otherwise, female characters are witches, wicked stepmothers or other demonic characters—which abound in Disney's work. Disney's coquette, a starlet in the most traditional Hollywood style, is the ultimate token archetype, both revered and feared by men. In short, the world of Disney—a universe where no sex occurs—is "an asexual sexuated world" (Dorfman and Mattelart, 1975: 39).

Dorfman and Mattelart claim that it is in the name of innocence, chastity and decency that Disney keeps children from being exposed to any reference to sexuality, while paradoxically constructing a world full of sexual stereotypes and connotations. The world of Disney is a perpetual orphanage. But without having a biological birth, how could these orphans have grown up? They are "forced to imitate their creator and spiritual father . . . The emasculated slave [the hero] is condemned to others, as he is condemned to Disney" (Dorfman and Mattelart, 1975: 36). Without a biological family, these characters are free to enjoy immortality and eternal life.

Love, affection and loyalty are absent. In Disney comics, the dominated are obedient, humble, disciplined and subjected to the orders of the dominators, who are not above employing constant repression, threats, and physical, moral and economic coercion. Scrooge McDuck, Donald's uncle, exploits his great-nephews and Donald in a relation of dominance, and does not tolerate any complaints from his victims. Scrooge is the boss, and they are his victims. Despite their submission, the victims themselves uphold Scrooge's values advocating the virtues of notoriety and fortune. "So the child's 'natural disposition' evidently serves Disney only in so far as it lends innocence to the adult world, and serves the myth of childhood" (Dorfman and Mattelart, 1975: 35). In situations where the system fails due to an adult's incompetence, it is up to the children to re-establish the order, not so that their imaginations can rule, but to restore the order of adult domination. Thus, the child "contributes to his own colonization" (Dorfman and Mattelart, 1975: 36).

In the world of Disney, children, who in reality are mostly responsible, spontaneous, imaginative and affectionate, become envious, ruthless and cruel exploiters of the weak. In the absence of affection, "children learn through Disney fear and hatred"; thus, as Dorfman and Mattelart have asserted, Disney becomes "the worst enemy of family harmony" (1975: 35). However, the stereotypes transmitted in this "un-natural" world are not limited to images of children and women: they include all that is not American, white or male.

The Noble Savage

Disney's is a "natural" world in which his creators present every character in a "humanized" animal form. Urban characters dream of a return to nature, a classless universe populated with "noble savages" only. Every Disney comic story is constructed on the basis of the discrimination between the city and the countryside that infantilizes nonindustrial communities and portrays the city/countryside relationship in terms of dichotomies: dominator/dominated and colonizer/colonized. Any attempts at a rebellion by the dominated is ridiculed and belittled as a form of momentary disorder, which is quickly resolved. Finally, the cleavage between the dominated characters divides them into two clans: the rural clan (positive-popular-countryfolk) and the urban clan (negative-popular-proletarians).

First and foremost, the world of Disney yearns to be the "natural" world of the child. To achieve this "naturalization," Disney suggests an animal universe, with which children tend to identify. These small animals, that is, Disney's endearing characters, are in reality "monstrous human beings" (Dorfman and Mattelart, 1975: 41). All are city dwellers who long to return to nature, but live in the inferno of bureaucratic cities, regulated by police, where penalties are imposed on whoever contravenes the law. This city life, in which

Donald and company experience countless inconveniences and injustices, is what feeds their desire to return to nature. When, at last, the characters find themselves in nature, they are confronted with (big and small) primitive and exotic characters of a different race and colour, each one dressed in a simple loincloth. These exclusively male primitives are "noble savages": somewhat lazy characters who speak a language not unlike that of infants. They subsist on hunting, fishing and tourism, and never seem to work. Even though they are ruled by a king, they are all equal, have no religion and never die.

Dorfman and Mattelart (1975) have thus remarked that there are two types of children in Disney stories: those from the city, who are superior and intelligent, and those from the periphery, who are innocent, clumsy and easily fooled. Urban children are active and, armed with technology and intellectual maturity, dominate the natural world in the name of civilization. In contrast, nature's children are passive and immature, and do not project the image of adulthood that the urban children do. According to Dorfman and Mattelart (1975), the noble savages represent Disney's image of underdeveloped peoples. They are naive, not very bright and willing to give up their resources for next to nothing. They are portrayed as uncivilized beings, from whom it is easy to take things, since they do not have the means to exploit their own resources. Progress comes from the outside in the form of trinkets or other cheap products manufactured by industries in so-called "civilized" or capitalist countries. Like the noble savages, "underdeveloped" countries will never be able to join the "civilized club." These are the two models of childhood that Disney presents its young readers, and it is one of these that they must choose as their model for behaviour: the small, active, competitive, clever, victorious and resourceful duck, who is made in the image of grown-ups; or the passive savage, who never wins anything.

Within the context of these stories, imperialism is portrayed as "the impartial judge of the interests of the people, and their liberating angel" (Dorfman and Mattelart, 1975: 52). In fact, the savages are never stripped of their natural means of existence, for this would mean risking their discovery of the existence of the production economy. Thus, Donald and his nephew are sometimes placed in situations where they support the natives in a "disinterested" way when the latter are confronted with bad guys who are even "more bad" than they are. Thus, in addition to the authoritarian atmosphere, the noble savages must contend with the paternalism of benevolent strangers, the dispensers of justice and defenders of the rights of the underprivileged to eat and survive. "Defending the only thing that the noble savage can use (their food), the lack of which would result in their death (or rebellion, either of which would violate their image of infantile innocence), the big city folk establish themselves as the spokesman of these submerged and voiceless peoples" (Dorfman and Mattelart, 1975: 53). Among all these characters, the proletariat is absent. Even though the underprivileged classes themselves are present, there is no visible production process in which to put them to work.

The Missing Production Process

In Disney comics, no one earns a living as a labourer in a company beset by employee/ employer conflicts. On the contrary, money is obtained from either out of the blue or some playful activity such as a treasure hunt. Regardless of the form of the treasure, once it is discovered, it is transformed into coins. The process of production—the human participation in the extraction of precious metals and the manufacturing of material goods—is absent from the story. This strategy not only eclipses the existence of commodity production, but also disseminates the idea that it is the gold treasure that replaces the production process. Consumption, however, is unbridled and justifies the obsession for money that brings Disney's characters to life. This obsession is shared by bad and ugly robbers, who represent the underprivileged classes of society. These characters are the personification of public enemy number one and constitute the essential threat looming over wealth, even though they never manage to appropriate it. Strong, but stupid, robbers always come up against the good, intelligent, little characters.

Dorfman and Mattelart (1975) have noted that in every *Donald Duck* story, more than three-quarters of the action revolves around trips taken by the urban ducks in their quest for gold, while the other quarter shows the ducks back in the city struggling to keep their fortune and trying to achieve glory. The treasure hunt—that is, the hunt for the ancient object dating back to ancient civilizations which has disappeared without a trace or heir—is the main focus of the ducks' activities. The nobel savages are never descendants of the ancient civilizations that once occupied the land, and therefore cannot be the rightful heirs to these treasures; at any rate, they ignore the value of these treasures. The treasure-trove, the origin of which remains a mystery, therefore legitimately belongs to whoever discovers it. The owner of the treasure "creates it the moment he thinks of setting off in search of it. It never really existed before, anywhere" (Dorfman and Mattelart, 1975: 62). As soon as the object falls into the hands of Uncle Scrooge, for example, it is transformed into money, or dollars to be specific. The most beautiful jewel loses its history and shape; it melts and mixes in the pool of coins, in which Scrooge bathes in ecstasy. This leads Dorfman and Mattelart to claim that "Disnification is Dollarfication: all objects . . . are transformed into gold" (1975: 62). Moreover, there is never any end to the quest. And traces of the fabrication of these objects are nowhere to be found: no mining, no drilling, no miners, who are the real-life labour power required to extract mineral ores. Once the gold is found, all that matters is to accumulate it.

In this context, the worker—the true producer of objects—disappears along with class conflicts and antagonistic interests. Thus, Disney removes from children's imaginations all reference to social reality; he serves up a world without conflict, contradiction or class struggle: a classless world. For Dorfman and Mattelart, "Disney's is a world of bourgeois interests with the cracks in the structure repeatedly papered over" (1975: 65).

Though production may be absent from the world of Disney, consumption is everywhere. Characters work in service-sector professions associated with the sale and purchase of thousands of objects. The Disney comic never ceases to glorify overconsumption, thereby instilling the concept in children: purchase objects, throw them away and purchase new ones, all for the sake of perpetuating the system. It is this thirst for money that characterizes every Disney character: the almighty dollar can buy any object, even though objects are never seen being produced.

In this world that is thirsty for money, there is a clear distinction between good and bad. The good guys are those who respect others' property. Thus, when Donald's nephews fight over the $10 bill they found on the street, they are scolded by Donald, who insists that it should be returned to its legitimate owner. Next, a young girl dressed in tatters appears, and the bill she lost earlier is rightfully returned to her. The message is clear: the bad guys are those who try to appropriate others' goods. The bad guys, however, never succeed, for the good guys are more clever. Disney pits muscle against brain, manual labour against intellectual labour. And who comes out the winner? "The good guys have 'cornered the knowledge market' in their competition against the muscle-bound brutes" (Dorfman and Mattelart, 1975: 68–9). Charity is the virtue of the wealthy, and any good deed done in a poor neighbourhood will be described as a sign of morality in the comfortable bourgeois homes. It is never said that the good bourgeois possess society's wealth and own the means of production only because they have constantly exploited others to make profits and accumulate capital. Thus Disney defends the argument that it "was always the ideas of the bourgeoisie which gave them the advantage in the race for success, and nothing else" (Dorfman and Mattelart, 1975: 69). Once again, it is in the name of this ideology that Disney defines Donald Duck's work.

Donald the Worker

The world of Disney, where everything exists without having been fabricated and can be purchased although no one earns money, is also the world of work that is both easy to find and do. Such work may be described as adventure-work or leisure-work. Donald is fired from his job only because of his clumsiness. He will do his utmost to find a new job as soon as possible, and for his troubles he will be quickly rewarded with a well-deserved rest: tranquility bordering on boredom. This is not only a world where all efforts are rewarded, but also where work becomes a pastime and is associated with the unusual—not with routine and normality, as in real life. Uncle Scrooge, the true bourgeois that he is, is portrayed as a lonely being, who is poor in appearance. He is sensitive and sentimental, since he loves gold for the sake of gold. He conveys the myth of the *self-made* man, namely that everything is possible to whoever is desiring and deserving enough; a myth certain sociologists refer to as "meritocracy."

Thus Donald, an incorrigible consumer of the superfluous, spends his time looking for work, but never has problems finding it in a world that abounds in jobs. Nevertheless, he is regularly fired and develops the fear of losing his job. To the reader, Donald remains eternally unemployed, not because of the structural contradictions of the capitalist system, but because of his personal faults and clumsiness, and the endless catastrophes that afflict him, and which ultimately result in his dismissal. This situation therefore conveys the idea that if people are unemployed it is because of their own doing, not because of a lack of work. Thus:

> Despite all the masks, Donald is sensed as the true representative of the contemporary worker. But the wages essential to the latter are superfluous to Donald. What the real life worker searches for desperately, Donald has no trouble finding. While the worker produces and suffers from the material conditions of life and the exploitation to which he is subjected, Donald suffers only the illusion of work, its passive and abstract weight, in the form of adventure (Dorfman and Mattelart, 1975: 73).

In this world of easy work, the trials Donald faces ultimately earn him his crown of laurels, that is, leisure and rest. Every story begins with idle scenes of leisure, tranquility or sometimes outright boredom, which characterize the ambiance of Duckburg, and from which the hero will extricate himself for wild, difficult adventures (work or travel) that will end with a vacation and a well-deserved rest. According to Dorfman and Mattelart, this "apparent opposition between work and leisure is nothing but a subterfuge to the advantage of the latter. Leisure invades and imposes its laws upon the whole realm of work. In the 'Hard-Working Leisure-Lovers Club' . . . work is nugatory, a leisure activity, a vehicle of consumerism, and a means of killing time" (1975: 75). Work is also something strange and abnormal that has lost its real meaning, namely that work is associated with banality and routine.

This caricature of work is a reminder of the role that leisure and entertainment play in capitalist society. Donald fills his free time and chases away boredom with adventures that will give him the means to escape, much like the contemporary consumer who escapes boredom by feeding on mass culture. "Mickey is entertained by mystery and adventure. The reader is entertained by Mickey entertaining himself" (Dorfman and Mattelart, 1975: 76). Disney applies the modern concept of mass culture, namely that only media entertainment can liberate humans from everyday anxieties and hardships, and reconcile the conflicts between work and leisure, the commonplace and the imaginary, the social and the extrasocial, body and soul, production and consumption, and city and countryside. The imaginary seizes reality, coats it with a veneer of innocence and magic, and returns it to the consumer, who interprets it "as a magical, marvellous paradigm of his own common experience . . . " (Dorfman and Mattelart, 1975: 76). Yet this fantasy is the opposite of reality and does not incorporate any facet of it. Let us now take a closer look at the set of values conveyed in Disney comics.

The World of Disney: "New" Simply Means More of the Same

Disney comics do not help children become familiar with the world they live in or understand reality. Contrary to reality, Disney characters are hyperactive and yet psychologically immobile—that is, they do not grow—and, despite apparent struggles, both the dominator and the dominated remain trapped in their respective positions. The history of the past is a reproduction of the predominant norms and values of the present. Thus, the power of the ruler is portrayed as natural, not as something socially acquired. In a reversal of reality, the ideas that are conveyed come from nature, not from humans evolving in a given social and historical environment.

For Disney, fast-paced action and turmoil are everything. Yet, nothing ever really changes in the world of Disney, and variations revolve around the same theme; for instance, endless scientific and technological innovations are created and consumed, then perish and are replaced. However, these innovations are never placed in the context of the labour involved in the production of consumer commodities. Science is there to service this wonderful world: objects are versatile and are not synonymous with progress, since they disappear with the closing of the episode in which they were given life. As Dorfman and Mattelart have pointed out: "For there to be progress, there must be memory, an inter-related chain of inherited knowledge. In Disney, the object serves only the moment, and that moment alone" (1975: 81). Thus presented, objects are an invitation to consumption and disposal. Gadgets are a dime a dozen, and are related to transportation (planes, rockets, submarines, etc.) and mass culture (television, radio, records, etc.). Once again, commodities are entirely cut off from any ties with their fabrication: they come from nowhere.

Each adventure prides itself in being a new adventure. Yet, each "new" episode is just more of the same themes of the old episodes. For Dorfman and Mattelart (1975), the characters' frenzy and agitation are but an illusion of movement and change: there are two clans, one of masters (the citizens of Duckburg) and one of the dominated (the docile, noble savages and the wicked bandits), and no one can escape their situation. What is more, by reducing the past to the present, Disney achieves "his schematization and moralization of Third World history" (Dorfman and Mattelart, 1975: 85). Thus, an episode relates the ancient history of conquistadors (portrayed by The Beagle Boys) who tried their best to take away the wealth of the Aztec Indians (played by the ducks). Another finds Uncle Scrooge's head on an Egyptian sphinx. In this way, Dorfman and Mattelart concluded, the dominant classes perceive and interpret history only on the basis of facts that reinforce its universality and eternity.

Thus "Disney, the bourgeoisie's eulogist and flattering mirror, has distorted history so that the dominant class sees its rise as a natural, not social, phenomenon" (Dorfman and Mattelart, 1975: 86). Of all of Disney's characters, Mickey distinguishes himself as a sort of god obsessed with good, and disinterested in honours and wealth. He sees himself as the symbol of America, its most famous representative and its ambassador to the world. Because he does not subscribe to the same aspirations to power as the other characters, he could be construed as a "maternal" character, and as such would fill the void of the absent mother in Disney's work. Disney sometimes also uses Mickey to criticize the defects of the system, out of concern to "democratize" his publications. For example, Disney deals with inflation without mentioning that it is the proletariat and the dominated classes who suffer most of its consequences; he also addresses the issues of pollution and drugs without pointing to their causes. Incorporating these social problems is only a "facade of democratic debate, which while it appears to open up the problems defined by the bourgeoisie as 'socially relevant,' really conceals the subtle censorship they impose. This 'democratic debate' prevents the unmasking of the fallacy of 'free' thought and expression . . . " (Dorfman and Mattelart, 1975: 93).

Donald the Impostor

The world of Disney is immaterial: industrial, sexual and historical production are all absent. Conflicts have no social basis and do not emerge in response to economic or political control. Instead, they pit the good against the evil, the resourceful against the foolish, the lucky against the unlucky. There are no grey areas. This situation is all the more disturbing given that the characters evolve in a world that bears a close resemblance to everyday life: they are frenetic consumers, abide by market rules and delight in the joys of leisure. Yet they are never motivated by material needs, and their only concern is to find something to pass the time. In short, Disney's ideas take the form of inherently material productions which convey a set of values, opinions and judgments that correspond to the image capitalist society creates of itself. These ideas, however, are completely unrealistic, since they do not reflect a large part of the social experiences of both the young and old. True, these ideas are entertaining; but they are in no way instructive for the young, since the immateriality and immobility of characters and situations do not help children develop the imagination and skills required to adjust harmoniously to a society in constant evolution.

This deformation of reality is all the more threatening when Disney inundates people in Third World countries with stories that sing the praises of the American model, and attempts to instill values that have nothing to do with their reality. Because this interpretation is disconnected from social realities, Dorfman and Mattelart accuse Donald not only of being an impostor, but also of promoting underdevelopment: "reading Disney is like having one's own exploited condition rammed with honey down one's throat" (1975: 98). Through so-called "innocent" literature, values and ideas originating in Western societies are massively disseminated and presented as the only valid ones for all societies.

> Putting the Duck on the carpet is to question the various forms of authoritarian and paternalist culture pervading the relationship of the bourgeoisie among themselves, with others, and with nature. It is to challenge the role of individuals and their class in the process of historic development, and their fabrication of a mass culture built on the backs of the masses (Dorfman and Mattelart, 1975: 98).

Today, this analysis may appear to be outdated, for have the times not changed and comics too? Let us see if a more recent study draws the same conclusions.

THE DECONSTRUCTION OF DONALD THE IMPOSTOR

Martin Barker (1989) has conducted a critical analysis of American comics, including those produced by Disney, by drawing on various studies of the subject. Barker has maintained that Dorfman and Mattelart's (1975) study remains one of the most extensive and important analyses of Disney characters, despite the existence of a body of research that interprets the various themes of Disney comics differently. Barker has made a comparison between the analysis of Dorfman and Mattelart and those of other researchers.

For Dorfman and Mattelart, humour is a mask, a stratagem aimed at justifying what would otherwise be openly considered imperialism. Other authors, Barker has argued, have drawn different conclusions. For example, Reitberger and Fuchs (in Barker, 1989) placed greater emphasis on the satirical aspect of Disney comics. They have interpreted Uncle Scrooge as a buffoon, a caricature of someone who is so successful that he can detect the smell of gold or money miles away, and revels in plunging into a pool full of gold coins. This caricature of money relates the possession of wealth with comicalness and absurdity. For Reitberger and Fuchs, humour modifies the message by poking fun at capitalist exploitation through absurdity.

Another researcher arrived at conclusions diametrically opposed to those of Dorfman and Mattelart (1975). Indeed, Dave Wagner has construed that Disney comics are a critique of capitalism. According to him, Uncle Scrooge is a scathing parody of the typical bourgeois capitalist. Scrooge's personality can be summed up by his quest for capital and his ridiculous passion for money. "If he keeps his capital in the money form, he won't be able to expand, and all will be lost. But if he invests he will be deprived of his only source of delight, which is to swim and bathe in piles of the stuff" (cited in Barker, 1989: 286). For Wagner, humour keeps Scrooge "alive" in the sense that if readers did not find him funny, he could not survive as an object of derision.

Mike Barrier has also attenuated Dorfman and Mattelart's (1975) arguments. Barrier has claimed that it was only natural for Carl Barks, Donald's official artist, to write and draw stories revolving around money for contemporary America, just as it was natural for a Renaissance artist to draw the Virgin Mary. "Good artists," Barrier wrote, "work with what is around them, but they are not limited by it. Barks *used* the American preoccupations with wealth and idleness and work; he wasn't imprisoned by them . . . His real subject-matter was not money, but the way in which human beings deceive and destroy themselves—and how funny they can be when they do it" (cited in Barker, 1989: 286–7). Humour thus represents a parable of human absurdity and creates a bridge between Scrooge and human obsessions.

In summing up these studies and his own research, Barker has identified four important issues that characterize Walt Disney's cultural politics.

1. Disney wanted to control everything and have only his name appear on all his company's productions.

2. He was interested not in culture or art, which he hated with a passion, but only in sales. He prided himself in speaking the language of the people, the language of massive sales.

3. In this context, every fairy tale redone by Disney underwent "Disneyfication" thanks to brilliant techniques that transformed a tale into a "folksy, gag-ridden" and innocent story. Disney made extensive use of techniques available to him at the time: he was one of the first to use sound, then colour, in movies.

4. Finally, each Disney production was so sugar-coated in innocence that "Disney" became *the* name in mass culture productions, as well as a form of morality. He "became the embodiment of the 'American way of life'" (Barker, 1989: 290). For this reason, Dorfman and Mattelart's (1975) analysis of Disney productions must be considered as a critique not of an art form, but of the morality transmitted by his productions.

For Barker, this morality—this representation of the "American way of life"—raises the question of cultural imperialism. He has emphasized the importance of David Kunzle's research which traces the various stages of Carl Barks' work. Kunzle showed the extent to which Barks' stories were influenced by the political context in the United States. For example, in the 1950s, at the height of McCarthyism, Barks' stories were imbued with explicit anticommunism. But what is most important to note is that Kunzle showed the extent to which the various stages of American foreign policies were reflected in Disney comics. Kunzle agreed with many of Dorfman and Mattelart's points on this issue. In short, Walt Disney comics are far from being as innocent as they appear to be. If they are not children's literature, can they be considered infantile literature?

ARE COMICS INFANTILE LITERATURE?

It has been constantly observed that the cultural industry, tailored to answer the simultaneous needs of immense groups of people, levels off its messages at the so-called lowest common denominator, creating only that which everybody can understand effortlessly. This common denominator (as has also been pointed out frequently) is based on a construct of—what else?—the median, quintessential North American common man, who has undergone secular canonization as the universal measure for humanity . . . People can be treated as children because they do not, in effect, control their own destiny (Dorfman, 1987: 145).

Comics are part of this mass culture. Dorfman (1987) believes that mass culture, especially comics, infantilizes people, adults and children alike. Disney and his superheroes offer the adult reader the means to relive childhood and the possibility of maintaining a form of innocence. These products, typically American, have taken off and attained their cruising speed in a century marked by phenomenal technological developments and growth of consumption. Americans have found themselves in a privileged position, where they have engendered a host of lasting and popular symbols. According to Dorfman, it is the history of the United States, the way the country developed, that appears to have made the infantilization process of adults possible.

America has always been associated with innocence. In just over two centuries the United States has become an *empire*. And yet, Dorfman (1987) has argued, its citizens have always maintained the belief that they are "good, clean and wholesome," without considering themselves members of an empire and without being bound by responsibility. Unlike people from certain European countries (for example the French, the Spanish and the British), Americans have not established permanent institutions with laws, rules and doctrines to rule over their territory. Instead, they look for openings for the American market to sell their large production of goods. While Americans have sought to impose their vision on other countries through aggression, they have simultaneously tried to maintain an image of naivety and give the impression "of being reborn at every crossroads" (Dorfman, 1987: 147). Americans view themselves simply as young and as new as their own country. They have forgotten its tyrannical legacy and its mistakes of the past, and only remember the outcome of the American revolution—which was considered a battle and a victory for democracy and liberty. They tend to view themselves as superior to and different than the rest of humanity, and nurture the belief that they are its best hope of survival. This explains their dream of converting pagans to the real way of life and their encouragement to others to follow their example, an example which is accessible to anyone as long as the world remains a market. Dorfman asserts that Americans believe that all foreign cultures should emulate them, and that these foreigners have but to consume American products to become their equals.

Americans also firmly believe that North America is a *melting pot* and that anyone can become American, regardless of one's culture, interests, religion, beliefs, race or age. "To become one, all we have to do is consume and dream the good dream" (Dorfman, 1987: 147). It is because of this combination of elements that Americans consider themselves as "untainted children." With the historical development of this image, America has been able to project a universal category—that of childhood—onto foreign cultures that are subjected politically and economically to American influence. "American mass culture appealed to the child the audience would like to be, the child they remembered . . . " (Dorfman, 1987: 147–8).

Nevertheless, Dorfman has noted that historical circumstances cannot by themselves explain the success of mass culture. " . . . the infantilization that seems to be such an essential centerpiece of mass media culture may be grounded in a certain form of human nature that goes beyond historical circumstances" (Dorfman: 1987: 148). This tendency to maintain an infantile mentality at adult age is a twentieth-century phenomenon. In the spirit of modernity, people do their best to stay young in mind and in body for their entire lives. Mickey Mouse himself was not an exception to the rule. In his early days, in the 1920s, Mickey was a sort of wicked bandit, an adult with hostile features. With the passing of time his behaviour changed, and he became friendlier and younger-looking, most notably with a larger head and bigger eyes; in short, he adopted all the traits of juvenility. This infantile-looking character became the ambassador and the symbol of American society.

> Mickey does nothing more than go the way of all North American mass culture. He joins power and infantilization . . . and lets an innocent smile disarm all criticism. The famous mouse, like the mass culture into which he was born, automatically reconciles the adult and the child by appealing to a biological attribute in us, the fact that humans are instinctually conditioned to protect their young and are prepared by nature to react well to anything that resembles juvenility (Dorfman, 1987: 148).

Disney, therefore, targets not only the child inside every adult, but, as Dorfman warns, also real children, who are equally subjected to the influence of his productions. How can they be protected from these images, which teach them how to be competitive, which show them dominance as the only model capable of replacing submission, which presents them with stereotyped sexual roles, and which suggests deformed visions of history? These images show them "how to grow up, adapt, and succeed in the world as it presently is. They are learning not to ask questions" (Dorfman, 1987: 150). Dorfman has suggested that people should be trusted, for they have a critical mind.

> The enemy is inside. . . . We have been produced by the same world that produced the *Digest*, Babar, Superman, Mampato, and Donald Duck. We have grown accustomed to the way they whisper to us. . . . There is in men and women a deep refusal to be manipulated. We have in ourselves intimations of another humanity . . . (Dorfman, 1987: 150).

This refusal to be manipulated leads individuals to work towards making social changes in various spheres, including the realm of the arts and the media.

But, above all, Dorfman concludes, we must have faith in children. Aided by their parents, in a language characterized by respect and open-mindedness, children can distinguish between what is real and what is false, and—"with the mutual patience that comes from building together a future for which no insurance policy can be bought" (Dorfman, 1987: 151)—make the effort to reinterpret reality. In short, child audiences, like adult audiences, *negotiate* media content.

CONCLUSION

Are comics an innocent genre of literature? As we have just seen, the answer is no. Like all the other forms of mass communication that we have examined, comics convey values and ideas that are not so easily detected on the surface. It must not be forgotten that comics, like any mass media product, are fabricated to make a profit and convey an ideology. Whether it is *Donald Duck* or *Superman*, each story transmits the values that creators and producers intend to convey, and is *constructed* with a particular form that attempts to satisfy the largest possible number of people.

Nevertheless, even if the ideas expounded in comics do not appear to be the most educational and formative for the young, they—much like soap operas and Harlequin Romances—can certainly serve as a springboard for instigating discussions between young people and adults on more serious topics. As Dorfman remarked, children must be trusted not only to interpret these contents in their own way, but also to put up resistance against certain ideas and to discuss others.

On the basis of what we have seen in previous chapters, it is obvious that mass cultural creations are not a vehicle for *avant-garde* ideas or revolutionary values suggesting profound changes aiming for social equality or liberation of the oppressed. Nevertheless, most analyses have shown that the content of comics is a catalyst for discussions of personal or social problems. There do not appear to be any studies of this form of communication. It could be expected, however, that as mass culture, its impact would be similar to that of other types of content.

Another form of communication that is even more widespread than the ones we have looked at so far is advertising—a ubiquitous feature of everyday life. Even inside the home, individuals are bombarded with advertising. Are these messages also constructed in such a way as to convey particular values? This is the issue that will be addressed in the next chapter.

ADVERTISING AS MASS CULTURE

INTRODUCTION

Advertising is also a form of communication diffused through various mass media. Because it is so ubiquitous in both the written and oral media it warrants a chapter devoted to its analysis. Advertising is closely linked to the mass media because they have mutually dependent economic objectives: advertising agencies provide the money that enable the mass media to operate, and the media give companies the required public exposure to stimulate sales of products or services. How do ad agencies use this exposure? What is the response of audiences? To answer these questions, it is important to first look at exactly what messages are transmitted. Also, because the advertising images sometimes closely resemble pornographic images, we believe it is also worthwhile to compare these two types of communication. This analysis will be made in the last section of the chapter, and it is our hope that it will stimulate interesting discussion on the subject. But first, let us look at some of the characteristics of advertising as a specific form of communication.

THE TRANSFORMATION OF ADVERTISING INTO MASS CULTURE

Modern advertising was born at the advent of the Industrial Revolution, at the end of the nineteenth century. The development of technology and the division of labour led to the creation of mass production systems. Modern advertising was then developed in direct response to mass production. How else could the surplus of commodities resulting from the process of mass production be sold, if not by encouraging mass consumption?

It was necessary to develop a commercial system of persuasive and informative "devices for organizing and ensuring the market" (Williams, 1980b: 186). Advertising became a privileged sector of the modern enterprise because of its unique role in the process of mass distribution. In the words of Rutherford (1994), television advertising represents the "gospel of consumption." Indeed, with the establishment of the new order of mass consumption, it became necessary to accustom people to respond to the demands of production. The role of modern advertising was to condition labourers both culturally and ideologically to adhere more closely to the values of the new mass consumption order (Breton and Proulx, 1993). To this end, markets needed to be restructured, national advertising systems developed and previously ignored markets—namely the working classes and the middle classes—tapped.

Without transforming the relations of power of labourers to ownership and use of the means of production, there was a gradual increase in wages and reduction in working hours—a change that was perceived as a qualitative improvement in people's lives. This extra time was to be used for mass consumption and, for industry, it became just as important as time allocated for production. Henceforth, it was necessary to correlate the aspirations of the workforce with those of capital. "Now priorities demanded that the worker spend his wages and leisure time on the consumer market" (Ewen, 1979: 235). While mass production controlled the factory workers, consumption began controlling and standardizing the consumer. Advertising, the bastion of the *establishment*, was given the task of creating desires and consumption habits for the consumer. Thus, advertising was slowly transformed into mass culture.

Advertising has changed considerably since its emergence at the end of the nineteenth century. As early as the 1920s it played an important socio-cultural role. Beyond selling goods and services, it developed the universal notions that defined the *consumer*. Stuart Ewen (1979), who has done a great deal of research on the phenomenon of advertising, has explained the important transformation of values that American society underwent as a result of advertising. Advertising evolved from promoting thriftiness, a value dearly embraced by the country's puritan fathers, to promoting spending, thereby establishing a new moral order: that of the consumer. Ewen noted that advertising served the interests of capitalists: "By transforming the notion of 'class' into 'mass,' business hoped to create an 'individual' who could locate needs and frustrations in terms of the consumption of goods rather than the quality and content of his life (work)" (Ewen, 1979: 239).

To develop these techniques of persuasion, the advertising industry turned to psychologists for help. Breton and Proulx (1993) point out that these advertising experts had favourite themes revolving around a personal fault which could be seen by others, but which could be corrected by consuming a particular product.[1] Detergent ads made at that time are good illustrations of this approach. Thanks to psychological concepts, it was possible to keep the critical eye of consumers focused on themselves instead of the product advertised, which, it was said, could resolve everyone's personal problems.

According to Ewen (1979), it is therefore impossible to examine the functioning of advertising without acknowledging that the product being plugged is only part of the message conveyed. The other, and probably most important, part of the message is the intent of the ad to create a uniform social image which even immigrants—who were then numerous—could identify with. Advertising was therefore one of the components of the "American Dream." Consequently, advertising can be seen as a form of communication that conveys values on behalf of mass culture. As was mentioned in Chapter 6, the concept of *modernity* transformed the properties of an object into human characteristics, so

---

[1] From this perspective, advertising has not changed greatly over time.

that in buying the object, one also buys social respect, health, beauty, success, and control over one's environment.

According to Wernick (1991), this multidimensional nature means that modern advertising has expanded into something larger, what he calls promotionalism and *promotional culture*. This has occurred because the distinction between the commodity being advertised for consumption and the signs that do the advertising has become increasingly blurred. He has traced the origins of this back to the advent of the mass market and advertising itself, and has noted that as the latter developed as a distinct form of communication and persuasion, the commodity was reconstructed as an advertisement for itself in the way that it was consciously designed, packaged, labelled, etc. The result is a kind of circularity in which it is no longer possible to identify one simple thing that is being urged on the consumer. When Michael Jackson appears in ads for Pepsi, Michael Jackson is himself being promoted as a musical performer and commodity, along with all the values of the modern, consumerist way of life.

Advertising in The Mass Media

The advertising industry developed at the same time that the mass media began to expand. Breton and Proulx (1993) have noted that the technical means of persuasion, combined with the means of mass communication (the press, radio, cinema, etc.), made it possible to organize the first nation-wide publicity campaigns during World War II, inciting men to enlist in the army, recruiting women for war factories, broadcasting national unity propaganda, etc. In short, advertising had become a veritable system of communication.

Today, advertising is the economic engine of the entire communication system, including all forms of communication, from the written press to the electronic press. As was mentioned earlier, advertising income is the principle means of financial support of the media industry and, therefore, plays a role in media production. In 1993, television broadcast licensees reported to the Canadian Radio-television and Telecommunications Commission (CRTC), a Federal government agency, that their earnings from advertising were more than $1.6 billion.

The advertising industry, however, also generates profits by investing money in the media. This is especially true since television advertising activities are monopolized by a few powerful corporations which, until now, have managed to resist most regulations. In fact, the high level of profitability of television advertising enables advertisers to create expensive products with broad appeal, using, among other strategies, sophisticated technological means and well-known personalities (Yerza, 1995: 6).

According to Rutherford (1994), the English Canadian television advertising industry is now monopolized by a few of the biggest American multinationals such as Procter & Gamble, General Motors, Coca-Cola and Pepsi. The process of monopolization occurred mostly in the 1980s, with an increasing number of mergers of Canadian companies with American conglomerates. One serious consequence of this process, for the Canadian cultural industry, was the appropriation of Canada's best creators by foreign companies. Rutherford found that in 1968 only two American agencies had financial investments in the Canadian advertising industry. The 1970s and early 1980s were the glory years of Canadian advertising, when such agencies as Jerry Goodis' and Graham Watt and Jim Burt's companies created outstanding advertisements with an authentic Canadian accent. By 1992, however, "only one top-ten agency remained fully owned and managed by Canadians: Cossette Communication Marketing," a Québec company (Rutherford, 1994: 88–9).

Within this economic and political context, Breton and Proulx (1993) have maintained that audiences act as consumers of both advertising and products, and are also used as bait for obtaining more advertising investment. How does advertising create a link between consumers and investors? By using the technical means of persuasion, advertising can artificially create "needs" in order to encourage consumption. In practice, these "needs" are social constructions adjusted to serve capitalist industries. Through an imagined "middleman," consumers are lured into purchasing a certain lifestyle that is said to improve their social status.

Would a baby-boomer consider going on a holiday without his or her American Express card? The card that lets you travel in security, without any financial worries, and that admits you to a select club, a privileged class for which honours are rights, and which gives you free access to previews of the best shows and exhibits? As a form of communication, however, advertising cannot create such "needs" on its own. This is why it is integrated into a much larger process: *marketing*, the creative and economic force behind the media industry. The unique goal of marketing is to sell commodities that are, or will be, produced. Thus, marketing encompasses three functions: sales promotion, public relations and advertising policy development.

Williams (1980b) has claimed that large firms have developed the marketing sector in order to ensure that products are commercialized more efficiently through enhanced communication between the sponsor, the broadcaster and the target audience. Marketing ensures the depersonalization of commercial relations between the producer and the consumer. Market research and polls contribute to extending control over the social environment and to guiding production according to the "needs" of consumers. In reality, as the marketing function expands, so does the power of the advertisers within the production system. In this context, the economic reality of the production system takes precedence over the socioeconomic reality of the individual consumer. Nevertheless, advertising is based on social "needs." How does advertising manage to conceal the economic reality behind the social reality?

What is Hidden Behind Advertising?

Advertising tries to adjust its notion of consumption to criticisms raised by oppositional forces. The existence of consumer protection groups is a clear indication of the gap that exists between consumer satisfaction and the promises made through advertisements. In Canada, women's groups were the first to lobby the CRTC against offensive gender portrayals through sexual stereotypes in different media (Timble in Yerza, 1995: 7). Modern advertising attempts to conceal this reality by adding to the object of consumption the notion of the desire for satisfaction, by polishing the ideal of success, social status, beauty, health, and so on.

Williams (1980b) has asserted that the model of advertising is the same as that used in so-called primitive societies, namely *magic*. When the values entertained by society cannot respond to the problems of solitude and frustration or to the need for identity and respect, the "magic system" is used as a means of enchanting the potential customer. The dream market must make the consumer believe that decisions about production, priorities, manufacturing methods and styles are made on the basis of consumer needs, not those of capital. However, as we have noted in the previous chapters, decision-making is a prerogative of the minority who determine the choices available to the majority. This majority is seen as "the masses," and even though capitalists take their opinions into account, they disregard the more specific opinions of groups or individuals that constitute "the masses." The reason, according to Williams (1980b), is that large firms are not interested in individuals: they do not aim at just one target audience, but all of society, namely the world. To put it more concretely, they do not simply want a full-page newspaper ad, but a whole corporation with information systems at their disposal to conduct their advertising.

To conquer the advertising industry and consumer markets, advertising firms produce messages using codes based on sexual differences. In her analysis of advertising, Denise Kervin (1990) has identified several types of codes—nonverbal codes (facial expression, body stance, etc.), codes referring to social roles (active/passive, in charge/subordinate, etc.), and aesthetic codes (colour, lighting, etc.)—which, depending on how they are used, give a message feminine or masculine connotations. For example, a feminine message would be a woman smoking a Capri cigarette in an obscure, hazy, pastel-coloured atmosphere, as opposed to a man smoking a Marlboro under the bright blue sky of a blazing desert landscape. But even without humans in the image, the codes can be used to suggest a feminine or masculine context, as is often the case in perfume advertisements.

The notions of masculinity and femininity that are developed during the process of socialization are taken to extremes in advertising. Kervin (1990) has claimed, however, that times have changed, and today female characters often appear more confident and more resistant than before, whereas advertising for men contains strong connotations of seduction that did not previously exist. Let us examine in greater detail the image of women and then the image of men in advertising.

THE IMAGE OF WOMEN IN ADVERTISING

The image of women in advertising is similar to that in other mass production processes: it is constructed on the basis of feminine stereotypes, which, as we saw earlier, are instilled during the period of primary socialization, and maintained throughout our lives by values and images conveyed in society. As such, feminine stereotypes are reassuring and, as a result, are constantly repeated in an infinite number of ways to fit the fashion and context of the day.

By dint of repeatedly seeing images of women concerned with household chores, obsessed with being beautiful and able to manage both a career and family life (the super-woman), people gradually come to assume that this kind of behaviour is characteristic of all women. "It is true (if somewhat reductive) to say that in a patriarchal culture most representations of women are readable as connoting 'otherness' or difference—difference from the norm of patriarchy, that is" (Kuhn, 1985: 19). This difference is the creed of advertising: more often than not, it is images of women that promote the consumption of food, detergent and beauty products. Men, on the other hand, are used to sell cars, alcoholic beverages, insurance, credit cards, banking services, etc.

The Social Construction of Women in Advertising

In her study of the representation of women in advertising, Denice A. Yanni has contended that "the underlying identity of a culture is revealed through the positioning of goods in relation to each other and to people as well as through the institution designated for representing and influencing that relationship—advertising" (Yanni, 1990: 71). Because of their position in society, women play a different role in this relationship than do men in that they occupy both sides of the relationship as persons and objects. In advertising, the representation of women is based on a negative meaning of the word "woman," since the modern mediation of the person/object relationship perpetuates the ancient patriarchal system, which defines women as objects. Let us take a closer look at how women are represented in advertising.

An image, or a representation, is structured on the basis of the relationship between its spectator and its producer. In other words, the negative image of women conveyed in advertising is only the result of the system that produces these images. In this way, the social inequalities that exist in the cultural context are reflected in advertising.

In Chapter 5 we saw that in our patriarchal society women are defined in relation to men, in other words, as the "other." In identifying women as the "other," societies usurp the subjectivity of women by turning them into objects or things. In advertising, Yanni (1990) has told us, this concept is manifested by prostitution-like images: cars are sold using the body of a woman stretched out on a hood, or women's stockings are sold using a businessman turning around as he passes by a young woman with a shapely bottom. In advertising, the key is to make certain that the women are seen. Women are examined as objects. In a culture like ours, this "objectification" of women is, above all, concerned with women's sex.

Women are given a material and symbolic value, much like the value that is attached to commodities. And, as all commodities are transformed into a monetary value, the process of quantification applies to women also. "It is the functioning of advertising to be the synapse between goods and social meaning. Through this cultural institution, the economy of sexuality is perpetuated" (Yanni, 1990: 74). Women's bodies have sold cars, trips to sunny destinations, rock music and even hardware supplies (see Figure 10.1).[2]

---

[2] Figures can be found at the end of this chapter on pages 222–237.

Servant-woman, femme fatale, child-woman, woman-as-mother, loose woman and object-woman: these are the different facets of a unique model that is based on generally negative personality traits, Yanni (1990) has told us. Yet, this model appears to be natural, an inherent part of the object described in advertising instead of a construction based on the message system within a given social context. On their own, these different identities of women are meaningless; attached to these identities a symbol has been created, namely that of "woman."

According to Yanni, this symbol plays an important role in the construction of reality, and contributes to a distortion of awareness. The "woman-as-mother" is fostering, protective and caring; it is therefore easy to represent her next to her child's bed, rubbing his chest, at her husband's bedside, massaging his back, or, while we are at it, being woken up in the middle of the night by her cold-infected husband so that she may get him cough drops. One of the strategies of advertising is to attract the audience's attention by showing an easily recognizable symbol. Because modern society is in constant evolution, advertising must keep pace. However, regardless of society's evolution and the transformations it has brought about in the advertising industry, the representation of women remains stereotyped.

Representations of the "New" Woman

In the realm of advertising, there is an ongoing proliferation of new stereotypes revolving around the image of the "new woman." They join other well-established images of the submissive, considerate mother. As we saw in Chapter 4, the new or "modern" woman is characterized by her femininity and sexuality. She is fashionable, works outside the home and consumes many products to satisfy her "needs" and those of her family. Advertising creates the image of the perfect woman's body constructed to arouse the desire to consume. A number of feminist studies (Dyer, 1987; St-Jean, 1989) have shown that, more than ever, these images involve placing women under male scrutiny. The typical image is that of a beautiful, tall, slender, fit, somewhat provocative woman in her twenties, sometimes even younger. By itself, this image is not reprehensible. The problem lies elsewhere, in the fact that women's bodies are used as bait for commercial purposes. More than anything, this object-body is fragmented and depersonalized: the legs are used for selling shoes, the hair for shampoo, the bosom for perfume, the buttocks and belly-button for jeans, and so on. In fact, the use of only certain parts of women's bodies to sell products, which sometimes have nothing to do with each another, is the ultimate expression of the objectification of women. If, on top of it all, this fragmentation is accompanied with nudity, the object becomes blatantly sexual (see Figures 10.2a, b and c).

Without abandoning images of women in the kitchen, advertising also reflects women's integration into the labour market, showing them in every profession imaginable to sell just about anything. Advertising agencies have rapidly and clearly identified that the phenomenon of women's liberation represents a potential market to be exploited, and have done their best to capture it by creating the modern woman from scratch. For some researchers like Dyer (1987), appropriating this image is a process by which the dominant ideology ensures its continuity. It neutralizes the threat of protest by adapting and absorbing, in an apparent show of tolerance, some of the elements of threatening ideologies. As we saw in Chapter 4, the dominant ideology is capable of *adapting* to, and using to its own ends, oppositional ideologies.

Advertising relies on the "sure values" exemplified by the so-called traditional feminine trades to exploit the romantic model of the mother chiefly for the purpose of supporting sales of household products and medicine. "A woman is complete if her children have gleaming, white clothes and the dishes sparkle. She is shown in soft, dreamy focus in the bosom of the ideal family" (Dyer, 1987: 10).

Fashion magazines such as *Vogue*—which consists of almost 70% advertisements—have been one of the privileged means for defining the needs of the "new woman." Since the 1970s, *Vogue* has managed to reach middle-class women who have been at the forefront of the women's movement, and achieve a monopoly of the *baby-boomer* market. With these new markets, *Vogue* has tried to define modern femininity by representing the "new woman" as an androgynous and schizophrenic subject, in other words, caught between the desire for a home and the desire for a career, thereby wielding her ambiguous and sexualized power (an image closely resembling that offered in pornography: for instance, is there much difference between the pictures in Figures 10.2a and 10.3?). With new alternatives available, fashion magazines have assembled an image of what the new woman wants: "she wants everything" (Griggers, 1990: 96). In other words, a career, sex, a family, etc.

Women's aspirations have shifted from the traditional notion of a better life to that of social success, and finally to "megadesire": the desire to have everything. This desire irreparably binds them to the consumer society since, in their desire for everything, they are confronted with perpetual change. Moreover, the mass media thrive on the instability of the very notion of the "new woman" by constantly offering women new images: working woman, career woman, liberated woman, professional woman, university student, sporting woman, and so on, while preserving the images of the woman-as-mother, married woman, etc. All these images are created and exploited by the advertising machine of fashion magazines and newspapers, which profit by representing the fragmented desires and multiple social identities of their female readers. Given that women have multiple identities, Griggers (1990) has remarked, a number of markets have been created to respond to the multiplicity of their needs and desires. And only the mass media have the means to present the rich possibilities of consumption.

By looking at the pictures mentioned above, we can see that the degree of the objectification of women in advertising varies depending on the country where the ads are shown. France, for example, is especially liberal in this regard (see Figures 10.1 and 10.2a). In Canada, these excesses are controlled by municipal, provincial and federal laws. Let us take a closer look at the impact of these laws.

Is Advertising Sexist?

In 1979, the Council on the Status of Women defined sexist advertising as that which rigidly divides social roles and functions along gender lines. Such a division alienates the potential for individual development. One of its main consequences, according to Lord

(1979), is the oppression of women. What forms does sexism take in advertising? What are some of the discriminatory and degrading images shown in the Canadian marketplace?

First, here in Canada and elsewhere, women are portrayed as an entity called "woman," whose qualities, faults, aspirations and dispositions are defined on the basis of gender, with no differentiation made according to class. As Rutherford (1994: 26) has put it, "the most important source of definition of an ad is gender." Advertisements embody "a highly sexist view of men and women with roots that stretch back to the nineteenth century" which suggest to women that only two elements are of importance in their lives: "the pursuit of beauty and the cult of domesticity." In the 1950s, for instance, "woman" in ads was represented "as something of a domestic drudge," and was shown doing such domestic chores as shopping, cleaning, cooking and looking after others. At the same time, men were shown in activities such as sports, driving or repairing cars, drinking, relaxing, or entertaining. Although advertisements have changed over the years, Rutherford (1994: 26–8) has argued that gender remains their main subject of definition.

Lord (1979) reported on a 1978 study conducted by the Council on the Status of Women of 248 ads televised during a one-week period on Radio-Canada (the French CBC). The study revealed that 77% of ads for food, laundry, personal hygiene and household cleaning products starred women, while 73% of advertisements for alcoholic beverages, banks, real estate services, cars, transportation, communications, gasoline and government services featured men. The same study showed that only 14% of television ads depicted women working outside the home, although the real proportion of women in the labour market at the time was 35%. As for their roles, women were typically portrayed as objects of decoration or as being anxious about aging, worried about their shape or body odour, obsessed with the desire for beauty, desirous of a man's approval, jealous of other women and responsible for their families' health.

Rutherford reported his findings on ads in English Canada, which he drew from an analysis of the Bessie Collection. He found that, in the late 1970s and early 1980s, men and women in advertisements were not only represented as different, but were also "depicted in quite different ways. The man watches, the women display" (1994: 107). Moreover, men were more frequently represented than women: in all the ads examined, both men and women were represented together 540 times, men alone 415 times and women alone 113 times. The only ads where women outnumbered men were those with subjects considered to be typically feminine such as health, beauty and the like.

Still, since the mid-1980s, gender stereotypes have changed. Women are now seen displaying their bodies in different ways, being preoccupied with turning themselves into a work of art, as well as caressing different objects: their bodies, their clothes, their legs, etc. (Rutherford, 1994). Men, in contrast, are seen caressing only their beautiful companions, as well as possessing the ability to do valued tasks efficiently, and mastering different obstacles that may stand in their way. However, they are also positioned as voyeur, capable of appreciating female beauty (Rutherford, 1994).

In the late 1980s, the Service d'action-femmes of the Council on the Status of Women believed that sexism still existed in advertising, but was manifesting in more subtle ways. It appeared that pressure groups set up during the intervening 10 years had successfully raised public awareness of this issue thus causing advertising agencies to modify their approach somewhat. Lord (1989) reported on two cases which clearly illustrate the importance of developing a critical perspective within the population so that they will react to overly coarse sexist advertising.

In January 1988, Suzuki launched a nation-wide advertising campaign using billboard ads. The image on the billboards showed a motorcycle roaring at full speed along a valley road. A closer look revealed that the road traced the outline of a woman's chest: the motorcycle was shown leaning slightly to the left, as if ready to negotiate the curve of a breast. Women's groups from across the country raised such an outcry over this ad that the Canadian Advertising Foundation issued the most severe recommendation in its history: the interruption of the advertising campaign.

In the fall of 1989, the spotlight was on the Domicil ad scandal. The advertisement showed a young, innocent-looking girl with blond curls of about four or five years old sitting on the edge of a bed with a man at her side wearing an open shirt. The child wore over-sized women's lingerie which left her shoulders bare. She was shown tying his shoe laces while he read his newspaper. The petitions that followed the appearance of the ad denounced its incestuous nature and the erotic use of the child.

In Canada, a number of organizations are devoted to monitoring the advertising industry. Moreover, the influence of the *Déséritas-Éméritas* prize (which the Council on the Status of Women used to award), the increasing vigilance of women, and the evolution of the public's mentality have made it possible to reduce the number of sexist advertisements. In addition, pressure groups have managed to influence the CRTC to intervene with regard to the representation of women in advertising.

In 1969, the Royal Commission on the Status of Women (RCSW) wrote a report condemning the use of sexual stereotypes in media images of women, with the recommendation that men and women be portrayed accurately. Federal and provincial government agencies responded by imposing regulations on television advertising, restricting or prohibiting ads on diverse subjects, including birth control products, patent medicines and pharmaceutical products, commodity sex, alcoholic beverages, tobacco, and certain food products. In addition, these laws placed limits on the types of claims that television advertisers could make about their product. It became unacceptable, for instance, to claim that a product could make a person stronger or younger without scientific proof. However, Yerza has noted that "the lack of gender portrayal regulations indicate that for many years the same governments were not concerned with sexism or truth in gender portrayals" (1995: 8).

Thus, in 1979, the Canadian Advisory Council on the Status of Women (CACSW) presented a plan advocating equality for both sexes, proposing that the CRTC address the Council's concerns towards sex-role portrayals in broadcasting. This intervention followed the United Nations' recommendation that a plan of action be developed regarding equality of women and sex-role stereotyping in the broadcast media. The Honourable Jeanne Sauvé, then Minister of Communication, acting on the CACSW's report, "charged the CRTC with 'the task of seeing that guidelines and standards were established to encourage the elimination of sex-role stereotyping from the media regulated by the CRTC'" (cited in Yerza, 1995: 10). Sauvé's successor, David MacDonald, even spoke of the lack of women in various occupations in broadcasting organizations as a cause of negative and stereotyped television portrayals. The CRTC was "'to set in place a monitoring program to ensure that the broadcasters were eliminating stereotyping, especially in advertising'" (cited in Yerza, 1995: 10).

The federal government agency then announced the creation of the Task Force on Sex-Role Stereotyping in the Broadcast Media, a mitigating strategy to meet both the pressures coming from the governments and the opposition coming from the advertising industry. Let us look at the Task Force's action and influence in greater detail.

The CRTC Task Force, composed of six public representatives appointed by the Department of Communication, developed four recommendations regarding guidelines for advertising: 1) "sex-role stereotyping was to be considered nothing less than a problem of inequality and injustice"; 2) priority was to be given to advertising because it was considered as "the most blatantly offensive"; 3) emphasis was to be placed on sex-role stereotyping of women; 4) the existing body of evidence was to be considered sufficient to prevent delays in implementation on the pretext of requiring new research (Yerza, 1995: 11–2).

The Task Force, which had to recommend how to implement its guidelines, "opted for CRTC monitored industry self-regulation for a trial period of two years" (cited in Yerza, 1995: 12). In 1984, the Erin Research organization was commissioned to conduct a content analysis to verify the progress brought about by the guidelines. The organization reported "that little, if any, improvement in the portrayal of gender had occurred during the period of voluntary self-regulation" (Yerza, 1995: 13). Following these findings, in 1986 the CRTC made "self-regulation a condition of licensing" (cited in Yerza, 1995: 13). Two years later, the Erin Research organization again conducted another content analysis. One year prior to its 1990 Report, the CRTC was already declaring that "important progress has been made to eliminate the most offensive forms of sex-role stereotyping" (cited in Yerza, 1995: 13). Then, shortly after the publication of the report, the CRTC declared "that most of the concerns about sex-role stereotyping had been largely satisfied" (cited in Yerza, 1995: 13), and then disbanded the Task Force on Sex-Role Stereotyping.

Nevertheless, it is obvious that sex-role stereotyping was, and still is, part of the advertising industry's strategy, though ads such as the ones by Suzuki and Domicil are no longer part of the sophisticated means employed by most advertising agencies to mark gender differences. In cultural discourse, the inequality of the social relations between men and women has a detrimental effect on women's self-image, as well as their public image. To be sure, women are not alone in terms of having a negative image reflected through advertising. For some years now, advertising has also begun to treat men's bodies as objects.

THE IMAGE OF MEN IN ADVERTISING

In a study conducted on the image of men in advertising, Jacques Primeau (1989) has largely refuted the argument that media advertising degrades women only. Many analyses on this theme, Primeau has argued, are based on a biased interpretation of sexism in which most men have dominating, exploitative or manipulative roles from which they profit. But the real question is, who imposes or controls this sexist advertising, and who reaps the benefits? Primeau says it is doubtful that whomever controls advertising is also its target.

For Primeau, the classic image of a woman stretched out across the hood of a car is completely disrespectful to men, for it suggests that ad agencies believe they can trap men into making mindless purchases. While it is true that advertising clearly exploits gender relations to the benefit of one gender, not every member of the privileged gender enjoys this advantage. According to Primeau, some men object to the dominant image that advertising generally attributes to them. In this sense, one can detect a divergence or resistance among men with respect to the values conveyed by the dominant ideology. Does this divergence apply to the "new" image of men in advertising as well?

In his study, Primeau (1989) revealed that not only are more and more men appearing in ads, but these men are clearly set up as objects. He claims that advertising uses men's bodies in the same way that it uses women's, namely for the purpose of promoting commodities. Primeau has called this new form of sexism "neo-sexism." The concept refers to the fact that men are portrayed in four major roles: man as an object of desire, man as lovemaker, man as a phallic object and man as an erotic object. In these roles, men appear partially or completely nude in order to advertise hair salons, potato chips, perfume, underwear, wine, etc.

One of the most obvious signs of the objectification of men in advertising is that they are now being shown "in pieces" (a close-up of a man's feet, head, naked chest, genitalia, etc.), as has long been the case with women. This phenomenon, however, is new and still not widespread. Until recently, in contrast with women, men had always been shown in full in advertising. Even more important, Kastner (1991) has pointed out that the silhouette of a fragmented male body has never been used, whereas the female figure has always been clearly exploited. Men were portrayed in whole, as individuals with distinct personalities, choosing to get together to talk in their underwear!

Today, advertisements aimed at men are much more sexual than, for example, 10 years ago—even those in which they are shown in full. Ad agencies use codes (discussed earlier) to emphasize this sexuality. Below are Kervin's (1990) comments on a male advertisement run by Calvin Klein which depicts a man with a washboard stomach wearing only close-fitting Calvin Klein briefs. He is leaning against a distinctly phallic form in a cocky pose.

> In the Klein advertisement the rich skin colour contrasting with the bright white of the underwear emphasize (sic) the near-nakedness of the male model. Similarly, the tactile cues from the strategic shadowing on the underwear suggest the feel of the material against the skin, creating a sensuousness usually associated with representations of women. However, elements of the advertisement do strongly mark the male (and by extension, the underwear) as masculine. For example, shadows are used to emphasize bulging muscles, a conventional sign of masculinity. The model withholds contact with the viewer through his raised head and closed eyes; the connotation, as Richard Dyer (1982) argues, is that the model does not care that he is being surveyed. . . . Perhaps the strongest, and almost self-parodying, "masculinizing" element of the advertisement is the

combination of the phallic monument, against which the model leans, and the camera's extreme low angle, an aesthetic choice that places the viewer in the position of worship (Kervin, 1990: 67).

Male Advertising: Neo-sexism?

Primeau (1989) has attributed the emergence of men as objects—an important development, he has claimed—to the fact that more and more women work in advertising agencies. He refers to this development in advertising as reversed sexism or neo-sexism. Not everyone, however, agrees with this hypothesis. For instance, some adwomen claim that men still control much of the decision-making power in agencies; it is men who generally choose to present men as objects because they believe it is profitable. In a newspaper article (*La Presse*, January 12, 1991), Claire Bowé, of the Montréal-based agency Publi-Mix, even suggested that men began using men in this way to justify the exploitation of women's bodies. Bowé claimed that the exploitation of women is as rampant as ever.

Spokeswomen at the Council on the Status of Women add that it is not because men are portrayed as objects in advertising that there is necessarily such a thing as reversed sexism. The situation is much more complex. Of course, men are portrayed as objects in some ads, for example, the Man from Glad (or the boy who sometimes replaces him), who ensures that our garbage makes it to the roadside thanks to his green plastic bags. Thus, ad agencies do maintain the structure of institutionalized representation based on sexual stereotypes. However, in a patriarchal society, the image of men as objects is still not a widespread problem and does not represent a symbolic identity. The use of male models has no bearing on the structure of representation, no more than it challenges the fact that women are perceived as objects in the cultural discourse transmitted by advertising. Figures 10.4a to 10.4f clearly show this reality. This "story" of a couple features a man always completely dressed and in a constant *pensive* state, while the woman is always partially undressed and constantly suggesting her *abandonment*—she is photographed in sexually suggestive positions, as if offering her body shamelessly. The same attitude is reflected in Figure 10.5a, where a saucy woman sells jeans by exposing part of her chest, while the men in Figure 10.5b, confident and smiling, are each wearing a jacket and tie. Such sexist representations abound in advertising.

The advent of advertising involving the use of men as bait cannot be perceived as compensation for sexism against women. If the image of men as objects in advertising is said to be symbolic of the new distribution of male and female roles in society, this illusion can only benefit those people who manipulate consumption habits. Far from creating a new order in the distribution of roles in society, this neo-sexist image, Primeau (1989) has argued, has played a role in masking or camouflaging social reality. It has helped ridicule ancient social practices without presenting new realities or roles for men and women.

In fact, because society is in transition, the content of today's advertising is often ambiguous: the idea of the new man is not as well defined as that of the new woman. Faced with women's affirmation and increasing unemployment in general, today's consumer can no longer identify with a dominating male model. As a result, modern advertising is attempting to define new social realities—with limited success. According to Primeau (1989), the image of men in "neo-sexist" advertising does not suggest equality of the sexes. Instead, it reveals the ambiguity of men's role in current social structures. New advertising no longer appeals to men's virility, and men are sometimes portrayed as being insecure, worried, immobile and often inactive. In addition, they are sometimes unapologetically substituted for women models: they are portrayed as men who have managed to reconcile their masculinity with traditionally female tasks. From this perspective, there does not yet appear to be a coherent male counterpart to the feminist ideology.

Advertising, therefore, does not do justice either to men or women. Both are exploited as objects for the sole purpose of generating sales of the commodities advertised. Let us now see if the same phenomenon occurs regarding racial representations.

THE IMAGE OF CULTURAL MINORITIES IN ADVERTISING

In her study of racial representation in advertising, Ellen Seiter (1990) has claimed that, like the notion of "woman," the notion of "race" is a social category that tends to create distinctions, to separate from the "other," to differentiate and lead to relationships of dominance. To identify what is conveyed through the media in terms of race, Seiter (1990) has referred to two kinds of stereotypes: *positive* stereotypes, which characterize dominant and active roles, and *negative* stereotypes, which are attributed to passive and subordinate roles. An analysis of these sheds light on the structure of the class system and the ideology conveyed in the mass media. Through a study of the use of children in advertising, Seiter has shown how positive and negative stereotypes interact. The roles played by white children tend to confirm "dreams of a great and inevitable destiny" (Seiter, 1990: 32). Their importance is emphasized by allusions to their future economic value; one need only think, Seiter (1990) has argued, of the advertisement showing a baby's bare buttocks with the following caption: "One day this little bottom may sit on the board of directors. Today it needs Johnson's."

But the promise of a bright future does not constitute the only difference between the roles attributed to white and black children. The measurement of intelligence is an implicit component of stereotypes and of the relationship between mental aptitude and economic status. In advertising, it is extremely rare to see, if at all, non-caucasian models selling educational games, video systems, etc. On the whole, black children serve as playmates to white children. Seiter has pointed out that one of the most prevalent stereotypes of white children in advertising is the "go-getter."

> The go-getter is not a stereotype available for the representation of Black children, who tend to be shown in advertising as passive observers of their white playmates. If Black children were pictured in the same aggressive postures used for white boys, the available stereotype with which they are likely to be associated by whites is the "pushy" Black or the hoodlum. Thus the same set of behaviours, descriptively speaking, can be negatively or positively evaluated in racial stereotypes (Seiter, 1990: 33).

The norm of all media representation is white culture, and advertising is no exception to the rule. Advertising agencies generally use only one black character to represent all "minorities," while white characters are infinitely varied and unique, and sometimes even have particular habits or idiosyncrasies. Ad agencies are incapable of recognizing the same diversity in blacks, Natives, Asians, Hispanics, etc. Seiter (1990) has stated that, for fear of alienating or losing clients and consumers, firms will decide to include a black character in an ad, but only if he or she blends into the background, or is portrayed in a situation (involving sports or music, for example) where one would expect to see a black person. There is, however, possibly more to this than simply financial concerns. It could be that whites, blinded by their mentality as dominators, are incapable of distinguishing between the personal characteristics and physical traits of people of other races. Nevertheless, whatever the reasons may be, advertising never shows domestic scenes or family relationships that reflect the multiethnic reality of society.

Williamson (1986) has interpreted the attitude of ad agencies with respect to noncaucasian races as a form of colonization. Like women, the coloured races are portrayed as the "other," that is, as those whose existence is known, but who cannot be accepted in mainstream practices unless their image is adapted or transformed to correspond to the dominant ideology. For example, as was mentioned in Chapter 6, it is quite fashionable to show images representing well-tanned people, or people wearing turbans, and so on, if they are white. Conversely, the people who, physically or culturally, inherently have these characteristics are considered to be "different"—"strange" even—and unrelated to the dominant culture.

What is more, the racist stereotypes used in advertising underscore socioeconomic differences as well. As we saw in the first part of this book, the ideological function of stereotypes is to attribute characteristics to a group by implying that these attributes are innate and natural, and are not caused in any way by the socioeconomic system. Seiter (1990) has said that social realities such as slavery, immigration from Third World countries exploited by colonization, on-the-job discrimination, educational systems with assimilation instead of integration policies, and insalubrious housing cannot possibly convey the message of material happiness and satisfaction. Consequently, these themes are never used by advertising agencies.

In the United States, some black-owned ad agencies have attempted to feature middle-class black families. However, these images are simply another version of the same stereotype, namely that all blacks can be successful. In Toronto, industry consultants have tried to explain to advertisers the importance of communicating with minority groups using their own cultural code. These growing markets have attracted the attention of ad agencies; their clients, who are beginning to tap these markets, have their advertisements shown in the media within these ethnic communities only. Thus, corporations are not worried about being associated with values that could seem negative to white consumers, consequently scaring them away from their products; nevertheless, it does not stop these actions from being discriminatory.

In short, in the mainstream mass media the image of any given visible minority is reduced to a minimum. To target this market, advertisers prefer running campaigns within the target community itself. Nevertheless, sponsors do not have a monolithic view of racism. Concerned with satisfying a large audience and aware of fashions, they attempt to corner the market by regularly revising their racial representation.

However, the ideology of differentiation imposes limits on attempts to find positive images. Even the efforts undertaken in American minority-owned agencies are circumscribed by this ideology and the fear of offending white consumers. Seiter (1990) has noted that the advertising approach of agencies such as Burrell in Chicago is based on two concepts: psychological distance and positive realism. Thomas J. Burrell describes psychological distance as that which separates African-American consumers from mass products. In order to remove the impression that a given product is not for them, Burrell associates this product with a "positive reality" such as people working relentlessly, family activities, good neighbours, good parents, people with dreams or ambitions, and so on. In practice, however, the only effect that this kind of positive realism has is to depict African-Americans embracing the dominant values of American culture. In general, Burrell's advertisements present a more realistic image of the situation of working mothers—who are no threat to dominant culture—than other agencies. However, the utopian ideas inspired by the dominant ideology and used in advertisements do not make it possible to allude to the real problems of the black community in North American society—problems which, it is generally acknowledged, are more acute, at least in appearance, in the United States than in Canada. Let us see if advertising in Québec reflects this subtle difference.

Multiracial Representation in Advertising in Montréal

Niemi and Salgado (1988) reported that in 1988 the Centre for Research-Action on Race Relations (CRARR) published a study on the representation of visible minorities on billboards in the Montréal subway system. The study sounded the alarm about the lack of accuracy with which the multicultural and multiracial reality of Québec was depicted in the advertising. Out of the 311 posters examined in the study, only 10 (3.2%) featured a non-caucasian; out of 44 advertisers, only one (2.3%) included a non-caucasian—it was none other than the Ontario Ministry of Tourism. For Niemi and Salgado (1988) the findings of the study were interesting given that 80% of immigrants to Québec settle in Montréal.

Despite the presence a few years ago of musical performer Boule Noire for Loto-Québec, of radio and television personality Normand Brathwaite for GM and the milk producers of Québec, and an advertisement for Hydro-Québec featuring black children gathered around singer Jean-Pierre Ferland, Montréal-area advertising completely ignores the new face of Québec. Advertising, according to Niemi and Salgado (1988), transmits a message which implies that all Québécois belong to one and only one racial group.

As Niemi and Salgado (1988) have pointed out, CRARR concluded its study by stating that it is hard to believe that the complete absence of non-whites in advertising in Québec is purely coincidental or due to a lack of awareness of the growing diversity of Québec society. The "bleaching" of advertising in Montréal's subway stations—and certainly in all other media in Québec—is a reflection of a type of ethnocentrism whose objective is to protect the white face of society. It also represents a form of discrimination, since the advertising industry appears to offer few job opportunities for non-white models.

The evidence, at this stage, leads us to conclude that advertising is sexist and racist, and that the situation in Québec is not exceptional. Indeed, Signorielli, McLeod and Healy (1994) found similar characteristics in a study examining MTV commercials in the United States. They discovered that in all the commercials analyzed, "9 out of 10 characters (95%) were white" (1994: 95). Is this done consciously for economic reasons? Is it the result of an unconscious mentality among whites? It is not our aim here to answer these questions. Whatever the reasons may be, however, these observations are alarming, given the omnipresence of advertising in Québec society and Canadian society at large. The question that remains to be asked is, what impact does advertising have on people? Does it have as much power over people as some would have us believe?

THE POWER OF ADVERTISING

As we saw in the General Introduction to this book, an individual spends roughly 24 hours a week watching television, and between five and seven hours of this time is spent watching commercials. In fact, as much as 40% of television viewing time is taken up by advertisements (Derevensky & Klein in Yerza, 1995: 23). Some researchers argue that by the age of 16, a child has viewed more than 300,000 television ads (Singer in Yerza, 1995: 1). Thus, advertising is very much a part of media socialization, all the more so when one considers that the average person also spends time looking at other types of advertising: billboard ads in subway stations, on roadways and other public places, newspaper and magazine ads, etc. Clearly, then, this type of advertising invasion must have a certain effect on our values and desires, and on the image we have of ourselves and society. In fact, the power of advertising lies in its ability to create a link between the multitude of modern objects placed on the market and the traditional values conveyed in society.

In Chapter 4 we saw that, within the context of a society that promises to continuously improve people's comfort and aspirations, every individual is concerned with the need to base his or her life on familiar social relations that will foster a sense of security. Advertising creates such a link between the familiar and the modern and contributes to forging a public image accessible to all, in which people can ground their own experiences. In this way, advertising contributes to the reinforcement of dominant values and sexist stereotypes. However, it has also been observed that, when confronted with mass culture, individuals are not gullible and willing to absorb everything they see and hear.

Kervin (1990) has stated that the ad-reading public offers as much resistance to advertisements as other types of audiences do to other forms of mass communication. The way people interpret advertisements is based on their social and personal history; in other words, an ad can be read in different ways. Readers can choose their own link between an advertised product and its image, and make their own interpretation of the connotation associated with the product. Reading an advertisement is therefore influenced by the following factors: the reader's gender, social class, race and education.

For example, a men's underwear ad that is too masculine can be rejected by some women who dislike the "macho" style. Blacks can dismiss a series of ads if they never use non-white models. Finally, again according to Kervin (1990), middle-class people are not interested in the same kinds of ads as people from the working classes. It would appear that resistance to sexism and racism in advertising is due to people's interpretations of advertisements.

Thus, advertising appears to be similar to other forms of communication examined in the previous chapters. Advertisements are constructed to express particular ideas, but the audiences who receive these messages do not always interpret them in the way intended. Audiences "negotiate" advertisements and give them meaning: sometimes this meaning is biased, and sometimes it is the complete opposite of what was intended. In the same way that some advertising images are quite erotic, it is pertinent, at this point, to ask whether another explicitly sexual and highly controversial type of mass culture, namely pornography, adheres to the same rules of interpretation.

IS ADVERTISING RELATED TO SOFTCORE PORN?

We have seen that, in advertising, images of women are constructed in order to sell commodities. In pornography, Annette Kuhn (1985) has explained, these images are bought, sold and—within a socioeconomic context—given a value at the time they are consumed. Therefore, it is the images themselves that constitute the commodity, not the product advertised: they circulate as commodities through television, cinema and magazines. This socioeconomic and cultural system helps determine the meaning given to these images, for as Kuhn says, "Meanings do not reside in images, then: they are circulated between representation, spectator and social formation" (Kuhn, 1985: 6). Feminist theory attempts to develop a critical analysis of pornographic representation on the basis of the socioeconomic and cultural context by trying to understand the unique position women have in the person/object relationship.

Kuhn, who has used this approach, has confirmed that "it is unlikely that it is *only* about sex. Moreover, it works in highly specific ways, deploying particular modes of representation in particular socio-historical contexts" (1985: 23). She adds that "crucial among the concerns of certain types of contemporary pornography is a construction, an assertion, of sexual difference" (Kuhn, 1985: 23). Graham Knight has added that "male dominance . . . takes sexual difference as its main rationale and alibi" (1986: 2). We have seen that, with regard to the representation of women, advertising also attempts to underline the sexual difference of women. As industries, both advertising and pornography fabricate "woman" and femininity to the benefit of specific audiences and for the purpose of selling commodities. Women are portrayed as sexy: in advertising, it is to *sell a product*; in pornography, it is to *sell themselves*. Pornography is distinct from advertising in that the former is concerned with the sexualization of women to the benefit of male audiences, while the latter is directed to female audiences.

There are two types of pornography: *softcore porn* and *hardcore porn*. According to Kuhn (1985), softcore porn refers to situations where women are generally represented only among themselves; in other words, there is no male presence in the photographs.

Hardcore porn involves a male presence, and often portrays a couple having sexual relations or engaging in sodomy. The parallel drawn here between advertising and pornography is, of course, limited to softcore pornography. What we wish to emphasize is that many of the codes used in advertising to highlight women's femininity and sexuality are very similar to those used in pornography. If, for example, we compare Figures 10.2a, 10.2c and 10.4f with Figure 10.6, or Figure 10.7 with Figure 10.8, it is difficult to identify which was designed as pornography. Is pornography, then, a question of intent? To answer this question, it is important to understand how pornography works. Kuhn and Knight have expressed differing views on the matter.

While Kuhn has claimed that pornography situates the male as the subject (the spectator) and the female as the object (the observed), Knight has stated that the subjects and objects are interrelated, or interdependent "though of course not in any necessary relationship of equality" (Knight, 1986: 4). The process of objectification is a social construction consisting of turning a person into "the object of a controlling and inquisitive gaze" (Knight, 1986: 5), the object of desire. But Knight has noted that the subject, the "voyeur," is also the product of such a social construction.

Knight has suggested that objectification is part of "pornography's promise"—it is its ideology. However, it is a promise and ideology that porn fails to achieve. He denounces all narrow critiques of objectification because, he has said, they offer no explanation for the diverse forms of oppression found in pornography. For a long time, feminists have emphasized that while pornography is not always openly violent and sadistic, it is no less vicious and degrading in its representation of women. Rosalind Coward (in Knight, 1986) has identified three codes used to construct pornographic representations: fragmentation, submission and availability. The fragmentation of a woman's body is achieved by means of photographic close-ups, which sexualizes parts of the body and dehumanizes women. Submission refers to the way in which models are asked to pose almost always prostrate, with the eyes cast down. Finally, availability is expressed by models in constantly sexualized poses, with no other *raison d'être* than *sexualized desire*. In pornography, models have a provocative or teasing look, with bodies always ready for sex. According to most feminist researchers, these three notions reinforce the equation that objectification equals oppression. Moreover, they are what differentiates advertising images from pornographic images.

Knight has expressed a different perspective on the matter. He has argued that the objectification of women cannot by itself explain their oppression and degradation. According to him, people usually relate with objects in a functional, rational and non-emotional way. If, in pornography, women are nothing else but objects, why do voyeurs experience emotion, confusion or depravation from looking at pornography? For Knight, the reason is that:

> Pornography is a "performance" text that works by evoking a response that is emotionally laden and confused, a perverse mixture of desire and contempt, submission and control, viciousness in the name of the sexual. It is only towards objects that act as subjects—wilfully, independently, actively—that the desire to oppress and punish is expressed (Knight, 1986: 4).

For both Knight and Kuhn, however, the notion of sexual difference constitutes a threat to male dominance. Thus, pornography is concerned with controlling this threat, with reassuring the voyeur of the superiority and validity of his beliefs, and with providing him with a substitute, the object-female, which denies the threatening difference. In other words, in the object-female of pornography, the aspect of "woman" as subject represents the sexual difference that threatens male power, whereas the aspect of "object" denies the existence of this threat. But can we not do anything we want with an object? Femininity and the female state are constructed as a set of bodily attributes and are reduced to a form of sexuality for the benefit of the male spectator. In this way, the system of pornographic representation "invites the spectator to participate in a masculine definition of femininity" (Kuhn, 1985: 43). Therefore, this image has a pornographic structure, based on the *construction of sexual desire*, which does not exist even in the most erotic photographs in advertising.

The Pornographic Look

Photographs are given meaning based on their authenticity and visibility. But in the end, it is the "solicited" gaze of the spectator that provides meaning and is essential to the interpretation of photographs. One can leisurely look at a photograph, simply glance at it, take a second look, or slowly analyze its details. Kuhn and Knight agree that an important part of photographic intent lies in the spectator's look. The pornographic look is thus described as that of both the voyeur and participant. The spectator can look without being seen, but at the same time the image projects a visual "come-on"—which is always absent from the advertising image—"inviting" the spectator to take part in the pleasure, or *constructing* his desire.

The audience looks in voyeuristic pleasure, Knight has claimed, but also in a narcissistic way, by identifying with what is being looked at. The dynamics are like a mechanical process of action and reaction: the spectator looks at an object which does not look back and, as a result, seems to exert power; but the spectator transforms what he is looking at to make it correspond, through a process of symbolism, to an image of himself, that is, *his* representation of femininity.

Kuhn has also defined the look of contemplation as voyeurism: "The voyeur's pleasure depends on the object of this look being unable to see him: to this extent, it is a pleasure of power, and the look a controlling one" (Kuhn, 1985: 28). In pornographic photography, the spectator has the assurance that the woman does not see him. And so he can desire the female body. "He can gaze as long as he likes at her body, with its signs of difference on display" (Kuhn, 1985: 30). But after spending a certain amount of time investigating the photograph, the artifice of the representation is revealed and the photograph is seen for what it is: only an image. According to Kuhn, the absence of the "woman" can add to the voyeur's pleasure, but can also lead to ungratified desire. Thus, without being assured of the woman's pleasure, "he is condemned to endless investigation" (Kuhn, 1985: 31). But in order to pursue his investigation, the male spectator must perceive women as being different from him, as an object of study.

The nude woman stretched out on a sunny beach, her legs spread open and head tipped back, evokes the concept of "natural" realism and fidelity, but after examining it long enough, the spectator realizes that it is only an image. However, the picture, which simultaneously offers itself as both "spectacle" and "truth," suggests that "the woman in the picture, rather than the image itself, is responsible for soliciting the spectator's gaze" (Kuhn, 1985: 43). In this way, reality is replaced by its effects; it is abandoned for our interpretation of the image. As Knight has claimed, the "real meaning gradually recedes: the surpassing of reality by reality effects, of power by power effects, of desire by desire effects, and yes, of sex by sex effects" (Knight, 1986: 11).

The pornography business produces a mass product fit for mass consumption, an industrialized sexuality that necessitates investment and effort to fabricate pleasure, a bureaucratized sexuality that requires material, a distribution network, various levels of quality control, a moral police, a censor bureau, trade laws, operational codes and, above all, a system of symbols. Pornography is thus an industry to the same extent as is advertising. The two industries utilize sexual, "objectified" images of women. Is advertising, then, a form of pornography?

Advertising is not Pornography

Though it may sometimes be seen as excessive, *advertising is not pornography*. At first glance, advertising appears to be similar to pornography in a number of ways. In both cases, the "sexualization" of women serves to mark a sexual difference which dominant groups try to maintain as a means of ensuring their power, and which they seek to neutralize as a way of preventing eventual threats to this power. In both systems of representation, women are beautiful, fragile and submissive.

Also, like advertising, pornography is a complex system of representation, with different forms, cultural variations, modes of production and consumption involving various technical means, and the status of industry. Both systems convey an ideology, that of the dominant classes, though sometimes in limited ways. How else can one explain the existence among diverse social groups of protest movements against pornography or risqué advertising? The two forms of communication also attempt to impose a system of symbols, a representation of reality that guarantees the dominant classes' status as the point of reference. Moreover, advertising and pornographic images often use the same codes: attitudes of submission or abandonment, and expressions that tend to amplify the sexual difference in women, which are very popular strategies in the two genres of mass cultures. It would appear, then, that advertising is a form of pornography.

But, while they may use similar codes, the intent that motivates the *design* and interpretation of these two types of communication are *profoundly* different. Furthermore, the construction of desire, which is the force governing the production of these images, is based on different motives. Advertising is designed to *sell a product by using the image of women*; pornography is designed to *sell women themselves*. Moreover, readers buy pornographic magazines because they want to see nude or partially nude women, whereas readers buy fashion magazines such as *Vogue, Cosmopolitan* and *Chatelaine* not primarily because of the advertisements, even if they happen to be of nude women. There is therefore a marked difference with respect to the *intent* behind the creation of the desire.

Based on this difference in intent in terms of design and interpretation, there follow other differences in representation and interpretation. These are sometimes subtle: they can result from a slight movement, a look, a stance, or even a minute detail. For instance, the looks of women appearing in pornography are direct and always inviting, whereas models in advertisements generally have an evasive look. Sometimes these details are so small that they can be misjudged by the unsuspecting eye. When looking at Figures 10.2a, 10.3 and 10.6, it is not evident at first glance that the first is indeed an ad and the latter two are pornography. Even in photographs of nude women, the subtle details can be difficult to discern. Nevertheless, it is usually easy to recognize photographs intended for advertising by their softer lighting. But the earmark for identifying nudes produced for pornography is that the model's pubic hair is almost always visible (see Figure 10.7), which is never the case in even the most risqué advertisements. To put it in Williamson's words (1981), advertising nudes are "cooked," whereas pornography nudes are "raw."

Williamson (1981) used the concepts "raw" and "cooked" developed by Lévi-Strauss to describe the transformation of natural objects. "Cooking" raw objects (such as meat) refers to the complex system in which objects can be culturally differentiated, since the way an object is cooked can differ from one culture to the next. Similarly, images of nature are "cooked" by a culture so that they may be integrated into its symbolic system (for example, a garden must have a well-mowed lawn and a well-organized floral and arboreal arrangement). Williamson has applied these concepts to gender representation. For her, sexual images in advertising are always "cooked" in the sense that they utilize symbols, innuendos, and so on, to express the sexual object. "Thus again the illusion is that sex is being revealed, while in fact it is concealed behind its own references" (Williamson, 1981: 120). Once sex is "cooked," it offers a safe appearance and may be consumed. Conversely, hardcore pornographic sex is "raw," that is, it is shown as such, without any disguise.

In short, it is usually possible to distinguish between photographs used for advertising and pornography. Even in softcore pornography, the intent is obvious. The situation regarding the lack of legal restrictions on pornography is all the more remarkable today, particularly in Canada, where there are laws governing the publication of advertising images.

CONCLUSION

Advertising, like pornography, is both a social construction that reflects the values of the dominant ideology, and a representation of reality that reinforces the status of the dominant classes as the point of reference. To survive, advertising must rely on the marketing process, and since marketing constitutes a large profit-oriented capitalist industry, it cannot allow itself to have dissatisfied clients. As a result, the industry produces advertisements that it believes will please consumers. Since, in a patriarchal society such as ours, it is men who generally have the money to purchase commodities, publicity ads are created to satisfy this particular market. Furthermore, since most of the mass media are completely dependent on advertising agencies, they are not in a position to censor advertisements—supposing they would want to—since these constitute their means of existence. In this context, the exploitation of women to sell all sorts of products remains a prevalent aspect of advertising, despite mild regulations restricting advertisers.

Until now, Part II of this book has focused on cultural productions of the mass media. We have seen that they are created according to well-defined rules founded on "sure values," or stereotypes, created by the dominant ideology. We have also seen that audiences do not always interpret these social constructions in the way intended by their creators. Can the same be said about news production? This is the topic that will be addressed in the next chapter.

Figure 10.1

SOURCE: Astrid Berrier, UQAM.

Figure 10.2a

SOURCE: *Votre Beauté*, 646, April 1991.

Figure 10.2b

Figure 10.2c

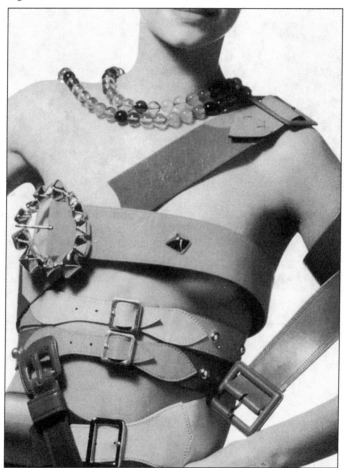

SOURCE: *Votre Beauté*, 646, April 1991.

Figure 10.3

Figure 10.4a

SOURCE: *Domino*, September 1990.

Figure 10.4b

SOURCE: *Domino*, September 1990.

Figure 10.4c

SOURCE: *Domino*, September 1990.

Figure 10.4d

SOURCE: *Domino*, September 1990.

Figure 10.4e

SOURCE: *Domino*, September 1990.

Figure 10.4f

SOURCE: *Domino*, September 1990.

Figure 10.5a

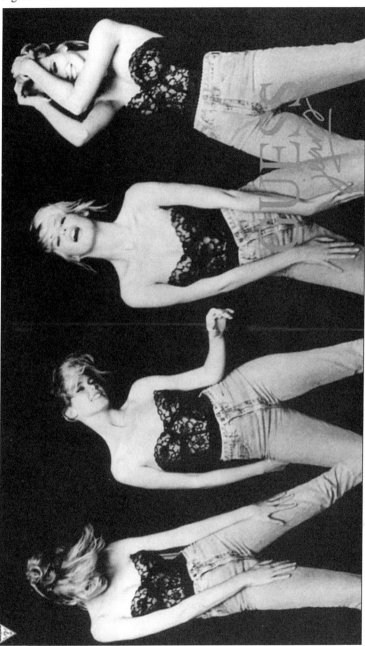

SOURCE: Guess Jeans.

Figure 10.5b

SOURCE: Hugo Boss.

Figure 10.6

Figure 10.7

Figure 10.8

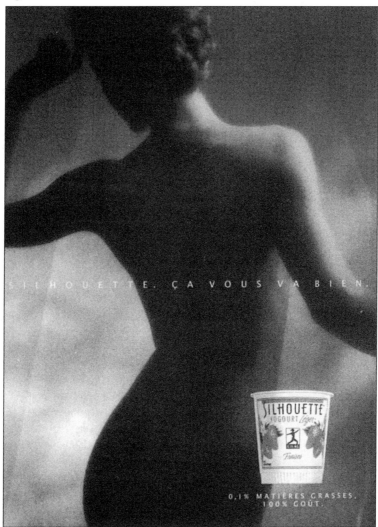

SOURCE: Delisle Ltd. Ad created for Silhouette yogurt in 1991/92.

THE NEWS:
SHOW, PROPAGANDA OR CONSENT?

INTRODUCTION

The news world has evolved considerably along with the expansion of the mass media. The written press, for instance, emerged at the same time that printing was developed, around 1440. However, the history of the beginning of printing is testimony to the bitter struggle that ensued in the quest to win the freedom to report the news. For example, in England, a country recognized as being democratic, people did not obtain the right to *print* newspapers and *report the facts* without prior scrutiny until the 1700s. Furthermore, it was only after a long-fought battle that people won the right to *criticize*. In the United States, these rights were not secured until 1787.

The printing press came to Canada in the 1750s and 1760s with the consolidation of British colonialism, but the newspaper industry grew slowly due to widespread illiteracy. By 1800 there were only nine printing establishments in what was then British North America (Rutherford, 1978). The early newspapers, or gazettes, were usually published by the local king's printer who was also responsible for printing official government documents, etc., so the tie between the press and the ruling class was a close one. Even the first unofficial newspapers such as Anthony Henry's Halifax *Chronicle* (1769–70) rarely set themselves up as champions of the ordinary people against the local elites, but strove instead to curry favour with them. In large part this was due to the fact that, unlike today, where advertising is the main source of the press's revenue, newspapers supported themselves chiefly through subscription revenues. As a result, a newspaper had to cater to the interests of readers wealthy enough to afford to pay for their news. It was not until after the War of 1812 that a more diverse and competitive press began to grow, though, as Rutherford has pointed out, there was "astonishing uniformity" in the essentially bourgeois social and economic message of the nineteenth century press in Canada: "the press idealized the progressive farmer, the busy workingman, and above all the entrepreneur" (1978: 24).

In Québec, censorship of the press was carried out by the Church and the ultramontane[1] movement. The large majority of newspapers were thus controlled by the clergy.

---

[1] Ultramontanists were a conservative group that supported the submission of the state and, by extension, all of Québec society, to the Catholic Church.

Many of these papers had nationalist leanings characterized by a kind of conservatism that isolated French-Canadians from non-Catholics and from the social changes occurring in other societies. There was, however, resistance. Some critical newspapers supported the workers' cause, while other more radical papers defied the Church leaders. The liberal press was situated between these conservative and radical extremes: though it was subjected to the clergy's censorship, it still found ways of getting around it.

There were few means of escaping the clergy's scrutiny. One was to offer apologies, the day after publication, for having allowed a "radical" article to "slip through"—while in fact editorial clearance had been given. Some chose more radical ways to protest against censorship. For example, de Bonville (1988) reported that the editor of *Canada-Revue*, Aristide Filiatreault, filed a lawsuit against Monsignor Fabre for condemning his newspaper and disallowing the publication of an article. This proved to be an efficient and unequivocal means of protesting against the Church, which was subsequently forced to be more cautious in condemning the media. Despite such protests, the clergy's influence over the press remained a determining force in Québec society, while in some other countries the state played this role. In yet other countries, the press had almost complete freedom, which is not to say it was any more "objective."

Researchers have developed two perspectives to explain the workings of newspapers on the basis of different social and political contexts: the authoritarian theory and the liberal theory. According to the authoritarian theory, the press is controlled by a minority with complete authority over all published material. This was the case in Québec, where the clergy had the upper hand with regard to the press; in the Soviet Union, this power was wielded by the state. But such control can also be exerted by a small group of politicians (the party in power, for example) who control all the news being published. In contrast to the authoritarian model, the liberal theory assumes that the press is not controlled by either the government or the clergy, or any group of elites. According to Agee, Ault and Emery (1988), this kind of press reports on every event, and judges the masses to be capable of distinguishing the truth from lies and of taking all sides into consideration. But even in the most liberal enterprise, can the press truly report on reality? Can one ever be certain that it is unbiased? Is the press not also a social construction? To answer these questions, it is important to look at *who* fabricates the news and *how* it is fabricated. It is also important to examine *why* audiences consent to read or listen to the type of news that is presented to them. These are the questions addressed in this chapter.

THE NEWS WORLD: A MALE WORLD

The general perception is that the news is a serious and objective field which one can turn to for the truth. But, like soap operas, novels, comics and advertising, the news is *constructed*. The people who work in the news field do not report all they know. They make choices. How are these choices made? Who makes these choices?

In 1978, Harvey Molotch claimed that the news is "essentially men talking to men" (Molotch, 1978: 180). Ten years later, Colette Beauchamp (1988) arrived at the same conclusion in her study. There can be no doubt: the news world is male-dominated. We recall that in Chapter 5 we saw that there are still very few female journalists working in newsrooms. However, the dominance of men in this field extends well beyond there. Marlene Mackie (1983) has described why the news is a male-dominated world.

1. The business people who control news production, that is, those who control the social definition of the news—editors, wire service owners, newspaper owners, desk editors, reporters—are generally men.

2. Women are rarely newsmakers, since the social definition of important news is that it must relate to important people or events: in other words, there is a link between the news and power, and very few women hold dominant positions in our patriarchal society. At any rate, the fact that an event involves a man makes it important. A good example is the case of Lynda Durand, a lawyer and law professor at the Québec bar association's training centre, who was named vice president of the workers' compensation board of Québec. The heading of the short paragraph describing the event referred to Ms. Durand as "the wife of Jean-Luc Mongrain," a popular television personality in Québec. One wonders whether the newspaper would have done a similar inversion of his title had the roles been reversed.

3. Studies have found newspapers to be guilty of sexual discrimination in their treatment of newsmakers. For example, in municipal elections held in Canada between 1950 and 1975, the media frequently mentioned the marital status of a female candidate as well as her husband's social status, a practice that was not deemed necessary in the case of male candidates.

4. The news focuses on the "news needs of men" and ignores, or relegates to the women's section, the daily reporting of events concerning women, unless these have a sensationalist value.

5. News stories revolving around the women's liberation movement are usually reported from a male perspective. For example, such reports focus less on the activities women engage in to have their rights recognized and more on alleged bra-burnings.

6. Lastly, Mackie has pointed out that placing news about women in separate sections intended for this purpose reinforces the idea that these items are less important than those placed on the front pages of the newspaper.

According to Mackie, there are several reasons to explain this distorted image of the relations between men and women as conveyed by the news media. First, since television and written news address the whole family, they focus on satisfying the news needs of the "head of the family" while targeting women through separate sections or programmes (on fashion, cooking, social life, etc.). "Once again, we see men being treated as the norm and 'women as the deviation from the norm'" (Mackie, 1983: 216). Second, the news media may be viewed as ideological institutions of society and agents of socialization, since it is they who organize the symbolic aspect of society. Because women have been excluded from the production of ideas and symbols, "Men attend to and treat as significant only what men say" (Mackie, 1983: 216). Men have therefore assumed the role of producing the means of thought and imagination on behalf of women. Under these conditions, what place do women have in the news?

The Image of Women in the News

Armande Saint-Jean (1989), who has conducted an analysis of the news world, has observed that, although the news talks about women and their interests, and sometimes presents extensive articles or series of reports on the injustices and discrimination they face, women's reality continues to be absent from the news. The difficulties they encounter in the workplace, in the home and with their children, and the conditions of poverty and the emotional distress faced by certain specific groups (e.g., single mothers and female seniors) are completely ignored in the news. Saint-Jean (1989) has argued that instead of discussing the conditions of poor women, the news blows out of proportion reports about those who succeed.

Michèle Mattelart (1981) has added another dimension to the issue. In liberal democracies such as Canada and France, she has claimed, the political role of the media is the reproduction of the concept of a harmonious coexistence of the different social classes and social groups that make up society. Thus, the media contribute to reducing social tensions by showing that, after all, everyone has their role to play in society. At the same time, Mattelart (1981) has argued that society seeks cohesion by reproducing the legitimacy of public opinion, which is defined as that of the average citizen. This abstract individual— for he or she does not belong to reality or any particular class—fosters social inertia and represents the norm through which social change occurs and is mediated. It is by maintaining this norm or basic profile that the equilibrium between news and fiction in the media is established. In fact, the roles women play vary depending on whether they appear on a fiction or a news programme. As we saw in Chapters 7 and 8, in fiction women are almost exclusively represented in roles of mother or wife, whereas in the news they must be shown in the actual roles they play as newsmakers. Why?

In the news, the media are obligated to cater to the various, often divergent, interests of the public. It is important to emphasize the difference between the private and public media with respect to this obligation: the former are by definition associated with variety and entertainment, while the latter, because of their status, have to respect pluralism and, consequently, different social tendencies. The role of the media also varies according to the type (magazine, television, etc.) and genre of programming they tend to favour. Some magazines, for example, have a penchant for variety, while others wish to reflect society's pluralism by reserving space for diverse social groups. There are also specialized magazines which target specific audiences.

It is the duty of television, especially state-run networks, to foster the personal growth of responsible citizens by creating awareness of their rights and the various currents of opinion in society. This is not to say, Mattelart (1981) has claimed, that public television can allow itself to be transformed into an *avant-garde* medium. The function of television, which is to maintain the social order, implies that it must strictly codify the pluralism that justifies its role within the political system to preserve a definite conservatism for society as it presently stands. It is the interrelation between the conformist role of women projected in works of fiction and their more progressive image in the news that are the underpinnings of this conservatism.

With reference to the book about the Radio-Canada programme *Femmes d'aujour-d'hui* by Canadian political scientist Anne Légaré (1980), Mattelart (1981) has defined the limits of the coverage of women's issues in the media imposed by mass media pluralism. *Femmes d'aujourd'hui*, always broadcast in the afternoon on Radio-Canada (the French CBC), was an information programme devoted to issues concerning women in the home. The programme went through several phases during the dozen or so years of its existence. It first helped women fulfil their traditional roles as mothers and wives by valuing their knowledge and opinions. Later, it focused on increasing women's awareness of their condition and of social changes occurring in Canadian society, changes which were instrumental in the development of the present condition of women, the couple and the family. Mattelart (1981) has thus claimed that *Femmes d'aujourd'hui* will go down in history for having explored the new democratic answers put forth by the (organized and non-organized, formal and informal) women's movement.

The conflicts that subsequently arose between the female public, the production team and Radio-Canada management concerning this TV program have shown the efficiency of the regulatory mechanisms of the established order and the limits of pluralism. In 1981, riding the crest of success thanks to its popularity and its development of the theme of women, *Femmes d'aujourd'hui* went through what Mattelart has referred to as a positive growth crisis ("crise de *croissance positive*"). The crisis pointed to the necessity of broadening the programme's formula and of airing the show during a better viewing time slot, while creating other programmes corresponding to the diverse needs of the public and the different levels of treatment of the theme of women. But, as Mattelart (1981) has argued, the "feminine genre," as conventionally established and understood by the media, cannot escape the place it has been assigned without challenging the criteria which determine entire programming schedules.

For Mattelart, even if many types of programmes can coexist within the same programming schedule, each has its own legality that is reflected, among other things, in its scheduling, which corresponds specifically to the conventional division of time that reproduces the traditional division of roles along gender lines (Mattelart, 1981). Thus, while the mass media concede many ways of perceiving the role and image of women, Mattelart has emphasized that they require one form of femininity which must be subjected to its own unique set of programming rules. How does the well-regimented world of information organize the daily news? We will begin by examining the organization of the news in Canada, especially in Québec, and then extend our analysis to the news produced around the world.

THE NEWS IN CANADA: SOME BASIC FACTS

In *Le silence des médias* (1988), journalist and researcher Colette Beauchamp studied the production of the news in Québec with reference to Canada, and discovered that here too the news is male-dominated. It constantly reports on wars and catastrophes, the underlying issues of which are unknown, or on violence, fights, political wrangling, etc. It is this type of sensational event that makes the news, for, according to Beauchamp (1988), everything else is simply too dull. The press and reporters have a penchant for politics, more specifically when it concerns male politicians: their reactions, remarks and behaviour. All the same, reporters' investigations remain superficial. For instance, the coverage of an event like the tabling of a budget by the federal finance minister will focus only on generalities (such as "smokers will pay more"), while the details of spending cuts in various sectors and their impact on certain social groups are barely mentioned. Beyond the personalities of politicians, political scandals are also regular headline material: personal profiles, patronage, conflicts of interest, etc. Beauchamp (1988) has pointed out that more details and column inches are provided to these topics than to budget issues with much graver consequences on the lives of the entire population.

The economy is another subject covered in the news, especially in relation to politics, finance and the business world. News treatment includes recessions, deficits, inflation, free trade, unemployment and factory closings and openings. In this male-dominated field, Beauchamp (1988) has maintained, reporters discuss the recession from the perspective of different experts who offer solutions for improving the business and economic situation, while barely mentioning the people who suffer most from the effects of economic downturns: the unemployed, laid-off workers, people in compulsory retirement, women, etc. Moreover, there is little talk about the growing poverty mirrored in the increasing number of homeless people living on big city streets, and the fact that these figures include more and more young people and women. It seems that the male press prefers to cover the financial and business world and provide more panel discussions, advice and tips on stocks held by a minute segment of the population.

What this points to is the way that news reporting is shaped in accordance with the general division of labour that the news media impose on their sources. Most news information is gathered by interviewing other sources, so the way the media select those sources and the kinds of information they seek from them—the kinds of questions they ask of whom—have a crucial bearing on what the reader or viewer ultimately sees. Broadly speaking, there are three types or levels of news sources organized along hierarchical lines in terms of their importance and credibility (Knight, 1988). The most important are the primary sources who normally represent the professional and managerial culture of society's chief political, economic, intellectual and control institutions. These are the officials, such as politicians or police officers, and experts, like academics and scientists, who are deemed the most credible source of information. The primary sources are those who basically define the essential aspects and features of a newsworthy event or issue; they are the ones who tell the media—and us—what the event is really all about.

On the next level in terms of importance and credibility are secondary news sources, of which there are two general types. The first are "ordinary" people who are featured in the news as a source of moral and emotional reaction to an event or issue. Very often, these secondary sources fill the role of actual or potential *victims*, those who are in some way afflicted, harmed or deprived as a result of some newsworthy occurrence. The other type of secondary source are representatives of oppositional groups or social movements, such as environmentalists, who also play a reactive role, responding, usually in negative emotional ways, to the actions of primary sources like politicians. In contrast to victims, who normally speak only about how they feel, oppositional sources are sometimes allowed to speak about what they think and to offer alternative strategies on an issue to those being pursued by the powerful.

Finally, there are those who are excluded altogether from the news, even though the event or issue does impinge upon them in some way. As such, they are not really sources at all since, by definition, they remain voiceless and unrepresented. These missing voices often come from the extremes of the class structure: at the bottom are those who lack the power to make their point of view newsworthy; at the top are those who have the power to conceal their point of view from the news. In coverage of the Gulf War, for example, very little was said about the ramifications of the cost of the war for poor, developing countries who were witnessing the expenditure of massive amounts of money for the purposes of destruction rather than economic development. Nor was very much said about the massive economic benefits the war had for the arms manufacturers whose profits ultimately depend on the continued pursuit of violence.

As we have noted, women often fall into this tertiary level of missing voices. When they do appear in the news, moreover, they are normally assigned the status of secondary sources where their role is to provide negative emotional reaction. This is what Voumvakis and Ericson, in their study of Toronto press coverage of sexual assault, have called the "fear and loathing" angle (1984: 53). Voumvakis and Ericson also found that the press used the police as primary sources to define the issue of sexual assault in terms of the victim. This was done in two ways. Firstly, news reports about attacks on women described the circumstances of the event in terms of the whereabouts and actions of the victim. Thus, for example, they cited one news story that informed its readers that "'the woman was taking a shortcut through a ravine'" when attacked. Secondly, and relatedly, the coverage referred to police concerns that women should take precautions and police themselves in order to avoid becoming the victim of an attack. When these items are considered together, the researchers have argued, this kind of reporting places the "locus of blame" for sexual attacks on the female victims, rather than the male offenders, and reinforces "the dominant image that women who are attacked are in some way responsible since they did not take the necessary precautionary measures required of them" (1984: 76).

To redress the problem of gender bias in the news media, Beauchamp (1988) has expressed the hope that the press concentrate more on investigative journalism. This type of reporting requires more in-depth research of topics, and exposes previously unknown information of interest to the public, news which would otherwise never be revealed by those who possess it.[2] It would replace the current norm, namely sensationalist journalism, which simply attracts the public's attention without deepening their knowledge.

Beauchamp (1988) has also complained that newsrooms are not possessed of the spirit of journalistic adventure. There is, of course, an obsession for the latest scoop and for current events. The competition between the media is so fierce that reporters will stare at their fax machine, waiting for the latest breaking news, which is essentially obtained from news-agency dispatches and press conferences. The fax rolls out hundreds of dispatches everyday, sent by the four largest Western news agencies (United Press International and

---

[2] Woodward and Bernstein of the *Washington Post* used this journalism technique brilliantly to uncover the Watergate scandal, which, in 1974, led to the resignation of the president of the United States, Richard Nixon.

Associated Press in the United States, Agence-France-Presse in France, and Reuters in Britain) and the Canadian news agency Canadian Press. Telbec, a Québec-based message distribution company, transmits press conference invitations and press releases to paid subscribers. In the newsrooms, those responsible for handing out reporter assignments make a selection of the news; journalists' responsibilities include rewriting texts and attending press conferences. According to Beauchamp (1988), press coverage in Québec is essentially carried out by Telbec, and consequently by those who can afford its services. Thus, Beauchamp (1988) has stated, the media and reporters are used as middlemen by those who wish to reach an audience. Among the many subjects to be covered (politics, the economy, current events and sports), the decision about which press conferences journalists may attend is based on the priorities of the dominant ideology that accords primary news sources their importance and credibility. When forced to choose between an invitation from a minister or a multinational corporation and a community-based group, Beauchamp (1988) has said that the press will obviously favour the former, since it best corresponds to its immutable criteria.

In short, the press reserves its headlines for a select number of subjects. Politics, the economy and violence are some of the most appreciated topics, while social problems are relegated to a position of secondary importance. But who decides on this order of things?

Who Wields the Power?

Although the press blurs the distinction between those who wield the power and those who are subjected to it by not discriminating in its classification of pressure groups,[3] a few small groups control many aspects of the news. In our society, the groups that wield this power also have the resources to pay for a professional communications staff, while other groups do not. Consequently, the former control the information they would like to have broadcast. Not only do the latter have no power, but their discourse, often in opposition to dominant values, is generally viewed as suspect and as subjective, if not subversive, by the press. In some exceptional cases, the press will provide coverage to an oppositional group if, for example, there is internal dissension within it, or in other words, in the case of conflict.

Telbec provides newsrooms with information written by communications professionals, public relations experts and press *attachés* who have come straight out of journalism school and work for social institutions, companies, multinational corporations or the government. This raises questions concerning the manipulation and control of information, since it is the journalistic material which they produce that is transmitted to reporters in press rooms and broadcast in its original form or somewhat modified. Under these conditions, reporters delegate much of their own work and the privilege to define current events to this group of experts.

---

[3] For example, under the heading "pressure groups" are randomly classified powerful financial, industrial and commercial associations, churches, professional associations, unions, grass-roots and community-based groups, women's groups, youth, senior and tenants associations, as well as unemployed and ecological groups.

The institutions of power who hire these communications experts have more material and human resources at their disposal than do journalistic enterprises. Beauchamp has noted (1988) that even though the latter are profitable and earn millions in profits, they invest only minimally in their news departments and newsrooms. Conversely, the former possess the economic and political power to control the information broadcast by owners of media empires who are concerned about making profits and producing information at a reduced cost. Is it not true that such well-known media magnates as Conrad Black and Pierre Péladeau reinvest their profits by purchasing new enterprises without increasing the quality of the media they already own? According to Beauchamp (1988), Péladeau's newsrooms are short of resources and have very few journalists.

The news produced by communication experts is long-winded, since it relies on the opinions of personalities or journalists in order to fill columns. These opinions are rarely based on scientific reasoning, but instead on the prejudices and partisanship of these experts, and are without subtlety. Beauchamp has given the example of radio phone-in shows where people such as Gilles Proulx (in Montréal) and André Arthur (in Québec City) have acclimatized audiences to their vulgar tone and narrow-mindedness. This kind of journalism is also practiced by Wally Crouter in Toronto.

In the printed press, editorials must respect the opinions of newspaper owners. For example, Beauchamp (1988) recalled that during the 1980 Québec referendum, *La Presse* ran a bold "*non*" across its front page, accompanied by an enthusiastic editorial by the newspaper's president. However, the editorial in support of the "*oui*" side, written by editorialist Guy Cormier, had been pushed aside. Thus, it seems that during important political debates some newspapers become overtly politicized, and take sides in the same fashion that newspapers did prior to mass production. However, newspapers that do not openly take sides can be more insidious in the sense that although they pretend to be impartial, all or most of their articles and editorials might support a particular politician or party. Beauchamp (1988) has also noted that newspapers tend to substitute quantity for quality of information by providing journalistic columns on a wide variety of topics: politics, television, books, seniors, computers, etc. The printed press has shifted from providing critical content to providing opinion columns. Opinions have replaced documented facts, and topics are selected on the basis of journalists' personal preferences rather than the public's news needs.

Sections like "Letters to the Editor" and "Commentary," where readers can express their opinions, must also meet specific requirements. They will allow organizations to express their opinions, but only if their commentaries are signed by one individual. By appearing as the opinions of one person, when in fact they represent those of many individuals, they carry less weight. Beauchamp (1988) has stated that these sections are a means for media owners to clear their consciences by providing a forum for the critical discourse of those who complain that their activities and opinions are never covered by the media. She has also pointed out that the information found in these sections is not only essential, but should more often be the subject of investigation and coverage by professional journalists.

Although news production is controlled in a general way by those who wield substantial financial power, the detailed business of gathering news information, processing it and packaging it into its final forms is a process that requires the negotiation of relations between reporters, editors, producers, technical support staff (camera operators, videotape editors) and news sources. Although in agreement with the critical perspective of news as generally reproductive of dominant ideology, Ericson et al. (1987, 1989, 1991) have nonetheless argued that this negotiation involves a constant struggle for control between these various parties. Based on ethnographic research conducted in newspaper, radio and television newsrooms in Toronto, Ericson et al. claimed that there is more tension and conflict within newsrooms, particularly between reporters and editors, than previous research had revealed. The reality of the newsroom, they concluded, is that in which "ideological cleavage, personal self-interest, and attendant conflict" are not uncommon, and where reporters have more autonomy and interpretive discretion than that implied by the cohesive, consensual portrait of the typical newsroom painted in earlier research (1987: 211).

Similarly, relations between reporters and sources can also be problematic as each side tries to manage and control the other. Sources vary in terms of their power to reveal and conceal information, and in their need for secrecy or publicity. In the case of crime news, the police hold a virtual monopoly on the source of credible information, yet at the same time, like any complex organization, they need favourable media publicity. In the case of politics, however, the adversarial nature of democracy means that the media have competing sources who are in search of favourable coverage, providing reporters with potential leverage to get both sides to talk. At the same time, much of the decision-making that determines the practices of source organizations like government or the police occurs in backrooms from which the media is normally excluded. Much of the superficiality for which the media are criticized is due to these limitations regarding access to sources, rather than an overt complicity in supporting the powerful.

At the macro level, however, the structure of news is ultimately determined by those who have the financial and/or political power to support the mass media; the ability of reporters and other news professionals to renegotiate news frames and practices is restricted to the details of individual story assignments. It is those with the financial control who decide what general ideological line is to be followed. Furthermore, most of the news broadcast in our society is produced by international conglomerates. Here, too, the range of information is controlled by a small group of people who decide what is important and what is not. In this context, we must ask the following question: is the news objective?

Objectivity in the News: A Myth?

Beauchamp (1988) has contended that the sacrosanct principle of objectivity in the news is in fact nothing but pure male subjectivity, which generates a male product. Objectivity is used as a veil to cover the real interests of news producers. For centuries the dominant male gender has had a tight monopoly in defining the world and creating knowledge and language. Men have defined everything, including femininity. And on this point, Beauchamp has noted that with a sleight of hand men have attributed subjectivity to women. Furthermore, they have reduced women to a sort of silence: men listen without paying heed to women's opinions.

Feminists have often challenged the validity and neutrality of objectivity, without suggesting the existence of female objectivity to counteract male objectivity. Moreover, for women, there are ways of looking at reality other than that based on the objectivity/subjectivity dichotomy, for these notions are too narrowly defined to reflect the pluralism of society and the diversity of human experiences adequately.

Since the 1970s, feminists have appropriated and redefined a number of concepts while maintaining their opposition to male objectivity. For example, Beauchamp (1988) has noted that for women the private sphere is political. She has stated that this explains the press's readiness to discredit feminism as a biased, partial and subjective ideology, thus justifying their role in preventing its diffusion, or, worse yet, their reappropriating of it so as to neutralize it. As is vividly confirmed in the news, objectivity does not tolerate women's perspectives. Beauchamp has remarked that objectivity serves those in power. To dispel the myth of objectivity is to dispel that of the impartiality of the press. Male subjectivity is biased: because it is based on the values of power, money and competition, it provokes a disequilibrium in the news to the advantage of the elite.

Beauchamp (1988) has asserted that the concept of neutrality or impartiality of the news is a myth that is hard to swallow. Journalists perceive reality through their values, their understanding of the world and their professional and personal existence. It is therefore impossible for them to be neutral, even if the press has made neutrality a rule of conduct and a code of ethics. The only ethic possible in the news revolves around the concept of equality, that is, the consideration of as many aspects of an issue or problem as possible. According to the concept of equality, journalists should enable those involved in events to have their voices heard, should refrain from making anecdotal remarks, and should attribute the same media coverage to men and women and likewise to the dominated and dominators. The principle of equality re-establishes an equilibrium in the news, which extends beyond simply stating the pros and cons of an issue, and embodies a more accurate reflection of pluralism and the diversity of schools of thought and courses of actions available to society.

For Beauchamp (1988), however, the present ethic of the media, based on the golden rule of objectivity, is the other face of media propaganda, which raises the question of the political role of the media in maintaining the legitimacy and the very foundations of the institutions in power. For example, with respect to the issue of health, the media are quick to ridicule or find fault with non-traditional approaches such as alternative medicine, even though the population is relying on them more and more. The media prefer to promote *science* and the power of traditional medicine, as if these are the only authorities deserving of attention and credibility. In this particular case, the news media dilute the "alternative" discourse. The same applies to the issue of ecology, where the news focuses on the economic unfeasibility of military and industrial enterprises to stop polluting, instead of on the senseless degradation of the planet. By leaving no room for the economic ideas, solutions and techniques of the ecological movement, she claims that the media have managed to convince the population that it cannot but resign itself to live and die by pollution.

As we saw in Chapter 4, media coverage of the issue of peace is made from the perspective of the dominant ideology of war. Little space is provided for the different pacifist movements around the world. On the contrary, Beauchamp (1988) has contended that the news coverage is like an act of war. It disseminates its spirit, gives warriors the red-carpet treatment and portrays them as heroes. It engenders the psychosis of the inevitability of war, suppressing the idea of peace as naive, and as a childlike and feminine understanding of the situation. What is more, the media support the ideology of war but only if it originates with Western powers. One need only recall the news coverage of the Gulf War to realize that the war was condemnable because it was begun by Iraq.

During this conflict, the public was inundated with a constant flow of news coming almost exclusively from the United States, where CNN[4] ruled. As a result, the press described the war activities of the Americans and allied forces as clean warfare and their air strikes as "surgical" operations. Although these operations dropped tons of explosives over Iraq, the media never mentioned the word "kill" and rarely spoke of "deaths."[5] Conversely, Iraq, which fired off a few old-style missiles, was denounced for causing incredible fear (worse than death?), even though its arms were basically harmless.

We could also draw attention to other cases. For example, the media clearly approved of the American invasion of Panama and strongly condemned the activities of the poorly armed Panamanian forces. In the case of Afghanistan, however, it was the rebels who received media support against the evil "Soviets" (who in the end sided with the "good guys"). It is therefore clear that the media take sides in their so-called "objective" news. Why? Do they simply side with those who are the most entertaining?

The News as Show

The show-news ("*information-spectacle*")—the news that exploits blood, tears, human misery, violence and death—is the type of news programme favoured by today's media. Around the globe, the media are searching for the war "of the day" or deadly earthquakes, spectacular plane crashes or victims of terrorist bombs. Sensationalism, Beauchamp (1988) has argued, banks on the unusual, the unknown and the unexpected; it exaggerates news items and makes no distinction between propaganda and information, between respecting and violating privacy, and between transmitting and exploiting emotions.

Religious personalities are also considered newsworthy material. Indeed, Mother Teresa and the Pope are two religious subjects who have become the darlings of the media. The show-news attained new heights during the Pope's visit in 1984, when, Beauchamp (1988) claimed, all the Québec media were in a "state of grace." For example, during his 11-day tour, Radio-Canada turned the Pope into its exclusive programming hero. As for the printed press, they succumbed to their own kind of verbiage by reporting on the "love affair" between the shepherd and his flock, and on the young and their "new idol." Reporters converted en masse and were swept off their feet by the

---

[4] This American network received Saddam Hussein's permission to remain in Iraq.

[5] There were exceptions, however. Some columnists, such as Pierre Foglia in the Montréal daily *La Presse*, were sometimes very critical of the media and the allied forces.

Pope's charisma, and, consequently, lost all sense of critical judgment. They were so pre-occupied with showering praises upon the Roman Pontiff, they neglected to discuss his rigid positions on abortion, contraception, divorce, the role of women in society, and homosexuality, which clash, for instance, with those of many Canadians who advocate freedom of choice with respect to motherhood and abortion. Instead, the journalists were simply blinded by the glitter of the show-news.

Another favourite subject of the show-news is human misery, especially that of immigrants. In August 1986, 156 Sri Lankan Tamils landed in Newfoundland. What made this situation show-like was the fact that their spokesperson had lied, claiming they had arrived from India, when in fact they had come from West Germany. For the media, the lie was the news, and the Tamil refugees became the victims of both the reporters and the public: the Tamils found themselves at the receiving end of all sorts of threats and racist comments. According to Beauchamp (1988), the media presented a biased view of reality by blowing the lie out of proportion. That is, the media never discussed the conflict raging in Sri Lanka between the Hindu Tamils and the Buddhist majority in which thousands of people have disappeared or been murdered over the past many years. Instead, faced with a wave of "lying" illegal refugees, the media fuelled racism and rumours, and emphasized the spectacle of the situation, while carefully withholding the fact that Canada accepts only 1% of the millions of refugees worldwide who are looking for sanctuary, fleeing torture, death, poverty and misery and who are demanding the right to life.

What is most worrisome is that the news has become a form of entertainment, whose star attraction is undoubtedly images of violence and misery. The phenomenon of show-news has spread to all Western countries. Gilles Perrault (1988), a journalist at the French monthly *Le Monde Diplomatique*, has reported, with a touch of humour, that a French television network summed up the French Revolution during a news bulletin by showing images of cut-off heads brandished at the ends of spears. Perrault's views agree with those of Beauchamp in that mediocre, vulgar, voyeuristic sensationalism takes precedence over hard journalism, and likewise, news flashes over in-depth stories. As a result, a nation can lose its sense of history. Moreover, such decontextualization transforms the news into a sort of global video clip which audiences are invited to watch, but not necessarily understand. Thus, both democracy and liberty are endangered.

Claude Julien (1988), the editor of *Le Monde Diplomatique*, has flatly denounced the show-news concept, calling it an abomination. For him, communication bigwigs have no patience for worthy ideals that could turn the media into a genuine window on the world, a place of exchange and information about education, understanding and thought. Julien (1988) has indicated a desire for the media to represent the real world, rich in differences and constantly undergoing social conflicts fuelled by the concern for growth and development, not for winning the war. But he has deplored the fact that this ideal is far from being achieved: for the powerful forces controlling the media, the view is that "the show must go on." What will happen, he asks, when the public wakes up the morning after the show? It will realize that its fate has not played out on the stage it was led to believe, but elsewhere. It will discover that the monetary system, the mechanisms of financial markets or the goods and services markets, the strategic arms systems—that is, all the difficult problems the show-news organizers did not want to bore their public with—have steered the course of its fate. The public will realize that it is too late, that other power structures have emerged and other power relations have been established. It will continue to respect the ritual of democracy, but it will discover it is not grounded in reality. There will then be a public outcry, Julien has concluded. The public will want to know why it was kept in the dark for the sake of a show that was not even all that good.

But does the show not have its limits? The international news, considered a prestigious realm in the journalistic hierarchy, must surely be more serious.

The International News: An American Production

With modern technology, the media can cover any event they want, whenever and wherever it takes place around the world. The international news that is shown in Canada is generally filtered by the United States, and the coverage of the realities of other countries is made from a Western, factual perspective. For instance, Québec television networks are teeming with American images. As for the printed press, Beauchamp (1988) has claimed that newspapers are at the mercy of news agencies and present the international news from a pro-American bias. Thus, when Québec newspapers such as *La Presse* and *Le Devoir* covered the crisis in El Salvador, they reported the government's "wrongdoings" in short paragraphs, but discussed the "guerillas'" activities in large articles crowned with bold headlines. The same partiality can be observed in the papers' coverage of the shooting down of a Korean Airline passenger jet by the USSR in August 1983. The American press referred to the event as a "tragedy." Conversely, the death of 47 patients in a hospital in Grenada, following the American invasion in October 1983, was described as an "error." Finally, the American press emphasized the efforts and desires of former American president Reagan to democratize Nicaragua, but remained silent about how the United States waged war against that country by financing and providing material support to the anti-government Contras.

Canada, however, is not alone in transmitting international news originating in the United States. In fact, the Americans provide this information to many parts of the world, including South America. This is why it is essential to examine this news production more closely. Edward Herman and Noam Chomsky (1988) have conducted a study on the news produced for the international market by American firms. They have argued that the American political and economic elite provide a structure and shape to all aspects of the news originating in the United States according to a specific and well-organized propaganda line. In fact, for these researchers, the international news is not a show. Even worse, it is propaganda.

THE AMERICAN INTERNATIONAL NEWS: PROPAGANDA AND DISINFORMATION

Herman and Chomsky (1988) have stated that the primary objective of the mass media is to entertain, inform and instill in individuals the values, beliefs and codes of behaviour that will help them integrate into the institutional structures of society. To meet these objectives, the media must transmit content that will mobilize audiences to integrate into society, not rise up against it. "In a world of concentrated wealth and major conflicts of class interest, to fulfil this role requires systematic propaganda" (Herman and Chomsky, 1988: 1). For the media, especially the news media, content must be constructed in a way that conceals part of reality and emphasizes its more positive aspects. This is what the authors call the *propaganda model*; it is a crucial element to the proper economic functioning of the media industry. In their study, Herman and Chomsky (1988) looked at the way American international news agencies have constructed various news items and distributed them in such a way as to underscore viewpoints approved by the American dominant ideology. They identify five elements responsible for the construction of news as propaganda: a) the media as profit-making enterprises; a) advertising as the income source of the media; c) groups in positions of power as sources of information; d) the media as controlled by those in power; and e) anticommunism as the dominant ideology. These are discussed below.

The Profit Orientation of the Mass Media

With the expansion of the free enterprise system since the beginning of the century, the media and the press have become industrialized. In 1986 there were 1,500 daily newspapers in the United States, most of which were small papers, covering local news and owned by large press corporations. The concentration of ownership of the press is a reality in the United States, where the owners of the *New York Times*, the *Washington Post*, the *Los Angeles Times* and the *Wall Street Journal* rule over genuine media and economic empires with incomes in the billions. The market integration and the breathtaking economic expansion of press companies occurred at the same time as the liberalization of the rules governing or attempting to control concentration of ownership. Restrictions over the placement of advertising have also gradually disappeared.

Thus, in order to meet the needs of the market and respect their essentially economic vocation, modern press corporations focus primarily on profitability. This would explain the close ties they maintain with players in the financial and industrial community (such as General Electric and Westinghouse in the United States), which have become directly involved in the management and decision-making of press corporations. It is also important to emphasize that press corporations depend greatly on governments, since it is the latter that grant licences and franchises to the media. Governments use this legal dependency as a kind of instrument to discipline the media, and the media protect themselves by cultivating good relations with the political world.

> The great media also depend on the government for more general policy support. All business firms are interested in business taxes, interest rates, labour policies, enforcement and nonenforcement of the antitrust laws. . . . The media giants, advertising agencies, and great multinational corporations have a joint and close interest in a favorable climate of investment in the Third World, and their interconnections and relationships with the government in these policies are symbiotic (Herman and Chomsky, 1988: 13–4).

In short, the media giants are first and foremost large capitalist corporations. They are controlled by millionaire directors or managers who are obliged to conform to tight constraints imposed by owners and other profit-oriented market forces. Finally, these media enterprises have a number of important common interests with other large corporations, banks and governments. *Profit* is therefore the most important factor influencing the selection of the news, and is generated by the major income source of the media: advertising.

Advertising: The Primary Source of Income of the Media

Advertising is the mainstay of press corporations because, within the context of the free market, without its support newspapers would cease "to become economically viable." However, in the free market, the use of advertising as a source of income does not constitute a neutral system in which, ultimately, the consumer has the last say. On the contrary, "The *advertisers'* choices influence media prosperity and survival" (Herman and Chomsky, 1988: 14). Advertisers wield enormous power. In a way, they are "patrons" who buy the advertising exposure from the mass media that will enable them to prosper financially. As for the media, they develop services to solicit advertisers by offering them programmes adapted to their needs.

According to Herman and Chomsky, advertisers choose to advertise on television or radio programmes that most correspond to their principles, and with "rare exceptions these are culturally and politically conservative" (Herman and Chomsky, 1988: 16). It is also rare for large corporations to sponsor shows with a critical bent, dealing with issues such as the environmental deterioration of the planet, the military industry or the profits made by Western countries supporting Third World tyrannical regimes. "Advertisers will want, more generally, to avoid programs with serious complexities and disturbing controversies that interfere with the 'buying mood.' They seek programs that will lightly entertain . . . " (Herman and Chomsky, 1988: 17). Thus the financing from *advertising*, which generates profits for media enterprises, clouds the issue of objectivity in the news and the authenticity of reality projected by the press. But even though *capital* wields considerable power over the news, it must nevertheless share it with other groups in power.

Political Leaders, Private Enterprise and Experts as Sources of Information for the Media

In the United States, the media obtain most of their information from sources such as the White House, the Pentagon and the State Department, where press conferences are held regularly. Each of these institutions has its own information and communication departments with thousands of employees at their disposal and considerable financial means. For example, in 1982, the Pentagon alone published 1,203 periodicals. At the local level, the role of public-information sourcing is assumed by city halls and the police. Herman and Chomsky have added that major corporations are also considered credible sources of information: "Government and corporate sources also have the great merit of being recognizable and credible by their status and prestige" (Herman and Chomsky, 1988: 19). This reinforces the image of concern for objectivity, which is so dear to the media. It also helps reduce costs. Indeed, as Beauchamp (1988) has pointed out as well, drawing information from presumably credible sources is less costly than undertaking more in-depth journalistic investigations.

The connection between power and information sources is maintained by experts whose discourse is often biased and adapted to that of the market and government. Herman and Chomsky recalled Henry Kissinger's remark about these experts, which he considered to be "those who have vested interest in commonly held opinions; elaborating and defining its consensus at a high level has, after all, made him an expert" (cited in Herman and Chomsky, 1988: 23). The media too have their own experts who, despite claiming to present personal opinions and analyses, regularly recite the official view. Another type of expert who represents the voice of power is the former radical who has returned to the "straight and narrow."

> The motives that cause these individuals to switch gods, from Stalin (or Mao) to Reagan and free enterprise, is varied, but for the establishment media the reason for the change is simply that the radicals have finally seen the error of their ways. . . . The turncoats are an important class of repentant sinners. It is interesting to observe how the former sinners, whose previous work was of little interest or an object of ridicule to the mass media, are suddenly elevated to prominence and become authentic experts. . . . who will say what the establishment wants said (Herman and Chomsky, 1988: 25).

They are given all the more credibility because they were once in the opposite camp. However, the various forms of power that control media information are not without their critics, who are not only from groups opposed to the dominant ideology. The media must also face critics from certain powerful groups concerned about so-called "abuses" of freedom of the press.

Criticism and Discipline of the Media

Criticism from individuals or groups with direct ties to power, which Herman and Chomsky refer to as "flak," is aimed at the media when the latter deviate from the line that institutions of power expect them to follow. This kind of criticism can take the form of letters, telegrams, telephone calls, lawsuits, speeches, petitions or other types of complaints, threats and punitive action. Flak can be produced either as a large-scale campaign or through (direct or indirect) individual action. In the United States, there are even associations specializing in this kind of action.

The Media Institute, founded in 1972 by rich corporations and employers, has a particular interest in monitoring the media treatment of American foreign policy. The Center for Media and Public Affairs, founded in 1980, defines itself as a "non-profit, non-partisan research institute" acclaimed by Ronald Reagan, whose mandate is "to demonstrate the liberal bias and anti-business propensities of the mass media" (Herman and Chomsky, 1988: 27). The older Freedom House, which was established in 1940, also focuses on American foreign policy, and expresses the view that the American media should enthusiastically support all national enterprises abroad. "In 1982, when the Reagan administration was having trouble containing media reporting of the systematic killing of civilians by the Salvadoran army, Freedom House came through with a denunciation of the 'imbalance' in media reporting from El Salvador" (Herman and Chomsky, 1988: 28). Although such "flak machines," with propagandistic roles, regularly attack the media, they are still treated with respectful attention by the latter. Finally, the government itself is often the source of flak, threatening and regularly "correcting" the media, and "trying to contain any deviations from the established line" (Herman and Chomsky, 1988: 28). Consequently, the media must adjust their production so as not to contradict the ideas of the government in power. In the United States, one of these fundamental ideas is anti-communism.

Anticommunism as a Control Mechanism

The final component responsible for the transformation of information into propaganda is the American ideology of anticommunism. "This ideology helps mobilize the populace against an enemy, and because the concept is fuzzy it can be used against anybody advocating policies that threaten property interests . . . It therefore helps fragment the left and labor movements and serves as a political-control mechanism" (Herman and Chomsky, 1988: 29). Hence, liberal-thinking people were often accused of being pro-Communist or insufficiently anti-Communist, and were "kept continuously on the defensive in a cultural milieu in which anticommunism is the dominant religion" (Herman and Chomsky, 1988: 29). For the two authors, it was clear that this national anticommunism had a profound influence on the media. Thus when the Iron Curtain was lifted in Eastern Europe, it was a great relief to some journalists, who claimed that at last the Communists could be put in their place.

The five components of information construction we have just discussed do not act independently of one another: they constantly interact and reinforce one another. Their basic material, namely the news, is adjusted according to these elements before being broadcast. The dominance of the media by the elite and the marginalization of dissident perspectives that results from this filtering operation occur so "naturally" that those working in the press, certain of their integrity and goodwill, "are able to convince themselves that they choose and interpret the news 'objectively' and on the basis of professional news values" (Herman and Chomsky, 1988: 2). Yet, there is a huge discrepancy on the part of the media when it comes to selecting what is and what is not likely to be published or broadcast. It is at this stage that the media define and choose between "worthy" and "unworthy" causes which, as Herman and Chomsky have emphasized, is a political choice.

INFORMATION AS PROPAGANDA: A MANIPULATION OF "WORTHY" AND "UNWORTHY" VICTIMS IN THE NEWS

The propaganda model developed by Herman and Chomsky describes the American mass media as propagandistic because they portray the oppressed in enemy states of the United States as "worthy" victims, while portraying those in friendly countries as "unworthy" victims. To support their assertion and to better demonstrate the accuracy of their propaganda model, the researchers applied it to the treatment of two cases of coverage in the American media: the 1984 murder of a Polish priest, Jerzy Popieluszko, in Poland, an enemy country of the United States, and the murders of Archbishop Oscar Romero in El Salvador and of numerous priests in Guatemala, two "client" countries of the United States. Through a quantitative analysis of the content of the American news media, the authors highlighted significant differences in the journalistic treatment of these two cases.

Coverage of the Murders of Popieluszko in Poland and Romero in El Salvador

On several occasions, the murder of the Polish priest Jerzy Popieluszko made the front page of America's major dailies, including the *New York Times*, and was the top story on many television networks. The media presented many in-depth reports about his life and personality, and denounced his assassination by providing generous coverage of the sordid violence that "had occurred in a Communist state" (Herman and Chomsky, 1988: 38), which was therefore an enemy state of the United States. To make matters worse, the murderers were identified as police officers of this totalitarian country. The trial of the murderers was covered with much interest, with the media expressing indignation and demanding that the police officers, as well as the high-ranking Polish-government officials involved, be brought to justice.

By comparison, the media remained silent about a great number of murders of priests in Latin American countries with friendly ties to the United States. For example, the American public never heard about the assassinations in Guatemala of the father superior of the Franciscan order, Augusto Ramírez Monasterio, in November 1983, and of Father Miguel Ángel Montufar, a priest who disappeared in the same month that Popieluszko's murder took place. According to Herman and Chomsky (1988), none of the victims murdered in Latin America, including Romero and four female American religious workers assassinated in Salvador, received as much media coverage as that given to the Popieluszko murder.

By the time Archbishop Romero was assassinated in El Salvador in 1980, he had become an activist and an outspoken critic of the murderous repression that was so rampant in his country. In a letter to Jimmy Carter, then-president of the United States, written a few weeks before his assassination, Romero denounced American military aid to the Salvadoran junta as "destructive" of the interests of the Salvadoran people. "The Carter administration had been so disturbed by Romero's opposition to its policies that it had secretly lobbied the pope to curb the archbishop" (Herman and Chomsky, 1988: 48). The U.S. intervention explains why the American press treated Romero, despite his religious status, not as a martyr, as was the case with Popieluszko, but as the victim of a "bad" cause. The press provided scant details about his murder and made no statements demanding that the murderers be brought to justice.

While in the case of the Polish priest the media attempted to place the responsibility on the shoulders of high-ranking government officials, they made no such effort in the Romero case, and even alleged in the early stages that the identities of the murderers were a mystery. Then, with deep regret, Salvadoran and American officials claimed that the murder had been committed by the extreme right and the extreme left, not by the Salvadoran armed forces or their agents, who were trying their best to contain the violence of these extremists. For Herman and Chomsky (1988), the image of the Salvadoran junta as moderate, centrist and neutral was a myth. Did Romero not write to President Carter that the Salvadoran military "knows only how to repress the people and defend the interests of the Salvadorean oligarchy," and write in his diary that the security forces were instruments "of a general program of annihilation of those on the left"? (cited in Herman and Chomsky, 1988: 53–4).

In October 1979, the military junta declared all-out war against all progressive individuals and organizations in El Salvador. Ten thousand civilians lost their lives in 1980 alone. It was in response to this extreme violence that leftist and centrist groups launched a guerilla war and began criticizing the Carter administration's support of the junta. Far from being centrist or reformist, the Salvadoran government was a rightist military regime with close ties to paramilitary forces such as the death squads and the terrorist force ORDEN, which "had extensive interlocking relationships with the official military and security forces and their U.S. counterparts. . . . The paramilitary did jobs for which the official forces wished to disclaim responsibility" (Herman and Chomsky, 198: 50). Given this context, then, is it a surprise that Romero's assassins were never officially found or tried? The Archbishop joins the ranks of tens of thousands of Salvadorans who disappeared or were assassinated under "mysterious" circumstances. And in contrast to the case of Popieluszko, the American media seemed uninterested in finding the murderer and demanding that justice be done.

But in 1983, following an investigation, two American journalists claimed that Roberto D'Aubuisson, a member of the junta, was at the centre of a military conspiracy to assassinate Romero, and had in fact planned and ordered the murder. "Further evidence of D'Aubuisson's involvement in the murder came to light with the confession of Roberto Santivánez, a former high official in Salvadoran intelligence. According to Santivánez, the murder of Romero was planned and carried out by D'Aubuisson with the aid of former national guardsmen of Somoza, but 'under the protection of General García and Colonel Carranza'" (Herman and Chomsky, 1988: 57). D'Aubuisson, recalled Herman and Chomsky, was a subordinate and political ally of Carranza, the number-two man in El Salvador's military.

In short, there was substantial evidence that pointed to Romero's murderers and established significant links between them and high-ranking officials in the Salvadoran army. In fact, the Salvadoran judicial investigation headed by Judge Atilio Ramírez linked D'Aubuisson to the murder. In the wake of numerous threats and assassination attempts, Judge Ramírez was forced into exile. He later declared that "there was 'undoubtedly' a 'kind of conspiracy to cover up the murder' from the very beginning" (Herman and Chomsky, 1988: 57).

Neither Judge Ramírez's testimony nor the accumulation of evidence implicating D'Aubuisson in the murder of Romero made the headlines in the American media. This new information did not lead to expressions of indignation, emotional outbursts, or demands for justice on behalf of the American press. While the extreme right in El Salvador consolidated its power, the media were content to repeat their claim that the Salvadoran government was centrist or reformist. In fact, according to the media, it was a moderate government supported by the U.S. because it was plagued by terrorism from rightist and leftist extremists, which the country was incapable of controlling. What is more, Herman and Chomsky expressed their indignation that the press continued to refer to D'Aubuisson in terms of his responsibilities within the power structures of the Salvadoran government. Never was there any mention of his involvement in the murder of Romero or the fact that he was one of the known leaders of the death squads and therefore a mass murderer. Even D'Aubuisson's overt anti-Semitism was never mentioned. Herman and Chomsky claimed that "if an anti-Semite and professional assassin, who was suspected of having organized the murder of Popieluszko in Poland, ran for office and became head of the Polish legislature, there might have been a raised eyebrow or two in the U.S. media" (Herman and Chomsky, 1988: 58–9).

These specific examples of press coverage are clear evidence of the *social construction* of the news disseminated by the American mass media. The adoption of the dominant ideology by the media, which is encouraged, it must be said, by the financial requirements of profitability, greatly influences the *angle* from which they treat the news. These examples, however, illustrated an emotional issue, the assassinations of clergy members. Let us see whether the media are more "objective" in their treatment of more "rational" issues, such as politics.

News Coverage of Elections in El Salvador, Guatemala and Nicaragua

Herman and Chomsky (1988) discovered that elections in Third World countries were excellent cases to which they could apply their model of propaganda as observed in the American media. The elections held in El Salvador in 1982 and 1984, and in Guatemala in 1984–85—two countries friendly to the United States and governed by military juntas—received media coverage that carefully neglected to mention the signs of oppression, including state-organized terror, that prevailed during election campaigns in these countries. In fact, the media emphasized the "democratic conditions" in which they took place. Yet, five factors seemed to contradict the essential conditions recognized by the United States for holding a "free election." During both the Salvadoran and Guatemalan elections, there was:

1. a suspension of the *freedom of speech and assembly*;

2. a total absence of *freedom of the press*, accompanied by the murders and disappearances of native journalists, foreign correspondents or printers who supported the opposition;

3. a ban on the *freedom to organize and maintain intermediate groups*, accompanied by the murder of leaders and members of "illicit associations";

4. an absence of the *freedom to form political parties, field candidates and campaign for office*, a ban that also resulted in the assassination of contraveners;

5. *an implementation of state-organized terror and a climate of fear* justified by murders, disappearances, military violence and torture.

These factors, which prevailed during the so-called free elections in El Salvador and Guatemala, were also present in the 1984 elections in Nicaragua. Yet, the American media considered the elections in the latter an electoral farce, taking place in a questionable and suspect democracy. Why? According to Herman and Chomsky, the media's attitude was due to the fact that the "election held in Nicaragua in 1984, by contrast, was intended to legitimize a government that the Reagan administration was striving to destabilize and overthrow. The U.S. government therefore went to great pains to cast the Nicaraguan election in an unfavorable light" (Herman and Chomsky, 1988: 88). By conveying the dominant ideology, the media became involved in projecting this image in order to continue defending American political interests. The American press justified its actions by declaring that "Guatemala and El Salvador were 'new democracies' with 'elected presidents.' Nicaragua, in contrast, is a Marxist-Leninist dictatorship that does not have an 'elected president' and would never permit elections unless compelled to do so by U.S. force" (Herman and Chomsky, 1988: 141). How can one explain the double standard of the coverage by the news media?

According to Herman and Chomsky, the adherence of the American media to the state propaganda line was extremely functional. It enabled the Guatemalan government to exterminate, without repercussions, hundreds of people who, according to the American imperialist ideology, represented obstacles to the economic exploitation of these countries. In this context, these individuals were not real victims working for a worthy cause. The American government's political support of Guatemala, El Salvador and the anti-Sandinista Contras in Nicaragua was made possible because the media continued to broadcast only images of what they considered were worthy victims. "As their government sponsors terror in all three states (as well as in Honduras), we may fairly say that the U.S. mass media, despite their righteous self-image as opponents of something called terrorism, serve in fact as loyal agents of terrorism" (Herman and Chomsky, 1988: 142). In fact, in a democratic country like the United States, very few journalists dare to seriously criticize the conservative regime in place. How is this possible?

For Herman and Chomsky (1988), the press has adopted the propaganda model because the mass media are entirely under the guidance of the dominant ideology, as well as financially dependent on capitalist corporations that flourish under it. Americans adhere to an imperialist ideology that leads them to support regimes that they can dominate economically and politically—that is, regimes that allow them to exploit their resources. This privileged position also allows them to intervene in the internal affairs of these countries when they see fit. When they encounter opposition, they do all that is possible to eliminate it. The media's support of these ploys is reflected in their content. But how do they manage to make audiences accept this information?

Stuart Hall (1982) has stated that regardless of the form in which it is transmitted—as propaganda or entertainment—information is the product of a *social consensus* obtained under the leadership of a certain group of individuals. An analysis of the news must therefore be guided by a number of structural factors: the state's willingness to disseminate certain types of information, profit conditions, the constraints of social values, professional journalism practices and audience preferences. In short, Hall tells us the news must be analyzed as a battleground where the dominant classes attempt to come to some agreement with other classes on what meanings to give news contents by incorporating viewpoints obtained through compromise between divergent and even opposing ideas. This can therefore lead to the creation of a *consensus* about what is to be understood. This is a dynamic process: it is open to change and never closed in the sense of adopting the propaganda model in particular. In this way, Hall's model of consensus mirrors other models we have discussed in Chapters 3 and 4, and is more pertinent to analyzing resistance to the dominant ideology, which this book encourages.

CONCLUSION

This chapter has shown that the news world is controlled by male journalistic criteria which have guided the news media towards two types of production: show-news and propaganda-news. Are there any differences between these two types? Although they have a number of common features, they differ in many respects. But first, let us look at their similarities.

The five elements underlying propaganda-news are also applicable to show-news. In both cases information is transmitted by the media, which are profit-driven enterprises. We recall that because of their profit orientation, these enterprises have formed alliances with the advertising industry. Thus, the media are controlled by economic interests as well as political interests which ensure that all media productions are subjected to the dominant ideology. Finally, in both show-news and propaganda-news, information is supplied primarily by large, specialized media corporations or by economic and political institutions that have the power to hold press conferences attended by journalists. But how do these two types of news differ?

The difference lies in the *intention* underlying the social construction of the news. Show-news aims at *entertaining* audiences to attract as many viewers as possible. As a result, their content is light-hearted and rather inconsequential. Propaganda-news, on the other hand, involves a certain effort to *lead* audiences towards adopting specific ideas. The former *omits* the facts it considers too disturbing, while the latter *conceals* them. Thus, show-news selects the news with the *intention to entertain*, and propaganda-news with the *intention to lead*. These two types of news, however, are not mutually exclusive. Even propaganda-news always strives to entertain audiences and, consequently, is as sensationalist as show-news. Let us consider the example of the Gulf War to see the distinction between the propagandistic and the show-like features of this news event.

As we saw in Chapter 3, the Persian Gulf conflict was described in the Québec media as "*La guerre en direct*" ("The live TV war"). The conflict was covered by journalists and experts in military and Middle East issues. It was as if the news transported viewers to Baghdad itself, where it showcased the "high tech" firepower of the American military, which executed "clean" operations and precision strikes to destroy Iraq and its military installations. In the military bases of the "American" coalition, order and method were the rule of the day: the *boys* did the job, the "cleaning." From one hour to the next, the public was saturated with all sorts of news dispatches and every bit of news from the

United States and other allied countries. *This is what the show was about.* Exuberant Canadian journalists were quick to report the information, however raw, rolling off teleprinters, often presenting it in provisional terms. From one hour to the next, they rehashed the same lines, retold the same developments, presented the same headlines, and so on, all in an attempt to fill airtime. Since the show-news is an excellent means of improving ratings and making profits, it was important to provide as much of it as possible. Thus, as the show-news expanded, the news itself became a rarity.

In this non-stop flow of information, every bit of news was carefully filtered by the countries involved in the war, especially the United States. As in any period of conflict, state propaganda was coupled with war propaganda. For example, images from anti-American Arab countries showed hostile, disorganized crowds protesting against the armada sponsored by then-president George Bush's New Order, and images of war demonstrators in the West were invariably associated with clashes with the police and, therefore, with chaos. In this way, the propaganda-news presented a strange paradox: those who sought peace (the pacifists) were identified with violence, while those who waged war (the soldiers) with peace, for it was in the name of peace that they fought.

The propaganda-news also concealed the human dimension of the conflict behind endless descriptions of military strategies, hypotheses of political and military consequences, and constant reports of precision air strikes on Iraqi buildings, which viewers were invited to admire. How many people died during these bombings? The propaganda-news never said. Why did these people die? Once again, there was no answer. The Iraqis were not victims of a worthy cause, so why talk about them.

It is possible, therefore, to say that the *show-news* coverage of the Gulf War had an element of *propaganda* as well. This propaganda glorified not only the United States, but also antidemocratic Middle Eastern countries such as Kuwait and Saudi Arabia, while completely discrediting nations in the same region governed by more democratic leaders, such as the Palestinians and Iraqis. But the propaganda-show-news treatment of the Gulf War paid off, especially for the American media, which were in decline prior to the conflict. It is true that certain advertisers did not want their names associated with the "show," a move which resulted in smaller revenues than expected for the media. But these sponsors were a minority and, at any rate, a considerable ratings hike was good news for television networks, even if they did not generate the extra revenues expected. As Bureau (1991) has claimed, war is a ratings boon: the American network CNN, stationed in Baghdad for the duration of the conflict, increased its ratings sevenfold, and the other big American television networks recorded considerable ratings increases as well. Clearly, then, the "social construction" of media production is profitable not only in the case of artistic productions, but for news productions as well. Furthermore, as Hall (1982) has claimed, it is made with the complicity of viewers, with a social consensus.

Will mass media content be modified with the advent of new technologies (such as videotex and interactive television) as some experts claim? The last chapter looks at the impact of new mass communication technologies on our society.

CHAPTER 12

NEW MASS COMMUNICATION TECHNOLOGIES

INTRODUCTION

For a long time the term "mass media" has been associated with two technologies in particular: radio and television. But, as we saw in the General Introduction, this book uses a broad definition of the term. After examining diverse forms of television and printed content, we will now turn our attention to new technologies such as videotex, e-mail, the videocassette recorder (VCR) and interactive television. In this chapter, we will analyze these new forms of communication, the activities of those who use them, and the most significant effects they have had on different realms of society. Moreover, because some of these media are only in their initial stage of implementation, we will look at their effects more from a prospective angle than from the viewpoint of studies of existing data.

All the new forms of communication examined in this chapter are related in one way or another to computing and television. The computerization of communication has long meant the linking of high-performance computers with satellites, telephone exchanges, sophisticated television graphic imagery, as well as many other applications made possible by engineers or specialized technicians. In a short time, these innovations have improved the quality of transmission to the point where their effects are often imperceptible to audiences. However, few of these innovations have limited their impact to audio and visual improvements of radio and television. In particular, computerization has brought about multiple branching, in which networks can establish instantaneous links with other networks, other media, or the public. Moreover, new functions have been added, thus diversifying media use.

Because the first computer languages were complicated, it was not certain whether these innovations would be easily accessible to everyone. Nevertheless, the growing interest in technologies like calculators, television remote controls, automated banking machines, VCR programming units and video games has shown the capacity of most consumers to use simplified computers efficiently. From the development of these "technological skills" it has become possible to attain a new level of implementation of computer-based telecommunications technologies, namely the hands-on use of computer terminals. Audiences will then acquire unprecedented control over what the media offer them, though not over what they produce.

According to Mosco (1982), because of their interactive mode, the new media will correspond less and less with the classic image of the mass media as they focus increasingly on meeting individual needs. For a long time, radio and television audiences received the same information at the same time. Gradually, audio tape recorders and videocassette recorders have made it possible to delay programme reception until a convenient time chosen by the individual consumer. Also, the proliferation of media and transmission channels has fragmented audiences by delivering content better adapted to the particular needs of each consumer. Moreover, the development of communication satellites has greatly expanded the content possibilities available to audiences without necessarily providing greater variety. In all cases, the overall objective has been accessibility for the masses to a range of content considered to be of general interest, even though the means of transmission may be considered less of a "mass" process.

In the following sections, we will examine the implementation of some new technologies, as well as the services they offer and the effects they could have on society. We will begin by looking at videotex, followed by video, pay television and interactive television.

VIDEOTEX

Videotex is an information retrieval system, a technology that merges telecommunications with computing. Videotex transmits textual or graphic contents displayed on screen. We will study the specific features of videotex by making specific reference to the development of the system in France. The French videotex system, called Télétel, operates through the telephone system. The terminal device used to transmit on the Télétel system is called Minitel. This is a small information retrieval terminal consisting of a keyboard and monitor, which users are given free of charge, along with a list of services and a user guide. Some services are free (such as telephone directory consultation), while others involve a fee.

Minitel terminals have been in use since 1981 and offer over 20,000 services, including advertising, information retrieval services and interactive "social" messaging between users (for example, "chat lines"). These services are provided either by private enterprises for a fee, or by public agencies. In 1988, there were already 3.4 million Minitel users who made more than 20 million calls monthly.

According to Odile Challe (1989), since its implementation in France, Minitel has changed the communication habits of the French. The network is increasingly used as an information and communication medium, especially for special events such as elections. Although in its early days the press was hostile to the development of this new form of communication, it now uses Minitel to broadcast the latest news headlines. The advantage is that, in contrast to radio and television, the news is accessible at all times on Minitel. Challe (1989) has reported that the news column is the most used service on Minitel: 34.9% access the news, versus 17.4% for leisure, arts and culture. What makes this service all the more interesting is that it provides access to foreign news media such as the BBC and *USA Today*, which transmit the news in English.

A Videotex network such as Télétel is more than just an information system. It allows interactive communication, either by voice on the telephone or in print on screen. Moreover, Minitel makes international communication possible, since each terminal is connected to telephone cables that are part of a worldwide network. Therefore, the French telephone system, which has long been mocked for its inefficiency, has been transformed into a high-quality network equipped with a videotex system, using telephone lines, instead of a cable-distribution network, to transmit information. According to Kevin Wilson (1988), the economic advantages for the French government are twofold: first, by increasing telephone system use, Minitel has contributed to reimbursing the cost of modernizing the system; second, this government-sponsored initiative has stimulated indigenous development of a large electronic telecommunications industry.

Although this form of communication has also been developed in other countries (Europe, Great Britain, the United States, Finland, etc.), the scale of these networks and services has been much more modest than the Minitel example. The situation is similar in Canada, where attempts to implement videotex technology failed. A first attempt was made by the French organization CETI (the Centre d'excellence en communications intégrées) through the Minitel network, followed by Bell Canada through Alex. Bell Canada worked hard to push the implementation of its videotex network in Canada, but the system never made it past the initial development stage, launched in January 1989. Sales of Alex were disappointingly low. By the end of 1989 the system was expected to have as many as 20,000 subscribers, but it had only 16,000 users and, among these, 9,000 rented rather than bought the emulation software required to connect their microcomputer with the network. This lack of enthusiasm on the part of the population, Martin has told us (1989a), forced Bell to form alliances with the political and economic world by attempting to foster the participation of government agencies (Hydro-Québec, Loto-Québec, the Québec environment and revenue ministries, the Société des Alcools, etc.) and private enterprises (the Caisses populaires Desjardins and a number of department stores) in the network to provide a broad range of services to attract users (e.g. driver's and hunting and fishing licence applications; direct transmission of income tax returns to Revenu Québec; special wine orders; etc.). However, despite the relative success of Télétel in France, the implementation of the videotex system there has run into some difficulties.

Difficulties in Videotex Implementation

In France, research shows that the fee mechanism of the Télétel network is potentially a major obstacle to widespread acceptance of paid videotex services. Fee structures based on a "rate per page of information accessed" or on "total log-on time" have encountered resistance by consumers, who are wary of using a medium whose cost is not known ahead of time (Wilson, 1988: 22). Among the paid services, teleshopping could be presented as a means of rationalizing one's expenses if user charges were not too high. According to Wilson (1988), who has studied the Minitel network in France, research has suggested that monthly subscription fees and page advertising income would be the most viable financing arrangement. But videotex faces other challenges.

Wilson (1988) has claimed that the technical means currently available are insufficient to satisfy the needs of users. For example, teleshopping cannot be a viable service without high-resolution graphics, which would provide more attractive images of commodities offered. Thus, promoters are likely to have difficulty easing consumer mistrust about purchasing objects that cannot be examined prior to purchase.

Home banking services, however, should represent a particularly attractive videotex feature. Referring to market research conducted in the United States, Arlen (1983) claimed that there is great public demand for such services, which in turn could stimulate a rapid increase in the number of subscribers. Two facts, however, call for a more cautious interpretation of this market research. First, the implementation of automated banking machines (ABMs) has been a much slower process than originally anticipated.[1] Second, while a large number of customers use ABMs for cash withdrawals, few use them for more complex transactions: funds transfers, bill payments, etc.[2] Thus, only a small number of ABM functions have been implemented on a large scale.

In order to overcome these inconveniences, Wilson (1988) has claimed that videotex promoters have focused on the attractive feature of the network's sophisticated graphic capabilities. Although it has not yet been established systematically, graphic images, particularly animated images, could generate sufficient interest to motivate people to purchase the system. It is doubtful, however, that graphics alone could sustain the long-term interest required for membership to a system such as videotex.

Wilson (1988) has maintained that, in France, industry has shown growing interest in implementing a sophisticated domestic computer-based information system. Not only has more capital been invested in this venture, but a more sophisticated approach has been developed by proposing, among other things, to deliver in-house interactive electronic services. The problem is that there is no clear "need" for such a system. Demand must therefore be *created* and *nurtured*. After a number of failed attempts in the United Kingdom and Canada in which videotex was presented as a transaction system (home banking, bill payment, teleshopping, etc.), renewed efforts have been made to develop an attractive package of videotex services, including fire and burglar alarm systems, world news, video games, travel information, concert ticket reservations, e-mail, etc.

After determining what services would be made available, it has become easier for French industries to identify potential consumers who would not only *desire* such services, but who would also *pay* the additional charges to access them. It was therefore deemed preferable to target small markets with significant purchasing power, instead of a large market with little purchasing power. The ideal market was found to be that of two-income households with little time available for personal transactions. Promotional ads for the system focused on the theme of personal and business transactional technology. According to Wilson (1988), the combined telephone/mail-order shopping service met

---

[1] For example, the financial institution with which the author does business postponed the installation of an automated banking machine for two years because studies showed it would be underused.

[2] The Bank of Montréal recently offered a 25¢ credit to customers who used its ABMs to make deposits. The bank hoped that this would encourage people to use the machines for other types of transactions.

with the most enthusiasm. It soon became apparent, however, that data on these transactions could be stored in the memory of the computer system and that, indeed, this system could collect a phenomenal amount of highly diversified information on users. But who would have access to this information, and how could it be used?

A New Form of Social Control

Although they are seen as innovative, home networking systems such as Minitel are often perceived as simple extensions of technologies like the telephone and computers. Wilson (1988), however, has stated that the information collected by these systems will be used to augment social control. The issue extends well beyond the problem of privacy protection: it concerns the surveillance of social groups through the control of large-scale home networking systems. Wilson (1988) has warned that the strategy of industry and government will be to integrate households into a computer-based communication infrastructure for the purpose of increasing the extent of this social control. An interactive technology like videotex would be useful to achieve household integration. According to the author, generalized access to the Télétel network will lead to greater control because it will result in a larger number of network transactions, which in turn will increase the amount of data available for corporations. This mechanism will lead to a form of social management of the whole of society.

In France, however, laws aimed at protecting the private lives of individuals have been implemented not only with a view to ensure access to the system, but also to regulate it. Nevertheless, Wilson (1988) has stated that such legislation has had limited effects, for it does not impose restrictions on data collection, or hinder corporate ability to consult these data. It aims only at eliminating arbitrary practices and punishing routine data collection by individuals with malicious intent. Moreover, the system of surveillance of potential lawbreakers is difficult to apply because it would require universal application, which would involve exorbitant costs. People, therefore, must be trusted for their good will, knowing that a small number of contraveners will go unarrested. Thus, the problem of administrative control over the population in the form of public surveillance remains unsolved. But how can this be?

The more users there are, the more enterprises and organizations (banks, loan companies, pharmacies and other enterprises capable of providing information on the private lives of individuals) are likely to offer services, and the more it is possible to obtain information on a person. These records of transactions represent an opportunity to collect the information required to form user profiles. Furthermore, one of the characteristics of these transactions is that they occur almost instantaneously. According to Wilson (1988), this could lead to "real time" surveillance of activities of just about any client. And as more services are offered, the more pressing it will be for users to possess a standardized identification card to use the system. Users will then be required to have a "smart card" containing complete information on its owner.

Thus, home videotex networking integrates individuals into an expanding network of computer-based communication, which in turn results in a proliferation of contacts between individuals and institutions. For the institutions involved in public surveillance (banks) and social control (the police), such a network is becoming more and more important. However, Wilson (1988) has argued that as individuals become increasingly aware that information on their activities is being stored in institutional files, they will be forced to react to the consequences of using the system by rationalizing their interactions. This will result in a form of "self-compliance." For Wilson (1988), then, it would appear that the future under videotex technology is rather bleak. The development of computerization, which has made data collection and consultation possible, is one of the reasons for Wilson's pessimism. Let us take a look at one of the videotex services that enables the collection of large amounts of personal data on users: electronic mail, or e-mail.

E-MAIL

We have just seen that computer-based networks such as Télétel and Alex can be connected to personal computers. For this reason, we consider that e-mail, which forms an interrelated system, could potentially emerge as a mass medium. E-mail systems are not only available to Videotex users. Indeed, for a fee, anyone who has access to a computer can use what is increasingly known as the information highway, or the electronic highway. The information highway project has become the hottest topic of discussion in politics and the media, even though most people do not know exactly what it is. As the number of services offered on computer-based networks increases, so does the number of people using them. Moreover, as the number of options offered increases, so does the level of skills required of users. It is therefore important to look at the impact that such developments can have on society. As we have seen, computer-based networks can store a phenomenal amount of data on users. For this reason, we believe it is also necessary to examine the ways in which information is treated. In this section, we will attempt to give a definition of the information highway, and then describe what appears to have become its prototype, the "Internet" network. After addressing a number of political and economic issues, we will conclude with a critical discussion of the state's role in this sphere.

Definitions

Despite the media attention towards this new technology, there still is no formal definition of the information highway. Lemieux (*Le Devoir*, January 19, 1994) explains that the development of the highway has been possible because of digitizing and its growing use in information communication networks. In Canada, a project called CANARIE has been set up to research the possibilities of transforming the existing network in order to increase the pass-band[3] and thus create technological conditions that would be favourable to the development of the information highway. Achieving this goal will require laying down an information infrastructure at a cost of $1 billion. The highway is to be constructed on the

---

[3] The pass-band of a signal is the range of frequency at which it is transmitted. For example, in the case of the telephone network, the pass-band ranges from 300 to 3400 Hz, which corresponds to the range of human voice. Beyond these frequency limits, an audio signal cannot be perceived.

CANET network, which provides a communication link between computers at universities, research centres and certain private firms. The CANET network, however, is outdated because it can transmit only 56,000 bits (the "0's" and "1's" of computer language, which are arranged to create pieces of data) per second. Eventually, the information highway will make it possible to send *45 million bits per second* (enough to transmit all 33 volumes of the *Encyclopaedia Britannica* in 4.7 seconds). Several major technological transformations will therefore be required to complete the development of the information highway.

From a purely technological point of view, the information highway is made up of a bundle of wires, fibre-optic cables,[4] switches and routers, which digitize information so that it can be transmitted and routed directly to a desired address. Beyond the technology itself, research on the information highway has focused primarily on its applications, such as e-mail, which is the computer equivalent of the traditional mail system. Instead of writing a message on paper and sending it by mail, users communicate via a central terminal. When communication is established, users simply input their text directly into the terminal and indicate the receiver's address. If the latter is on the network, his or her computer will display a list of the messages received since the last time the system was used. The message will be stored in the computer memory until the user erases it.

More than One Information Highway?

At this stage, it may be more appropriate to speak of several information highways, or collector lanes adjoined to the information highway. Indeed, information about the new technology is often reported in a confused manner by the print media—and scientific works are little better. We will therefore attempt to shed some light on the conditions in which the information highways are currently emerging, and then examine the types of information highways that will be developed in the future.

It seems that the emergence of the concept, or at least the initial move towards developing it, was linked to the 1992 electoral campaign of American President Bill Clinton. To be more specific, Vice-President Gore was given the mandate by the president to clear the way for the eventual development of a super information highway where citizens could participate in a variety of information and entertainment activities, from which the private sector could generate profits. According to the White House project, the information network of tomorrow would be developed on the existing network of telephone lines.

However, this political vision of the information highway project was soon picked up by large American corporations who, instead of waiting for the implementation of a coherent and integrated network, began developing several separate information highways. As a result, the telephone and cable-distribution industries have essentially taken over the project by gradually installing fibre optics in their networks. For example, the digital revolution will eventually allow cable-distribution companies to transmit a large volume of information (text, audio and video data) in a bidirectional manner to over 60

---

[4] Fibre-optic cables will become the means of transmission that could allow for extreme speeds in transmitting large quantities of textual and numerical data, as well as audio and video data (both animated and fixed). The large-scale installation of fibre-optic cables is very costly.

million households. Consumers with the financial and technological means will be able to "zap" through hundreds of interactive television channels, order a video, purchase goods via video catalogues, as well as play video games. The information highway will also use the telephone network to circulate all kinds of data, particularly educational and commercial databases, around the world.

In short, the concept of the information highway will combine cable-distribution, telecommunications, telephone, wireless and satellite communication networks in a single integrated network. This technological integration, however, is not yet reality because it is still unknown as to what form it will take. Indeed, multimedia integration is still an abstract notion.

The "Internet"

During the 1992 American presidential election campaign, Vice-President Gore claimed that the Internet was the prototype of the information highway. While some researchers do not share this vision, the Internet is considered to be the "mother of all networks," that is, the network that encompasses all other networks.

Development of the Internet began some 20 years ago when the American Department of Defense was keen to link all research centres working on military projects. The network later turned into a "civil" system, developed in an anarchic manner by governments, universities, researchers and students who wanted to communicate among themselves through computers. The Internet was thus transformed into a communication network of an almost inconceivable size. The popularity of this form of messaging seems to be growing and spreading incessantly. In 1988, as many as 3 billion messages were transmitted by e-mail in the United States alone, and that number was expected to reach 10 billion in 1991. Today, e-mail correspondents can be reached all over the globe. Salwyn (1993) has explained that in 1993 the Internet network consisted of 47,000 public and private networks, representing as many as 20 million users in 91 countries. Its Canadian users are connected to the Internet via either the CANET network or the Québec-based RISQ network. Dutrisac (1994) has pointed out that the Internet user and services directory comprises 1,200 pages, featuring as many as 50,000 "servers" (i.e., nodes, local networks and databases). The Internet also includes 7,500 interest groups involved in a wide variety of areas (nuclear physics, medicine, antique cars, and so on).

The number of Internet users is growing at a spectacular rate. In Canada, between 1994 and 1995 there was a 117% increase in the use of the information highway and a 2% drop in the use of fax machines in Toronto and Montréal (Durivage, 1996). Network specialists predict that in the year 2000, or possibly even before, 50 million private enterprises will be connected to a worldwide clientele via the Internet. In 1995, the Internet already had 25 million users—5 million more than in 1993. The Internet also features a host of non-commercial services: people can use e-mail, share software belonging to the public domain, consult databases accessible to the public, etc. The Internet has become a genuine information marketplace that provides any user (who has the financial means) with instantaneous access to hundreds of databases. Users can also readily find expert advice on countless topics.

According to Smith and Balka (1988), the services available through electronic bulletin boards can be very useful for linking people with common interests, but who are geographically dispersed. The two researchers put together a bulletin board specializing in feminist issues, which has enabled them to:

- access bibliographies on a variety of subjects;
- access lists of network participants, including their interests and current projects;
- engage in an ongoing dialogue with network participants on subjects related to women and technological change;
- collaborate on publishing or other projects;
- share information concerning conferences, recent publications, job openings and other activities related to their fields of interest.

For Smith and Balka (1988), the advantage of e-mail is that it is an inexpensive way of delivering messages, even when receivers are not there to receive their messages right away. Also, messages can be looked at by any authorized person from any terminal. The sender does not have to worry about whether receivers are there or whether it is a convenient time to reach them. This service, however, does not only have its advantages; it has its drawbacks too.

For the time being, no one owns the network—a rather incongruous situation for a capitalist society. The Internet is a federation of several thousand networks administered by a society of volunteers in the state of Virginia (*The Economist*, Dec. 1993-January 1994). Deutsch, who operates a leading Internet server located in Montréal, explains that cooperation between the different network components (universities, companies, etc.) enables the system to function. No one can change the rules of the game without unanimous consent, Deutsch has pointed out, adding that anyone who refuses to cooperate is simply ejected (in Fortin and Poissant, 1994).

To gain access to the Internet, one needs only a computer equipped with a modem and communication software, and to pay a monthly fee and know the complex codes required to access the network. In addition to the monthly fee, agencies specializing in electronic messaging charge a fee for every message sent. The combination of these costs is what stands in the way of universal access. However, to those who can fulfil these conditions, e-mail provides endless advantages. For example, by using the Internet, a person can send the same message to thousands of people for no additional fee. For a private enterprise, this represents a considerable economic benefit.

Economic and Political Implications

Given the astronomical investments required to operate the Internet, the information highway has major economic implications. The United States government has pledged more than US$3 billion over a five-year period to expand the highway and transform the Internet into a "national research and education network." The government has promised that this will create thousands of new jobs. At the same time, the government has been deregulating the telecommunications industry in order to attract large investments in the Internet from telephone and cable-distribution companies.

In Canada, competition between the telecommunications and cable-distribution companies is fierce. The Stentor Alliance, which represents nine telephone companies, has announced plans to develop an information highway called "Sirius" before the year 2005 (Tremblay, 1994). This $8 billion project is expected to generate a total of 12,000 jobs. In Québec, investments are expected to reach $2.1 billion, with a payoff of three thousand new jobs. The money invested by Stentor will mainly be used to upgrade the simultaneous telephone call-out systems from copper wires to fibre optics.

"Sirius" will initially offer clients the opportunity to exchange video messages, order films, consult databases, and use public services in health, education and culture. With this project, Stentor will compete directly with the $750 million information highway project sponsored by Vidéotron. The first phase of the Vidéotron project, also known as "UBI" (Universal Bidirectional Interactivity), was supposed to be implemented in Québec's Saguenay region by the spring of 1995.

A few days after announcing "Sirius," Stentor invited cable-distribution companies to take part in the construction of its network (Tremblay, 1994). Stentor, of which Bell Canada is a member, has also asked the government to completely deregulate the telecommunications sector so that it can move into the cable-distribution industry. As for the Vidéotron corporation, it has kept the door open to the possibility of working with Bell in developing a segment of the information highway in the province of Québec.

The Government of Québec has announced that it will contribute $50 million to implementing the information highway. This investment is part of an economic partnership which saw the acquisition of Softimage by the American software giant Microsoft for the purpose of creating the main technological component of interactive games which will be used by young people on the newly emerging information highways. Following the acquisition of Softimage, Microsoft was made an economic partner of the Government of Québec. Microsoft has also signed a letter of intent with Rogers Cablesystems (Canada's leading cable-distribution company) with a view to offering services on the information highway (Turcotte, 1994).

Thus, even though the Government of Québec lost all rights to legislate in the telecommunications sector to the federal government, it is still making major investments in the information highway project. This is simply evidence of the government's infatuation with the technology; indeed, the state is perfectly willing to invest large sums of money in the technology recklessly, since, as was mentioned earlier, the information highway project has not yet been formally defined. It seems the state is afraid of falling behind on a project which is based on a concept that does not even exist yet!

The debates surrounding the advent of the information highway in Canadian society are a reflection of the complexity of the issue. The print media often tend to highlight the grandiloquent aspects of the project (massive job creation, mammoth investments, revolutionary home services, etc.), to emphasize the scale of the challenges arising from the stiff competition between Stentor and the cable-distribution companies and the state's willingness to undertake large-scale deregulation of the telecommunications sector, as well as the promotion (followed by the denunciation) of megaprojects (e.g., Futuropolis). A critical study conducted by Mosco (1994) has provided a more sobering take on the advent of the information highway. Mosco (1994) has argued that, as is common with any new technological innovation, the current discourse surrounding the information highway tends to focus on the "novelty" aspect of the project. Mosco has also expressed reservations about the state's willingness to evade its responsibilities *vis-à-vis* the eventual regulation (or deregulation) of these information highways.

Mosco (1994) has drawn a parallel between the arrival of electricity in the cities and the advent of the information highway. In both cases, he says, the period preceding the implementation of the new technology took on the appearance of a social spectacle. Indeed, a hundred years ago, the announcement of the electrification of cities engendered a surprisingly "prospective" discourse, comparable to that which can be heard today about the information highway. Yet, Mosco has explained (1994: 4), electrification, like many other technologies, attained its real potential long after it was no longer seen as a novelty.

Mosco (1994) has raised concerns that the trend towards deregulation seems to confirm the *laissez-faireism* of the industry. If the market is given free rein to determine the future course of the information highway, including the services it will provide, the gap between those who can and have the means to access these services and those who cannot (most notably less-educated people, low-income earners, people who are in technologically deprived areas and small businesses in financial difficulty) will widen, since there will not be any guidelines fostering universal access to these services. The researcher has estimated that the state is abandoning its traditional responsibilities in this sphere. He cites, among other things, the example of the policy to provide universal access to the telephone which made it possible to connect almost 99% of Canadian households to the telephone network. It was not private, but state, initiative that made it possible to connect remote regions to the network. Today, the government is no longer able to offer a monopoly to telecommunications firms in exchange for universal access.

Finally, Mosco (1994) has estimated that whatever form regulation takes, individuals must be at the centre of attention. To achieve this, it would be helpful to present recommendations guaranteeing the protection of an "information public sphere." The recommendations should safeguard the principles of universality, diversity, accessibility, participation, equality and choice. To be sure, it is easier to grasp these principles in theory than it is to spell out their application in real life, but reference to these values is still essential for the development of such a large-scale project.

Technological Illiteracy

As technology becomes increasingly complex, the means of interacting with machines are growing in number and diversity, and users need to acquire more and more new skills to use them. What is more, new communication technology designers have not yet managed to identify optimum interaction procedures; as a result, these procedures are still not yet completely standardized. People who wish to use the new computer-based media face a changing technological environment in which they are constantly required to develop new skills. Some people adapt well to inconsistent procedures when they are aware that the changes will bring about improvements or provide new options. Others have great difficulty in making constant adjustments, especially if they believe the effort that is required of them far outweighs the potential benefits.

Consequently, the use of these new communication tools is limited by a lack of time or motivation to acquire necessary skills. For various reasons, a large number of people remain on the fringe of communication-technology developments. As a general rule, the underprivileged classes are the most disadvantaged in this respect.[5] Wealthier groups, especially those who are more educated and more favourably disposed towards these innovations, are clearly at an advantage. This is particularly true in the case of technologies that call for special skills. It is pertinent, then, to ask whether all classes of society in France have the knowledge required to benefit *equally* from using the Télétel network, and whether certain services are readily available to housewives, for example. The lack of relevant training to ensure efficient use of new technologies is referred to as technological illiteracy.

It would be a mistake to believe that the growing power of computers will result in more user-friendly services. Until now, computers have only enhanced the knowledge of those who already know how to use these machines well. No attempts have been made to compensate for knowledge gaps or the sloppiness of people who have problems understanding how to use computers. We do not know how much technological illiteracy will hinder the implementation of certain technologies that require particular skills for them to function properly. This issue, however, is but one of the challenges facing the implementation of a new technology.

The Issue of Data Base Construction

As we saw in the first section of this chapter, Wilson (1988) was concerned about the capacity of computer-based media, such as Minitel, to collect data pertaining to the private lives of individuals. The computerization of the media is gradually transforming telecommunications networks into data bases. Personal computers can easily be used as terminals, and the finetuning of internationally used conventions has given birth to telecommunications protocols, which have become true standards. Moreover, there has been a development of an information market with rates increasingly within the means of individuals, at least those belonging to the wealthier social groups.

With the ever-growing capability of computers to list and preserve huge stocks of information in memory, and the high transmission speed of networks, individuals or institutions can have rapid access to information that is directly relevant to their field of interest. Whoever possesses the appropriate technology and sufficient knowledge of the

---

[5] As we will see in the following sections, this is not the case for all media.

organization and structure of data bases can have access to detailed information that is generally not found in other mass media. The temptation is great for social and financial institutions to consult the data contained in the personal files of individuals who perform confidential transactions via computer networks. Unfortunately, this information can be used to increase the control of certain aspects of people's lives.

An important limit in terms of the ability of computer systems to ensure the validity of the information they disseminate resides in the archival processes that must be used to store information. In order to make crosschecking easier and increase data processing speed, archivists must often enter information by indicating the category to which it belongs. Thus, archivists will emphasize that a person is single, married, widowed or divorced, while overlooking particular aspects of this individual's situation. For example, some married women must assume all family responsibilities on their own while their husbands work abroad for months at a time. Such specific details are not reflected in the data. Moreover, the state considers people living in communal settings, and couples whose status is not legally recognized, to be single. No distinction is made between married, remarried, divorced or widowed people. Thus, data directories constructed by categories often involve information loss or value judgments by archivists. In this way, computer-based networks can affect the validity of information retrieved from data bases. What is more, it is not uncommon for errors to creep into the data. The CBC's *MarketPlace* (November 5, 1991) reported on a survey of 200 people who had asked to consult the personal information collected by financial institutions about them. Roughly 43% of those surveyed noted that some of the data in their files was inexact; 14% of those files contained errors that were serious enough for financial institutions to refuse any credit to these individuals.

Archivists who analyze information—first to construct a set of categories, and then to insert each individual case—must regularly evaluate the data in terms of what they believe are objective criteria. But it must be acknowledged that such objectivity is unrealistic. For example, when compiling data bases for the purpose of resolving complex social problems, archivists select the information categories *they believe* are relevant. This choice is subjective. A researcher who decides to list cases of drug abuse among violent persons will do so according to what he or she *believes* are the causes of violence. As a result, anyone consulting these data will be accessing biased and incomplete information on the individuals and events reported.

There is, therefore, a risk that information collected in a data base may be confused with reality, since this information is the result of a choice made during the categorization stage; in other words, it is a *social construction* of the lives of individuals. This trap is all the more dangerous when we consider that a computer-based system provides access to masses of data in which one easily becomes lost. What is more, Wilson (1988) has noted that the size of these data bases will continue to grow over time, as computer-based systems such as Minitel and Alex are used more and more. Nevertheless, this impact on the degree of social control of the population is somewhat attenuated by certain factors.

One of these factors is the resistance of some people to e-mail practices. It must be acknowledged that the interest in this type of technology, though widespread, is still far from equalling that in television or VCRs, for instance. There appears to be a certain lack of public trust in the security of computer procedures. Aware of the speed with which a computer can perform thousands of transactions, users still fear that an error could ruin them before they would even have a chance to respond. In this type of application, it is important for technology to increase the control of users over the consequences of their actions, not the inverse. But is this fear justified?

Thanks to their transmission speed and capacity to stock information, the new means of communication could constitute additional instruments of social control. The use of new media for these purposes, however, is not enough to prove that technology is responsible for this consequence. The will to control the masses existed well before the implementation of these technological innovations. Social control depends on the *political* (or *economic*) *will* of a few who could use technology to increase their power, but who use other means when such technology is not available.

In China, population records are not computerized as in the West, but residents in even the most remote villages are under surveillance of a party informer who reports directly to the central party organization. This role of investigator and supervisor is usually given to an older woman who is familiar with the lives of residents in her neighbourhood and who agrees ideologically with the government. This system is more efficient than any computerized system in many respects. The memory of these women allows them to store objective information, but also to take into account emotional reactions and recall even the smallest details which at first could have been considered unimportant. The female party informer is a living memory, which the computer is not. In this way, she constitutes a channel through which information may be widely transmitted, while remaining closely adapted to the particular nature of each micro-community. She knows what information will be met with resistance and what arguments are most persuasive. She is also aware of the level of tolerance of receivers. The automation of telecommunications may help improve the performance of a system in terms of speed and the precision of certain types of information, but it may reduce its quality considerably. Thus, it can never be held responsible for transforming a democratic society into a totalitarian society, in which a small group of administrators control the rest of the population.

If technology enables the ruling classes to refine their methods of social control, it must be said that lower production costs of computer equipment also results in increased access of other social classes to these instruments, which could help them *avoid this form of control*. For example, if real estate owners compile a list of people they believe are bad tenants, the latter can respond by putting together a list of bad landlords.

In the past, the high cost of information technologies provided an advantage to the well-to-do, and for many years these people took advantage of highly efficient computer tools. Present forecasts, however, suggest that it is the middle classes who will benefit the most from present innovations. For example, as a general rule, electronic bulletin boards are used as a means of broadcasting by the middle classes—perhaps because it is associated with writing. Other new technologies, however, have had more success among the working classes.

VIDEO: AN EMERGING MEDIUM

The videocassette recorder (VCR) is a technology that combines a sound and image cassette-recording system with a computerized programming system. Over the past 15 years this technology has developed at an astounding pace; in fact, video is one of the media whose use has spread the quickest. As early as 1987, 36% of households in the United States possessed a VCR: 45% in urban centres, 32% in rural communities and the remainder in small towns. Who owns a VCR? A number of studies (e.g., Roe, 1987) have shown that 5% more men own VCRs than women and that this figure is constant across all milieus. Gunter and Levy (1987) reported that 84.5% of VCR owners are married and 66.4% have at least one child. Moreover, the highest rate of ownership is found among the working class (57.9%); the lowest rates are among professionals and managers. Finally, 71.5% of video owners have at least two television sets in their households.

The Sony corporation was the first to introduce a home version of the VCR to the United States in 1975. According to Bettig (1990), as early as 1976 the movie companies Universal and Disney launched lawsuits against Sony to curb the public's use of this new technical means to copy their films; this, however, did not prevent the staggering household penetration of the new technology. The American government predicted that before the end of 1990 about one-third of American households possessing a television set would have a VCR (in Bettig, 1990). In 1990, in the United Kingdom and Australia, 60% of households with a television set owned a VCR; in Europe the percentage was lower, at 25% (representing an estimated 25 to 35 million VCRs), though in Germany the figure was as high as 55%. On a smaller scale, video has also made inroads in many Third World countries, as we will see later. But what is video technology used for?

According to Gunter and Levy (1987), video is most commonly used as a complement to television, that is, to record programmes that would otherwise be missed or that people would like to watch again. Video is therefore used to mediate contents previously mediated on television. This type of video use runs counter to the concept of spontaneous communication. The second most popular use consists of recording programmes or films, even those that users do not intend to watch immediately, to build up a home video library. Thirdly, video technology is used to watch films, which are either rented or bought.[6] What exactly do people watch on video?

Tastes differ according to age and gender. Among adults, preferences are clearly differentiated along gender lines: men say they like watching police serials and sports programmes, while women prefer to watch dramas and soap operas. Teenagers, however, do not display any marked sexual differentiation. Roe (1987) has informed us that both girls and boys spend an incredible amount of time watching videos. Weekly averages are as follows: 50% of teenagers watch between 0 and 3 hours of video per week, 40% between 3 and 10 hours per week, 7% between 10 and 20 hours per week, and finally 3% over 20 hours per week. The most frequently viewed programmes are police shows and horror and adventure movies, followed by martial arts movies and films with violent scenes, and finally pornographic movies. It seems that the VCR has been a means of spectacular penetration

---

[6] None of the studies examined here mention the production of home videos as a popular use.

of pornography into the home. In Japan, for example, some 300 porn films are produced every month; this sector of the video industry reports yearly revenues of more than $2.6 billion (*La Presse*, May 18, 1991). Although statistics on this specific topic are not available for Canada, the frequency of this activity has probably also increased here given that such movies can be viewed in the privacy of one's home.

Video-use differences between adults and teenagers are found not only with respect to content. There are clearly marked differences regarding the preferred social context of use as well. For example, Gunter and Levy (1987) have reported that although most adults in their study believed that video promotes family viewing practices, and a majority (73%) claimed that watching video is an enjoyable way for a family to spend time together, the data suggest otherwise: 59% of the videos viewed by the same adults during the two-week period preceding the investigation were watched alone. However, Roe (1987) has informed us that only 6% of teenagers tend to watch videos by themselves. As opposed to adults, teenagers overwhelmingly view videos in groups of three or four individuals. Thus, for young people, this activity is an occasion to socialize. What are the effects of the rapid expansion, at least in certain social classes, of this popular medium?

It appears that the effects of video are similar to those of other forms of communication examined earlier. Ownership of a VCR seems to stimulate interaction (organized viewings, cassette trades, programme taping for others, etc.) between different people. However, the data of video-use studies show that adults have developed individual viewing behaviour. Watching videos is "a kind of communications separateness, a privatized media experience, often unshared even between members of the same household" (Gunter and Levy, 1987: 491). Children watch videos in the company of friends, whereas men and women watch their favourite programmes by themselves and when they so choose. Why?

For many researchers, the reason for these patterns is that people use VCRs to mark their preferences for specific content. But as preferences become more marked, the more audiences become fragmented. If a woman's favourite soap opera airs at the same time as her partner's detective show, she can record her soap and play it back later or the next day. Video has therefore made more selective television viewing possible. Instead of watching a programme they do not enjoy, people can watch a programme or a movie they have recorded. Thus "passive" television users have become active video users who are more motivated to find programmes they enjoy, even if they are broadcast at times which would make television viewing impossible. This has led Rubin and Bantz (1987) to claim that video users have more control than television viewers over viewing time, place, partners and types of programmes watched.

In sum, during the past 10 years, video use has spread at a staggering pace all over the world. This rapid expansion has generated phenomenal revenues for the media industry, especially enterprises specializing in video technology. However, there is a flip side to this positive situation. Copying videocassettes is so easy that "piracy" of original content—which costs much less than producing content—has become child's play. It seems that piracy has become a genuine problem in the video world. It is therefore important to look at this phenomenon in greater detail.

The Piracy Problem

Ronald Bettig (1990) has conducted a study on the consequences of the expansion of video technology, especially with respect to piracy. Piracy has made it possible to make unauthorized recordings of films and television programmes for private or commercial use. Indeed, it appears to be quite simple to duplicate works (artistic, intellectual, etc.) originally produced on 35mm or 16mm film, or as television programmes, without authorization. According to Bettig (1990), video has had three major effects on the mass media industry: it has a) increased the availability of films and television programmes; b) reduced the cost and complexity of mass production, which was once reserved for specialists; and c) privatized the act of viewing pirated versions.

It comes as no surprise that the movie and television industries are concerned about these effects. The possibility of reproducing cassettes, films or television content without surveillance is a problem for producers who own the reproduction rights and who invest large sums of money into their legal reproduction. The fact that videos can be reproduced at will reduces the producers' control over the rights of intellectual property, and increases the audience's control over both the accessibility of creative works, and the viewing time and place of this material. For this reason, the American movie industry moved as quickly as possible to take over a large part of videocassette production and a significant share of the video market.

In 1989, seven of the largest movie production companies (Twentieth Century Fox, Columbia, Paramount, Warner, Disney, MGM and Universal) controlled 65% of videocassette production for the home market. Thus, what first appeared as a threat has become a new opportunity for these companies to increase profits. In 1989, wholesale videocassette sales provided production companies with $5.3 billion in revenues.[7] In spite of this, Bettig (1990) has explained that in 1990 companies reported losses of up to one billion dollars because of piracy.

These financial losses led the industry to request the American government's help in controlling the production of unauthorized material. But this begs the question: with the advent of new technologies such as cable distribution and satellite systems, how can the industry succeed in controlling international pirating of American productions? Many industrialized countries have developed a control mechanism in compliance with the Berne Convention for the Protection of Literary and Artistic Property. But rights cannot be protected internationally if they are not first protected on a national level. Bettig (1990) has claimed that this problem is particularly acute in many Third World countries. As we will soon see in greater detail, these countries are not interested in developing policies in this area, either because they do not want their cultural industry to be controlled by foreign monopolies, or because they do not want a flow of foreign currencies into their countries. Brazil, for example, requires a minimum of 25% Brazilian content in videocassette production, while Columbia demands 20%. It is therefore not surprising that so much piracy is occurring. But what exactly is piracy? Does piracy include recording a film on a videocassette recorder for personal use?

---

[7] Sales in America alone were as high as $3.37 billion, in comparison with $1.18 billion in other countries.

When a cultural work is put on the market or made public, its owner (the creator, or in most cases the person who agrees to produce it) legally receives the exclusive reproduction rights for commercialization. In this context, piracy occurs when someone duplicates the work of another person (or even his or her own work if the rights were sold to a producer) without permission and monetary compensation, and sells it for personal or commercial profit. Bettig (1990) has identified six forms of piracy:

- making a videocassette copy of a film or any other audiovisual work, and using this copy for mass duplication;

- taping a programme (a film or any other show) broadcast on television, and using this taped version for mass duplication;

- distributing unauthorized copies of videocassettes;

- selling or renting unauthorized copies of videocassettes;

- importing authorized or unauthorized versions of videocassettes without the permission of a legally recognized importer;

- organizing unauthorized public viewings of videocassettes.

From this list one can deduce that those reproductions intended only for personal use do not constitute piracy. They may be viewed with a group of people in the privacy of one's home. It is forbidden, however, to project them in a public place without special authorization. All other forms of reproduction, viewing or broadcast are illegal and are commonly referred to as piracy. The material that pirates copy is almost exclusively popular films and television programmes which they are guaranteed to sell. Piracy naturally implies that those who practice it do not pay for copyrights, that their copies are of lesser quality than originals, and that they are sold at a lower price. Who engages in piracy?

As was previously mentioned, the lowest rates of piracy are in industrialized countries, including European countries, where a highly efficient and economically profitable protection system has been put in place. How can controlling pirated copies from foreign countries be made profitable? Because countries that produce and export videocassettes, such as France, Italy and the United Kingdom, are interested in seeing their own rights protected internationally, this means that they, in turn, are ready to accept that the rights of other countries, such as the United States, be protected as well.

The situation, however, is different in many Third World countries that have a small videocassette-production industry and almost no video exports to speak of. Not only do these countries have no economic interests to protect, but most of them also consider that the universal property rights system puts them in a position of economic dependence with respect to the producing countries because it would require them to pay to import culture from these countries. As a result, they refuse to adopt property rights protection policies. According to Bettig (1990), it is a means of resistance against this new type of dependence on industrialized countries. Moreover, some Third World countries argue that cultural or intellectual works should belong to all humanity and therefore be available to all nations, especially poor countries, at no cost.

This is particularly the case in Middle Eastern countries because they have no agreements with producing countries regarding copyrights (Bettig, 1990). In addition, two other factors contribute to piracy in these countries: a) as a result of the economic boom stimulated by the oil crisis in the seventies, these countries now have the means not only to purchase copies, but also to obtain the technology for mass duplication of works originating in producing countries, which they can then distribute throughout Africa and Europe; b) because these countries have few movie theatres, their movie industries are underdeveloped and therefore incapable of producing original works. As a result, residents of these countries are particularly interested in foreign productions, notably British television content produced by the BBC and movies produced by American companies. Kuwait and Saudi Arabia are the two countries with the highest rates of piracy. Despite intense pressure, especially from the United States, Middle Eastern countries are major importers of pirated videocassettes, as well as large-scale reproducers of the same cassettes and exporters of these duplications.

The situation is similar in Asian and Pacific countries (Singapore, Taiwan, South Korea, Thailand, Malaysia, the Philippines and Indonesia) that have a weak movie industry largely incapable of producing original works, and where rapid proliferation of the means of videocassette duplication has occurred. These factors create ideal conditions for piracy. Furthermore, these countries also view the universal property rights system as creating a new form of dependence on Western countries. It appears that Hong Kong is an exception to the rule. In fact, it has the most highly developed protection system of all the countries in this region of the world.

In this context, videocassette reproducers have economic interests to protect and therefore have the tacit support of the state. But the situation is also partly the result of cultural factors. Bettig (1990) has informed us that in these countries it is traditionally seen as an honour to have one's work copied. Thus residents, and even governments of certain countries are far from convinced that piracy is a criminal act.

We can see that videocassette piracy is a complex problem involving factors other than economics. Thus, a study of the problem must take into consideration the cultural practices, among other things, that are unique to each country. "Deviant" countries cannot be forced to comply with the universal property rights system, especially given that most are acting in good faith. For Bettig (1990), the reason for the American government's support of multinational corporations in this struggle is that by reinforcing the system of intellectual property, this will help American producers dominate the world's cultural production. It is precisely this kind of intervention that Third World countries are resisting. But how long will they be able to resist? Some researchers predict that in a few years a dozen multinationals, mostly American, will have a monopoly of the world's cultural production.

In the meantime, videocassette piracy continues to have negative effects on the local development of Third World movie and television industries. Movie theatre attendance and television viewing have fallen considerably since piracy has become a systematic practice. One of the reasons for this is that local movie industries are so disorganized that pirated copies of films, for example, are available before official versions are released in theatres. Furthermore, piracy deprives these countries of large quantities of foreign currencies, and reduces revenues from theatre ticket taxes. Finally, far from diminishing American cultural imperialism, piracy enhances it by enabling large-scale distribution of its products. American producers are not calling for copyright protection for altruistic reasons. They intend to make a profit over the long term from their cultural imperialism that is flourishing in the present system. Thus, an intellectual rights protection system would not necessarily re-establish the cultural balance between industrialized and non-industrialized countries.

In short, the videocassette recorder is a new instrument of communication that has been widely adopted by the more modest classes and developing countries. While video technology has provided users with numerous advantages, it is causing an increasing number of problems for producers, a major one being that its simplicity renders them vulnerable to large-scale duplication of their products. Let us see if this is also the case for other new technologies such as interactive television and pay television.

NEW FORMS OF TELEVISION

Television has changed considerably in the past decade. Satellite systems have dramatically increased the breadth of broadcasting capacities and the range of content available to users. Moreover, cable distribution has created new ways of perceiving television by delivering a tenfold increase in channels, which in turn has made pay television (pay TV) and interactive television possible.

Pay Television

Pay television is a private television programming system in which users must pay a fee to access. Pay TV has financial advantages not only for cable distribution companies, but also for content suppliers. For example, Norm Green, one-time owner of the former Minnesota North Stars hockey club, agreed to have each of his team's games broadcast on a pay TV channel for half the price of a ticket to a home game. Of course, the games were not broadcast on regular television stations. This way, the owner of the hockey team sold enough pay TV time to make substantially more money than if he only sold a limited number of tickets at the sports arena (*La Presse*, May 12, 1991).[8]

This type of television is so popular in the United States, and regular networks are losing so much revenue, that governments have felt the need to intervene. For example, the State of Minnesota had harsh words for Norm Green, arguing that the air waves and the right to cable television belong to the public. The State claimed that depriving audiences of the right to view a national league playoff series runs counter to the spirit of American laws (*La Presse*, May 19, 1991). One can understand the State of Minnesota's

---

[8] Mr. Green had such success that Peter Pocklington, former owner of the Edmonton Oilers, thought of adopting a similar strategy.

concern when one considers the enthusiasm of hockey fans here in Canada. Imagine if the owners of the Toronto Maple Leafs or the Vancouver Canucks, for example, were to restrict access to the club's Stanley Cup playoff television broadcasts, thereby eliminating the CBC's *Hockey Night in Canada*? Of course, only those viewers with the financial means to subscribe to such a channel would be able to watch these games. This kind of application of pay television would clearly be antidemocratic, not to mention that it would deprive the CBC of an important source of revenue. Producers would potentially apply pay TV programming to any show they like. If these shows were broadcast on pay TV networks, their price would go up proportionally.

Interactive Television

Interactive television is a technology that was introduced only recently. In Québec, this new service is currently offered by the Videotron cable company under the name of Videoway. It consists of a box about the size of a compact disc player connected to a television set which offers different information retrieval services such as video games, horoscopes, lottery results, stock exchange quotations, pay television and a channel entirely devoted to interactive programming (Latouche, 1991). More than 40,000 Montréal residents subscribe to the interactive network, which offers more than 12 hours of programming (hockey games, news, etc.) per day.

Interactive television is seen by its promoters as a means for viewers to personalize their television consumption. "Conventional" networks such as the CBC, CTV and the Global Television Network are viewed as "basic menus," while pay TV and interactive television are seen as offering "gourmet menus." Why? First, the latter often provide more recent content than regular television. Second, because their programming is usually specialized in an area, they offer subscribers a wider variety of programmes to choose from. There are other advantages as well. An executive at an interactive-television distribution company emphasized that viewers who want longer news broadcasts, for instance, can request additional news (Latouche, 1991). Similarly, a viewer watching a hockey game can choose to follow a particular player or order replays.

In this context, one can assume that interactive television will have an effect on various aspects of television communication, namely audiences, content and even financing. Audiences may be the first to be affected by these technological changes. Because audiences can interact and ask for what they want, viewer categories will become increasingly diversified. It will be possible (and necessary) to distinguish, for example, between viewers who are news-hungry and those who are not, and those who prefer watching one particular hockey player over another, etc. Consequently, this new form of television will have an influence on content, which will need to take audience diversity into account. As a result, content could become more varied to satisfy more categories of viewers.

Finally, advertising, the financial engine of television, will also have to adjust to interactive television. The executive mentioned earlier claimed that the interactive nature of this new form of television could be an opportunity to increase advertising revenues, since sponsors will be able to vary their ads according to a viewer's programme choices.

You don't use the same approach to sell an automobile to someone who has chosen in-depth coverage of economic issues and someone looking for all the latest sports scores. With our system the same advertising slot can be used to reach four different audiences and more fragmented audiences (Latouche, 1991: 54).

Thus, interactive television could introduce interesting variations to a mass medium whose form has not changed since its invention. However, it is certain that pay TV and interactive television (for which additional fees must also be paid) are not as democratic as regular television, which is broadcast in all households without discrimination. If television networks begin reserving general interest programmes for pay TV channels, there will be cause for concern about the future of television for everyone.

CONCLUSION

One might think that the proliferation of transmission channels would foster the wide spectrum of viewpoints expressed via the mass media. Indeed, the more channels there are, the more a variety of people should be able to express diverse opinions. Theoretically, then, the more television channels there are, the easier it should be to present content opposed to the dominant ideology. This book has shown that in practice this is not the case. Why?

The reasons all revolve around the fact that television is a capitalist enterprise. Its primary objective is therefore to be profitable and, in order to achieve this, it must present content that will attract the financing (advertising) required to continue operating. This reason alone is enough to explain a large part of television production. What is more, television operates in a patriarchal capitalist society and adopts the values of that society, which support the groups in power. Is it realistic to think that a pay TV channel can specialize in content with feminist tendencies? It is not in the interests of groups involved in mass media financing and production, and who control their operations, to support oppositional ideologies. These groups represent the financial mainstay of all large-scale projects of communication development.

The success of projects such as the Télétel network in France was made possible only because of large-scale financing from, and the concentration of, large communication enterprises. However, up until now, the success of the new media has occurred outside this context. For example, the development of large networks of electronic bulletin boards began through the initiatives of small groups which operated their own bulletin boards independently of one another. These small groups gradually joined together without losing their autonomy, first within the scope of regional associations, and later as associations extending across North America. This was accomplished without the help of a government infrastructure or the financial support of major private corporations.

The difficulties in implementing a videotex system in North America compared with the rapid proliferation of electronic bulletin boards suggests that consumers are more interested in using the new media to acquire some control over broadcasting instead of simply obtaining the right to choose from a limited set of options. This could mean that the frequency of use of these media is determined primarily by how well they meet the needs of people for whom they are intended.

There are a number of protest movements that are opposed to the implementation of certain technological innovations. This opposition is manifested in different ways, depending on whether or not the movements accept the ideology underlying the media. Mosco (1982) has claimed that the movements can be divided in two categories. On the one hand, there are "alternative" groups which agree that all media production should be based on the dominant ideology as long as they foster socially acceptable values. When the media fail to do this, alternative movements express their opposition by attempting to control content. For example, Mosco has noted that if a television network attempts to broadcast sexist or violent television programmes, alternative pressure groups will be formed to counter this tendency. On the other hand, there are "oppositional" groups which believe that the media simply do not have the right to represent dominant values only. For these people, neither the dominant ideology nor oppositional ideologies should monopolize media content.

GENERAL CONCLUSION

Throughout this book, we have seen that media productions (written, televised and otherwise) are anything but flawless reproductions of social reality. On the contrary, we have seen that media contents are *social constructions of social reality*, in other words, the result of a selection process involving not only creators, but also producers and the financial and political institutions that support them.

The social constructions of the media are nevertheless not entirely imagined. They are based on certain aspects of our existence, or real social experiences; consequently, fiction is made to *look like* reality. In other words, because social constructions are inspired by reality, media content is perceived as reality by certain audiences and can even take its place. What makes this situation all the more disturbing is that the media project a *constructed image* of social reality. For example, we saw that the portrayal of soap opera and popular novel characters corresponds with the sexist stereotypes that are attributed to women and men in Canadian society—in fact, these stereotypes are often exaggerated by the media. Thus, male characters are typically portrayed as physically strong and intellectually superior to women, and tend to be chauvinistic and fill dominant roles. Female characters, on the other hand, are represented as more physically fragile, kind and often passive, and play dominated roles. And yet Canadian society is full of kind, passive men and intelligent, active women.

One of the more damaging biases of media production is that content does not reflect the cultural diversity of Canadian society. For example, although most soap operas are set in urban areas, which in real life consist of many different cultural groups, almost all the characters come from white ethnic groups. One would be tempted to conclude that no other social groups exist in our society. Why is media content constructed in this way?

Media industries produce different means or forms of communication in order to reach a variety of audiences. But it would appear that these forms have stopped evolving: aside from slight, superficial adjustments, they still convey the same ideas and values in spite of social changes occurring in society. For example, Harlequin Romances are still based on the same type of sentimental scenarios, although in order to adjust to "modern" ideas, authors have had to add certain scenes that would have been unthinkable when these publications first appeared. For example, scenes describing the hero's sexual conquests, and even the idea of a career for the heroine, would have outraged female readers.

In short, although media productions are important socialization agents in the lives of individuals, and could therefore be used to put forth oppositional ideas, they have been confined to a reactionary role, reluctantly adjusting to social change when there was no choice but to accept it. Why are the mass media so reluctant to allow ideas promoting social change to emerge?

Given that the media are private enterprises functioning within the framework of a capitalist patriarchal society, they are obliged by the logic of capitalism either to seek forms of financing to generate profits, or to operate under government funding. In the case of profit-oriented enterprises, they cannot allow themselves to take too many risks. For example, denouncing abuses of power, the dominance of certain groups, and so on, could scare those who usually provide capital investments, namely powerful institutions. In the case of publicly funded media, financing is secured from governments, which are just as unlikely to tolerate open criticism. Thus, media industries are supported by powerful capitalist institutions and must therefore disseminate the dominant ideology that keeps these institutions in power. Because the media are subjected to economic and political control, they cannot present revolutionary productions or information. The type of communication produced by these industries is therefore a reproduction of the most traditional ideas in Canadian society. In this context, "modern" ideas are presented only after social change has occurred.

The fact that the media are subjected to various forms of control may not be the only reason why they essentially represent dominant values. It may also be due to the fact that audiences are guilty of a certain complicity with media content. Because the dominant ideology plays an inherent, though often unconscious, role in the socialization process, a consensus is formed around some of the ideas and activities that support it. For example, people from different classes *implicitly* agree on what is considered socially acceptable. Given this situation, isn't it likely that a majority of audience members would resist content that is strongly opposed to dominant values?

Clearly, media activities are closely related to the social conditions in which they are produced. Media communication does not occur in a vacuum: it is a *social, socialized* and *socializing* phenomenon. Every hour spent watching television or reading a novel constitutes a social act during which consumers interpret content—that is deliberately constructed by a medium—in different ways depending on their living conditions and backgrounds. Thus, both content production and consumption are influenced by social factors.

In this book we saw that people of different classes have divergent interpretations of identical content. People from the working classes tend to have more materialist interpretations than people from the middle classes, who need not worry about making ends meet at the end of every month. Interpretations can also vary from one culture to the next. Consumers belonging to different cultures will place their own emphasis on different aspects of content. Finally, women and men have different preferences and therefore different interpretations of media content: it seems that women prefer romance, and men prefer aggression. Because of this divergence, some audiences resist certain types of content. Even two women from the same social class can have dissimilar opinions about violence in the media. The interpretation of media content is therefore mediated by the notions of *class, culture and sex.*

This is why audiences are said to *negotiate* the content they consume. In other words, people rarely accept what they are shown at face value. Contrary to the claims of the psychological model, audiences are not passive, but *active* media users. They *make decisions* during the process of media consumption of all kinds (newspapers, television, radio, literature, etc.). Which newspaper or book shall I buy? Which television network shall I watch? What will I *decide* to believe in based on what I read or hear in the media? Thus, not only do audiences choose content but, within the scope of this choice, they use various mechanisms to achieve a *negotiated* reading of this content.

The notion of negotiating media content is important because it constitutes the only means for audiences to resist media producers. Economic control of the media by a number of small groups appears to be an *immutable* aspect of media production. It seems that audiences have no leverage to negotiate on an economic level. Instead, audience negotiation occurs in relation to consumption, that is, on an ideological and cultural level. Nevertheless, the power of audiences to resist, as well as their influence on production financing, should not be underestimated. For instance, many big-budget television programmes have been taken off the air in their infancy due to rejection by the public.

What do these facts tell us? That communication is a link between people which cannot be considered in isolation. It is important to be aware of this link in order to develop critical media consumption habits. It is also important to understand that the news, even when it is done live, is always mediated by journalists, and that cultural programmes are not created for purely artistic reasons, but are constructed with a view to please audiences. In fact, the difference between the two types of programmes is not nearly as clear as some would imagine: the news contains elements of artistic creativity and cultural programmes contain elements of reality.

In the end, there may be little difference between news and fiction. Michèle Mattelart (1981) has commented on the grey area between the two. She has argued that fiction suggests a certain lifestyle just as much as the news does. Fiction programmes, such as soap operas, are a vehicle for ideologies aimed at reinforcing and promoting the values, roles, beliefs and practices that are accepted by the majority and acceptable by the minority in power. For Mattelart (1981), this is a privileged area of mass culture where power does not need to talk about politics to do politics. It is important to remember that the aim of all content—cultural works and the news—is to attract audiences to secure the funding required to meet the media's profit objectives, and that content is *constructed* with these objectives in mind. However, achieving this task is increasingly difficult because audiences have a greater say about which media they *decide* to use and which content they *decide* to consume.

This book has looked at many aspects of mass media and communication; however, there are many other issues that we have not addressed, for example, the production of such media as film, theatre and radio. Are the assertions we have put forth about certain media applicable to other types of media? Similarly, many questions concerning forms of communication have not been raised. For example, we only touched on the representation of minority groups—that is, cultures or sexual orientations different from that of the majority—in soap operas, advertising, and the news, as well as the images by which they are portrayed. A more in-depth analysis of these issues could lead to interesting findings.

Many questions regarding audiences and media consumption have not been tackled. An analysis could be made of "unexpected" audiences, that is, audiences that were not targeted by media producers because they were not expected to consume a particular mode of communication, for example, women who read detective novels, men who watch soap operas, etc. Do these audiences "negotiate" content the same way that intended audiences, which have already been studied, do? There is an incredible number of mass media phenomena that have not yet, or only superficially, been explored. It could be said that the possibilities of mass media studies are endless.

Bibliography

Agee, W.K., Ault, P.H., and Emery, E. *Introduction to Mass Communications*. 9th ed. New York: Harper & Row, 1988.

Arlen, G. "Videotex battlefield." In *Videotex Canada*, Winter 1983, 15–9.

Ash, S., and Quelch, J. *The New Videotex Technology and Its Impact on Retailers in Canada*. Ottawa: Department of Industry, Trade and Commerce, 1982.

Attick, R. D. *The English Common Reader*. Chicago: University of Chicago Press, 1957.

Bacon-Smith, C. *Enterprising Women: Television Fandom and the Creation of Popular Myth*. Philadelphia: University of Pennsylvania Press, 1992.

Barker, M. *Comics: Ideology, Power and the Critics*. New York: Manchester University Press, 1989.

Beauchamp, C. *Le silence des médias*. Montréal: Editions du Remue-ménage, 1988.

Beaud, P. *La société de connivence : média, médiations et classes sociales*. Paris: Aubier Montaigne, 1984.

Beauvoir, S. de. *The Second Sex*. New York: Alfred A. Knopf, 1953.

Bell, J. *Guardians of the North*. Ottawa: National Archives of Canada, 1992.

Bettig, R.V. "Extending the Law of Intellectual Property: Hollywood's International Anti-Videocassette Piracy Campaign." In *Journal of Communication Inquiry*, 1990, 14(2), 55–70.

Bettinotti, J. *La corrida de l'amour : le roman Harlequin*. Montréal: Université du Québec à Montréal, 1986

Bettinotti, J.; Bédard, H.; Gagnon, J.; Noizet, P.; Provost, C. *La corrida de l'amour: Le roman Harlequin*. Montreal: XYZ, English version, 1990.

Bonville, J. de. *La presse québécoise de 1884 à 1914 : genèse d'un média de masse*. Québec: Presses de l'Université Laval, 1989.

Boyd-Barrett, O. "Media Imperialism," in J. Curran et al (eds.) 1977 *Mass Communication and Society*, London: Edward Arnold, pp. 116–135.

Breton, P., and Proulx, S. *L'explosion de la communication*. Paris: Boréal, 1993.

Brown, M.E. "Conclusion: Consumption and Resistance, The Problem of Pleasure." In M.E. Brown (ed.), *Television and Women's Culture*. London: Sage, 1990.

Bureau, S. "Les premiers vainqueurs." In *La Presse*, Montréal, February 4, 1991.

Butler, J. "The Force of Fantasy: Feminism, Mapplethorpe, and Discursive Excess." In *Differences: A Journal of Feminist Cultural Studies*, 1990, 2(2), 105–126.

Carey, J. W. "Editor's Introduction: Taking Culture Seriously." In J.W. Carey (ed.), *Media, Myths, and Narratives: Television and the Press*. Newbury Park, CA: Sage, 1988.

Carey, J.W., and Dreiling, A.L. "Popular Culture and Uses and Gratifications: Notes Toward an Accommodation." In J.G. Blumler and E. Katz (eds.), *The Uses of Mass Communications*. Beverly Hills: Sage, 1974.

Challe, O. "Le minitel: la télématique à la française." In *The French Review*, 1989, 62(5), 843–856.

Clanchy, M.T. *From Memory to Written Record*. London: Arnold, 1979.

Christian-Smith, L.K. *Becoming a Woman Through Romance*. London: Routledge, 1990.

de Certeau, M. The Practice of Everyday Life, trans. by S. Randall, Berkeley: University of California Press, 1984.

DeFleur, M.L., and Ball-Rokeach, L. *Theories of Mass Communication*. 5th ed. New York: Longman, 1989.

Dorfman, A. "The Infantilizing of Culture." In D. Lazère (ed.), *American Media and Mass Culture*. Berkeley: University of California Press, 1987.

Dorfman, A., and Mattelart, A. *How to Read Donald Duck*. New York: International General, 1975.

Dubino, J. "The Cinderella Complex: Romance Fiction, Patriarchy and Capitalism." In *Journal of Popular Culture*, 1993, 27(3): 103–118.

Dubois, J. "Les femmes et l'information. Étude statistique de la place des femmes dans les médias québécois." In *Communication/Information*, 1988, 9(2), 111–22.

Dubuc, A. "Le Futurarium." In *La Presse*, 4th May 1994.

Durivage, P. "Les Montréalais adoptent l'Internet." In *La Presse*, 4 March 1996, p. B.1.

Dutrisac, R. "Autoroutes électroniquqe: au-delà de la tuyauterie, il faudra créer des appplications." In *Le Devoir*, 29th January 1994.

Dyer, G. "Women and Television: an overview." In H. Baehr and G. Dyer (eds.), *Boxed In Women and Television*. New York: Pandora, 1987.

Eaman, R.A. "Putting the 'public' into public broadcasting." In H. Holmes and D. Taras (eds) *Media Power and Policy in Canada*. Toronto: Harcourt, Brace Jovanovitch Canada Inc. 1992, pp. 58–76.

Eisenstein, E.L. *The Printing Press as an Agent of Change*. Cambridge: Cambridge University Press, 1979.

Eisenstein, E.L. *The Printing Revolution in Early Modern Europe*. Cambridge: Cambridge University Press, 1983.

Elliott, P. "Uses and Gratifications Research: A Critique and a Sociological Alternative." In J.G. Blumler and E. Katz (eds.), *The Uses of Mass Communications*. Beverly Hills: Sage, 1974.

Englander, D.; Bearden, M.; Kelly, B.; Kitzmiller C.; and Dahlin, R. "What I did for Love: Academics, Booksellers, Executives, Lawyers, Police Officers—All These Writers Learned to Write What They Loved to Read." In *Publishers Weekly*, 1995, 242(20): 36.

Ericson, R., et al. *Visualizing Deviance: A Study of News Organizations*, Toronto: University of Toronto Press, 1987.

Ericson, R., et al. *Negotiating Control: A Study of News Sources*, Toronto: University of Toronto Press, 1989.

Ericson, R., et al. *Representing Order: Crime, Law and Justice in the News Media*, Toronto: University of Toronto Press, 1991.

Escomel, G. "La 'pub' en France : toujours aussi sexiste?" In *La Gazette des femmes*, November–December 1986, 16–20.

Eudes, Y. "La Société Disney, un modèle de 'communication totale.'" In *Monde diplomatique*, Paris, November 1988.

Ewen, S. "Advertising as Social Production." In A. Mattelart and S. Siegelaub (eds.), *Communication and Class Struggle*, vol. 1. New York: International General, 1979.

Ewen, S., and Ewen, E. *Channels of Desire*. New York: McGraw-Hill, 1982.

Febvre, L., and Martin, H.J. *The Coming of the Book*. London: NLB, 1976.

Ferguson, M. "Images of Power and the Feminist Fallacy." In *Critical Studies in Mass Communication*, 1990, 7(3): 215–230.

Fiske, J. "Women and Quiz Shows: Consumerism, Patriarchy and Resisting Pleasures." In M.E. Brown (ed.), *Television and Women's Culture*. London: Sage, 1990.

Flichy, P. *Les industries de l'imaginaire*. Grenoble: Presse universitaire de Grenoble, 1980.

Fortin; et Poissant "Entrevue avec Deutsch." In *Voir*, 17th February 1994.

Foucault, M. "Subject of power." In *Critical Inquiry*, 1982, 8, 777–95.

Fox, B.J. "Conceptualizing 'patriarchy.'" In *Canadian Review of Sociology and Anthropology*, 1988, 25(2), 163–82.

Franco, J. *Plotting Women*. New York: Columbia University Press, 1989.

Frisby, D. *Fragments of Modernity*. Cambridge, MA: M.I.T, 1988.

Fritz, K.A., and Kaufman Henever, N. "An Unsuitable Job for a Woman: Female Protagonists in the Detective Novel." In *International Journal of Women's Studies*, 1979, 2(2), 105–28.

Garnham, N. *Capitalism and Communication*. London: Sage, 1990.

Gitlin, T. "Media Sociology: The Dominant Paradigm." In *Theory and Society*, 1979, 6, 205–53.

Goody, J., and Watt, I. "The Consequence of Literacy." In *Comparative Studies in Society and History*, 1963, 5, 304–45.

Gottlieb, L.C., and Keitner, W. "Images of Canadian Women in Literature and Society in the 1970s." In *International Journal of Women's Studies*, 1979, 2, 513–27.

Greenberg, B.S., and Heeter, C. "VCRs and Young People." In *American Behavioral Scientist*, 1987, 30(5), 509–21.

Griggers, C.J. "A Certain Tension in the Visual/Cultural Field: Helmut Newton, Deborah Turbeville, and The Vogue Fashion Layout." In *Differences: A Journal of Feminist Cultural Studies*, 1990, 2(2), 76–105.

Gunter, B., and Levy, M.R. "Social Context of Video Use." In *American Behavioral Scientist*, 1987, 30(5), 486–94.

Hall, S. "Encoding/Decoding." In S. Hall et al. (eds.), *Culture, Media, Language*. London: Hutchinson, 1980.

Hall, S. "The Re-discovery of 'Ideology': Return of the Repressed in Media Studies." In M. Gurevitch et al. (eds.), *Culture, Society and the Media*. New York: Methuen, 1982.

Hall, S. "Signification, representation, ideology: Althusser and the post-structuralist debates," *Critical Studies in Mass Communication, 1985*, 2, 2: 91–114.

Hayes, F., and Baran, N. "A guide to GUIs." In *Byte*, 1989, 14(7), 250–7.

Herman, E.S., and Chomsky, N. *Manufacturing Consent, The Political Economy of the Mass Media*. New York: Pantheon Books, 1988.

Hiltz, S.R., and Turoff, M. "Computer-Mediated Communications and the Disadvantaged." In S.R. Hiltz and M. Turoff (eds.), *The Network Nation: Human Communication Via Computer.* Reading, MA: Addison-Wesley, 1978.

Hobson, D. "Women's Audiences and the Workplace." In M.E. Brown (ed.), *Television and Women's Culture.* London: Sage, 1990.

Hoskins, C, & Mirus, R. "Reasons for the US dominance of the international trade in television programming," *Media, Culture and Society,* 1988 10: 499–515.

Hudson, V.M.A. *Harlequin Romances: The Significance of a Changing Genre as a Chronicle of Women Readers' Changing Concerns and Social Situations.* [M.A. Thesis]. Ottawa: Carleton University, 1989.

Innis, H. *Empire and Communications.* Oxford: Clarendon Press, 1950.

Jay, M. *The Dialectical Imagination.* Toronto: Little, Brown and Company, 1973.

Jenkins III, H. "Star Trek Rerun, Reread, Rewritten: Fan Writing as Textual Poaching," *Critical Studies in Mass Communication,* 1988, 5, 2: 85–107.

Johnson, B. "The cult of ISDN." In *PC/Computing,* 1989, 2(4), 144–51.

Jones, M. "Filling the Shelves." In *Publishers Weekly,* 237(17): 16.

Julien, C. "La communication victime des marchands." In *Monde Diplomatique,* Paris, November 1988.

Kastner, S. "Underwear Ads Degrade our Men." In *Toronto Star,* Toronto, February 17, 1991.

Katz, E., Blumler, J.G., and Gurevitch, M. "Utilization of Mass Communication by the Individual." In J.G. Blumler and E. Katz (eds.), *The Uses of Mass Communications.* Beverly Hills: Sage, 1974.

Katz, E., and Lazarsfeld, P.F. *Personal Influence.* New York: Free Press, 1955.

Katz, E., and Liebes, T. "Interacting with 'Dallas': Cross Cultural Readings of American TV." In *Canadian Journal of Communication,* 1990, 15(1), 45–65.

Kervin, D. "Advertising Masculinity: The Representation of Males in Esquire Advertisements." In *Journal of Communication Inquiry,* 1990, 14(1), 51–70.

Klapper, J.T. "Mass communications: effects." In *International Encyclopedia of the Social Sciences.* New York: Macmillan and The Free Press, 1968.

Knight, K. "Stratified News: Media, Sources and the Politics of Representation," in P. Bruck (ed.*) A*

Proxy for Knowledge, Ottawa: Carleton International Proceedings, 1988.

Knight, G. "Fetishism and Pornography: The Images of Male Looking." Presented in the Humanities Lecture Series, McMaster University, 1986.

Knight, G., O'Connor, J. "Social Democracy Meets the Press: Media Coverage of Industrial Relations Legislation."In *Research in Political Sociology,* 1995, 7, 185–205.

Kuhn, A. *The Power of the Image.* Boston: Routledge & Kegan Paul, 1985.

Kunzle, D. "Introduction to the English Edition." In A. Dorfman and A. Mattelart, *How to read Donald Duck.* New York: International General, 1975.

Lacroix, Y. "L'Avènement de la BD québécoise (1930–1950)." In *Actes du premier colloque de bande dessinée de Montréal,* Montréal, 1986, 7–19.

La Presse. "Après la femme-objet, voilà désormais l'homme-objet." Montréal, January 12, 1991.

La Presse. "L'industrie japonaise du sexe connaît un essor sans précédent." Montréal, May 18, 1991.

Latouche, D. "Television and the Harsh Reality of Audience Fragmentation." In *Forces,* 1991, 92, 50–1.

Lazarsfeld, P.F., Berelson, B., and Gaudet H. *The People's Choice.* 2nd ed. New York: Columbia University Press, 1948.

Le Bon, G. *Psychologie des foules.* Paris: Retz-C.E.P.L, 1895.

Légaré, A. "Le cas de l'émission 'Femme d'aujourd'hui' (Canada)." In *L'influence des médias audiovisuels sur le comportement socio-culturel des femmes. Deux exemples : le Japon et le Canada.* Paris: Unesco, 1980.

Lemieux, R. "L'autoroute informatique: sans limite de vitesse à 45 millions de bite par seconde." In *Le Devoir,* 19th January 1994.

Lemonde, A. *Les femmes et le roman policier, anatomie d'un paradoxe.* Montréal: Québec/Amérique, 1984.

Levy, M. "Some Problems of VCR Research." In *American Behavioral Scientist,* 1987, 30(5), 461–70.

Liebes, T., and Katz, E. "Dallas and Genesis: Primordiality and Seriality in Popular Culture." In J.W. Carey (ed.), *Media, Myths, and Narratives: Television and the Press.* Newbury Park, CA: Sage, 1988.

Lord, C. *La publicité sexiste c'est quoi?* Québec: Conseil du statut de la femme, October 1979.

Lord, C. "La publicité est-elle moins sexiste?" In *La Gazette des femmes*, January–February 1989, 10 (5), 31–3.

Lorinc, J. "Romance Language." In *Quill & Quire*, 60(5 May): 13–14, 1994.

MacGregor Davies, J. "Pornographic Harms." In *Feminist Perspectives*. Toronto: University of Toronto Press, 1988.

Mackie, M. *Exploring Gender Relations*. Toronto: Butterworths, 1983.

Madden, J. *Videotex in Canada*. Ottawa: Minister of Supply and Services of Canada, 1979.

Manning, R. "First-class maii." In *PC/Computing*, 1989, 2(8), 159–60.

Margolis, J. "Romancing the East." In *Report on Business Magazines*, 8(6 Dec.): 57–60, 1991.

Martin, M. "Capitalizing on the 'Feminine' Voice." In *Canadian Journal of Communication*, 1989, 14(3), 43–62.

Martin, M. "Racoleur ou libérateur: le Minitel comme moyen de démocratisation." Unpublished paper, 1989a.

Martin, M. *Hello Central? Gender, Technology and Culture in the Formation of Telephone Systems*. Montréal: McGill-Queen's University Press, 1991.

Martin, M. and Proulx, S. *Une télévision aux enchères : programmations, programmes, publics*. Ste-Foy, QC: Les Presses de l'Université du Québec, 1995.

Marx, K. *The Eighteenth Brumaire of Louis Bonaparte*. New York: International Publishers, 1963.

Marx, K. *Capital*, vol. 1. New York: International Publishers, 1967.

Marx, K., and Engels, F. *Manifesto of the Communist Party*. Peking: Foreign Languages Press, 1973.

Mattelart, A. *Multinational Corporations and the Control of Culture: The Ideological Apparatuses of Imperialism*. Brighton, GB: The Harvester Press, 1979.

Mattelart, A. "Introduction." In A. Mattelart and S. Siegelaub (eds.), *Communication and Class Struggle*, vol. 2, 1983.

Mattelart, A., and Dorfman, A. *Donald l'imposteur*. Paris: Alain Moreau, 1976.

Mattelart, A., and Mattelart, M. *Le carnaval des images*. Paris: La documentation française, 1987.

Mattelart, A., and Mattelart, M. *Rethinking Media Theory: Signposts and New Directions*. Minneapolis: University of Minnesota Press, 1992.

Mattelart, A., Mattelart, M., and Delcourt, X. *La culture contre la démocratie?* Paris: La Découverte, 1984.

Mattelart, A., and Piemme, J.M. *Télévision : enjeux sans frontières*. Grenoble: Presse universitaire de Grenoble, 1980.

Mattelart, A., and Siegelaub, S. (eds.) *Communication and Class Struggle*, vols. 1, and 2. New York: International General, 1979, 1983.

Mattelart, M. "Préface." In A. Mattelart and A. Dorfman, *Donald l'imposteur*. Paris: Alain Moreau, 1976.

Mattelart, M. *Les femmes et les industries culturelles*. Paris: Unesco, 1981.

Mattelart, M. *Women, Media and Crisis*. London: Comedia, 1986.

McLuhan, M. "A Historical Approach to Media." In *Teachers College Record*, 1955, 57(2), 104–10.

McLuhan, M. *The Gutenberg Galaxy*. Toronto: The University of Toronto Press, 1962.

McLuhan, M. *Understanding Media*. Toronto: McGraw-Hill, 1964.

McQuail, D. (ed.) *Sociology of Mass communications*. Harmonds-Worth: Penguin, 1972.

McQuail, D., Blumler, J.G., and Brown, J.R. "The Television Audience: A Revised Perspective." In D. McQuail (ed.), *Sociology of Mass communications*, 1972.

McQuail, D., and Gurevitch, M. "Explaining Audience Behavior: Three Approaches Considered." In J.G. Blumler and E. Katz (eds.), *The Uses of Mass Communications*, 1974.

Méar, A., Pons, C.M., Martinez-Mailhot, A., Bellafiore B., and Mercier, F. "Le téléroman, genre hybride : réalité et fiction à la télévision." In *Études Littéraires*, 1981, 14(2), 293–306.

Miège, B. "The Cultural Commodity." In *Media, Culture and Society*, 1979, 1(3), 297–311.

Milliot, J. "Harlequin's U.S. Sales Rose 11%, to $174 Million, in '93." In *Publishers Weekly*, 241(24): 10, 1994.

Milliot, J. "Harlequin's American Division has Gains in Sales and Earnings." In *Publishers Weekly* 242(21):16, 1995.

Minister of Education of Ontario. *Media Literacy*. Toronto: Queen's Printer of Ontario, 1989.

Modleski, T. "The Disappearing Act: A Study of Harlequin Romances." In *Signs: Journal of Women in Culture and Society*, 1980, 5(3), 435–48.

Modleski, T. *Loving with a vengeance*. Hamden, CT: Archon Books, 1982.

Molotch, H.L. "The News of Women And the World of Men." In G. Turchman, A.K. Daniels and J. Bénet (eds.), *Hearth and Home: Images of*

Women in the Mass Media. New York: Oxford University Press, 1978.

Mosco, V. "Critical Research and the Role of Labor." In *Journal of Communication*, 1983, 33(3), 237–48.

Mosco, V. *Pushbutton Fantasies: Critical Perspectives on Videotex and Information Technology.* Norwood, NJ: Ablex Publishing Corporation, 1982.

Niemi, F., and Salgado, M. *Un visage français, oui, mais . . . multiculturel et multiracial, aussi!* Montréal: Centre for Research-Action on Race Relations (CRARR), 1988.

Nightingale, V. "Women as Audiences." In M.E. Brown (ed.), *Television and Women's Culture.* London: Sage, 1990.

Penley, C. "Feminism, Psychoanalysis, and the Study of Popular Culture," in L. Grossberg et al. (eds.) *Cultural Studies,* New York & London: Routledge, 1992.

Perreault, G. *Le monde diplomatique.* Paris, November 1988.

Pomerleau, L. "La BD en librairie au Québec." In *Actes du premier colloque de bande dessinée de Montréal,* Montréal, 1986, 115–9.

Pool, I. de S. "Extended Speech and Sounds." In R. Williams (ed.), *Contact.* London: Thomas & Hudson, 1981.

Pool, I. de S., and Ableson, R. "The Simulatics Project." In *Public Opinion Quarterly,* 1961, 25(2), 167–83.

Press, A.L. "Class, Gender and the Female Viewer: Women's Responses to Dynasty." In M.E. Brown (ed.), *Television and Women's Culture.* London: Sage, 1990.

Primeau, J. "L'image de l'homme à travers la nouvelle publicité." Unpublished Master's Thesis, Université Laval, 1989.

Raboy, M. "Canadian Boradcasting, Canadian Nationhood: Two Concepts, Two Solitudes, and Great Expectations." In H. Holmes and D. taras (eds) *Media Power and Policy in Canada.* Toronto: Harcourt Brace Jovanovitch Canada Inc., 1992, pp. 156–173.

Radway, J. "Women Read the Romance: The Interaction of Text and Context." In *Feminist Studies,* 1983 9(1), 53–73.

Radway, J. *Reading the Romance.* Chapel Hill, NC: University of North Carolina Press, 1984.

Rinehart, J.W. *The Tyranny of Work.* 2nd ed. Toronto: Harcourt Brace Jovanovitch, 1987.

Roach, C. "The movement for a New World Information and Communication Order: a second wave?" *Media, Culture and Society,* 1990, 12: 283–307.

Robinson, G.J., "Women and the Media in Canada: A Progress Report." In H. Holmes and D. Taras (eds), *Seeing Ourselves: Media Power and Policy in Canada.* Toronto: Harcourt, 1992.

Rocher, G. *A General Introduction to Sociology.* Toronto: Macmillan, 1972.

Roe, K. "Adolescents' Video Use." In *American Behavioral Scientist,* 1987, 30(5), 522–32.

Roth, M. *Foul and Fair Play: Reading Genre in Classic Detective Fiction.* Athens, GA: University of Georgia Press, 1994.

Rubin, A.M., and Bantz, C.R. "Utility of Videocassette Recorders." In *American Behavioral Scientist,* 1987, 30(5), 471–85.

Rutherford, P. *The Making of the Canadian Media,* Toronto: McGraw-Hill Ryerson, 1978.

Rutherford, P. *The New Icons? The Art of Television Advertising.* Toronto: University of Toronto Press, 1994.

Sadoul, J. *93 ans de BD.* Paris: J'ai lu, 1989.

Saint-Jean, A. "Le système." In *Pour en finir avec le patriarcat.* Montréal: Primeur, 1983.

Saint-Jean, A. "L'image des femmes dans les médias." In *La parole métèque,* Winter 1989, 8.

Salter, L. "L'étude de la communication : évolution d'une discipline au Canada." In *Canadian Journal of Communication,* 1983, 2(3), 37–62.

Salwyn, A. "20 millions d'utilisateurs dans 91 pays: l'incroyable expansion d'Internet." In *Le Devoir,* 8th December 1993.

Samson, J. "Rencontre avec Albert Chartier." In *Actes du premier colloque de bande dessinée de Montréal,* Montréal, 1986, 55–70.

Sarfati, S. "Harlequin, des livres importants pour femmes . . . seulement." In *La Presse,* Montréal, September 23, 1990.

Schulhafer, J. "Embracing the Niche: Publishers are Developing New Imprints, Series and Sub-Genres to Capitalize on a Diverse Readership." In *Publishers Weekly,* 1993, 240(24):43.

Seiter, E. "Different Children, Different Dreams: Racial Representation in Advertising." In *Journal of Communication Inquiry,* 1990, 14(1), 31–48.

Settel, I. *A Pictorial History of Television.* New York: Frederick Ungar, 1983.

Seymour, J. "The GUI: An Interface You Won't Outgrow." In *PC Magazine,* 1989, 8(15), 97–109.

Siegelaub, S. "Preface." In A. Mattelart and S. Siegelaub (eds.), *Communication and Class*

Struggle, vol. 1. New York: International General, 1979.

Siegelaub, S. "Preface." In A. Mattelart and S. Siegelaub (eds.), *Communication and Class Struggle*, vol. 2. New York: International General, 1983.

Smith, J., and Balka, E. "Chatting on a Feminist Computer Network." In C. Kramarae (ed.), *Technology and Women's Voices: Keeping In Touch*. New York: Routledge & Kegan Paul, 1988.

Snitow, A. "Mass Market Romance: Pornography for Women Is Different." In *Radical History Review*, 1979, 20, 141–61.

Sohet, P., and Desaulniers, J.P. "Le téléjournal et le téléroman, le papa et la maman." In *Mine de rien*, Montréal: Saint-Martin, 1982.

Spano, S. "Flower Power; Romance Category Closeup." In *Publishers Weekly*, 1992, 239(54): 31.

Stoessl, S. (1990) "Women as TV Audience: A Marketing Perspective." In H. Baehr and G. Dyer (eds.), *Boxed In Women and Television*. New York: Pandora, 1987.

Tremblay, F. "La guerre des autoroutes électroniques aura-t-elle lieu?" *The Canadian Press* published in *Le Devoir* 14th April 1994.

Tremblay, F. "Développement de l'autoroute électronique au Québec: Vidéotron ne s'en laissera pas imposer par Bell Canada." *The Canadian Press* published in *Le Soleil*, 9th April 1994.

Tremblay, F. "Stentor lance un projet d'autoroute électronique." *The Canadian Press* published in *La Presse*, 6th April 1994.

Turcotte, C. "Microsoft multiplie les partenariats." In *Le Devoir*, 25th May 1994.

Tydeman, J., Lipinski, H., Adler, R., Nyhan, M., and Zwimpfer, L. *Teletext and Videotex in the United States: Market Potential, Technology, Policy Issues*. New York: McGraw-Hill, 1982.

Variety "The global 50," *Variety*, August 28–September 3: 27–60, 1995.

Varis, T. "The International Flow of Television Programmes," Journal of Communication, 1984, 34, 1: 143–152.

Voumvakis, S. & Ericson, R. "News Accounts of Attacks on Women: A Comparison of Three Toronto Newspapers," Toronto: University of Toronto Centre of Criminology, 1984.

Washington Post "Digital Comics: An Old Art Form Finds a New Home on Line." In *The Ottawa Citizen*, 1995, Dec.11, p. B3.

Wernick, A. *Promotional Culture: Advertising, Ideology and Symbolic Expression*. London: Sage Publications, 1991.

Whitworth, S. "Feminist Theories: From Women to Gender and World Politics." In R.P. Beckman and F. D'Amico (eds) *Women, Gender and World Politics*. London: Bergin & Garney, 1994, pp. 75–88.

Williams, R. *Culture and Society*. New York: Columbia University Press, 1958.

Williams, R. *Keywords: A Vocabulary of Culture and Society*. London: Fontana/Croom Helm, 1976.

Williams, R. *Television and Culture*. London: Verso, 1976.

Williams, R. *Television*. London: Fontana/Collins, 1978.

Williams, R. "Means of Communication as Means of Production." In R. Williams (ed.), *Problems in Materialism and Culture*. London: NLB, 1980.

Williams, R. "Advertising: The Magic System." In R. Williams (ed.), *Problems in Materialism and Culture*. London: NLB, 1980.

Williamson, J. *Decoding Advertisements*. London: Marion Boyars, 1978.

Williamson, J. "Woman as an Island." In T. Modleski (ed.), *Studies in Entertainment*. Indiana: Indiana University Press, 1986.

Wilson, K.G. *Technologies of Control: The New Interactive Media for the Home*. Madison, WI: The University of Wisconsin Press, 1988.

Winkler, C. "Diskazines Go to Press." *PC/Computing*, 1989, 2(4), 179–80.

Wood, L., and Blankenhorn, D. "State of the BBS nation." In *Byte*, 1990, 15(1), 298–304.

Yanni, D.A. "The Social Construction of Women as Mediated by Advertising." In *Journal of Communication Inquiry*, 1990, 14(1), 71–82.

Yerza, F.N. *The Good, the Bad and the Ugly: Gender Portrayal in Advertising in CRTC Regulated Television*. Unpublished Masters Thesis, Ottawa: Carleton University, 1995, used with permission of author.

Index

Action heros, 172
Advertising, 106
    children in, 212
    creation of needs, 202
    and dominant ideology, 206
    history of, 200, 201
    image of cultural minorities, 212–15
    image of men, 209–212
    image of women, 203–209, 221–37
    and interactive television, 282
    and myth of modernity, 110–12
    and news media, 253
    objectification of women, 217
    ownership of, 201–202
    and pornography, 216–20
    power of, 215–16, 253
    relation to mass media, 201–202
    sexist, 206–209
    use of exotic images, 111
Agence-France-Presse, 245
Aird Commission, 26
Alternative media, 56–57
American Dream, 200
Amplificatory media, 56–57
Anticommunism, 255
Archival practices, 13
    computer-based, 274
Associated Press (AP), 63, 245
AT&T, 24–25
Atomization, 30, 34
Audiences, 55. *See also* Mass audience
    as commodity, 63
    of detective fiction, 170–75
    female, 104, 112–26
    of game shows, 122–26
    international, 140–42
    of popular romances, 153–70, 173–75
    of soap operas, 114–19, 140–47
Audimeter, 13
Authoritarian theory, of newspapers, 239
Automated banking machines (ABMs), 265

Baby boomers, 206
Backle, Leo, 179
Barker, Martin, 194
Barks, Carl, 186, 195
Barrier, Mike, 195
Beauchamp, Colette, 239, 242ff
Beaud, Paul, 12, 39, 79–80
Beauty, 204, 207
Behaviourism, 30
Bell Canada, 264
Bell, John, 178
Bettig, Ronald, 278ff
Bias, *see* Communication bias
Bidimensional communication bias, 39
Black, Conrad, 246
Blacks, image of in advertising, 212–15
Boivin, René, 180
Book publishing, 85
Books
    censorship of, 18–19
    copyright, 16–17
    manuscripts, 12–14, 16
    printed, 15–21
Bourgeois ideology of communication, 67
British Broadcasting Corporation (BBC), 24
Brown, M.E., 117
Brownmiller, Susan, 165
Bureau of Broadcast Measurement (BBM), 5
Bush, George, 261
Byrne, John, 179

Calkins, Dick, 178
Calvin Klein ads, 210
Canadian Advisory Council on the Status of Women
    (CACSW), 208
Canadian Broadcasting Corporation (Radio-Canada),
    76, 77, 101, 242, 249, 282
Canadian Press (CP), 245
Canadian Radio Broadcasting Commission
    (CRBC), 26
Canadian Radio-Television and
    Telecommunications Commission (CRTC), 201,
    208–209
Canadian School of Communication
    communication bias, 39–42
    hot and cold media, 42–45
CANARIE, 267
CANET network, 268, 269
Capitalism, 47–51
    media production process, 84–86. *See also*
    Production
    patriarchy and, 92, 95–97, 101–102

Carnival, TV game shows, 123–24
Carter, Jimmy, 257
Censorship
    of books, 18
    of comics, 178
    during Gulf War, 58
    of press, 239
    of radio, 23
    of television, 58
Center for Media and Public Affairs, 254
Centre d'excellence en communications intégrées
    (CETI), 264
Centre for Research-Action on Race Relations
    (CRARR), 214
Challe, Odile, 263
Chartier, Albert, 180
Children
    in advertising, 212
    and Disney images, 185
    effect of TV violence on, 133–34
    and videos, 277
Children's programs, 78
Chomsky, Noam, 251ff
Class, *see* Social class
Clinton, Bill, 268
CNN, 62, 249
Codes
    in advertising, 203
    decoding of soap operas, 142
    negotiating message, 76, 115, 286
Colbert, Jean Baptiste, 19
Comely, Richard, 179
Comics
    Disney, 183–96
    in English Canada, 178–79
    in French-speaking Europe, 180–82
    in Quebec, 179–80
    superheroes, 182–83
    in U.S., 182–83
Comic strips, 182
Commoditization of culture, 53
Communication, 2–3, 79
    control of, 54
    human vs. mechanical modes of, 56
    oral, 3
    techniques of, 77
Communication bias, 39–42
Communication studies, 28
Community, 75
    radio and television, 81

Computers/computing, 262–63
Consumerism, and *The Price is Right*, 123–24
Consumption. *See also* Advertising
    of content, 112–14
    in Disney, 190
    mass, 199–203
    woman as consumer, 106–108
Content
    construction/production of, 57–58, 84–85, 239,
        258, 285
    consumption of, 112–14. *See also* Audiences
    negotiation of, 76, 115, 215, 286
    television, 132–36
Control. *See also* Power
    corporate consolidation, 61–63
    forms of, 54–59
    of press, 239
    resistance to, 59–64
Cooked and raw, 220
Cooking, 73–74
Copyright Act, 16–17
Corporate concentration, media ownership, 61–63,
    101, 252
Council on the Status of Women, 206, 207
Coward, Rosalind, 217
Critical decodings, 142–43
Critical school of communication, 46
Critical theory, 52
    mode of production, 53–54
Crouter, Wally, 246
Cultural commodities, 60–61
Cultural imperialism, 195
    and video piracy, 279–80
Culture
    dominant, 72
    elite, 52, 53, 74
    flow, 61
    international, 77–79
    mass, 74–80
    popular, 52–53, 72–74, 80
    promotional, 201
    property rights, 278–80
    relation to ideology, 67–71

Dallas, 141–45
Darwin, Charles, 31
Data base construction, 273–75
D'Aubuisson, Roberto, 257–58
de Beauvoir, Simone, 83, 89, 95
Decentralization, of media, 79–81

Democracy, 75
    and mass culture, 79–80
    in print culture, 20–21
Democracy of desires, 111–12
Desaulnier, Jean-Pierre, 139
Des dames de coeur, 139
Detective novels, 153
    analytic vs. hard-boiled, 171
    compared to Harlequin Romance, 173–75
    hero of, 171–72
    place of women in, 172–73
Dingle, Adrian, 179
Discrimination, against women, 99–102, 132
Disney
    absent parents, 187–88
    amusement parks, 184
    Donald Duck, 187, 190, 191–92
    image of women, 187
    and innocence, 196
    international presence of, 183–85
    Mickey Mouse, 193
    missing production process, 189–91
    noble savage, 188–89
    production, 185–86
    Uncle Scrooge, 194
    work and worker in, 191–92
Disney, Walter Elias, 186
Domicil ad scandal, 208
Dominant code, 76
Dominant culture, 72
Dominant ideology, 63, 67–68, 84, 104, 113, 169, 210
    advertising and, 206
    and Gulf War, 70
    news media and, 254
Dominant paradigm, 28, 29, 46, 152
Donald Duck, 187, 190, 191–92
Dorfman, Ariel, 185ff
Durand, Lynda, 240
Durative media, 56–57
Dynasty, 145–47

Elite culture, 52, 53, 74
El Salvador, news reporting on, 251, 256ff
E-mail, 267
Employment, women in media industry, 99–103
Engels, Frederick, 47
English-language media, 61
Entertainment, news as, 249–51, 260
Erie County study, 32–33
Ewen, Stuart, 200
Exotic images, 111
Experts, communications, 245–46, 253

Family Feud, 124–25
Family
    role of women and, 105–108, 116, 138–39, 168, 204
    in soap operas, 147–49
Fan writing, 120–22
Fanzines, 120
Fashion magazines, image of women, 206
Febvre, L., 14, 15ff
Feminism
    early, 89–90
    explanations of patriarchy, 92–95
    French model, 114–16
    North American and English model, 116–20
Femininity. *See also* Gender; Women
    in advertising, 203
    social construction of, 89–95, 106–108, 204–209
Femmes d'aujourd'hui, 242
Ferguson, Marjorie, 94
Film industry
    Disney, 183
    funding of, 61
Film, resolution in, 148
Flak, 254–55
Flow culture, 61
Form, 44
Frankfurt School, 51–53
Freedom House, 254–55
Freeman, George, 179
Functionalist theories, 28, 31
    critique of, 37–39
    theory of gratifying uses, 34–37
    two-step flow theory, 32–34
Funding, 60–63

Game shows, female audiences, 122–26
Gender
    in advertising messages, 203
    and reading habits, 152, 152–53
    social construction of, 89–95, 204
    stereotyping, 90, 97, 132, 136, 174, 202ff
Gitlin, T., 30, 37
Globalization, media control, 61–63
Gore, Al, 268
Gramsci, Antonio, 69
Gratifying uses, theory of, 34–37
Green, Norm, 281
Greer, Germaine, 165
Grignon, Claude-Henri, 180
Guatemala, news reporting on, 256ff
Gulf War
    and dominant ideology, 70
    television/news coverage, 58, 70, 244, 261

Gurevitch, M., 35
Gutenberg Galaxy, The, 19

Hall, S., 37, 76, 259
Harlequin Romances
    characters, 156–58
    compared to detective novels, 173
    contrasted to soap operas, 160–6
    as escapist, 167–70
    essential elements of, 158–60
    history of, 153–56
    reader profile, 156
    reasons for popularity of, 162–64
Hegemony, 69–70
Herman, Edward, 251ff
Hero
    in detective fiction, 171–72
    in romance novels, 156–58
Heroine
    in detective fiction, 172–73
    in romance novels, 156–58
He Shoots, He Scores (Lance et compte), 139
Historical materialism, 49, 59
Hot and cold media, 42–45
Housewife, woman as consumer, 106–108
Human modes of communication, 56
Hurt comfort, 121
Hypodermic model, *see* Psychological theory

Ideological decodings, 142
Ideological struggles, 68
Ideology
    dominant, 63, 67–70, 75, 84, 104, 169, 206, 210
    of modernity, 106
    patriarchal, 92
    relation to culture, 67–71
    of war, 249
Illiteracy, technological, 272–73
Immigration, news coverage of, 250
Individualism, 75. *See also* Atomization
Industrialization, and mass culture, 75–76
Industrial Revolution, 199
Infantilization, 196–97
Information highway, 267–69
    access to, 272
    regulating, 272
Innis, Harold, 28, 39ff
Integrated production process, 85
Interactive television, 282–83
International culture, 77–79
    and soap operas, 140–41
International news, *see* News, international

Internet, 269–70
    economic/political implications, 270–72
Invisible labour, 96
Iron Man, 179

Jay, Martin, 52, 53
Jazz, 53
Journal de Spirou, 181
Journal de Tintin, 181
Journalism. *See also* News
    ideology in, 67
    investigative, 244–45
    women in, 99, 102
Julien, Claude, 250

Katz, E., 32ff, 142ff
Kervin, Denise, 203, 215
Knight, Graham, 216ff
Kuhn, Annette, 216ff
Kunzle, David, 185, 186, 195–96

Labour
    Disney representation of work, 191
    invisible, 96
    media production process, 85
    women and, 95–96, 98
Lacroix, Yves, 180
Lasswell, H.D., 229–30
Lazarsfeld, P.F., 23, 24ff, 37
Legaré, Anne, 242
Leisure, 192
Lemonde, Anne, 170ff
Les Filles de Caleb, 61
Liberal theory, of newspapers, 239
Lucas, Tom, 180

Mackie, Marlene, 240
Magic, 203
Marketing, 78
    international, 110–11
    relation of advertising to, 202
Martin, Vic, 180
Marxist theory, 47–51
    Frankfurt School, 51–53
    historical materialism, 49, 59
    media production analysis, 59–64
Marx, Karl, 47ff, 83
Masculinity. *See also* Gender; Men
    in advertising, 203
    social construction of, 89–95
Masochism, 165

Mass audience. *See also* Audiences
    atomized individuals, 30, 34
    vs. crowd, 4–5
Mass culture, 74–77
    internationalization of, 77–79
Mass media
    impact of, 35–36, 38
    power relations in, 53–64
    profit orientation of, 252
    social construction of, 5–7, 55, 258, 285
Mass production, *see* Production
Mass reproduction, 53
Mattelart, Armand, 59–60, 65, 68, 72, 74, 77–78
Mattelart, Michele, 108ff, 140, 184, 241ff, 287
McCall, Ted, 178
McLuhan, M., 19–20, 28, 39, 42ff, 55, 79
Mechanical modes of communication, 56
Media
    biases, 39–42
    content, 1. *See also* Content
    control of, 54
    public vs. private, 60, 241
Media imperialism, 63
Media Institute, 254
Media ownership
    corporate concentration of, 61–63, 100, 252
    male dominance, 100
Megadesire, 206
Membership milieus, 88
Men. *See also* Masculinity; Patriarchy
    dominance of, 93
    image of in advertising, 209–212
    and sports, 136
Meritocracy, 191
Microsoft, 271
Milieus, *see* Membership milieus
Miller, Vernon, 179
Minitel, 263–66, 273
Minorities
    image of in advertising, 212–15
    television and, 134
Mode of production, 53–54
Modernity
    advertising and, 200–201, 205–206
    feminine ideal, 106–108, 205–206
    myth of, 105–112
Modleski, Tania, 138, 147ff, 164ff
Molotch, Harvey, 239
Monasterio, Augusto Ramírez, 256
Montreal, multiracial representation in advertising, 214–15

Montufar, Miguel, 256
Morissette, Gabriel, 179
Mother, role/image of women as, 106–107, 168, 205, 206
Multinational firms, 61–63, 77–78, 110. *See also* Disney
    advertising industry, 201
Mumford, Laura S., 138–39
Myth of modernity, 105–112
Myth of permanence, 114–16

Natural selection, 31
Negotiated code, 76, 115, 286
Neilson Ratings, 5
Neo-sexism, 211
News. *See also* Journalism
    agencies, 244–45
    angle of, 258
    in Canada, 242–47
    censorship of, 238
    as entertainment, 249–51, 260
    Gulf War coverage, 58, 244, 261
    history of, 238
    image of women in, 241–42
    international, 251, 255–60
    as male-oriented, 101, 239–40, 247–48
    objectivity in, 247–49
    propaganda model, 252–60
    role of communications experts, 245–46
    as show, 249–51, 261
    sources, 243–44, 247, 253–54
Newspapers, 24
    authoritarian vs. liberal theory of, 239
    editorials, 246
    ownership of, 252. *See also* Media ownership
    reader opinions/letter to editor, 246
New World Information and Communications Order (NWICO), 63
Nicaraguan elections, news reporting on, 258–59
Nightingale, Virginia, 112
Nowlan, Phil, 178
Nudes, in advertising vs. pornography, 219–20

Objectification of women, 204–205
    fragmentation of the body, 217
    in pornography and advertising, 217–19
Objectivity, in news, 247–49
Oppositional code, 76
Oral communication, 11
Oral cultures, 12–13
    perception in, 19–20, 43

Panama invasion, 249
Patriarchal capitalist ideology, 92, 113. *See also*
    Dominant ideology
Patriarchy, 83, 92, 211
    feminist models explaining, 92–95
    temporality imposed by, 115–16
Pay TV, 281–82
Péladeau, Pierre, 246
Perfect Match, 125
Perrault, Gilles, 250
Photographs, the pornographic look, 218–19
Pilote, 181
Piracy, VCRs and, 278–80
Planned obsolescence, 108
Pleasure, 76
Poaching, 120
Pope, news coverage of, 249–50
Popieluszko, Jerzy, 256ff
Popular culture, 52–53, 72–74
    vs. mass culture, 80
Popular literature, 152–53. *See also* Harlequin
    Romances
Pornography
    relation of advertising to, 216–20
    softcore vs. hardcore, 216
    VCR and, 276–77
Positive realism, 214
Postal services, 23
Power, 42. *See also* Patriarchy, 92–95
    control of media, 54, 252–53
    ideological, 75
    in media production process, 97–103
    and news, 240, 245–47, 254
Press, Andrea L., 145ff
Press, the, *see* News; Newspapers
Pressure groups, 245
Primeau, Jacques, 209ff
Primordiality, 144
Print culture, 12–21
    and democracy, 20–21
    in Far East, 18
    Latin vs. vernacular, 20
    and paper industry, 15
    role of state, 17–19
Printing press, 12
Production
    Disney, 185–86
    examples of, 85
    integrated process of, 84–86
    mass, 199
    means of, 50, 86

mode of, 53–54
    patriarchal processes, 95–96
    power relations, 97–103
Professionalism, 75
Profit orientation, of mass media, 252–53
Promotional culture, 201
Propaganda
    anticommunism, 255
    flak, 254–55
    in international news, 251–60
    radio broadcasting, 23
Propaganda model, 252–56
Property rights, international, 278–81
Prostitution image, in advertising, 204
Proulx, Gilles, 246
Psychological decodings, 142
Psychological distance, 214
Psychological theory (hypodermic model), 28
Public media
    vs. private, 60, 241
    women in, 101, 102
Public opinion, 32
Public relations experts, 245–46

Racial minorities, image of in advertising, 212–15
Racism, 175
Radio
    community stations, 81
    elite, 23, 24, 25
    financing, 25
    as hot medium, 44
    serials, 137
    women announcers, 98–99
Radio broadcasting, 21, 22–26
    propaganda, 23
    state control of, 23
Radio-Canada, *see* Canadian Broadcasting
    Corporation
Radio Luxembourg, 137–38
Radway, Janice, 167ff
Ramírez, Atilio, 257
Rape, in popular novels, 152, 165
Reagan, Ronald, 259
Record industry, production process, 85
Referential decodings, 142
Reformation, 19
Reinforcement theories, 36, 38
Religious figures, in news, 249–50
Reuters, 245
Rogers Communications Inc., 62

Romance
    popular literature, 152–53
    TV shows, 125–26
Romero, Oscar, 256ff
Royal Commission on Radio Broadcasting, 26
Royal Commission on the Status of Women, 208
Ruling class, 69, 73, 80

Saint-Jean, Armande, 139, 241
Seiter, Ellen, 212
Sensationalism, 249
Seriality, 144
Sesame Street, 78–79
Sexism, in advertising, 206–209. *See also* Women
Sexuality, women, 109, 125, 163–64
Shainblum, Mark, 179
Show-news, 249–51, 261
Shuster, Joe, 178
Siegelaub, S., 3, 71
Siegel, Jerry, 178
Sirius, 271
Slash fiction, 121, 122
Snitow, A.B., 164
Soap operas, 114–16
    classic formula, 138–39
    contrasted to romance novels, 160–61
    Dallas, 141–45
    Dynasty, 145–47
    family in 147–49
    fan community, 120–21
    gender representation in, 137–40
    international audiences, 140–41, 142
    in Quebec, 139–40
    as source of confusion, 148–498
    and women's culture, 116–17
Social class
    and audiences, 65
    and gender, 97
    in Marxism, 49–50, 65
    ruling class, 69, 73, 80
    working class, 73
Social control
    and computer data bases, 275
    and videotex, 266–67
Socialization, 86–89, 96, 203, 240
    advertising's role in, 215
Sociological decodings, 142
Sohet, Philippe, 139
Sony corporation, 276
Sports, women and, 136
Standardization, 75
    of consumer, 200

Star Trek, 121
State control
    and early print culture, 17–19
    radio broadcasting, 23–24
State intervention, 63–64
Stentor Alliance, 271
Stereotypes
    cultural and racial, 212–15
    gender, 90, 97, 132, 136, 174, 202ff
    regulation of, 209
Stimulus/response theory, 30
Superman, 178
Surveillance, 275
Suzuki ad scandal, 208

Task Force on Sex-Role Stereotyping in the
    Broadcast Media, 209
Technological determinism, 44–45
Technological illiteracy, 272–73
Technology, new developments in, 262–83
Telbec, 245
Telephone
    early history of, 21–22
    in France, 264–65
    women operators, 98
Telefon-Hirmondo Telephone, 22
Telephone Herald, 22
Teleshopping, 265
Télétel, 263–66, 273
Television
    accessibility of, 56
    camera angle, 58–59
    as cold medium, 44
    construction of content, 57–59
    decentralization of, 81
    employment of women in, 102–103
    female audiences, 112–14, 140–47
    Gulf War coverage, 58, 244, 261
    image of women, 134–36
    interactive, 282–83
    networks, 60
    pay TV, 281–82
    piracy, 278
    public, 60, 241
    sports, 136
    time spent watching, 215
    violence, 133–34
Temporal divergence, 115–16
Thatcher, Margaret, 73
The New Price is Right, 123–24
Third World, copyright agreements, 278, 279–80
Thomas J. Burrell, 214

Time Warner, 62
Tintin, 180–81
Tremblay, Michel, 73
Turner Broadcasting System, 62
TVA, 76
Two-step flow theory, 32–34

United Press International (UPI), 63

Values, transmission of, 88
Videocassette recorder (VCR), 262, 276ff
Video technology
    advent of, 276
    democracy and, 80–81
    piracy, 278–81
    and Third World countries, 278, 279–81
    use of, 276–77
Videotex, 263–64
    defined, 263
    difficulties in implementing, 264–66
    as form of social control, 266–67
Vidéotron corporation, 271, 282
Videoway, 282
Violence, on television, 133–34
Vogue, 206
Voyeurism, 219

Wagner, Dave, 195
Walt Disney Co., 62
War, ideology of, 249. *See also* Gulf War
Whitworth, Sandra, 93–94
Williamson, Judith, 107ff
Williams, Raymond, 2, 4, 5, 54ff, 202, 203
Wilson, Kevin, 264
Women
    beauty and, 204, 207
    discrimination against, 99–101, 132
    Disney image of, 187
    family/private sphere, 105–108, 116, 138–39,
    168, 204
    female television audiences, 112–14
    image of in advertising, 203–209
    image of in detective novels, 170, 172–73
    image of in news, 241–42
    media employment, 99–103
    myth of modern woman, 105–112, 205
    objectification of, 204–205, 217
    as "other," 204
    in radio, 26, 98–99
    role/image of mother, 106–107, 168, 205, 206
    sexuality, 109, 125, 163–64
    social construction of gender, 89–95, 106–108,
    203–209

    stereotypes of, 90, 97, 132, 136, 174, 202ff
    telephone operators, 98
    television image of, 134–36
    wages, 91
    wartime labour, 95–96
Working class, 73, 146–47
Written culture
    perception in, 20, 43
    rise of, 13–21

Yanni, Denice A., 204–205